Untimely Matter in the Time of Shakespeare

Untimely Matter in the Time of Shakespeare

Jonathan Gil Harris

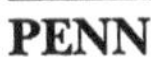

University of Pennsylvania Press
Philadelphia

Published by
University of Pennsylvania Press
Philadelphia, Pennsylvania 19104-4112

Printed in the United States of America on acid-free paper
10 9 8 7 6 5 4 3 2 1

Library of Congress Cataloging-in-Publication Data

Harris, Jonathan Gil.
Untimely matter in the time of Shakespeare / Jonathan Gil Harris.
p. cm.
Includes bibliographical references and index.
ISBN 978-0-8122-2146-6
1. English literature—Early modern, 1500–1700—History and criticism—Theory, etc. 2. Literature and history—Great Britain—History. 3. Literature and society—Great Britain—History. 4. Great Britain—History—1066–1687—Historiography. I. Title.
PR421.H26 2009
820.9′003—dc22 2008022363

To Madhavi Menon,
because it's about time

CONTENTS

ILLUSTRATIONS

INTRODUCTION

Palimpsested Time

Toward a Theory of Untimely Matter

An object, a circumstance, is thus polychronic, multitemporal, and reveals a time that is gathered together, and with multiple pleats.
—Michel Serres, *Conversations on Science, Culture, and Time*

OVER THE PAST decade, Renaissance historicism has witnessed something of a sea change. If the new historicism of the 1980s and early 1990s was preoccupied primarily with the fashioning of early modern subjects, a pronounced tendency in the new millennium, evidenced in the turn to so-called material culture, is to engage with objects. This new preoccupation has been showcased in several anthologies that offer readers wonder cabinets of material goods from the time of Shakespeare.[1] Feathers, textiles, Communion wafers, mirrors, coins, laundry baskets, graffiti, embroidery, mantles, stage beards, and furniture are all read by literary critics as closely as literature used to be.[2] For a growing number of Renaissance and Shakespeare scholars, the play is no longer the thing: the *thing* is the thing.

The new millennium, then, is arguably the time of material culture.[3] But this declaration should also provoke some suspicion, for the temporal rupture it asserts glosses over a significant continuity—one that concerns the very idea of time. Despite its novelty, the "new" new historicism of the object (as one critic has called it) cleaves to the same understanding of temporality that informs the "old" new historicism of the subject.[4] Fredric Jameson's well-known injunction, "always historicize," has often been invoked to authorize a critical practice that interprets historical phenomena chiefly in relation to their cotemporal contexts, whether cultural, social, or economic.[5] Such a practice works to separate time into a linear series of units—whether these be the *longues durées* of French Annales history or the single years of recent Shakespeare biography[6]—each of which is partitioned from what precedes and follows it. We might call this the national sovereignty model of temporality. Although it licenses trade between different moments (allowing, say, the "modern" to import elements from the "early modern" and to export others to the "postmodern"), it grants each moment a determining authority reminiscent of a nation-state's: that is, firmly policed borders and a shaping constitution. As a result, any historical phenomenon tends to be regarded as a citizen solely of one moment-state. And from the vantage point of the present, the past becomes a foreign country, or rather several foreign countries.

The national sovereignty model of temporality may have done much to puncture an uncritical universalism that naturalizes the assumptions of the present: if we understand early modern subjects to have been constituted differently from their modern counterparts, we can also begin to grasp the contingency of "our" moment. But it is perhaps time to question this notion of time, particularly when it is applied to material culture. How might things chafe against the sovereignty of the moment-state? What do we do with things that cross temporal borders—things that are illegal immigrants, double agents, or holders of multiple passports? How might such border crossings change our understanding of temporality? What, in short, is the time of the thing?

For scholars of Renaissance material culture, this last question might seem unremarkable and even tautological. After all, they might say, early modern things are early modern: a thing's time is its own, not any other's. As if to underscore this respectful insistence on temporal propriety, critics have often treated the Renaissance object as an ethnographic curio that materializes an early modern moment unfamiliar to us. Indeed, a recurrent strategy in scholarship on Renaissance material culture is to allege that its things are particularly worthy of attention because of their *strangeness*, at least to the palate of the modern literary and cultural historian. Championing a critical fascination with "marginal and strange details," one such study claims that "the everyday in the Renaissance can be the uncommonly strange to modern taste"; another characterizes early modern domestic matter as "enticingly alien."[7] Thus the Renaissance object is made to belong univocally to a foreign moment-state whose supposed integrity and singularity are guaranteed by that moment's difference from our own.

For philosophers of science, however, the question of a thing's relation to time is likely to entail a more complicated answer. Recent work in the field has increasingly drawn attention to how an object is never of a singular moment but instead combines ingredients from several times. As Bruno Latour notes, "Every cohort of elements may bring together elements from all times. In such a framework, our actions are recognized at last as polytemporal. . . . I may use an electric drill, but I also use a hammer. The former is thirty-five years old, the latter hundreds of thousands. . . . Some of my genes are 500 million years old, others 3 million, others 100,000 years old, and my habits range in age from a few days to several thousand years."[8] In light of Latour's recognition that all things and actions are "polytemporal," it perhaps becomes easier to understand the words of Michel Serres in my epigraph to this chapter: "An object, a circumstance, is thus polychronic, multitemporal, and reveals a time that is gathered together, and with multiple pleats." Philosophers of science offer accounts of the polytemporal object that, to current scholars of Renaissance material culture, may seem every bit as strange as the things they study. Yet these accounts may also make considerable sense. Many "Renaissance" objects were not of the Renaissance as such but survivals from an older time: think, for example, of the medieval monastic garments that, post-Reformation, were recycled for display in the public playhouses; or of London's old Roman walls, still visible in Shakespeare's lifetime alongside subsequent additions and renovations.[9] Such polytemporal objects—of the English Renaissance, yet not of it—might be characterized as untimely matter.

In this book, I adapt Serres's account of objects to argue that the untimely matter of the English Renaissance is, in his words, both polychronic and multitemporal. What may at first seem like a pair of synonyms for "polytemporal" are, on closer inspection, two subtly different concepts, and this difference points to a significant disjunction in the meanings of "time." "Time" can refer to a moment, period, or age—the punctual date of chronology. Hence "the time of Shakespeare" can be demarcated and numerically represented as a finite temporal block (1564–1616, or the sixteenth and seventeenth centuries). But "time" can also refer to an *understanding* of the temporal relations among past, present, and future. In this sense, "the time of Shakespeare" is not a historical period but rather a conception, or several conceptions, of temporality. As we shall see, time in Shakespeare's plays is sometimes a progressive line that follows the arc of the sun, but it is also counterintuitively a plane in which the future is behind and the past ahead, and a preposterous folded cloth in which before and after are coeval.[10] Serres's notion of the polychronic draws on the first, chronological meaning of time in asserting that objects collate many different moments, as suggested by Latour's polytemporal toolbox and genes. By contrast, Serres's notion of the multitemporal evokes the second meaning of time. In its polychronicity, an object can prompt many different understandings and experiences of temporality—that is, of the relations between now and then, old and new, before and after.

The distinction between the polychronic and the multitemporal is particularly helpful for understanding theories of matter in the time of Shakespeare. A strikingly wide array of sixteenth- and seventeenth-century forms of English literary and cultural activity—devotional lyric verse, urban chorography, vitalist philosophy, and, most insistently, Shakespeare's own drama—expound or enact theories of the polychronic nature of matter. These theories range from the explicit to the implicit, the philosophical to the practical, and the religious to the secular. But each understands matter to collate diverse moments in time. In the process, these theories do more than just recognize the polychronicity of the object; they also insist on its multitemporal properties—that is, its materialization of diverse relations among past, present, and future. In some instances, Shakespeare and his contemporaries use objects to theorize a supersessionary temporality according to which the present or future differs and distances itself from the past. The object's polychronic multiplicity, however, readily suggests modes of historical and cultural relationality other than supersession. Within the object's many temporal "pleats," as Serres characterizes them, the past sometimes acquires an explosive power to tear apart the present.[11] And in yet other instances, past matter is also allowed to assume a more dialogic relation to the present, suggesting affinity and proximity rather than difference and distance between elements of then and now.

Contrary to our either/or habits of local and universal reading, English Renaissance theorists of matter regard it as neither of an age nor for all time. Rather, they see it as out of time with itself—that is, as untimely. In the stone tablets of religious typology, the city walls of urban chorography, the compounded substances of vitalist philosophy, and the matter of the Shakespearean stage—histrionic actors' bodies, malodorous special effects, and even trifling hand properties—time is repeatedly, to use Hamlet's well-known phrase, out of joint. Renaissance theories of matter thus challenge conceptual organizations of time that often predominate in our own moment, including the very idea of the "moment" as a self-identical unit divided from other moments that come before and after it.[12] In medieval and Renaissance Europe, the smallest unit of time as well as matter was dubbed the "atom."[13] But, as we shall discover, the polychronic and multitemporal matter theorized by Shakespeare and his contemporaries repeatedly splits the atom in its dual temporal and physical senses, revealing it to be a hybrid assemblage rather than a singular entity. As a result, we might think more carefully about how we temporally frame our studies of Renaissance material culture.

The Time of Material Culture

The turn to objects in Renaissance studies has prompted considerable critical discomfort in many quarters, most notably in Marxist criticism. Even though the new scholarship on early modern things has repeatedly situated itself within a broadly materialist tradition of historicist criticism, the materialism it models—as Douglas Bruster has noted in an important and insightful essay—is one that "neither Karl Marx nor Fredric Jameson would be likely to recognize."[14] Studies of Renaissance objects have tended to offer little or no analysis of labor, class struggle, or relations of production, which are for most Marxists every bit as material as objects. And whereas material culture's chiastic double, the cultural materialism of the 1980s, remains passionately invested in Marx's dictum that the goal of philosophy is not just to understand the world but also to change it, the newer work on objects often has no express political commitment.[15] This difference in political purpose translates into notably different temporal orientations. Cultural materialism, in its wish for social change, is ostensibly future oriented; studies of material culture, by contrast, are often fueled by an antiquarian desire to recover and preserve the past as it "really" was.

But the reaction against the new scholarship on material culture amounts to far more than dismay with its insufficiently Marxist understanding of materialism. Lurking in the dismissals is a tangled knot of often unspoken assumptions about the critical overvaluation of "mere" objects and, more fundamentally, the temporal impropriety of such matter. Wittily noting that the many recent anthologies of essays devoted to early modern objects can seem like little more than scholarly versions of J. Crew catalogs, Bruster suggests that such studies run the risk of degenerating into "tchotchke criticism."[16] This critique does a great deal of rhetorical work. With the figure of the tchotchke, Bruster not only transforms the object of material culture into something cheap, trifling, and even in bad taste. Just as important, he reads into the object the specter of a backward-looking anachronism: "tchotchke" is, of course, a term that is a relic from an old Yiddish-speaking European Jewry largely erased or displaced by World War II and the foundation of the modern, Hebrew-speaking state of Israel. It thus quietly communicates a sense that the objects studied by what Bruster terms the "new materialism" are overvalued idols that belong more properly to an old, superseded culture. In Bruster's critique, then, the tchotchke has much the same valence as the fetish does for Marx and Freud.

Indeed, many theorists, including Bruster himself, have pursued the equation between the object of material culture and the fetish.[17] This equation often recasts questions about the object as a problem of the subject. Bill Brown, for example, has argued that the American fascination with material culture provides a fetishistic means to repudiate a lack—less the mother's missing penis, as in Freud's classic account of the etiology of sexual fetishism, than a more profound absence within the subject herself. Trifling things thus offer the empty subject the promise of a phantasmatic plenitude in the form of what Brown, after Lacan and Žižek, calls "the Thing."[18] This psychoanalytically derived approach to objects has often been accompanied by a more traditional materialist discourse of fetishism. In his study of the fetish character of the commodity form in *Capital*, Marx considered how the reifications of capitalist exchange value invest mere things with a magical power that usurps and alienates the agency of human subjects.[19] Some Marxists have accordingly denounced the recent critical interest in the so-called lives of things—a recurrent phrase in work on material culture—as a fetishism guilty of "magical" thought, insofar as it allegedly anthropomorphizes inert objects by lending agency to them.[20] Both psychoanalytic and materialist accounts of object fetishisms pivot on category confusions—the standing in of the thing for the Thing, the misprision of the passive object for an active subject. But each account couches these confusions in the terms of a more profound temporal confusion. After all, both Marx and Freud regarded the fetish as a pathological stray from a foreign past, an anachronistic irruption within the European present of a "primitive" African belief system.[21]

Even as theoretical invocations of fetishism—whether indebted to Marx or to Freud—ostensibly seek to divert attention from the object to the primacy of the subject, I would argue that they respond, albeit in disavowed form, to a temporal conundrum posed by objects and matter itself. That is, things are often shrouded in anachronism. This is not simply because many objects are time travelers from the past (think, for example, of family photo albums with their frequently embarrassing evidence of out-of-date hairstyles and other fashion no-no's). Nor is it because present objects are sometimes coded as temporally obsolete in order to assert their social unacceptability or pathological nature (think of the *hijab*, or veil, which has in much of the west become an overdetermined figure for Islam's supposedly "medieval" attitude to women).[22] It is, more precisely, because the objects of material culture are often saturated with the unmistakable if frequently faint imprints of many times. Philosophers of science have repeatedly drawn attention to this property of things. We have already seen how Latour's toolbox contains both contemporary electric drill and ancient hammer. Similarly, Serres notes of the automobile that it is a transtemporal assemblage: it collates old and new, less in its actual matter than in its aggregate of technical innovations dating from wildly different periods.[23] And Steven Shapin observes how modern material goods often contain antique elements, such as the QWERTY keyboard of his laptop, patented in 1878.[24] The discourse of the temporally retrograde fetish, when applied to the study of material culture, can thus work to displace and dismiss the specter of anachronism that haunts objects in general. But the relations between matter and temporality have been largely occluded in recent scholarship on objects, which has tended to transform the "material" of material culture into a synonym for "physical"—thereby freezing not just the object in time but also time in the object.[25]

Marx provides one important corrective to this disavowal of temporality in the study of physical objects. In the "Theses on Feuerbach," he argues that understanding matter "only in the form of the object" ignores the dynamic dimension of praxis. Matter, he insists, should be conceived of less as a physical actuality than as a sensuous, workable potentiality that implies pasts, presents, and futures.[26] It is one of Marx's enduringly useful insights, therefore, that a materialism that attends only to the physical form of objects leaves out not only work but also time from its understanding of matter. This is hardly Marx's innovation, of course. In *De anima*, Aristotle draws a critical distinction between form and matter, according to which "form is actuality" and "matter is potentiality [*dynameos*]."[27] For Aristotle as much as for Marx, matter is both past material that has been reworked as well as present, reworkable potential that presumes a future. Materiality thus articulates temporal difference. But in collating the traces of past, present, and future, it also pluralizes and hence problematizes the time of the object. In this respect, materiality is not simply some kind of raw physicality prior to language and culture. It is rather a site of inscription and of *différance*. Matter is a surface that can be written on; but it is itself a species of "arche-writing" in Derrida's sense, inasmuch as it is characterized by an ontological and temporal self-differentiation and hence deferral.[28] Far from being an actuality endowed with self-identical presence, then, "matter" or "material" might instead be understood as designating a play of multiple temporal traces.

The non-self-identity of matter has been recognized by some scholars of materiality in the English Renaissance, including Jonathan Goldberg in his studies of "writing matter" and seventeenth-century atomic theory, as well as Mary C. Fuller in her analysis of Walter Ralegh's conception of gold.[29] The "material" of material culture, however, has for the most part not been understood in this sense. By constituting objects as self-identical physical presences, scholarship on early modern material culture attends to what Aristotle would have instead called "formal culture." In the process, both matter and time are understood to be positive, singular entities rather than protean, hybrid assemblages. This tendency can be seen in the most common critical procedure employed in discussions of early modern objects: that is, subjecting them to "thick description," in the sense of contextual elaboration as theorized by Gilbert Ryle and popularized by Clifford Geertz.[30] Hence a discussion of (say) early modern feathers as fashionable accessories will contextualize them within new networks of global trade; or an analysis of early modern buck baskets will read them in relation to contemporaneous discourses of witchcraft and women's agency.[31] Whether described as a form in relation simply to its physical environment or to the more complex networks of discourse and culture in which it is assumed to be embedded, the thickly described object assumes a synchronic temporal framework in the shape of a historical moment. Object and moment, small thing and larger cultural context, are thus both reified as temporally singular.

One seeming critique of this synchronic approach has been offered by the cultural anthropologists Arjun Appadurai and Igor Kopytoff, who have argued for greater attention to the social life or cultural biography of things. Objects, in Appadurai's words, possess "life histories" or "careers" that invest them with social significance and cultural value. According to this view, objects do not simply acquire meaning by virtue of their present social contexts.

Rather, the value a particular object assumes derives from the differential relation of its present context to its assumed or known past usages and its potential future usages. In order to read the significance of any object, then, it becomes necessary to trace its "cultural biography" as it "moves through different hands, contexts, and uses."[32] With its emphasis on the trajectories of things over time, Appadurai and Kopytoff's approach to objects has been helpful as a means of reading social and cultural transformation into the otherwise synchronic terrain of early modern material culture.[33] The cultural biography of things has proved particularly attractive to scholars of early modern stage properties, including myself. By tracing the transmigrations of objects from monastic vestries or guild shops to the tiring room and the playhouse, recent studies of the English Renaissance theater have begun to understand how stage properties were not only physical accessories to playtexts but also mobile commodities participating within larger networks of social change and exchange.[34]

But even though this biographical approach is designed to consider the diachronic properties of the object as it moves through different institutional and economic settings, it can in practice amount to little more than a multiple series of synchronic exfoliations that assume the self-identical presence of the object within any given moment and of the moment as materialized by any given object.[35] Although Appadurai and Kopytoff do recognize the differential logic that allows past and future uses of an object to contribute to its value and significance in the present, theirs is primarily a structuralist and linear understanding of temporality. Moments are temporally purified by virtue of not being what comes before or after them; indeed, the critical objective of cultural biography is to plot the progressive movement of a thing through a sequence of moments—object *a* has value *x* in moment 1, value *y* in moment 2, and so on. As a result, cultural biography cannot fully account for the multiple traces of time embedded in things, and the complex ways in which—as in Latour's toolbox, Serres's automobile, or Shapin's laptop keyboard—these traces play an active role in the present object.

One scholar of English Renaissance material culture who has consistently heeded the anachronistic traces of the past within the object is Peter Stallybrass. In a series of essays on Renaissance textiles and what he calls the "materials of memory," Stallybrass—often in collaboration with Ann Rosalind Jones—notes how clothes cannot be understood simply in terms of their cultural contexts or their "life" histories. Rather, they "both *are* material presences and they *encode* other material and immaterial presences."[36] These other presences are, in Stallybrass's brilliant analyses of theatrical garments inherited from the monasteries and the stage costume of the Ghost in *Hamlet*, the memorial marks of the past.[37] Textiles, multiply inscribed by corporeality and memory, are resistant to the synchronizations and temporal purifications of thick description and cultural biography. In Stallybrass's garments, we can glimpse another temporality that exceeds and complicates the reifications of the self-identical moment and the diachronic sequence. Stallybrass instead allows textiles to materialize the possibility of what Kathleen Biddick, arguing for an alternative to the linear, purified time of Christian supersession, calls "a temporality that is not one."[38] Yet this nonsingular temporality is a possibility more suggested than sustainedly theorized in Stallybrass's work on textiles. Stallybrass notes that clothes often bear the imprints of past wearers or encode the immaterial presences of memory, but he does not consider how such polychronic traces might be an intrinsic rather than contingent dimension of matter—or, indeed, how they might unsettle the fantasy of the self-identical moment that underwrites both synchronic and diachronic approaches to material culture. What we still need, in other words, is a comprehensive theorization of how matter tends to be out of time with itself, and how its properties lend themselves less to synchronic or diachronic than to polychronic analysis.

In this context it is salutary to return to Fredric Jameson's *Political Unconscious*, the work that not only provided historicism with its de facto imperative "Always historicize!" but also helped translate the very terms "synchronic" and "diachronic" from linguistic to historical analysis.[39] The new historicist and cultural materialist turn of the 1980s employed the terms of Jameson's study to advance two divergent ideals of what Jameson supposedly meant by "Always historicize!": always contextualize in relation either to a moment (that is, always synchronize!) or to a transition (always diachronize!). What got neglected was how Jameson's injunction is equally a call to polychronize. Noting the propensity of literature to resist any univocal reflection of the material circumstances of its production, Jameson writes of how literary "form, secreted like a shell or exoskeleton, continues to emit its ideological message long after the extinction of its host."[40] With his suggestively material metaphor of the exoskeleton, Jameson indicates that historicism needs to do more than simply read synchronically and/or diachronically; it also needs to consider how its objects are polychronic assemblages that are temporally out of step with themselves and their moment. In the process,

Jameson makes space for what Friedrich Nietzsche—or rather, Nietzsche's English translators—called the "untimely."[41]

The untimely is a particularly tricky concept, and it has a complex philological and critical history. The word Nietzsche used was *unzeitgemässe*; it derives from the negative *un* plus *Zeit*, meaning both "time" and "a time," and *gemäss*, a slippery term employed both as an adjective ("appropriate" or "fitting") and a preposition ("in compliance with"). The adjective *zeitgemässe* was popular among nineteenth-century German writers as a synonym for "modern, progressive, up-to-date"; it implied a sense of temporal propriety, of that which suits the time by being fully of it.[42] For Nietzsche, then, that which is *unzeitgemässe* is out-of-time, inhabiting a moment but also alien to and out of step with it. Hence it is often translated as "unfashionable" and "unmodern." Both terms suggest the anachronistic apparition of a supposedly superseded past in the present, a scenario that resonates with Nietzsche the philologist's fascination with etymological roots and Nietzsche the Hellenist's love of classical philosophy. Yet his *unzeitgemässe* does not simply connote the persistence of the past in the present; it also has a critical dimension. By resisting absorption into a homogeneous present, it brings with it the difference that produces the possibility of a new future even as it evokes the past. As he argues in "On the Uses and Disadvantages of History for Life," Nietzsche sees the untimely as "acting counter to our time and thereby acting on our time and, let us hope, for the benefit of a time to come."[43]

With its suggestion of dissident agency, Nietzsche's untimely has recently acquired a new life in a variety of theoretical ideolects. For Gilles Deleuze and Félix Guattari, the untimely is a temporal becoming-other that subverts the twin reifications of time as epoch and chronological sequence—what they elsewhere characterize as the false ontologies of the synchronic and the diachronic presumed by the idea of time as *chronos*.[44] And for Elizabeth Grosz, who grafts Deleuze and Guattari's emphasis on becoming to Nietzsche's investment in the subversive potential of the past, the untimely acquires a critical potential for feminist and antiracist movements.[45] But perhaps the most influential adaptation, and one of special interest to early modernists, has been Jacques Derrida's "hauntology" in *Specters of Marx*.[46] In a discussion that draws on Marx's conjurations of *Hamlet* and its Ghost, Derrida styles the untimely as a specter that haunts the present and renders the time "out of joint": specifically, it is the ghost of a superseded past that, by reintroducing radical alterity into an otherwise self-identical present, models the justice of the other. Derrida's figure of the specter works well for the untimely power of supposedly obsolete *ideas*, including those of Marxism after the alleged "end of history."[47] But a theory of untimely matter that seeks to understand how the past persists in and works through present *objects* might wish to resist Derrida's persistent characterization of the untimely as a ghostly revenant. Latour's toolbox, Serres's automobile, and Shapin's keyboard are hardly "haunted" by the specters of the past. Rather, the past works actively in and through them. How, one might then ask, is the past alive in the matter of the present—and in a way that doesn't assume its life to be merely spectral?

Jameson's exoskeleton, unlike Derrida's specter, suggests how a time out of joint can reside in living organic matter. Indeed, Hamlet's very phrase deploys a corporeal metaphor to represent temporal dislocation. Derrida discusses the various meanings and translations of "time out of joint" in *Specters of Marx*; but he focuses primarily on the meaning of "time" or "temps," and considers "out of joint" only in its literally disembodied French translations—"hors de ses gonds" (off its hinges), "détraqué" (broken down), "à l'envers" (upside down), and "déshonoré" (dishonored).[48] But Hamlet's phrase would have had a more insistently corporeal connotation for the play's early modern audiences. The OED notes that "out of joint" was used in Shakespeare's time primarily to refer to "a bone displaced from its articulation with another; dislocated; also of the part or member affected."[49] So when Gynecia's carriage crashes and turns over in book 2 of Philip Sidney's *Arcadia*, "the bruise of the fall" puts her shoulder "out of joint."[50] Hamlet's "time . . . out of joint" implies, like Jameson's exoskeleton, a bony matter out of time with itself. This intuition of the untimely is realized in *Hamlet* less by any ghostly apparition than by the play's insistence that the objects of today's material culture are riddled with the traces of antique bodily (and bony) matter. As Hamlet asks with regard to the matter of a wine cask in the gravedigger scene, "Why may not imagination trace the noble dust of Alexander till a find it stopping a bung-hole?" (5.1.187–89).[51] Alexander's "noble dust" may, in one context, be dead; but in another, it is still alive—and not as some spectral revenant but as an untimely agent within a larger network that includes not only the physical substance of the wine cask but also the "imagination" that "trace[s]" it.

Hamlet's reflections on what imagination can do to the dust of the past suggests that we need to do more than just understand the polychronicity of matter, or how it is marked by the traces of multiple times. We equally need to theorize matter's multitemporality: that is, the ways in which we physically and imaginatively rework matter to produce diverse organizations of time. Nietzsche's untimely is not just a descriptive theory of the polychronic, of the past-in-the-present. It is also a practical theory of how to rework temporality, of how we might use the past to imagine alternatives to the present and to chronology itself. Untimely matter likewise suggests the simultaneous agency of past matter and present subject in reworking our conceptions of temporality. To this end, I shall argue, scholars of Renaissance material culture might think more closely about the matter of the palimpsest. Few material artifacts better illustrate the untimely workings of a "temporality that is not one."

The Temporalities of the Palimpsest

The Walters Art Museum in Baltimore houses a peculiar and decidedly challenging manuscript called the Archimedes Palimpsest (fig. 1). Written on a sheaf of goatskin pages that are torn and riddled with holes and mold, its reading matter is unusually hard to decipher. Much of the manuscript consists of medieval Greek Orthodox liturgical materials handwritten by a monastic scribe who signs both his name, Ioannes Myronas, and the date on which he copied the text—April 29, 1229. The visibility of Myronas's writing is not just compromised by the damage the manuscript has sustained since the thirteenth century, including faux-Byzantine images painted over it by a twentieth-century forger. It is also interrupted by an eerie apparition from the past. Underneath Myronas's script, and often at right angles to it, are the faint traces of other handwriting. This under-text, also in Greek, most likely dates back to the late fifth century. Paleographic research has confirmed that the older writing consists in large part of the only surviving versions of two works by the Greek mathematician Archimedes: a study of hydraulics, *Floating Bodies*, and a treatise on the mathematical concept of infinity.[52]

The time of the Archimedes Palimpsest is flagrantly polychronic. Medieval liturgical script, modern forged image, and classical philosophical text are all legible in its matter. And the mold, stains, and wear and tear of all the intervening years supplement these multiple traces. But what work do these gathered temporal pleats do? And what work can we do with them? What relations between past and present, between old and new, might be generated from their folds? If the Archimedes Palimpsest is polychronic, it is also—to use Serres's subtly different term—multitemporal. That is to say, it can be

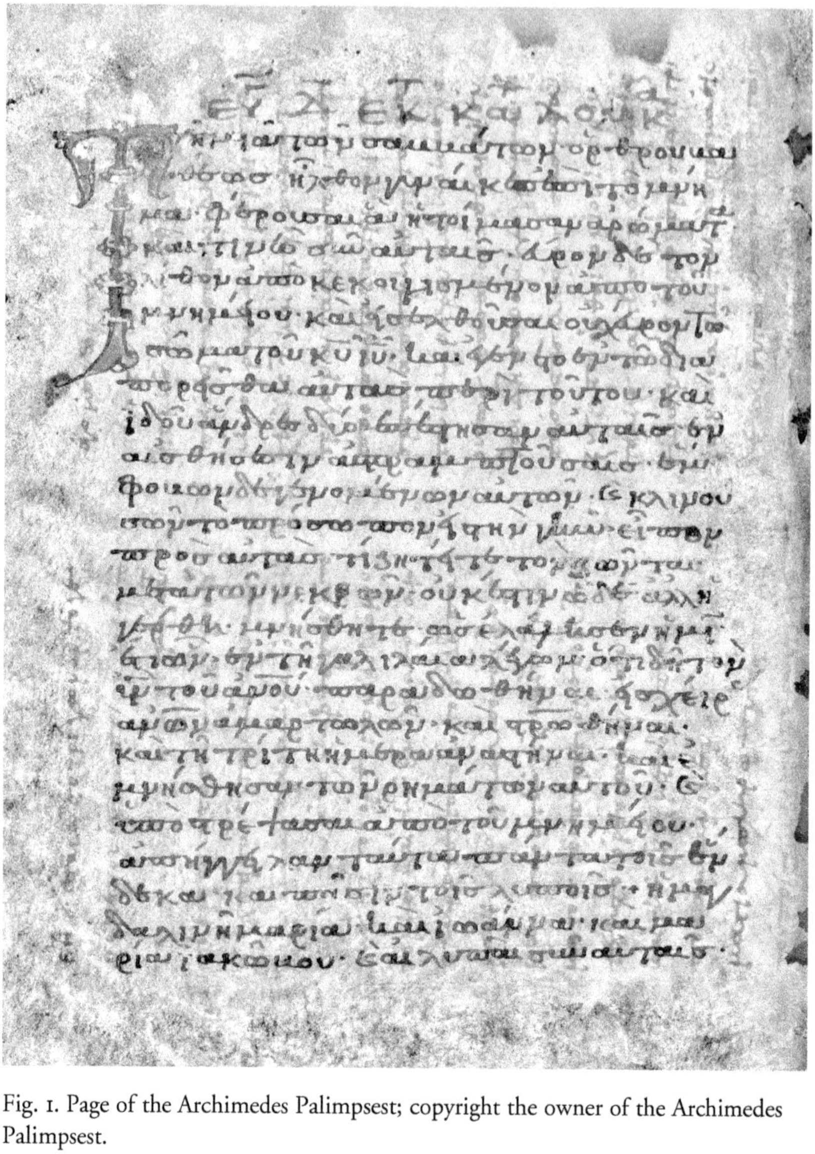

Fig. 1. Page of the Archimedes Palimpsest; copyright the owner of the Archimedes Palimpsest.

made to articulate several different organizations of time. I am interested in three in particular, and they will serve as templates for the temporalities of untimely matter I consider throughout this book.

Myronas had engaged in what was a common medieval practice—scraping and washing the pages of an old manuscript so that they may be written on anew, a process known as palimpsesting (derived from the Greek *palimpsestos*, meaning "scraped again"). On the one hand, the practice was a necessity born of the comparative scarcity of writing surfaces. But it was also suffused with a powerful symbolism. Myronas's manuscript performs the triumph of Christianity according to the logic of supersession—that is, of preserving, negating, and transcending rival religions and cultures deemed to be no longer coeval but "old" and of the past. Saint Paul had remarked, after all, that the Christian covenant canceled not only the law of the Jewish rabbis but also the *logos* of the Greek philosophers.[53] Just as the Bible transforms the Jewish scriptures into an Old Testament superseded by the living Word of God as revealed in the New Testament, so too does Myronas's palimpsest capture and cancel Greek philosophy, preserving it in the present yet banishing it to the past by overwriting it with Christian liturgy. Like the Bible, the palimpsest produces a supposedly purified temporality, a "living" after that is opposed to a "dead" before.

Yet this supersession is not, and cannot be, total. For the fifth-century under-text is not simply a dead letter buried beneath the living Word of a new covenant—it retains its legibility, albeit faintly. Thus even as it is temporally distanced from and by the liturgy written over it, it retains a power to speak, and hence to disrupt and transform its over-text. Myronas may have sought to cancel Greek philosophy with the up-to-date good news of Christianity. But the net effect of the Archimedes Palimpsest—within which, as the manuscript's official name suggests, the pagan under-text about floating bodies buoyantly rises through and above the Christian over-text beneath which it has supposedly been submerged—is not just one of supersession. It is equally one of untimely irruption.[54] I call this the temporality of explosion: the apparition of the "old" text shatters the integrity of the "new" by introducing into it a radical alterity that punctures the illusion of its wholeness or finality.

But the untimely relations between the Archimedes Palimpsest's over- and under-texts are not necessarily just supersessionary or explosive. The startling juxtaposition of mathematics and liturgy also potentially generates a third temporality. If the first two are grounded in a difference that bestows agency on present or past but not on both—supersession seeks to silence the pagan past, explosion allows that past to speak back—this third temporality is grounded less in absolute division than in affinity between classical Greek philosopher and medieval Christian scribe. After all, both Archimedes and Myronas are concerned with the subject of infinity. The former may imagine that concept mathematically, and the latter theologically. But without ever becoming identical, the infinities of classical past and medieval present can converse with each other. I call this dialogic temporality the temporality of conjunction.

The multitemporal dimensions of the Archimedes Palimpsest underscore how temporality is not simply a property intrinsic to a material object. It is also generated by the work we do with that object, and how we read and rework its polychronic marks of different times—how, to adapt Hamlet's words, "imagination" may "trace" matter. Temporality, then, is not just a singularity reified in an object. It is, more accurately, a polychronic network that collates various actors—human and inhuman, animate and inanimate, subject and object—from past and present.[55] On occasion, some of these "actors" might *seem* not to act at all. But even in such instances they are crucial to the polychronic network and the temporality it produces. The temporality of supersession needs the supposedly inactive past matter it negates; likewise the temporality of explosion needs the present matter that it shatters. It is only the temporality of conjunction that foregrounds what is suppressed by both supersession and explosion: how past and present work together, and how they are reworked by the imagination of the theorist, to produce the temporalities of matter.

How might the palimpsest illuminate the untimeliness of matter? The polychronicity of the palimpsest, like that of matter in general, is obstinately antisequential: superimposing past and present without insisting on any linear relation between them, it compresses different times within one surface. That doesn't mean the palimpsest's past layers are transparently legible. What interests me, rather, is that even in their very opacity or inscrutability, the most archaic inscriptions in a palimpsest have the power to transform and displace the texts that have been written over them, even as the latter equally transform and displace their predecessors. I should stress that I don't see either the palimpsest or matter simply as writing, at least not in any narrow sense of that word. I thus approach the palimpsest somewhat differently from how it has been employed in literary criticism and theory, where it has tended to be regarded simply as a species of textuality. Gérard Genette, for example, uses the palimpsest as a metaphor for an array of paratextual effects whereby past texts are echoed, parodied, and rewritten; new editorial theory has employed it to represent the changed and changing written elements of edited texts; Chantal Zabus has invoked it to characterize the "indigenized" English and French texts of West African writers.[56] But the palimpsest is more than a collation of diverse inscriptions that accrue over time. It is also a complex, polychronic assemblage of material *agents*: it includes a writing surface, whether parchment or vellum, that enables, even as it is transformed by, the writing on it.[57] And this network of agency, of course, presumes yet more actors—specifically, writers and readers from different times who work upon the palimpsest surface, transforming it but also exposing themselves in the process to the possibility of transformation. The palimpsest is thus not just a metaphor for untimely matter: it *is* untimely matter.

Take, for instance, a Renaissance genre of English palimpsest that has been recently studied by Eamon Duffy: copies of the Book of Hours, which were repeatedly annotated by their many readers in the fifteenth and sixteenth centuries.[58] As Duffy shows, Books of Hours—Catholic collections of psalms, prayers, and other devotional manuscripts—provided popular writing surfaces on which people left records of their lives and beliefs, supplementing or overlaying the books' original texts with biographical jottings, personal reflections, and pious alterations. The resulting collations of materials, as they were passed down from reader to reader, were subjected to ever new rounds of annotative reworking, especially after the Reformation. But their old textual matter could also get to work on the reader, prompting edification, nostalgia, or religious dismay. The annotated Books of Hours thus model "a temporality that is not one." Their polychronic pages articulate multiple temporal relations—supersessionary, explosive, conjunctive—among past, present and future.

These relations emerge in Peter Stallybrass's study of one such Book of Hours, a breviary first collated in around 1505.[59] Repeatedly transformed by its readers over the course of two centuries of religious reformation and schism, the breviary displays a variety of techniques of palimpsesting—scraping, overlaying, annotating—that not only update superseded texts but also juxtapose new and old matter (some printed, some handwritten) in surprising combinations (fig. 2). Stallybrass warns us against reading the breviary simply as a diachronic record of changing beliefs. Such an approach does not do justice to the text's polychronicity and multitemporality, which allow the old to do work alongside the new. Indeed, the breviary challenges periodization by being of several times: it shows how "book history should

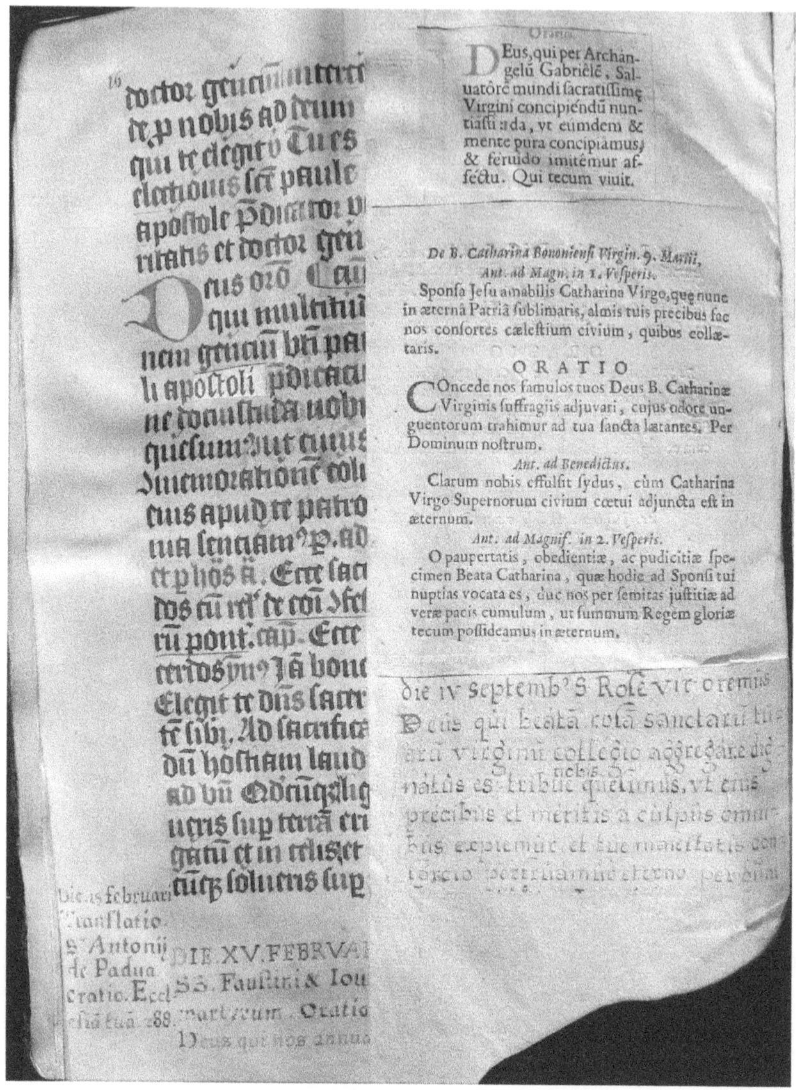

Deus, qui per Archangelũ Gabrielẽ, Saluatorẽ mundi ſacratiſſimę Virgini concipiendũ nuntiaſti: da, vt eumdem & mente pura concipiamus, & feruido imitemur affectu. Qui tecum viuit.

De B. Catharina Bononienſi Virgin. 9. Martii, Ant. ad Magn. in 1. Veſperis.

Sponſa Jeſu amabilis Catharina Virgo, quę nunc in æterna Patria ſublimaris, almis tuis precibus fac nos conſortes cæleſtium civium, quibus collætaris.

ORATIO

COncede nos famulos tuos Deus B. Catharinæ Virginis ſuffragiis adjuvari, cujus odore unguentorum trahimur ad tua ſancta lætantes. Per Dominum noſtrum.

Ant. ad Benedictus.

Clarum nobis effulſit ſydus, cùm Catharina Virgo Supernorum civium cœtui adjuncta eſt in æternum.

Ant. ad Magnif. in 2. Veſperis.

O paupertatis, obedientiæ, ac pudicitiæ ſpecimen Beata Catharina, quæ hodie ad Sponſi tui nuptias vocata es, duc nos per ſemitas juſtitiæ ad veræ pacis cumulum, ut ſummum Regem gloriæ tecum poſſideamus in æternum.

Fig. 2. Sixteenth-century breviary; Mortimer Rare Book Room, Smith College.

make us think of all history in terms of multiple (overlapping and intersecting) temporalities rather than the punctual time of specific dates and periods."[60] By disclosing the networks of transtemporal labor that both create period boundaries and collapse them, Stallybrass's analysis shows how the breviary is a text in the Latin sense of a "weaving together" of various elements—not just different fragments of writing but also different readers, times, and temporalities.

Reworking Matter in the Time of Shakespeare

The untimely matter I examine in the following pages is illuminated by this section's title, "Reworking Matter in the Time of Shakespeare." The phrase promises a reworking of material culture as currently understood in scholarship on objects in Shakespeare's England—specifically, a reworking that moves beyond the reifications of synchronic and diachronic analysis toward a polychronic account of matter. This means expanding the parameters of material culture not only temporally but also ontologically. Scholarship on objects has tended to privilege the visible thing; the latter offers the allure of a raw, unmediated physicality in contrast to the ineffable *mise-en-abîmes* of poststructuralist textuality. But the materials I consider here do not always make themselves known to sight. Some get to work on different senses, whether through the nose or through touch. Other materials I examine are not even things as such but blur the boundary between subject and object: for instance, the actor's histrionic body.[61] "Reworking matter in the time of Shakespeare" also means redressing a striking omission in studies of early modern things: that is, consideration of the various theories of matter—religious, philosophical, scientific—that shaped understandings of "material" objects. To this end, I take into account more abstract forms of materiality theorized by Shakespeare's contemporaries, such as the matter of Christian typology, the matter of Lucretian atomism, and the matter of vitalist philosophy. These theories do not always directly address objects of material culture. But they cannot be easily extricated from such objects, inasmuch as they inflect how material culture was understood, experienced, and worked upon by Shakespeare and his contemporaries.

As I shall show, these understandings and experiences of matter suggest a second meaning of this section's title. "Reworking Matter in the Time of Shakespeare" conveys how Shakespeare and his contemporaries saw matter as itself implicated in a dual process of reworking. For them, matter is always subject to change; but it also changes those who work on it. From George Herbert's typological reworking of Old Testament materials to John Stow's account of the refashioning of London's physical structures and Margaret Cavendish's vitalist theory of reworked compounds, English Renaissance writers repeatedly recognize the polychronic dimensions of matter—the many shaping hands, artisanal and textual, that introduce into it multiple traces of different times, rendering the supposedly singular thing plural, both physically and temporally. But they also recognize how these traces get to work on those who work with matter. Such recognition, I shall argue, is particularly pronounced in Shakespeare's work; and not just in his written work but also in the onstage material practices of his theater company. The stagecraft of the King's Men—their acting styles, special effects, and stage properties—arguably constitutes English Renaissance culture's most sustained practical theory of untimely matter.[62] This theory resists the confining rubrics of either the synchronic moment or the diachronic sequence. In its embrace of polychronicity, it suggests a distinctively Renaissance attitude to time—one that, inasmuch as it can unsettle the models of temporality informing much current scholarship on material culture, furnishes an illustrative instance of the past's untimely power.

As a result, this book does more than just rework understandings of material culture in the time (or age) of Shakespeare. More accurately, it recalibrates material culture with the time (or conceptions of temporality) of Shakespeare. "In the time of Shakespeare" is designed to communicate a sense less of a chronological period than of a tempo repeatedly theorized by Shakespeare and his contemporaries—that is, a tempo characterized by an untimely aggregation of matter, agents, and historical traces.[63] "The time of Shakespeare," then, is both of early modernity and also not of it. It is, to borrow Dipesh Chakrabarty's term, a *time-knot* that disrupts the supersessionary temporality informing the very terminology of the "early modern."[64] Whereas "early modern" presumes a diachronic movement from the past to the present, "the time of Shakespeare" suggests a polychronic alternative that is of the early modern era yet also problematizes the orderly progression from the early to the modern. "The time of Shakespeare," then, can be just as much our own "time"—though in laying claim to it we must no longer understand that time either as identical with itself or quarantined from what sequentially precedes or follows it.

This book is divided into three parts, each of which pairs a Renaissance writer's theory of matter with the untimely materials of Shakespeare's theater company. The parts outline the contours of the three different temporalities of polychronic matter I have already briefly sketched in relation to the Archimedes Palimpsest: supersession, explosion, and conjunction. My treatment of each temporality is framed by an engagement with a different philosophical tradition—in the case of supersession, the dialectical *Aufhebung* of G. W. F. Hegel; explosion, the weak messianic eschatology of Walter Benjamin; and conjunction, the actor-network theory of Bruno Latour—each of which, I argue, does not so much explain as bear the telltale imprint of a Renaissance production of untimely matter. Hegel's Aufhebung reworks medieval and early modern architectural practices of desecration; Benjamin's weak messianism is interarticulated with his reading of allegorical objects in seventeenth-century German *Trauerspiel*; Latour's account of actor networks pivots on Robert Boyle's demonstration of the air pump to the Royal Society in 1667. But while the three parts of this book draw broadly on these three philosophical currents, individual chapters engage with more specific trends in critical practice—among them, typology theory, the Marxist theater history of Robert Weimann, urban studies, historical phenomenology, French feminism, and Michel Serres's neo-Lucretian poetics of science. In the process, *Untimely Matter in the Time of Shakespeare* considers not only Renaissance theories of matter but also the ways in which these might speak to and even transform some of our most dynamic contemporary methods of interpretation and critique.

The first part, "Supersessions," outlines the basics of an English Renaissance theory of untimely matter with respect to notions of supersession and the supposed progression of spirit from orient to occident. Chapter 1 examines George Herbert's peculiar reworking of Pauline typology in *The Temple*, in which he views history as a providential palimpsesting of "old" Jewish matter with "new" Christian spirit. For Herbert, this temporal translation is accompanied by a geographical translation from east to west. Yet even as Herbert's poems assert progressive geographical and temporal movements, they also expose a recursive tendency that renders the illusion of progress problematic; supposedly superseded Jewish matter is never quite left behind, and instead keeps quilting the future with the past. Chapter 2 develops the implications of Herbert's polychronic compression of oriental past into occidental future by considering the bodily techniques of the Shakespearean actor. Shakespeare's second Henriad repeatedly palimpsests its characters with oriental despots, such as Cambyses of Persia, Tamburlaine of Scythia, Amurath of Turkey, and Herod of Jewry. These doublings not only conjure historical figures from the east; they also rehearse primitive acting styles from England's theatrical past in a display of histrionic versatility designed to suggest a new theatrical future. In the process, the plays perform the surprisingly untimely logic of supersession characteristic of Hegel's philosophy of history.

The second part, "Explosions," examines how the reworking of the past in the present need not serve just the temporality of supersession. Indeed, English Renaissance writers—like Walter Benjamin's historical materialist—often allow the untimely matter of the past to intervene in and fracture the present. Chapter 3 considers how John Stow's *Survey of London* inscribes the city's history onto its physical features, particularly with regard to the neighborhood of Old Jewry. Stow figures the district as a palimpsest that records diverse cultures and times. Even as his *Survey* seems to abide by the strictures of supersessionary time, however, Stow also uses past Jewish matter—in particular, a stone engraved with a Hebrew inscription that he finds in the Ludgate wall—to fracture the Protestant vision of London as a New Jerusalem. The explosive potential of this untimely matter is literalized in chapter 4, which considers the theatrical squib, the stinking low-tech gunpowder explosive used to produce the illusion of thunder and lightning in *Macbeth*. The smell of the squib entailed a palimpsesting of temporally discrete events and conventions: the contemporary Gunpowder Plot, the older stage tradition of firework-throwing devils and Vices, and the abandoned sacred time of Catholic ritual in which fair and foul smells signified, respectively, divine and satanic presence. This old religious time may be past, but it is not simply superseded; for *Macbeth* explosively registers the loss of the old system of value encoded in Catholic olfactory ritual.

The final part, "Conjunctions," traces a different, less antagonistic understanding of the relations between the polychronic traces at play in untimely matter. Chapter 5 examines the literally touching affinities between Hélène Cixous's theory of dialogic corporeality and Margaret Cavendish's vitalist theory of matter. Cixous and Cavendish both view materiality as palimpsested, containing within itself a potentially infinite number of alternate universes that touch each other; otherness—temporal as much as physical—is thus always inscribed within matter, which allows seemingly opposed entities (the female Cixous and the male Shakespeare, the Egyptian Cleopatra and the English Cavendish, the Jewish Cabbala and modern science) to conjoin and enter into untimely dialogue. Chapter 6 develops the notion of conjunction with respect to the one of the most fateful stage properties of *Othello*—the handkerchief—and Serres's model of crumpled or folded time. Building on Latour's theorization of the actor network, I show how both *Othello*'s treatment of its napkin and Serres's discussion of a crumpled handkerchief equally suggest a theory of palimpsested time grounded, like Cavendish's vitalist matter, in untimely conjunctions between seemingly opposed and bounded temporal elements, be they sexual, racial, or religious.

One of the most useful consequences of a new attention to the palimpsests of matter in the time of Shakespeare is how these can help illuminate a somewhat neglected axis in western understandings of otherness. Edward Said's *Orientalism* serves as a reminder that the orient is a trace that inhabits, often under erasure, the palimpsest that is Europe.[65] Said's invaluable study, however, offers a largely spatial, detemporalized template for understanding western representations of the east; it thus neglects the ways in which writers from Herodotus to Hegel have repeatedly constructed the orient as not just a present *space* but also a past *time* superseded by a west that embodies the present and the future.[66] And western Christian conceptions of supersessionary time have provided the foundation for the secular conceptions of developmental history critiqued by recent postcolonial, ethnographic, and actor-network theorists—be it the historicist time that, according to Dipesh Chakrabarty, places the non-west in "the waiting room of history"; the anthropological or "allochronic" time that, in Johannes Fabian's analysis, denies the coevalness of so-called primitive cultures; or the modern time that, for Latour, temporally partitions itself from the hybrid knowledge formations of what it slights as premodernity.[67]

These nominally secular constructions of the west's temporal and geographical others are illuminated by the instance of post-Reformation England, where not only pagan and Jewish but also Roman Catholic elements are temporally partitioned from the Protestant present. In the chapters that follow, I consider how the untimely matter of English Renaissance writing and Shakespeare's stage encodes a variety of temporal relations between England and its supposedly noncoeval others. If, in the Myronas/Archimedes manuscript, the past has become a foreigner—unassimilable Greek matter temporally deported by the good news of the Christian covenant—then English Renaissance writers even more insistently locate the past traces of matter in foreign space. Many instances of palimpsested matter I consider in this book code the past as "oriental" and the present or future as "occidental." We have come to regard these two terms simply as geographical and cultural. But in premodern usage, they also have a temporal dimension. The orient is where the sun rises and so connotes "early," while the occident is where it sets and implies "late."[68]

Shakespeare and his contemporaries understand what is temporally as well as geographically oriental in a variety of ways: the "antique" cultures of

Persia, Greece, and Egypt, the "outmoded" rituals of Roman Catholicism and, most insistently, the "old" covenant of Judaism. Indeed, as the repeated apparition of untimely Jewish matter in the following chapters make clear, English Renaissance writers' apprehension of polychronic matter was almost invariably shadowed by the figure of what Steven F. Kruger has termed "the spectral Jew," a paradoxically material and embodied ghost haunting the Christian spirit that has supposedly superseded it.[69] That Jewishness is such a pervasive metonymy for the oriental past in even supposedly secular theories of polychronic matter gives some indication of the shaping power of Christian conceptions of temporality in the time of Shakespeare. Yet contrary to the Bible's cancellation of Old Jewish Testament by New Christian Gospel, these conceptions are not always supersessionary.

Herbert's religious lyrics and Shakespeare's acting styles may seek to distance the orient temporally, whether that orient takes the form of pre-Christian Judaism or over-the-top histrionics associated with past despots and old theater practices. But Stow's chorographical discoveries and Shakespeare's stinking special effects allow the matter of Jewish and Catholic religious pasts to explode into and rupture the homogenous time of the present, converting material culture into *matériel* culture. And Cavendish's quasi-scientific treatises as well as Shakespeare's handkerchief in *Othello* fold the oriental past into the occidental present in ways that allow for relations of affinity and proximity rather than difference and distance between "then" and "now." To this extent, my project on the untimely is also entirely timely: it reworks the matter of early modernity to illuminate and critique the ways in which the west imagines and temporally distances itself from its orients in the twenty-first century.

Such a critique necessitates a new understanding of the temporalities of matter. In this book, I offer a polychronic and multitemporal account of material culture that abides by the following five directives:

1. Read matter not just synchronically in relation to its moment of production or use, but also for the traces of other times—past and future—legible within it; by doing so, recognize how matter, like a palimpsest, exhibits a temporality that is not one.
2. Resist the reflex of organizing the relations between matter's multiple temporal traces into a chronological narrative of progress, i.e. the diachronic movement from one "moment" to the next.
3. Pose the question of agency: how does matter participate within poly-

chronic actor-networks that work and rework it? By recasting matter as an actor-network, consider the traces of the past and the future within it, not just as that which is worked upon, but also as agents that work upon the present.

4. Determine the various temporal relations articulated by such work: supersession, explosion, conjunction.
5. Attend to both the production and the erasure of temporal partitions enabled by the actor-networks of matter; consider how untimely matter's temporal differentiations and de-partitions shadow differentiations and de-partitions, not just of geographical space, but also of culture, religion, and race.

When these directives are followed, time and matter need no longer remain the hostages of period purification and the sovereign moment-state. Instead, the untimely as well as the timely can find their voice. Greater critical attention to untimely matter can also help us realize that, contrary to a well-known apothegm in English Renaissance studies, communications with the past do not necessarily entail speaking with the dead—at least not in the sense of conducting séances with a superseded past that remains partitioned from us.[70] We instead speak with and from assemblages within which, like Jameson's literary exoskeleton or the Archimedes Palimpsest, the past is always potentially alive. And in its untimely life, that past speaks with and through us in the accents of the present and, in ways we can never quite predict, the future.

PART I

Supersessions

Fig. 3. Pisa Cathedral, detail from external wall; photo credit: Kidipede—History for Kids.

The negation [Aufhebung] *coming from consciousness . . . supersedes* [aufhebt] *in such a way that it preserves and maintains what is superseded, and consequently survives its own supersession.*
—G. W. F. Hegel, *Phenomenology of Spirit*

How can the temporality of supersession be untimely? At first glance, it might seem to be anything but. After all, supersession appears to guarantee a punctual progression from before to after, from early to late, from past to present. "That was then, this is now": the phrase, a neat summation of supersessionary time, presumes an absolute temporal rupture between two self-identical monads, one canceled, the other current. "Now" replaces "then," seemingly permitting no polychronic remainder, no untimely trace or survival of the not-now.

Yet one of the most influential theories of supersession constitutively depends on the trace of the then in the now. Hegel's conception of *Aufhebung*—sometimes translated as "negation" or "sublation," but also as "supersession"—is the irreducible kernel of his dialectics. It is also the basis of his faith in the teleological movement of Spirit toward perfection. As such, it informs his progressive conception of time: without Aufhebung, Hegel cannot imagine temporal as well as aesthetic, political, and philosophical progress. But as my epigraph from *The Phenomenology of Spirit* makes clear, his vision of supersession also "preserves and maintains what is superseded." Hegel's Aufhebung, which he views as a tripartite process of capture, cancellation, and transcendence, is the philosophical equivalent of the decidedly odd custom whereby we blow our noses into handkerchiefs that we then fold and put into our pockets—a desirable expulsion that is simultaneously a retention.

The dialectical logic of Aufhebung harks back to Socrates and Plato. But we should not privilege its philosophical and secular prehistory at the expense of its more immediate affinities with a religious hermeneutical tradition. For Aufhebung is uncannily close to the supersessionary temporality of Christian typology. In typological thought, the Jewish *figura* anticipates and is superseded by the Christian *littera*, so that Moses prefigures Jesus, circumcision baptism, the flood the Crucifixion, and so on.[1] The figura is temporally distanced, but it remains indispensable to the typological system. Hence the Christian Bible includes Jewish scripture even as it banishes it to the past by making it the "Old" Testament. Like Hegel's Aufhebung, then, Christian supersession operates by means of capture, cancellation, and transcendence; its forward temporal momentum is dependent on the untimely survival of what it supersedes.

Unlike its Hegelian counterpart, however, which trades in consciousness and subjects, Christian supersession is often grounded in material practices and objects. This is particularly the case with medieval and Renaissance instances of supersession, which repeatedly get to work on pagan as much as Jewish matter. We have already seen how the Archimedes Palimpsest is a material artifact that performs the supersession of a pagan past (the *logos* of Greek philosophy) by overwriting it with a Christian present and future. But the Archimedes Palimpsest is only one such object. Pisa Cathedral, constructed from 1063 to 1350, offers a revealing instance of how the effect of supersessionary temporality is generated by matter that is out-of-time with itself. Upon close inspection, the exterior walls of this "medieval" Christian structure reveal a startlingly polychronic palimpsest: its Romanesque buttresses are made in large part of stones cut from old pagan temples and civic monuments. One hefty and well-hewn stone, for example, pointedly upends an inscription referencing "IMPCAESAR," or Emperor Caesar, that was probably once part of an old civic monument or building (fig. 3). This is, in effect, a Christian precursor of Hegelian Aufhebung: the inscribed matter of the past is captured (taken from its original location), cancelled (through inversion and desecration), and transcended (by the holy structure it is subsumed within). Yet even as Pisa Cathedral's walls perform the triumph of Christian time—the Romanesque temple of the living word superseding the dead letter of pagan Rome—they also do not entirely allow the Christian "now" to replace the pagan "then." Visitors to Pisa Cathedral, like readers of the Archimedes Palimpsest, repeatedly find their eyes drawn to archaic matter—the Latin inscriptions on the cathedral walls—in ways that underscore how the medieval Christian break with the past paradoxically depends on its untimely retention.

Kathleen Biddick offers a particularly illuminating glimpse of this paradox in her book *The Typological Imaginary*, a sustained critique of ideas of supersessionary time from the Middle Ages to the twentieth century. Biddick's discussion suggests how what seems to be a unilinear temporality that presumes a pure, progressive movement from past to future is always shadowed by polychronicity. In a powerful psychoanalytic reading of the kernel of pleasure that drives repetitive Catholic fantasies of supersession in the Middle Ages and the Renaissance, Biddick argues that such fantasies are constitutively concerned with material practices—specifically, the rite of circumcision and technologies of inscription. In particular, she considers how Catholic supersession received a fillip from the invention of the printing press, which refined earlier technologies of pricking and cutting that she sees as crucial to the typological imaginary.[2] Biddick interprets these technologies as betraying a compulsion that manages the specter of Jewish circumcision by reenacting it at the expense of Jews, who are repeatedly "cut" from the present and banished to the past. Hence even as supersessionary time supposedly moves forward, it is inadvertently dogged by another, recursive temporality that not only retains the superseded past in the present but also discloses that present to be an uncanny reproduction of the abjected past.[3] Catholic supersession, which in Biddick's reading seeks to foreclose a "temporality that is not one," is thus paradoxically dependent on the polychronicity of circumcision, which is simultaneously past and present, Jewish and Christian.

The two chapters in this section consider the polychronic matter that enables two English Renaissance theories of supersessionary time—the first, George Herbert's Protestant reworking of the Catholic understanding of typology; and the second, a secular mode of dramatic performance, adopted by the Shakespeare and the Lord Chamberlain's Men, which I call intertheatricality. Both Herbert and Shakespeare demand to be seen as theorists of the untimely, preoccupied with the problem of polychronicity and the palimpsest-like nature of matter. In Herbert's *The Temple* and Shakespeare's second Henriad, the fantasy of supersessionary time is dependent on a constitutive anachronism redolent of the palimpsested Pisa Cathedral walls: in order to perform the very difference between past and present, the matter of the past must be incorporated into the present. This past matter is, in both cases, coded as "oriental" in its geographical as well as its temporal sense. In the process, Herbert and Shakespeare not only imagine hybrid oriental/occidental palimpsests. They also foreground the problem hinted at in my epigraph from Hegel—that what is superseded survives its own supersession and can thus call into question the very progress it is enlisted to facilitate. And once the past is no longer regarded as having passed but is instead understood to reside in the now, we can start to take stock of its agency. That is, we can start seeing the past not as dead and buried, or even as a spectral visitor from beyond the grave, but as alive and active. We can see it, in other words, as untimely matter.

ONE

Reading Matter

George Herbert and the East-West Palimpsests of *The Temple*

"Wait, this is yesterday's."

Fig. 4. "Wait, this is yesterday's," Victoria Roberts, *New Yorker*, September 18, 2006;

In a recent *New Yorker* magazine competition, readers were invited to supply a caption for a cartoon by Victoria Roberts (fig. 4). The cartoon depicts a recognizably bland scene of modern American life: a nondescript middle-aged couple, seated with their dog in a nondescript sitting room, read the news. Yet Roberts injects into this homely scene something *unheimlich*. The man and woman browse not newspapers but two engraved tablets that seem anachronistically to have materialized from biblical-era Mount Sinai. The winning caption pithily underscores the scene's temporal disjunction: "Wait," the man remarks to his wife, "this is yesterday's."[1]

The *New Yorker* cartoon may bring to mind to an episode from scripture that constitutes a primal scene not only of Jewish law but also of material culture.[2] The engraved tablets that Moses brings down with him from Mount Sinai are more than raw matter; they are matter that has been *reworked*, stones transformed into the Book of the Covenant. In other words, the tablets presume a network of agency—the agency of those who have reworked stones into engraved tablets, of those who derive meaning from the tablets, and even of the tablets themselves as they prescribe cultural systems of belief and practice. Yet Moses' stones have been reworked by no human hand, but rather by "the finger of God" (Exodus 32:18). Thus if Jewish worship of God is authorized by what we recognize as material culture, the latter is presented as the work of God alone, as if to cloak or annul the "material" of material culture by enveloping it in the pure spirit of its maker and its end, its *arche* and its *telos*. Significantly, the book of Exodus contrasts Moses' spiritually pure tablets with an impure material culture, one crafted by human tools. After revealing the Ten Commandments to Moses, God tells him that "if thou wilt make me an altar of stone, thou shalt not build it of hewn stone, for if thou lift up thy tool upon it, thou hast polluted it" (Exodus 20:25). Human labor "pollutes" the altar because it displaces God as Creator and incites idolatry. In the beginning, then, there is the Word; but there is also a lifeless stony matter that awaits refashioning, and with ambivalent consequences. Once it is transformed into material culture, it can either promise living spirit or revert to dead matter.

Material culture's primal scene, therefore, is marked by polychronicity. The reworked stone of Exodus signifies both a future-in-the-present (a law promised by the tablets' letters) and a past-in-the-present (a polluted altar shaped by a regressive death drive opposed to futurity).[3] Right from its inception, then, material culture articulates a temporal split between backward material and progressive culture, inspired by spirit. Later, in the New Testament, this split is given sharper focus by Saint Paul, who enjoins Christians to acknowledge God "not in tables of stone, but in fleshy tables of the heart" (2 Corinthians 3:3). Saint Paul's is the classic New Testament formulation of the Christian covenant of grace, and it is notably constituted by and against Moses' tablets: old engraved Jewish matter is now, quite literally, a thing of the past, replaced by the divine writing in the true believer's soul. As the deadly "hewn stone" of Exodus suggests, however, it is less that God's finger has retreated from the matter it once inscribed than that it had always already been pointed accusingly at it. One consequence of that accusation is the very illusion of consequence: both Exodus and Saint Paul's letter to the Corinthians express faith in the forward progression of culture by exiling matter to a supposedly superseded time and place.[4]

This is the logic of supersession from Exodus, through Saint Paul, to the time of Shakespeare. In its every iteration, supersession is constitutively grounded in material culture and its temporal splitting, whereby reworked matter functions ambivalently as both the progressive medium of spiritual transcendence and the regressive obstacle to it. Judaism refashions stony matter into the Book of the Covenant but also dispatches it into a superseded past of idolatry; early Christianity fastens onto Moses' tablets as an analogical figure for the faithful heart inscribed by God but also abjects those tablets as the accessories of a canceled Jewry; sixteenth-century Protestantism employs the Communion wafer as a symbol of Christ's body but also demeans belief in the wafer's divinity as a primitive Catholic idolatry.[5] In each of these instances, material culture is polychronic, simultaneously of the present and future and banished to a foreign, idolatrous past. Which is to say: supersessionary cultures have been saying for centuries what the *New Yorker* cartoon caption does—"Wait, this is yesterday's."

The cartoon and caption illuminate an untimely problem at the heart of George Herbert's extraordinary sequence of poems about the Christian heart, *The Temple* (1633). In Herbert's poetry as in Roberts's cartoon, material culture—again figured as engraved stone tablets—is split between past, present, and future. Calling on God in "The Sinner" to work on his "hard heart," Herbert says: "Remember that thou once didst write in stone."[6] The line evokes Saint Paul's declaration that the stone tables inscribed with the law of the old Jewish covenant have been superseded by the new law written on the heart of every believing Christian. Yet Herbert's line hints that Jewish material culture may be not out-of-date *enough.* Just as the cartoon's tablets are "yesterday's"—a term that suggests both antiquity and the nearly-now—Herbert's stone tables evoke a distant past yet are uncannily close to his own "hard heart." Throughout *The Temple,* a superseded "yesterday" is repeatedly materialized not only in stone tables that date back to an old people and covenant but also in the stone hearts of contemporary Christians whom, as Herbert observes in "The Bunch of Grapes," the Jews' "storie pennes and sets . . . down" (139, l. 11). Herbert's treatment of supersession, in other words, does not quite banish the Jewish matter of the past; rather, it paradoxically depends and even thrives on that matter's untimely persistence.

The Temple is not just concerned with the Jewish matter of the past and present. It also looks to a future. In this, too, it is reminiscent of the cartoon. Arguably the caption's coup de grâce is its first word: the man's "Wait" inaugurates a potentially indefinite temporal suspension that, extending beyond the instant it takes him to recognize the outdatedness of the tablets, anticipates the arrival of more current reading matter. The cartoon's scene of reading thus presents a polychronic palimpsest in the making. The tablet's text is no longer just legible in and of itself; it is now also overwritten by the promise of another text that supersedes it and makes it "yesterday's." In Herbert's "The Sinner," the engraved tablet is similarly incorporated into a stone-heart palimpsest within which can be glimpsed both the tablet's dead letters and the supposedly living Word of a future text that supersedes them. Yet like the man and the woman in the cartoon, Herbert confronts the prospect of an indefinite "wait" for this other text. His palimpsest strains away from the Mosaic characters engraved in stone toward the Word of God inscribed in the heart. But because it can never quite erase the traces of its Jewish past, the stone-heart palimpsest can also never fully deliver the living Word of the spirit. Its dead letters, in other words, refuse to die.

As this suggests, matter figures prominently—though perhaps unexpectedly—in Herbert's explorations of Christian spirituality. If, as Jonathan Goldberg has noted, *The Temple* claims "that all the world is the space of its writing," then Herbert's matter is likewise resolutely textual.[7] Indeed, I shall argue that the best way of reading matter in Herbert is to regard it *as* reading matter. But it is a special kind of writing, one that presumes processes of reworking intrinsic to material culture. The stone heart of "The Sinner" is one of many objects that, by collating old Jewish letter and new Christian Word, insist on matter's legibility as a polychronic palimpsest that retains traces of, even as it reworks, the past. And although Herbert's palimpsested heart claims to speak of and for a Christian God, its untimely Jewish matter tells other, sublunary stories about global geography, human history, and the impossibility of neatly dividing past, present, and future into an orderly progressive sequence. This untimeliness, I shall argue, is rooted in Herbert's peculiar reworking of Christian typology throughout *The Temple.*

Theorizing the Time of Typology

What is the temporality of typology? In Christian interpretive tradition, Old Testament events, people, and physical things are understood to foreshadow their corresponding antitypes in the life of Christ, the history of the church, and the soul of the individual Christian. Events before the time of Christ thus find their meaning and fulfillment in the Christian future. As Saint Augustine puts it, "In the Old Testament the New lies hid; in the New Testament the meaning of the Old becomes clear."[8] The task of reading the Old Testament typologically is explicitly prescribed by Saint Paul; in his letter to the Colossians, he invites them to regard old religious habits as "a shadow of things to come; but the body is Christ" (Colossians 2:17). Pauline typology, in other words, presumes not just a prophetic but also a teleological temporality, in which history progresses toward its full realization in the Word. Yet this temporality is polychronic, inasmuch as every past moment contains the trace of, by referring to, its certain future.

In secular twentieth- and twenty-first-century adaptations, however, typology has been made to reference a different future—one whose content is not necessarily messianic. In his influential essay "Figura," Erich Auerbach traced the historical origins of typology to pre-Christian prophetic and theatrical writing, unmooring it from its Christian telos in Pauline interpretive tradition. For Auerbach, what distinguishes typology is less the specific future it predicts than a mode of figuration that links diverse moments in time and thereby undoes their completeness and self-identity: "Figural prophecy implies the interpretation of one worldly event through another; the first signifies the second, the second fulfills the first. Both remain historical events; yet both looked at in this way, have something provisional and incomplete about them; they point to one another and both point to something in the future, something still to come, which will be the real, and definitive event."[9] Like Saint Paul, Auerbach views all phenomena, past and present, as containing the polychronic trace of the future: "all history . . . remains open and questionable, points to something still concealed."[10] For Auerbach, however, that "something" is always veiled. If there is still the ghost of messianic promise in his version of typology, then, its content is—like the future into which Walter Benjamin's angel of history is blown and like Jacques Derrida's eschatological future to come—radically unknowable.[11]

A more explicitly religious understanding of typology and its future-oriented polychronicity shapes Fredric Jameson's historicism in *The Political Unconscious*. In a discussion of medieval patristic hermeneutics, Jameson considers what he terms the allegorical mode whereby the Old Testament is assimilated to the New as both a record of historical fact and a system of figures that prophetically anticipate the life of Christ. He applauds—resorting to an implied metaphor of a palimpsest—the many interpretive possibilities this typological assimilation of Old to New generates: "Allegory is here the opening up of the text to multiple meanings, to successive writings and overwritings."[12] Jameson sees these "overwritings" not as extending ad infinitum, however, but as culminating in "the representation of History itself."[13] More specifically, the typological code that enables the Christian reader of the Old Testament to read its narratives as polychronic allegories of a later covenant demands several translations: interpreting scripture as a set of figures first for Christ, then for the life of the believer, and finally for the collective meaning of human history. Medieval patristic typology thus provides a template for Jameson's Marxist historicism, which also seeks to move from local textual instances and characters to a universal philosophy of history. Like new historicists, Jameson regards history as inaccessible other than through its textual mediations. But Jameson's method of historicist reading implies a temporality different from that of new historicism, and closer to Auerbach's. Rather than simply locating texts in the time and place of their production—what he terms "a *functional* method for describing cultural texts"—he proposes also an "*anticipatory*" method that projects those texts' power as the polychronic affirmation of collective unities that do not yet exist, and may never exist.[14] For Jameson, in other words, typology presumes a temporality of utopian possibility.

The future-oriented and universalist cast of Pauline thought has recently attracted the attention of Alain Badiou and Giorgio Agamben.[15] Both see Paul as a revolutionary who understood the Incarnation as a politically and temporally transformative event. By canceling the Jewish law engraved in stone in favor of a universal polity, Paul sought (as Badiou argues) to destabilize notions of ethnic identity and difference across time and (as Agamben argues) to articulate a messianic temporality that opens up the possibility not of a new law but of future lawlessness. Badiou's and Agamben's radical neo-Paulinism has been augmented by Julia Reinhard Lupton in her recent work on political theology. Critically departing from her earlier reading of typology as generating effects of temporal difference and historical period (including the very idea of "the Renaissance"), Lupton argues that Saint Paul's typological translation of Jewish law into universal polity is interarticulated with the figure of the citizen-saint—a civil servant-cum-divine messenger whose life prophesizes a more just future. For Lupton as for Auerbach and Jameson, then, the trace of the future polychronically resides in the past and the present.[16]

In marked contrast to these future-oriented embraces of Pauline thought, Kathleen Biddick offers a more pessimistic analysis of its legacy from the Middle Ages to the present. Considering the progressive timelines repeatedly fabricated by Christians to distinguish themselves from their Jewish and other non-Christian neighbors, Biddick argues that typology has been less open to universal futures and more invested in cutting Christians from other people, practices, and objects that it codes as "past." Typology's investment in the temporal cut underwrites a linear, supersessionary time that Biddick sees as surviving in contemporary secular hermeneutics from psychoanalysis to Foucauldian historicism and postcolonial theory. Biddick understands supersessionary time to be shadowed by polychronicity; but she sees this polychronicity as less a future-oriented untimeliness than the disavowed byproduct of a repetition compulsion that replicates the circumcising "cut" of the old covenant by excising the past, over and over again, from the present.[17]

What is the temporality of typology in *The Temple*? Even as Herbert's typological set pieces dream of a better future in a manner reminiscent of Auerbach, Jameson, or Lupton, they also repeatedly insist on the pastness of Judaism in a fashion that Biddick would recognize. But if Herbert abides by a supersessionary temporality, then his theorization of supersession is subtly different from Biddick's. I shall argue that the supersessionary temporality informing Herbert's use of typology is untimely just as I have suggested Hegel's Aufhebung is: it rematerializes the past in the present. And it does so in a way that does not entirely cut Jewishness (as in Biddick) but allows it to oscillate between obsolescence and activity. In *The Temple*, this oscillation is an effect of material culture's primal scene—a scene that, like the *New Yorker* cartoon's polychronic tablets, repeatedly prompts the observation "wait, this is yesterday's."

Herbert's typological conception of history certainly invests in the supersession of an old law by a new, spiritually superior covenant. Crucial to this temporal progression is an infrequently noted sense of geographical progression: throughout *The Temple*, he often presents the Old Testament type as oriental matter that must be translated in a western direction so that it may be both symbolically reworked and spiritually improved. But Herbert's Protestant treatment of typology entails more than a diachronic supersession of oriental past by occidental future. It also possesses an extra, synchronic dimension. He not only views typology as grounded in a decisive event (the Incarnation) around which all human history is organized into before and after, old and new, B.C. and A.D.; he also sees it as plotting an unresolved tension in each moment, even after Christ, between matter and spirit, dead letter and living Word, sin and love, stony table and pious heart. This compression of diachronic typological relations into individual moments has striking untimely effects throughout *The Temple*. As in Herbert's stone-heart palimpsest, the eastern Jewish type is not so much replaced as overwritten by the westward Christian antitype: it anachronistically persists in, even as it is reworked by, the occidental present. As a result, any "moment" in *The Temple* is out of time with itself. It is a polychronic palimpsest whose untimely traces of past oriental matter trouble even as they sponsor the goal of progressive westward movement.

In this chapter, I consider how untimely oriental matter is everywhere in *The Temple*, including in typologically dense lyrics about palimpsested objects, such as "The Altar" and "The Bunch of Grapes." But it most afflicts "The Church Militant," the long poem about the history of religion's "westward" course (193, l. 17) that concludes the sequence in its published form. The poem has been regarded as a problem within, and even as a text extraneous to, *The Temple*; indeed, many readings of the sequence have largely ignored it. By contrast, I argue that the complex treatments of matter and time in "The Church Militant" closely parallel those of the shorter and more widely studied typological lyrics. Taken together, they make the case for rereading Herbert as not "just" a religious poet but also a theorist of untimely matter. To view him this way, however, means questioning pervasive critical habits that have worked to dematerialize the matter of *The Temple*.

Dematerializing Herbert

In a well-known reading of *The Temple* (1978), Stanley Fish pondered the anomaly of what he called "criticism's two Herberts."[18] The first has been conjured by critics who imagine the poet as a cheerful if doctrinaire theologian, serenely comfortable in his beliefs (whether Anglo-Catholic, Anglican, or Puritan). The second is the projection of those who respond to Herbert's as a tortured and uncertain soul, divided against itself. How, Fish asked, can *The Temple* lend itself equally persuasively to both readings? And how can critics continue to pick between these two Herberts as if they were two absolutely opposed choices, without subjecting to critical scrutiny the dialectic that has pitted them against each other? Fish's solution was to propose a seeming synthesis: a poet-narrator who is simultaneously sure of himself and uncertain. This paradoxical disposition, Fish argued, is historically grounded in the Reformation tradition of catechizing, which is designed to coax the catechumen or potential convert toward certainty by submitting her to agonizing uncertainty in the course of spiritual questioning.[19]

Some thirty years after Fish's synthesis, we are again confronted with the specter of two contradictory Herberts. We might dub these latest versions the unworldly and the worldly Herberts. The first is inward looking, shunning earthly vanities for an intensely personal and dematerialized relation with God. The second is more *contentus* than *contemptus mundi*, in thrall to the social conventions of court and mercantile enterprise.[20] Perhaps the most articulate spokesman for the unworldly Herbert is Richard Strier, who argues that in poems like "The Church Floor," Herbert's pervasively inward spirituality "entirely eliminates the visual and material" and even repudiates the physical trappings of the church.[21] By contrast, the worldly Herbert is championed by Michael Schoenfeldt, who claims that, in appropriating the language of courtesy and sexuality for his religious lyrics, "Herbert welcomes the worldly reader and the profane world into the temple of his devotion";[22] and by Cristina Malcolmson, who argues that "for Herbert, 'heart-work' and 'business in the world' [are] inextricably linked."[23]

Paraphrasing Fish's response to the paradox of the certain and the uncertain Herberts, we might ask: How is it that a poet and the poetry he writes can be unworldly and worldly *at the same time*?[24] It is again hard not to see critics' reproduction of this conflict as a repetition of a shaping problem in *The Temple*. And it is again tempting to resolve the conflict by means of synthesis. Indeed, proponents of the worldly Herbert might argue that their vision of the poet is designed to synthesize his spirituality with his material investments. As a result they are more in tune with the strikingly paradoxical flavor of seventeenth-century biographies of Herbert, within which he emerges as both transcendent saint and practical handyman. In the opening letter to the reader of *The Temple*, Herbert's close friend Nicholas Ferrar characterizes him as "a companion to the primitive Saints" and asserts that "as for worldly matters, his love and esteem to them was so earnestly little." Yet these claims do not prevent Ferrar from noting the considerable love and esteem Herbert lavished on repairs to his parish church at Fuggleston-cum-Bemerton in Wiltshire, which "had layen ruinated almost twenty yeares."[25] We see the same balancing act in Izaak Walton's hagiographical biography of 1670. Even as he presents us with the figure of Saint George Herbert, who "liv'd, and . . . dy'd like a Saint, unspotted of the World,"[26] Walton locates Herbert squarely in that world, spotted or no, when describing the poet's lavish project of rebuilding and redecorating the Leighton parish church in Lincolnshire: "He, by his own, and the contribution of many of his Kindred, and other noble Friends, undertook the Re-edification of it; and, made it so much his whole business, that he became restless, till he saw it finisht as it now stands; being, for the workmanship, a costly *Mosaick*: for the form, an *exact Cross*; and, for the decency and beauty, I am assur'd it is the most remarkable Parish-Church, that this Nation affords. He liv'd to see it so Wainscoated, as to be exceeded by none."[27] If Walton's "unspotted" saint is the distant ancestor of Strier's absolute dematerializer of church floors, then Walton's extravagant and even competitive interior decorator anticipates Schoenfeldt's welcomer of the "profane world into his temple."[28] The biographies, then, suggest a simultaneously unworldly and worldly Herbert who, like Fish's catechizer, both corroborates and complicates the competing versions of him produced in literary criticism. Indeed, Herbert himself would seem to license a synthesis of the unworldly and the worldly. His Latin poem "De mundis et mundanis"—translated as "On the worldly and the unworldly"—insists that "ex profane Cosmico & Catharo potest / Christianus extundi bonus" (from unholy worldling / And the Puritan, a good / Christian can be hammered out).[29]

For all the attractions of a Fish-like solution that would synthesize the unworldly and worldly Herberts, however, we might do well to consider how Fish's catechizer is not, in fact, a straightforward synthesis. Instead, it implicitly favors one of the two poles in the opposition it is supposed to dissolve. Despite his interest elsewhere in self-consuming literary artifacts that resist closure, the historical frame Fish provides for his catechizing Herbert makes certainty the telos that *The Temple*'s performative uncertainty not only longs for but ultimately leads the reader toward.[30] Similarly, proponents of the worldly Herbert who seek to synthesize the poet's material and spiritual concerns tend to present the former as the means by which Herbert realizes the latter. Hence in her thoughtful study, Malcolmson sees Herbert in poems like "Business" and "Praise (III)" as "using the language of worldly employment and gain for exclusively religious purposes."[31] And even Schoenfeldt, despite his nuanced attention to the ways in which Herbert's spirituality potentially backslides into the world it "purportedly escapes," can claim that "Herbert does not just turn away from the social and political world but also turns the language of this world into the medium for his lyric worship of God."[32] Worldly matter or language, invoked as "the medium" by means of which Herbert can realize his "religious purposes," becomes—at least in these two instances—the expendable rocket fuel that transports him to his celestial destination.

The difference between recent criticism's unworldly and worldly Herberts, therefore, is perhaps less one of kind than of degree. The second Herbert may be more tolerant of matter than the first, but each ultimately supersedes it in his pursuit of spirit. In plotting this movement away from matter, both versions are arguably the latest instances of a striking tendency in Herbert studies throughout the twentieth century—a tendency that has worked to produce, in at least two guises, what we might call the dematerializing Herbert. An earlier generation of biographically minded critics had narrated Herbert's movement from matter to spirit as taking place over the course of his lifetime, with his maturation from ambitious Cambridge don and orator hoping for worldly advancement into humble Wiltshire priest seeking spiritual salvation.[33] Formalist critics in the 1950s and 1960s, turning away from biographical study, instead saw the dematerializing movement occurring within the sequence of *The Temple* itself. Influential readings of Herbert had already recognized in the title of the sequence an implied typological progression from Solomon's old physical temple on Mount Sion to the new spiritual temple of God in the heart of individual Christians.[34] But some wanted to see this historical movement from matter to spirit enacted within the space of the temple itself. One critic argued that the structure of *The Temple* is analogous to the architectural structure of the Hebraic temple; as such it traces a spatial progression from the semiprofane "Church-porch" or Outer Court into the more spiritual interior of the "Church" or Holy

Place, culminating in the supposedly transcendent éclat of "The Church Militant," which corresponds to the veiled inner sanctum, or Holy of Holies, in the heart of the old temple.[35]

Both the biographical and formalist versions of the dematerializing Herbert now hold little sway. A growing critical interest in Herbert's posthumously published treatise on the parish priest's duties in his community, *The Country Parson*, has helped deflate the fantasy that, after taking holy orders, he retreated from all material concerns.[36] Even as *The Country Parson* lays down rules for a pious life, it is difficult to see Herbert as having fully transcended worldly matter when he writes so enthusiastically about the English herbs in his wife's garden, the clothes a parson should wear, and his surprisingly colorful aesthetic of interior decoration: in a parson's house, he observes, "even the walls are not idle, but something is written, or painted there."[37] The formalist conviction that *The Temple* moves tidily from matter to spirit over the course of its progression from "The Church-porch" to "The Church Militant" has been similarly punctured; several readers have noted that the sequence concludes not with the Church Triumphant in Heaven but with a pessimistic intimation of the work that still needs to be done in the material world.[38]

Because the biographical and formalist versions of the dematerializing Herbert no longer have critical currency, it is perhaps all the more surprising that matter in the individual lyric poems continues to be seen as either what the unworldly Herbert erases altogether or the medium for the worldly Herbert to reach God. Critics have repeatedly noted Herbert's fears in *The Temple* of backsliding from grace to sin and from spiritual joy to carnal pleasure. But they have been more reluctant to take stock of Herbert's related fear that, for all his spiritual longings, the matter of his universe may be resolutely untranscendable—at least for now.[39] Part of the problem, I would argue, is that Herbert's matter hasn't been read as such, even though the status of matter as a special form of text is one of the abiding concerns of *The Temple*. That is partly because two interrelated interpretive frameworks modern critics have inherited from Herbert, the Augustinian theory of signs and the Pauline doctrine of typology, have predisposed them to dematerialize his matter. So long as Herbert is read from the vantage point of where he *wants* to be—close to God—each framework may seem to translate matter successfully into spirit: the Augustinian theory of signs through symbolic movement from material things to transcendent *logos*, the Pauline doctrine of typology through temporal progression from carnal law to divine grace. But if we read

The Temple also as a sustained reflection on the untimeliness of matter, we might see how the sequence simultaneously complicates both frameworks—not least because, for Herbert, neither offers a tidy, unilinear movement from matter to spirit.

Signs Taken for Matter

So how *are* we to read matter in *The Temple*? Complicating matters is that Herbert's attitude to it is so conflicted. There is no escaping the fact that he often views physical things with disgust, particularly when talking of flesh and food. "Look on meat, think it dirt, then eat a bit," he commands in "The Church-porch," "and say withall, Earth to earth I commit" (37, ll. 131–32). Because this edible "dirt" leaves the body as excrement, Herbert readily characterizes matter also as "dung": hence not only do "Sheep eat the grasse, and dung the ground for more" ("Providence," 131, l. 69), but also "foolish lovers," in thrall to worldly pleasures, "love dung" ("The Forerunners," 182, l. 25).[40] Dung producers beholden to dung, humans also become for Herbert a disease ontologically differentiated from God: "My God, Man cannot praise thy name," he complains; "How shall infection / Presume on thy perfection?" ("Miserie," 115, ll. 35–36). It is telling, then, that Herbert occasionally uses the word "matter" in a decidedly pathological sense. In "Love Unknown," his attempt to sacrifice his heart to God fails; his spiritual interlocutor, reprising the theme of the stony heart that we have already glimpsed in "The Sinner," tells him that the reason is "*Your heart was hard, I fear.*" Herbert concludes that "Indeed, 'tis true. I found a callous matter / Began to spread and to expatiate there" (141, ll. 37–39). "Matter" here is a sickness-unto-death that Herbert must cast off to acquire a state of grace and spiritual health.

Yet Herbert's many disgusted abjections of matter as dirt, dung, disease, and death are accompanied by another, more utilitarian attitude that runs through all of his writing. In *The Country Parson*, he observes that "They say, it is an ill Mason that refuseth any stone: and there is no knowledge but, in a skillful hand, serves either positively as it is, or else to illustrate some other knowledge."[41] Stony matter is redeemable, then, if it can be reworked by "a skillful hand" to a specific end: knowledge of God. Here we can see the pragmatic Herbert for whom no thing could be too mundane to be used as a lesson—the Herbert who spent a lifetime squirreling away proverbs in the hope that they might be put to effective pedagogical use, as emblematized by item number 70 in the collection of *Outlandish Proverbs* attributed to him: "Every thing is of use to a house keeper."[42] The use value to the "house keeper" of mundane, workable matter becomes a major theme for Herbert in *The Country Parson*, not least because of his experiences trying to impart spiritual lessons to his parishioners. Writing of Christ's exemplary rhetorical skills, he observes that

> Our Savior made plants and seeds to teach the people: for he was the true householder, who bringeth out of his treasure things new and old. . . . I conceive, our Savior did this for three reasons: first, that by familiar things he might make his Doctrine slip the more easily into the hearts even of the meanest. Secondly, that laboring people (whom he chiefly considered) might have everywhere monuments of his Doctrine, remembering in gardens, his mustard-seed, and lilies, in the field, his seed-corn, and tares; and so not be drowned altogether in the works of their vocation, but sometimes lift up their minds to better things, even in the midst of their pains. Thirdly, that he might set a Copy for Parsons.[43]

Material objects here become mnemonics (or "monuments") of Christian doctrine, especially for those of a humble vocation. Thanks to the parson's skillful hand, the "familiar things" manual laborers encounter in the course of their work can be dialectically transformed into the "better things" of God that transcend mere matter. Herbert seems to echo this theme with his assertion that "doubtless the Holy Scripture intends thus much, when it condescends to the naming of a plow, a hatchet, a bushel, leaven, boys piping and dancing; showing that things of ordinary use are not only to serve in the way of drudgery, but to be washed, and cleansed, and serve for lights even of Heavenly Truths."[44] But if Herbert believes that dirty physical objects can be spiritually "washed, and cleansed," it is not just because they can be transformed into utilitarian "monuments" to Christian doctrine. It is also because they are intrinsic rather than merely rhetorically convenient "lights . . . of Heavenly Truths" and, in particular, of the God that made them. In this, Herbert's attitude to the physical world bears the imprint of Augustine.

As several commentators have noted, Herbert's will indicates that he owned the works of Augustine; and Augustine's ideas, particularly his theory of signs, can be seen throughout Herbert's writing.[45] In Augustine's Platonized cosmology, the entire universe is a set of symbols of the Divine, a sublime poem written in the words of created matter whose silent voice is the logos of its Creator. A good reader of this poem will recognize in the matter of the universe the marks of God, and thus proceed from matter to spirit. A bad reader, by contrast, will perform an idolatrous and even fetishistic operation, mistaking the material thing as the end of signification and worshipping it for itself: "It is a servile infirmity to follow the letter and to take signs for the things that they signify."[46] Alternatively, the bad reader will concede the material thing to be a sign, but only of another material thing—thereby short-circuiting a chain of signification that properly leads back to God. The residue of Augustine's theory of divine signs in Herbert's writing again suggests how the activity of reading matter in *The Temple* demands that we treat it *as* reading matter.

In a sonnet he wrote at sixteen for his mother, the young Herbert warns against bad readers of the divine poem:

> *Sure Lord, there is enough in thee to dry*
> *Oceans of* Ink*; for as the Deluge did*
> *Cover the Earth, so doth thy praise, and doth forbid*
> Poets *to turn it to another use.*
> Roses *and* Lillies *speak thee, and to make*
> *A pair of Cheeks of them, is thy abuse.*
> *Why should I* Womens eyes *for Chrystal take?*
> *Such poor invention burns in their low mind*
> *Whose fire is wild, and doth not upward go*
> *To praise, and on thee Lord, some* Ink *to bestow.*
> *Open the bones, and you shall nothing find*
> *In the best* face *but* filth, *when Lord, in thee*
> *The* beauty *lies, in the* discovery.[47]

Herbert offers here a resolutely Augustinian view of the universe: its matter is textual, for all created phenomena are signs of God. However, love poets perform a twofold perversion of these divine signs. By worshipping women's faces, they succumb to idolatry, mistakenly believing the origin of beauty to reside not in God but in the flesh. Moreover, love poets idolatrously give signs material rather than spiritual referents. Herbert reserves special ire for poets' comparison of beautiful things like "Roses *and* Lillies" to a woman's "*Cheeks.*" He may sound here like the Shakespeare of Sonnet 130, who refuses to see "roses" in his mistress's "cheeks."[48] But while Shakespeare dispenses with such florid Petrarchan clichés by making a downward turn to the ground upon which his mistress walks, Herbert's rejection points "upward."[49] Unlike Shakespeare, Herbert wants to retain the rose as a sign—but only so long as it is granted its proper "use" as a signifier that points to God rather than being made to reference other matter, or what he demeans as "filth."[50]

This may suggest that the poem presents a straightforward translation of matter into spirit, of rose into logos. Yet things are surely not that simple. Herbert evokes the Augustinian conceit of the world as divine poem by means of an intriguing, double movement in the opening lines, from "*Oceans of* Ink" to the historical "*Deluge*" and "*thy praise*." All these phenomena, Herbert tells us, "*Cover the Earth*." If the "Ink" initially seems to refer to poetry produced by humans, the other homologous terms overlay and displace that reading: just as the deluge and praise are not human products but signs of God in the material world, so too is the ink.[51] Indeed, ink becomes here a master trope for how everything on "*Earth*" is a sign pointing to its Creator. But although the sonnet regards the material world as divinely inked text, that ink obscures even as it silently voices the logos: for while it supposedly gestures "upward"—a metaphorical operation that moves from matter to spirit—Herbert's "Ink" slips metonymically within the poem to other signs, via its typographical association with "Poets," "Lillies," "Roses," "Womens eyes," and "Ink" (again).[52] Each of these terms is nonitalicized and begins with a capital letter; each thus attempts to straighten out the otherwise bent matter of the sonnet, not by facing down like the italicized words but by pointing upward. But even as they grasp for transcendence, they remain firmly within the realm of physical things by referencing each other—and by leading inexorably back to "Ink" in the sonnet's fourth-to-last line. Herbert may long for a God who is signified by the ink of the world; but that ink leaks, producing a potentially infinite slippage of reference from thing to thing curiously similar to the Petrarchan abuse of the sign that Herbert derides. As a result, the world becomes legible as a palimpsest whose matter is superinscribed with the multiple inky traces of a supposed transcendence that keeps folding back into the materiality it seeks to shed.[53]

The sonnet may belong to Herbert's juvenilia. Yet in its treatment of matter as text that both promises and impedes transcendence, it eerily anticipates his more "mature" verse. In a number of ways, *The Temple* reproduces the simultaneously utilitarian and Augustinian attitude to matter that we have seen in *The Country Parson.* Herbert refashions the latter's proverb about the Mason and the stone when he asserts in "The Church-porch" that "The cunning workman never doth refuse / The meanest tool, that he may chance to use" (39, ll. 353–54); "God," he adds in "The Priesthood," "doth often vessels make / Of lowly matter for high uses meet" (168, ll. 34–35). But *The Temple* is also preoccupied with the potential resistances of matter to such "high uses." If Herbert can tell God that "Indeed the world's thy book, / Where all things have their leafe assign'd" ("Longing," 158, ll. 49–50), he can also ask, by means of a pun on the leaves of that book, "shall each leaf, / Which falls in Autumne, score a grief? Or cannot leaves, but fruit, be signe / Of the true vine?" ("Good Friday," 59, ll. 9–12) By questioning whether everything *is* a sign of God or Christ, Herbert extrapolates on a potential confusion in Augustine's *De doctrina Christiana.* Even as Augustine insists that the material world is a text whose every sign references its Creator, he also remarks that although "each sign is also in some way a thing. . . . It is however not the case that every thing is a sign."[54] Like the ink in Herbert's earlier sonnet, then, some matter can remain troublingly resistant to spiritual signification.

For the most part, Herbert dismisses this possibility by regarding untranscended matter as a problem less of matter itself than of bad readers. Like the earlier sonnet, *The Temple* diagnoses the failure to recognize the "high uses" of "lowly matter" as a species of misprision or idolatry in which material things are valued for themselves rather than for the transcendental signified of which they are sign. Herbert's unfortunate shorthand for such idolatry, as David Hawkes has noted, is Judaism.[55] This identification follows the precedent of medieval biblical exegesis, in which the "meer letter" or "carnal sense" of scripture was often equated with the "sense of the Jews," now wholly superseded by the new covenant.[56] With what amounted to an anti-Semitic adaptation of Augustine's theory of signs, Jews were understood, like Christians, to regard matter as text; but they were also understood, unlike Christians, as stopping at matter's "meer letter" rather than proceeding to the spirit it signifies. Hence in cataloging "those, who mock at Gods way of salvation," Herbert reminds his readers in "The Church-porch" that "The Jews refused thunder" (45, ll. 446, 449)—that they were incapable, in other words, of recognizing the thunder at Mount Sinai as a sign of God's revelation of his law. And in "Self-Condemnation," Herbert speaks of how "He that doth love, and love amisse / This worlds delights before true Christian joy"—that is, he who values the material signifier over the spiritual signified—"Hath made a Jewish choice" (176, ll. 8–10). This "choice" is, for Herbert, a choice of dead things over the living Word of spirit. It is a choice emblematized by the Jews, a "Poore nation" bereft of its life-giving "sweet sap" ("The Jews," 160, l. 1).

The Time of Jewish Matter

By making the misprision of signs a "Jewish choice," Herbert appears to offer a recognizably typological solution to the problem of untranscended matter: an object that fails to signify its Creator is literally a thing of the past, conjured by the misreading habits of an old covenant that predates the Christian church. The new covenant, in this reading, restores to the past object an Augustinian power to reference divine grace *in the future*. Hence Herbert's devotional poems invoke Old Testament types, a striking number of which are physical objects from the Jewish past—Moses' stone tablets, Aaron's priestly vestments, Solomon's gloriously decorated Temple of Sion, the grapes from Eshcol in Canaan. All these material things are superinscribed by their fulfillment as spiritual New Testament antitypes from a later time—the pious heart of the true believer, the spiritual accessories of the Christian priest, the new Temple that resides in each Christian's soul, the "wine" of Christ's sacrifice.[57] Herbert's typological solution to untranscended matter therefore adds a complex temporal dimension to Augustine's theory of signs. The movement from matter to spirit is not simply a logocentric operation enjoined on the reader of the world as text but also a teleological development through time, whereby old type is superseded by new antitype.

Yet typology's teleological schema does not entail only a diachronic progression. Thanks to God's providential design, the future antitype is also synchronically contained within the past type as its true meaning. The linear progression that distinguishes typological time is thus enabled by a constitutive anachronism. In *The Temple*, this anachronism does not simply make the future legible in the past; it equally materializes the past in the future. The first aspect permits the fantasy of dematerialization. But the second unleashes the specter of material reinscription: what might seem at first like irrevocable temporal progression toward spirit is, upon closer inspection, fraught with the risk either of delay or of anachronistic relapse into materiality. *The Temple* presents this risk through the sustained motif with which I started this chapter—the Christian heart that, longing for the joys of grace, nonetheless remains hardened in ways that resemble rather than transcend the "stone tables" of the Old Jewish law. In "Nature," Herbert asks God to "smooth my rugged heart, and there / Engrave thy rev'rend law and fear"; but resorting to language that recalls his "sap"-less vision of "The Jews" as well as their "stone tables," he asks also for a heart transplant, "since the old / Is saplesse grown, / And a much fitter stone / To hide my dust, than thee to hold" (65, ll. 13–18). In such poems, the anachronistic specter of stony matter typifies a sinful present that cannot muster the purity of faith needed to give Christ a home in Christian hearts.[58] Just as "of old, the law by heav'nly art / Was writ in stone," so Christ, "which also art / The letter of the word, find'st no fit heart / To hold thee" ("The Sepulchre," 61, ll. 16–19). These poems may offer an antitype to the stone tables of the Jewish temple in the form of the pious Christian heart; but that antitype cannot be fully realized in the present, thanks to the untimely persistence of the supposedly superseded past.

In other poems, the stony heart is a monument less to the sinful deferral of grace than to the constitutive anachronism of typology: "old" stoniness now provides the perfect medium for the inscription of the "new" covenant. This is illustrated by Herbert's most well-known pattern poem, "The Altar":

A broken ALTAR, Lord, thy servant reares,
Made of a heart, and cemented with teares:
Whose parts are as thy hand did frame;
No workmans tool hath touch'd the same.
A HEART alone
Is such a stone,
As nothing but
Thy pow'r doth cut
Wherefore each part
Of my hard heart
Meets in this frame,
To praise thy name.
That if I chance to hold my peace,
These stones to praise thee may not cease.
O let thy blessed SACRIFICE be mine,
And sanctifie this ALTAR to be thine.
(47, ll. 1–14)

For the Christian antitype to become legible as such, it must be written over the form of the Jewish type. That is why Herbert presents here not only the conceit of the "hard heart" as an engraved stone table reinscribed by God's hand ("nothing but / Thy pow'r doth cut"), but also a poetic meditation on Christian devotion that takes the typographical shape of a pre-Christian altar.[59] As a result, the altar-shape that the reader sees is at one and the same time "Christian" and "Jewish," a sign of divinity and base matter. It is a visible sign of the heart shaped by divine grace, which needs no "Workmans tools" to "frame" it—a reference to Exodus's primal scene of material culture. But it is also, like Solomon's Old Temple, the product of artful human labor. Just as Solomon's masons hewed and shaped stone in building the temple, so has Herbert skillfully reworked language to produce the "frame" of the poem.[60] As a result, what he produces is a stone-heart palimpsest that, contrary to the straightforward exchange promised by the prophet Ezekiel ("A new heart also will I give you, . . . and take away the stony heart" [36:26]), cannot entirely shed the traces of past Jewish matter and the temporally regressive material culture denigrated in Exodus.

It is perhaps telling that at least one of the seventeenth-century readers of "The Altar" found it and another of Herbert's pattern poems, "Easter Wings," too compromised by the matter from which each supposedly progresses. In an unmistakable swipe at both poems, John Dryden sarcastically advised his bête noire Thomas Shadwell to leave lofty subjects and confine his literary endeavors to poetic trifles in which "thou maist wings display and Altars raise."[61] Dryden's remark shows how a poetic genre designed to overwrite matter with spirit, Jewish type with Christian antitype, and old stony altar with new devoted heart could all too easily backslide into the abjected terms from which it sought to move forward. This suggests that although typology as *a system of divine signification* may promise spiritual progression, typology as *a technology of material reinscription* has decidedly different, untimely effects. In Herbert's case, I would argue that this second aspect of typology becomes visible partly because of his recognizably Calvinist understanding of history.

Since Rosemond Tuve, we have become habituated to reading *The Temple* as shaped by typological operations "deeply sunk in the matrix of orthodox Christian thinking."[62] For Tuve as for other scholars of typology, this matrix joins seamlessly to Catholic tradition: hence she explains the typological correspondences of *The Temple* with woodcuts from the fifteenth-century *Biblia pauperum*, in which Old Testament scenes are accompanied by the New Testament counterparts that supersede them.[63] Biddick's excellent study of the typological imaginary is unusually sensitive to how typology is not just a system of signification but also a set of material practices grounded in technologies of inscription. But like Tuve, Biddick illustrates her argument with exclusively Catholic materials—a fifteenth-century *Biblio cum glossa* and thirteenth-century *Bibles moralisées*—each of which works to present typology as only a progression from old to new.[64] As Barbara Lewalski has shown, however, Protestant adaptations of typology, most notably Calvin's, disrupt the diachronic, progressive trajectory of earlier Catholic versions. Even though Calvin recognized the importance of the Incarnation as a decisive historical turning point, he regarded the truly transforming event—in Alain Badiou's sense of an exceptional revolutionary occurrence that not only transforms what comes after it but also decisively revalues everything that has come before[65]—as the Last Judgment. Hence for Calvin, the ultimate victory of spirit has not yet happened but is to come. This postponement has important consequences for the typological relations between past and present, Jew and Christian. In Lewalski's words, "Calvin's revision of conventional typology presents both Old Testament types and New Covenant antitypes as alike referred to the supreme antitype to come at the end of time, thereby permitting Protestants to identify their spiritual experiences much more closely with those of the 'typical' Israel than medieval exegetes customarily did, and to regard history as a continuum rather than as two eras of time divided by the incarnation of Christ."[66]

Lewalski asserts a commensuration of the "spiritual" experiences of Jews and Protestants. But Calvin's revision of typology equally suggests an affinity between Jewish and Protestant *matter*: for both are now the material signifiers of a spiritual future that by definition can never coincide with the present. In Herbert's words, "Mans joy and pleasure, / Rather hereafter, then in present, is" ("Man's Medley," 142, ll. 5–6). Paradoxically, then, Calvinist typology encourages not just a radical future-oriented refusal of the material world (in anticipation of the spiritual transcendence ushered in by the end of days), but also an equally radical and anachronistic rematerialization of the past in the present. Untranscended "Jewish" matter is less the stuff of superseded history than the condition of the Protestant age, at least for now.

The Calvinist possibility of identity rather than difference between Protestant and Jew is foundational not just to *The Temple*'s fantasies of Jewish recidivism, evident in Christians' stony hearts or their "Jewish choice" to embrace earthly vanities. It is also apparent in Herbert's identification, in "The Bunch of Grapes," with the wanderings of the Israelites between the Red Sea and Canaan. Just as the Jews were lost in the desert, so does Herbert see himself as spiritually adrift: "I did toward Canaan draw; but now I am /

Brought back to the Red sea, the sea of shame" (139, ll. 6–7). This is but the first in a series of analogies that imagine the relation between old Jew and new Christian as structured by identification rather than supersession. Tellingly, the resistance to forward movement is modeled in the very story with which Herbert identifies:

For as the Jews of old by Gods command
Travell'd, and saw no town:
So now each Christian hath his journeys spann'd:
Their storie pennes and sets us down.
(ll. 8–11)

Herbert maps the Israelites' failure to progress geographically onto an apparent failure of Christians to progress in their devotion to God, so that the spiritual condition of Herbert and his fellow Christians mirrors rather than supersedes that of the Jews. For "we too have our guardian fires and clouds; / Our Scripture-dew drops fast; / We have our sands and serpents, tents and shrowds" (ll. 15–17). All these material phenomena—even as they assume a typological progression from manna to "Scripture"—are signs of the spiritual lot of Jew and Christian alike; both faiths have been the beneficiaries of God's bounty, and both have suffered great privations in their respective deserts. If anything, Herbert fantasizes that his miseries are greater because he lacks a counterpart to the one material object that gave hope and solace to the Israelites in their wanderings: the "cluster of grapes" from Eshcol that the spies had brought back as proof of the joys to be had in the Promised Land (Numbers 13:23). Where, Herbert asks, are *his* grapes? "Lord, if I must borrow," he pleads, "let me as well take up their joy, as sorrow" (ll. 20–21).

It is precisely joy's absence, though, that enables the poem's concluding volte-face, which abruptly asserts a temporal and spiritual progression away from the Jews. As many readers have noted, the poem presumes the conventional typological relationship between the grapes of Eshcol and Christ on the cross, the "true vine" crushed into the wine of grace by the press of the Passion (John 15:1, Isaiah 63:3).[67] Herbert's missing grape, therefore, is necessary for his supposedly greater joy: "But can he want the grape, who hath the wine? / I have their fruit and more" (ll. 22–23). As Lewalski remarks, this progression differs from earlier typological treatments of the Eshcol grapes by locating the relationship between type and antitype in the heart of the poet: "Tracing a progress within himself . . . he can finally affirm that this earnest of Christ's sacrifice affords him a less tangible but far more certain and all-embracing guarantee of spiritual joy."[68]

But the metaphors Herbert uses to represent this typological relation within his heart potentially trouble the unilinear progress to spiritual certainty that Lewalski asserts. When Herbert says that God "of the laws sowre juice sweet wine did make, / . . . being pressed for my sake" (l. 27), he resorts to a familiar typological metaphor of Christ as winepress (c.f. "The Agonie," 58, l. 11). Yet "pressed" surely has additional associations that recall *The Temple*'s preoccupation with writing on the heart. In "Praise (III)," Herbert claims that "my heart, / Though pressed, runnes thin" (166, ll. 37–38). It is hard not to hear in this line a subliminal pun on "printing press": his "pressed" heart flows with Christ's wine, but it is equally matter imprinted by God. If Herbert's heart is the Jewish grape transformed into Christian wine—a seemingly diachronic progression—we might also recognize in it the more untimely temporalities of the palimpsest: his heart demands to be seen as reading matter out of time with itself, doubly inscribed by the Jews' old "storie" that "pennes and sets us down" (l. 11) and the "press" of the new Christian covenant. The inscription of this "press" may rework, but it cannot efface, the traces of the Jewish writing that precedes it.[69] Nor can it fully transport Herbert to his desired spiritual destination. Just as the grapes materialize the promise of Canaan without bringing the Israelites there, so too does the wine of Christ promise a "spiritual joy" that only remains a promise.

Herbert's use of typology here and elsewhere thus offers only an incomplete solution to the problem of untranscended matter in the Augustinian theory of signs. Conventional typology temporally purifies the components of the sign by historically dividing old material signifier from new spiritual signified. But Herbert's version of typology undoes that purification by anachronistically collating the Jewish type and the Christian antitype within stone-heart palimpsests that promise yet impede the full arrival of spirit. In them, matter cannot be fully transcended, at least not for now. The most that can be achieved is movement in *the direction* of a spiritual future that, like the "Canaan" toward which both Herbert and the Jews "did . . . draw," nonetheless remains beyond the visible horizon.

West Is East

As "The Bunch of Grapes" suggests, Herbert often couches the twin pursuit and deferral of spirit in the language of geographical movement: in that poem, the movement is away from Egypt toward a Promised Land that remains, at least for now, inaccessible. His most typologically resonant fantasy of geographical movement is crossing the Jordan, the river over which the Israelites eventually passed to enter the Promised Land and in which Christ was later baptized. "Crossing Jordan" might seem to imply for Herbert a spiritual as well as geographical step forward. He twice invokes Jordan in the titles of his devotional lyric poems, and on both occasions he does so to suggest a supposed progression in his writing from baroque "*pretence*" to a plainer style more fitting for the praise of God ("Jordan (II)," l. 16). There is, of course, something a little disingenuous about artfully pleading one's commitment to artlessness. But this is just one way in which Herbert's fantasies of forward geographical movement tend to involve a simultaneous reversion to the matter he would leave behind. Tuve has memorably quipped that "Herbert's Jordans never stay crossed."[70] The simultaneity of Herbert's forward and backward geographical movements, however, might more accurately suggest that even as they are materially crossed, his Jordans are never spiritually crossed. Far from delivering him even only temporarily to his Promised Lands of grace, Herbert's journeys paradoxically return him to his points of embarkation—they are, as Goldberg resonantly puts it, "journey[s] without arrival."[71]

For Herbert, the paradox of the forward movement that is simultaneously an ineluctable return is most graphically represented by the progress of Sin. In "Sinnes Round," whose title ambiguously suggests both a lyric rondel proper to Sin and the notion that Sin is round or traces a circular course, Herbert records a causal sequence that leads back inexorably to its starting point. His "inflamed thoughts" engender ill words, which spawn ill deeds, which prompt "new thoughts of sinning" (ll. 7, 17), and so on. This circular course of cause and effect is typographically repeated in the poem's circular form. As is customary in rondels, the first line of each stanza reprises the last line of the previous one; and the poem's last line—"Sorrie I am, my God, sorrie I am" (l. 18)—is the same as its first, implying a potentially infinite cycle of progression-cum-regression. This cyclical conceit, as we shall see, lurks in Herbert's representations of untimely palimpsested matter and its supposed forward movement. And even when that movement is meant to be in the geographical direction of spirit, it is dogged by the recursive specter of Sin.

For the most part, Herbert's "spiritual" direction is westward. In this, he claims to follow the trajectory of the sun, which rises in the east but moves steadily to the west. This is the conceit of "The Sonne," a poem that celebrates the homophonic association of "sun" and "Son":

> How neatly doe we give one onely name
> To parents issue and the sunnes bright starre!
> A sonne is light and fruit; a fruitfull flame
> Chasing the fathers dimnesse, carri'd farre
> From the first man in th'East, to fresh and new
> Western discov'ries of posteritie.
>
> (173–74, ll. 5–10)

Like the sun, Christ the Son conveys light from orient to occident, progressing via the Holy Land from the "th'East" of the past to "fresh and new Western discov'ries" of the future. "East" and "West" thus refer not just to compass points but also to points in time: the orient is past, the occident is to come. The conceit is reworked in "Easter," which compares sunrise to the resurrection of the Son:

> The Sunne arising in the East,
> Though he give light, & th'East perfume;
> If they should offer to contest
> With thy arising, they presume.
>
> (62, ll. 23–26)

The material benefits of sunrise cannot hope to compete with the spiritual benefits of Christ's Easter "arising," which took place "in the East"—a term that again designates both a geographical and a temporal relation between Herbert's England and Christ's Holy Land. Here Herbert's English again facilitates his analogy. The word for Easter in other European languages etymologically derives from and hence typologically supersedes the Hebrew "pesach," or Passover (the Latin "pascha," the French "Pâques," or the Dutch "pask"). By contrast, the English word is descended from the Saxon pagan goddess of the dawn, Eostre, whose festival was celebrated at the spring equinox.[72] Herbert's Easter therefore contains the vestigial trace of not just a superseded pagan religious past but also—unlike its counterparts in other European languages—the easterly location of sunrise.

For Herbert, the new covenant's eastern dawn necessitates the geographical, temporal, and spiritual movement of the sun/Son's light. That movement is prefigured by "the starre, / That brought the wise men of the East from farre" ("The Sacrifice," 49, ll. 50–51). To achieve the fruits of grace, just as the wise men sought to locate the newborn Christ, one must follow the movement of celestial bodies, which, like the sun, go west. The steady linear movement of light from east to west, from past to future, may seem to provide a spiritual antidote to the circular matter of Sin. But Herbert is all too conscious that the path of the sun's light circumscribes the globe; rather than simply tracing a progression from a starting point to a final destination, its westward movement eventually returns it to the east. What seems like a progression from one discrete compass point to another can also, from God's perspective, work to blur the difference between those points: "East and West touch, the poles do kisse, and parallels meet" ("The Search, 169, ll. 43–44).

The seemingly progressive westward movement that reveals itself to be a simultaneous reversion to the east is the shaping, untimely paradox of *The Temple*'s long concluding poem, "The Church Militant." Even as Herbert narrates a global history of the Christian church's progression from country to country that is modeled on the path of the sun—"The course was westward, that the sunne might light / As well our understanding as our sight" (193, ll. 17–18)—he insists that this "course" leads inexorably back to its starting point:

> But as the Sunne still goes both west and east;
> So also did the Church by going west
> Still eastward go . . .
>
> (199, ll. 274–76)

This paradox has important consequences for how we understand progression in Herbert, both spiritually and temporally. Inasmuch as logocentric and typological progression in traditional Christian thought involves a supposedly unilinear movement away from dead letter to living Word and from physical object to spiritual grace, the paradox has consequences also for how we understand the status of Herbert's matter. If the west is Herbert's horizon of becoming-spirit and the east his horizon of becoming-matter, then the ineluctable return of west to east in "The Church Militant" suggests that his matter is less dematerializing than persistently rematerializing.

The Untimely "Atome" of "The Church Militant"

No poem in *The Temple* has provoked as much critical ambivalence as "The Church Militant." On the one hand, ingenious efforts have been made to justify the poem as an integral part of and rightful climax to the sequence, fulfilling Herbert's masterful design of *The Temple* as either an architectural structure, a hieroglyphic of the soul's movement in time, a typological map of religious history, or a graphic triptych illustrating the trifold aspects of the church.[73] By contrast, its more insistently negative reception has often shaded into a perception of the poem's untimeliness within the sequence and, more generally, within Herbert's writing career.

In both the extant manuscript versions in which it appears, the text of "The Church Militant" is separated from the main body of the other poems by one or more fly leaves.[74] For many readers, the suspicion that the poem may therefore be an unwieldy add-on has been exacerbated by its tone, which they see as being out of step with the rest of *The Temple*: in contrast to the dematerializing progression supposedly enacted in the movement from exterior "Church-porch" to interior "Church," "The Church Militant" does not culminate in a sense of spiritual triumph but rather backslides into uncertainty. As a result, some have argued that the poem should not be considered part of *The Temple*.[75] The suspicion that "The Church Militant" charts a spiritual regression has been at least partly displaced into a charge of temporal regression: namely, the claim that the poem must have been written at an earlier stage in Herbert's life. F. E. Hutchinson argued "The Church Militant" was most likely written in the 1610s or 1620s while Herbert was still at Cambridge.[76] Seizing on its infamous line about religion standing "Readie to pass to the *American* strand" (199, l. 236), many readers have seen the poem as responding to the activities of the Virginia Company, in which Herbert's family and stepfather had financial interests.[77] The company initially justified its activity as an opportunity to spread the light of Gospel to the New World's inhabitants, but in 1624 King James had taken over its charter and effectively shut down its evangelical mission. Herbert's composition of "The Church Militant," it is argued, must date to before then—which has allowed readers to explain its falling away from the spiritual progression and the formal elegance of "The Church" as what happens when a poet anachronistically chooses to conclude his adult masterpiece with an experiment from his immature years.

I do not want to enter the debate over when "The Church Militant" was written, or whether or not it should be included in *The Temple*. But I would observe that recuperations and rejections of the poem alike, as well as attempts to date it, are often informed by a desire for the dematerializing Herbert. Either the poem or his career must be slotted into the trajectory of movement from matter to spirit. Those who see the poem as a triumphant climax to the sequence want it to perform a purposeful movement to spiritual consummation. Those who argue for its exclusion from the sequence do so in order to allow *The Temple* to finish with the supposedly high spiritualizing note of "Love (III)," which commemorates Herbert's movement from "dust and sinne" to the final communion in heaven (192, l. 1).[78] And those who explain "The Church Militant" as the work of a much younger Herbert do so partly to narrate him as having moved from an immature didacticism and worldly concern with Virginia to a more exquisite command of poetic craft and spiritual discipline in his final years.

All these readings are designed to ward off the twin specters of rematerialization and anachronism which I have examined throughout this chapter and which, I have argued, are pervasive throughout *The Temple*. But it is precisely those specters that "The Church Militant" most insistently conjures: as Kathleen Lynch has cannily noted, the poem emphasizes "the circularity of human experience and the inevitability of facing the same experiences over and over again."[79] And if it is hard for many readers to admit these specters into Herbert's *Temple*, then that speaks in large part to the power of two related promises the poem seems to offer: that we can make an orderly progression from matter to spirit, and that we can make an orderly progression from past to future. It is less that Herbert breaks these promises than that he lays bare the untimely reinscriptions—reverting to matter in progressing to spirit, reverting to the past in progressing to the future—that quietly inform them. And it is because of this achievement, I would argue, that Herbert demands to be understood as a theorist of untimely matter.

In its opening lines, "The Church Militant" seems not simply to promise but also to insist on the subordination of matter to spirit:

> Almightie Lord, who from thy glorious throne
> Seest and rulest all things ev'n as one:
> The smallest ant or atome knows thy power,
> Known also to each minute of an houre. . . .
>
> (193, ll. 1–4)

The relation of matter to spirit here involves more than just the opening couplet's assertion of God's providential control over his creation. It becomes a good deal more complex with Herbert's reference to the "atome."[80] The term works as a salutary figure for irreducible smallness: not just the tiniest creature—an ant—but even the most minuscule particle of matter is under God's providential sway. In late medieval and early modern usage, the atom denoted not only the smallest particle of matter but also the smallest unit of time—one 376th of a minute.[81] The twin physical and temporal properties of line 3's "atome" provide a conceptual enjambment between the ant and the following line, in which God's power is known to "each minute of an hour." Herbert thus quietly signals his preoccupation with understanding God's relation not just to matter but also to temporality.

But the figure he selects to embody this relation comes with significant baggage. "Atome" derives from the pre-Christian materialist philosophy of atomism associated with Epicurus and his later Roman follower Lucretius, whose long poem *De rerum natura* Herbert may have encountered at Cambridge.[82] Epicurus and Lucretius both believed the universe to be composed of irreducible particles in constant motion, falling through a void. For many seventeenth-century English writers, atomism was a byword for atheism; as Lucy Hutchinson complained in her mid-seventeenth-century translation of *De rerum natura*, the philosophy undermines "the Soveraigne Wisedome of God in the greate Designe of the whole Universe."[83] Indeed, Lucretius asserts in book 2 of *De rerum natura* that nature is "free from the proud command / Of soveraigne power"; and he goes on to ask, "What power allmightie, sitting at the helme / Can guide the reins of such a boundlesse realme?"[84] Herbert cheekily answers this question by asserting a "power allmightie" that guides the motions of even particles that are definitionally independent of it. This leads to an unusual typological vision of spirit prevailing over not Jewish but pagan matter: godless atom is subsumed within, and superseded by, the providential cosmology of the new covenant. The "atome" is thus one of Herbert's many palimpsest-like objects within which the matter of the past is overwritten by the spiritual traces of its future. Yet like these other objects, the "atome"'s supposedly superseded matter continues to do untimely work. For even as "The Church Militant" places atomism under divine erasure, the poem uncannily reproduces aspects of an atomistic conception of the world.

For Lucretius, the world was divided into atoms and the void. The former move through the latter; but their course isn't linear and progressive. As they fall through the void, atoms exhibit a deviant and sometimes recursive motion, swerving or declining from the straight and narrow path of gravity's pull: "if they were not us'd to decline, / Like drops of raine, they all in a straight line / Would fall."[85] This declension is, for Lucretius, a repudiation of ironclad necessity: though atoms must fall downward, that fall cannot entirely determine their motion. In the words of Michel Serres, his most insightful and provocative exegete, Lucretius embraces "the creative science of change and circumstance" instead of "the physics of the fall, of repetition, and of rigorous trains of events."[86] For all their differences, Lucretius's and Herbert's poems share a vital preoccupation with movement through space and time. And though they are concerned with the movement of very different entities—atoms and the church—Herbert's understanding of motion in "The Church Militant" at times curiously resembles Lucretius's. In Lucretius, matter tends in one direction: downward. In Herbert, it likewise tends in one direction: westward. But in both cases, that tendency is complicated by local swerves and divagations that expose the impossibility of a unilinear, "rigorous train of events" toward an omnipotent telos or necessity. In Lucretius, that necessity is falling. In Herbert, it is transcendence of matter.

To assert as much is to fly in the face of not just the providential but also the powerful typological interpretive framework that shapes the opening section of "The Church Militant." In sketching the beginning of the global history of the church, Herbert develops a familiar metaphor—the grapevine growing with the rise of the sun/Son—in ways that seem to presume an orderly typological and temporal progression from old matter to new grace. Addressing God, Herbert proclaims that "Early didst thou arise to plant this vine" (193, l. 11). This divine vine represents a step forward from "the laden boughs / Of *Noahs* shadie vine" (193, ll. 14–15), whose "shadie" aspect suggests both a comparative lack of light and a *foreshadowing* of the new and more radiant vine that will supersede it. And if the vine image plots a typological progression from Old Testament to Incarnation, Herbert also implies a further progression to the future of Herbert's English present. "Spices come from the East," he observes; "so did thy Spouse" (193, l. 13). Herbert elsewhere offers versions of this sense-stimulating metaphor—spiritual joys are "th'Isle of spices" ("The Size," 147, l. 12), and Christ is "An orientall fragrancie" ("The Odour, 2. Cor. 2," 180, l. 5)—but these lack the topical relevance or portentous historical sense of "spices" in "The Church Militant." The church is here an oriental commodity that must move to other lands, just as spices are shipped into England by the Levant and East India Companies. Indeed, for spices to "come" from the "East," they must go to the West.[87]

The problem is what happens on the way. The expectation of ongoing historical progress generated by these typological figures—and by Herbert's brief summary of the movement of the ark from Noah and Abraham to Moses and Solomon, who "Finish'd and fixt the old religion" (193, l. 22) before its supersession by the new—is slowly but surely undermined over the course of the poem.[88] The sun/Son's light does indeed move from "eastern nations . . . to the western clime"—first "to *Egypt*" (194, ll. 35–37); "thence . . . into *Greece*" (194, l. 49); then "to *Rome*" (194, l. 60); and "At length to *Germanie*, still westward bending" (195, l. 81). But rather than a triumphal, incrementally spiritual march, Herbert presents this *translatio religii* as a beleaguered flight prompted by the withering rather than the flowering of religious devotion in each location. The force that impedes the unilinear march of history toward transcendence throughout the globe—and, by knocking it from the straight and narrow path, provides it with its Lucretian declension or clinamen—is Sin.[89]

Herbert elsewhere in *The Temple* treats Sin not just morally but also quasi-scientifically. We have already seen how, in "Sinnes Round," Herbert insists on Sin's recursive and circular perversion of causality. And in "The Agonie" he asks that philosophers give up measuring the heights of mountains and the depth of seas, and turn their attention instead to "two vast, spacious things, / The which to measure it doth more behove: / . . . Sinne and Love" (58, ll. 4–6). In "The Church Militant," Herbert combines these two interpretations of Sin, insisting on its circular motion and its ongoing struggle with Love. But whereas "The Agonie" sees Sin as the "presse" that by crushing Christ produces the wine of Love, "The Church Militant" does not offer any such functionalist recuperation of its effects. Instead Sin corrodes rather than facilitates progress. And in doing so, it generates the untimely effect of material reinscription that we have seen throughout *The Temple*.

If the Christian church plots what looks like a progressive westward course to spirit, Sin parodically replays that course in terms that collapse back into the inky and pathological properties of Herbert's matter:

Much about one and the same time and place,
Both where and when the Church began her race,
Sinne did set out of Eastern *Babylon*,
And travell'd westward also: journeying on
He chid the Church away, where e're he came,

Breaking her peace, and tainting her good name.
(195, ll. 101–5)

The Church and Sin, like Lucretius's atoms, together follow a turbulent rather than linear course, in which Sin collides with the Church and subjects it to material declension. Here that rematerialization takes the form of "tainting," a term that derives from both "attaint," meaning an infection, and "tincture," meaning ink.[90] Sin thus transforms the Church into a sick palimpsest.

Everywhere the Church goes, its spiritual practices are anachronistically rematerialized by Sin as a retrograde investment in things. In Egypt, Sin collapses the early advances of the Church into the fetishistic worship of food dug from the ground:

Ah, what a thing is man devoid of grace,
Adoring garlick with an humble face,
Begging his food of that which he may eat,
Starving the while he worshippeth his meat!
Who makes a root his god, how low is he,
If God and man be sever'd infinitely!
(196, ll. 111–16)

Yet if this garlic fetishism recalls what Herbert elsewhere in *The Temple* characterizes as a Jewish misprision of matter as spirit and signifier as signified, "The Church Militant" presents Sin's effects less as reversions to pre-Christian practices than as material reinscriptions of what should lead to spirit. In Rome especially, Sin makes "a jest of Christs three offices" (197, l. 174)—prophet, king, and priest—by investing in material riches and pleasures. Indeed, the Roman Church becomes legible as a palimpsest that rematerializes all the sinful matter of previous ages and nations: "From *Egypt* he took pettie deities, / From *Greece* oracular infallibilities, / And from old *Rome* the libertie of pleasure" (197, ll. 177–79). This results in a comprehensive orientalization of Catholic Rome. As Herbert notes, Sin did "in memoriall of his ancient throne / . . . surname his palace, Babylon" (197, ll. 181–82)—a reminder that one of the most recurrent strategies of English Protestant thought, evinced by writers as diverse as Edmund Spenser and Thomas Dekker, was to demonize the Roman Church as the Whore of Babylon, the apocalyptic figure in

Revelation. Thus was Rome recast in the English imagination as both geographically and temporally oriental.[91]

Sin's westward progress from Babylon to Rome is different from the true Church's. Some readers have seen in "The Church Militant" a justification of empire under the aegis of spreading the light of Gospel.[92] But in Herbert's pessimistic conception of history, it is Sin rather than the Church that possesses imperial powers of expansion. Sin, as its polychronic palimpsests suggest, grows in size and intensity with its every relocation. By contrast, the Church's movements diminish its virtue: "As in vice the copie still exceeds / The pattern, but not so in virtuous deeds; / . . . The second Temple could not reach the first" (198, ll. 221–22, 225). Although there is the prospect of a future westward relocation of religion to "the *American* strand" (199, l. 236)—a prospect that, as Hawkes has noted, is rooted in an idealizing vision of prelapsarian Native Americans happily indifferent to gold or other material goods[93]—Herbert is adamant that "as the Church shall thither westward flie, / So Sinne shall trace and dog her instantly" (199, ll. 259–60). "Trace" here suggests not only a pursuit but also a drawing, marking, or superinscription of the Church by Sin. Regardless of how much the Church flies westward in the ostensible direction of spirit, then, it is repeatedly overwritten by and rematerialized as the wicked past it would escape. No wonder that Herbert can insist "the Church by going west / Still eastward [did] go" (199, ll. 275–76). The only solution he can conceive of for this untimely conundrum is a Calvinist one—the apocalyptic promise of the Last Judgment in an indefinite future "time and place" (200, l. 277). For now, however, there can be no progression or transcendence, no matter how much we battle matter.

"The Church Militant" and *The Temple* thus embody a powerful contradiction rooted in Herbert's understandings of material culture, typology, and time. On the one hand, as the enduring popularity of the dematerializing Herbert shows, *The Temple* voices a powerful longing for supersessionary movements from fallen matter to pure spirit and fallen past to redeemed future. We cannot deny that longing, whose object is literally utopian—a good place and time that is also no place and time, the typological future theorized diversely by Auerbach, Jameson, and Lupton. On the other hand, *The Temple* provides equally powerful tools for showing how that utopian longing is haunted by the specters—though that may be too ghostly a metaphor for untranscended matter—of rematerialization and the untimely.[94] The implications of those material specters for understandings of temporality, beyond problematizing the notion of time as a linear progression from past to future, remain unclear in Herbert. What does the resurfacing of past matter in the present portend? And how might it invite different, heterodox conceptions of futurity? In subsequent chapters, I turn to the anachronistic specters identified by Herbert and the ways in which other English Renaissance theorists of untimely matter put these to critical use. Like Herbert in *The Temple* and Victoria Roberts in her cartoon, all these theorists understand the oriental reading matter of yesterday to be forever resurfacing as today's news, and with radically different implications for tomorrow. In the case of Shakespeare's *2 Henry 4*, as we shall see in the next chapter, that news takes the name of Rumour.

TWO

Performing History

East-West Palimpsests in William Shakespeare's Second Henriad

> I, from the orient to the drooping west,
> Making the wind my post-horse, still unfold
> The acts commenced on this ball of earth.
>
> —*2 Henry 4*, Induction, 3–5

AT THE BEGINNING of *2 Henry 4*, Rumour represents himself as a global communications system that spans "orient" and "drooping west." As in Herbert's "Church Militant," these compass points demarcate a space conceived not just geographically—from Asia to Europe—but also temporally: Rumour operates from sunrise to sunset and, by implication, from past to future. In this speech, "orient" and "west" also circumscribe the space and time of the theatrical, providing the imaginative limits within which Rumour can "unfold / The acts commenced on this ball of earth"—if not the aptly named Globe (built in 1599), then the stage on which the Lord Chamberlain's Men first performed *2 Henry 4*. But these compass points are not simply opposed outer limits for the play's spatiotemporal fields of representation. Indeed, throughout Shakespeare's second Henriad, the theatrical "unfold[ing]" of "acts" also entails a persistent palimpsesting of "orient" and "west" in both their temporal and their geographical senses. As in Herbert's "Church Militant," therefore, east bleeds into west and past into future, generating myriad untimely effects.

Henry 5's assertion of quasi-typological relations between historical figures from different eras—particularly the Chorus's "loving likelihood" that crosshatches the medieval Henry with both the classical Caesar and the Elizabethan Earl of Essex (*H5*, 5.0.28, 30), and Fluellen's comparison of Henry with Alexander the Great (4.3.22)—have attracted extensive commentary.[1] By contrast, the Henriad's persistent palimpsests of east and west have largely escaped critical attention. These palimpsests are most legible in the plays' ambivalent identifications of their English characters with a string of oriental despots from antiquity to more recent times: Cambyses of Persia, Tamburlaine of Scythia, Herod of Jewry, and Amurath of Turkey. By invoking these figures, the Henriad complicates Rumour's promise to "unfold" the "acts" of "the orient to the drooping west": instead the orient becomes folded into, or inscribed within, the west. This orient, however, is not the orient of historical fact or even of Elizabethan "orientalism." It is more specifically the orient of the English theater: an orient of over-the-top, histrionic bodily gestures and deafening verbal delivery.

The repeated allusions to oriental despots, all of whom were familiar to English theatergoers as larger-than-life stage villains, contribute to the metatheatrical quality of the Henriad in general. Of course, readers have long been attuned to the theatricality of the three plays. The tendency of critical readings since the 1980s, however, has been to subsume this theatricality within a statist politics that also provides a synchronic map of the "early modern." In Stephen Greenblatt's well-known essay on the Henriad, for example, Hal theatrically performs his power in much the same way the Elizabethan state apparatus performed its own, staging subversion so that it may be contained.[2] By contrast, I shall argue that the plays' metatheatricality—in particular, their allusions to oriental stage kings—demands a more polychronic analysis attuned to the untimely effects of actors' bodily techniques. For the Henriad's theatricality is not just about the *theatrum politicum* of the state but also about the institution of the theater itself. Or if the plays adumbrate a politics of playing, the power they seek to explain is not just that of the English monarch but equally their own. They do so with a keen self-reflexivity about styles of acting, past, present, and future: the ranting tyrants of the late medieval cycle drama, the Marlovian-era bombast popularized by Edward Alleyn and the Admiral's Men, and an emergent, more self-conscious style practiced by Shakespeare's company. In the process, Shakespeare's second Henriad offers what might be described as a politics of intertheatricality, where what is at stake is not just the realpolitik of the king or the destiny of the nation but also the skillful versatility, relative to both earlier and contemporary English actors, of the Lord Chamberlain's Men.

The performance of present versatility in relation to past histrionic styles amounts to a secular version of supersessionary time. This secular temporality, as we shall see, anticipates an influential theory of history associated with Enlightenment philosophy. Both imagine the temporal and cultural supersession of the east by the west as enabled by a refinement of self-consciousness. But far more than any Enlightenment philosophy of history, the second Henriad discloses how the temporality of supersession, and its assumption of timely development, is dependent on a constitutive untimeliness: the past needs to be performed in the present as that from which the present differentiates itself. Moving forward to the future, then, necessitates a simultaneous movement backward to the past. In the second Henriad, the remnants of supposedly superseded pasts take the form of untimely matter—specifically, actors' bodies whose techniques are legible as simultaneously out of date and cutting-edge. In Shakespearean intertheatricality, then, we see a versatile histrionicism that transforms the actor's body into a palimpsest of east and west, past and future.

Intertheatricality

To decode Shakespeare's intertheatricality, what is required is not a synchronic mode of analysis that would trace the circulation of discourse between the theater and larger social formations cotemporal with it, or even a diachronic analysis that traces the evolution of styles of acting. Rather, intertheatricality demands a polychronic hermeneutic that attends to the untimely performance within Shakespeare's present of its theatrical pasts (or "orients") and futures (or "wests"). Such a hermeneutic might have something in common with the method of criticism known as intertextuality, though it is also significantly different. This is partly because, in contrast to intertextuality's narrower focus on language (whether specific phrases or "discourse" in general), intertheatrical interpretation attends to the bodies of actors, their costumes, and their techniques of movement, gesture, and verbal delivery. A purely intertextual reading of, say, *2 Henry 4*'s allusions to Sultan

Amurath might investigate the play's verbal and thematic echoes of sixteenth-century treatises about Ottoman emperors or literary representations of Turks, but it will neglect the conventions of performance that shaped the Elizabethan actor's presentation of the oriental despot.[3] Intertheatricality, in other words, is concerned with the material culture of the stage—that is, the working and reworking of theatrical matter, including the actor's body and accessories.

An even bigger difference between intertextual and intertheatrical interpretations concerns the temporality of their hermeneutics. Though intertextuality is less invested in definitive origins than source study, it has often lent expression to a similar antiquarian impulse, showing how texts engage in dialogue with what has come before—the "already-written," in Roland Barthes's words.[4] This relation to the past can take many forms, be it wistful nostalgia (Paul Zumthor's "désir d'intégration"), Oedipal anxiety (Harold Bloom's filial revisionism), or playful assimilation (Julia Kristeva's mosaic *idéologème*).[5] By contrast, even as the intertheatrical performance resurrects the acting techniques of the past, its primary concern is the new ground opened up by histrionic versatility. The intertheatrical Shakespearean actor has at his command a variety of performance styles that he reproduces masterfully; the success of the performance, however, depends on audience recognition—of the styles, of their masterful rendering, but also of future opportunities that their performance engenders.

Intertheatricality serves as a reminder that the matter of the stage is not simply physicality existing in the here and now of the performance. It is also dynamic material, in both Aristotle's and Marx's senses of the term—material that is worked upon and transformed by theatrical praxis.[6] In the case of the Henriad's intertheatricality, the reworking of old acting styles signifies progress by modeling a new, "improved" form of histrionicism. Thus if intertextuality voices a desire for the past, the Henriad's intertheatricality generates a desire for what is to come. Despite its express nostalgia for a medieval Golden Age of expansionist English kingship, the Henriad's east-west palimpsests rework the past to produce new theatrical possibilities—possibilities that also have political applicability.[7] Shakespearean intertheatricality thus strives for the future-oriented temporality of supersession. And in doing so, it demands a critical sensitivity to the polychronic aspects of theatrical matter.

Few scholars of Shakespearean theater history have been as attentive to the polychronicity of the Renaissance stage as the Marxist critic Robert Weimann.[8] Among the many virtues of Weimann's work is the complexity with which he theorizes representation in Renaissance drama, in ways that illuminate the dynamics of theatrical authority. New historicism and cultural materialism have tended to imagine authority on the model of the centralized state: hence early modern drama is said to contain subversion in the manner of American Cold War foreign policy, and resistance to authority is styled as dissident.[9] By contrast, Weimann emphasizes the multiple forms of representational authority produced on and by the Renaissance stage. In the process, he proposes an alternative understanding of theatrical performance—one in which Shakespeare's drama is not subsumed within an all-pervasive, synchronic discourse, as it has tended to be in new historicist criticism. Instead he regards it as its own semiautonomous semiotic field, requiring special methods of critical analysis that are sensitive to the polychronic and multitemporal spaces of the premodern stage.

Weimann's well-known distinction between the "locus" and "platea" of the Renaissance stage might suggest a synchronic understanding of Elizabethan theatrical space. But the distinction does not so much map two opposing parts of the stage as articulate competing theatrical chronotopes.[10] The more representational locus of the Renaissance stage, specified in place and time, embodies what might be termed a historicist chronotope: its historical and geographical setting is determinate, and remote from that of the playhouse or its audience. The platea, by contrast, is "an entirely non-representational and unlocalized setting," from where the actor both comments on the action of the locus and speaks directly to the audience.[11] This space is typified by the "contrariety" of the theatrically ambidextrous Vice, who plays, in the words of Thomas Preston's *Cambyses*, "with both hands," participating in the dramatic illusion and stepping outside it.[12] Just as this space breaks down the barrier between audience and actor, so does it potentially intermingle past (as depicted in the playworld) and present (as instanced in the space of the playhouse and audience).

Weimann's account of the platea and its polychronic "contrariety" inflects his recent work on acting styles. In *Author's Pen and Actor's Voice*, he considers the rude mechanicals of *A Midsummer Night's Dream* in light of Peter Quince's peculiar direction "to disfigure, or to present, the person of Moonshine" (3.1.61). Even if it is a malapropism, Quince's equation of theatrical "presentation" with "disfiguration" suggests to Weimann how Shakespeare's actors frequently exploited the platea's unclear gap between "what is to be represented and what or who is doing the (re)presenting."[13] On the medieval stage, he argues, this gap was generated through nonnaturalistic, histrionic techniques of performance distinguished by "the *excessive*, the eccentric thrust in corporeal movement."[14] Even though medieval drama's "excessive" acting styles contrast Hamlet's mimetic ideal of holding the mirror up to nature, Elizabethan players were still very much in thrall to them—albeit in much more self-conscious fashion. So when the actor playing Bottom delivers an audition piece in the over-the-top manner of the ranting Hercules (1.2.22), and pronounces his bizarre performance to be "lofty" (1.2.32), he enacts a "bi-fold authority" that refracts theatrical space.[15] Displaying both the representational quality appropriate to the locus and the burlesque typical of the platea, he speaks simultaneously as an earnest Greek weaver and a comic English actor. That is, even as he rehearses an old, nonnaturalistic style that his audiences would have associated with the ranting despots of medieval cycle drama—"my chief humour," he says, "is for a tyrant" (1.2.21–22)—the sheer excess of that style offers metadramatic commentary on itself. His performance is thus an intertheatrical palimpsest, offering two voices in one.

The palimpsest is a particularly useful critical tool with which to read the intertheatricality of not just *A Midsummer Night's Dream* but also the Henriad. We can, of course, read the Henriad as a textual palimpsest, containing the telltale sedimented signs of earlier drafts in which the character we now know as Falstaff was called Oldcastle.[16] But Weimann's analyses of medieval and Shakespearean histrionics suggest that we might read the Henriad for a different kind of palimpsest, one that is literally embodied in the acting styles of the Lord Chamberlain's Men. Like Bottom's reproduction of medieval ranting, the Henriad compulsively recycles old performance conventions. But its intertheatrical palimpsests are subtly different from those of *A Midsummer Night's Dream*, at least as theorized by Weimann. In Weimann's analysis, the actor playing Bottom resurrects a traditional playing style that fractures the (re)presenter from what is represented; he is thus a descendant of the medieval actor, even if he performs in the twilight of a once vital tradition.[17] By contrast, the rehearsal of old acting styles in the Henriad widens the temporal gap between player and representational technique in a fashion that critically distances the past. Far more than the actor who performs Bottom, the players in the Henriad pointedly rework the histrionic techniques of the medieval stage in order to advance a newer style. And this newer style has little to do with the naturalism endorsed by Hamlet. Its ideal is not mimetic accuracy but versatile skill.

The innovative acting style demanded by the Henriad might be called, to borrow a coinage from Harry Berger, Jr., the "new histrionicism."[18] Its newness entails less a clean break with the theatrical past than a simultaneous retention and cancellation of it. Old styles of acting are performed; but they are performed in quotation marks, and in ways that draw attention to both the actor's and his character's histrionic versatility. Indeed, it is this versatility, and the theatrical self-consciousness it demands, that most characterizes the intertheatrical moments in the Henriad. The Lord Chamberlain's Men's bodily techniques become visible, and audible, as old modes of gesture and verbal delivery overlaid with and canceled by a new self-conscious skill. The "new histrionicism," in other words, performs the temporality of supersession. And because this performance affects the audience's perception of actor and character, supersessionary time shapes the claims that Shakespeare makes in the Henriad for the versatility both of his playing company and of Hal/Harry/Henry as prince and future king.

In a shrewd account of "projective transversality" in *Henry 5*, Donald Hedrick and Bryan Reynolds consider Henry's charismatic performances of his versatility in a number of scenes—at court with the traitors, on the battlefield with his own men, and in France with Katherine. Henry's performances are grounded in what Hedrick and Reynolds call "translucency," a mode of acting in which one semiotic code is "incompletely concealed within another."[19] Translucency involves an element of the playing style that Reynolds has elsewhere characterized (after Monty Python) as "Nudge, Nudge, Wink, Wink, Know What I Mean, Know What I Mean." This style asks the audience to recognize a semiotic excess within the performance, a self-reflexive supplement that turns a role into a palimpsest. Translucency demands that the actor "must do more than one thing at a time. Being 'in the moment' is not enough: one must also *point out* that one is in the moment; one must be in the moment in a way that is *about* the moment."[20] Henry performs the roles of king, warrior, and wooer in a way that signals his theatrical flair; his performances are translucent inasmuch as they overlay each role with a glimpse of something else—a self-conscious versatility that is as crucial to his political power as it is to the audience's theatrical pleasure. Thus defined, Henry's translucency is similar to the palimpsests of Shakespearean intertheatricality. Although Hedrick and Reynolds view Henry's performances of versatility as ultimately unconvincing—Henry does not, in their reading, entirely draw his onstage or offstage audiences into new experiences of subjectivity—they nonetheless insist on the heterodox potential of translucency as a theatrical practice.

Following Hedrick and Reynolds, I shall argue that translucency is the signature of Hal/Harry/Henry's performances *throughout* the Henriad. He is a palimpsest in which are visible both old styles of acting and a new, more versatile histrionicism. I am more interested than Hedrick and Reynolds, however, in folding such translucency back into an analysis of the claims the Henriad makes about the skill of the Lord Chamberlain's Men.[21] In doing so, I want to show how a more institutionally specific approach to Shakespeare's intertheatricality can bolster a reading of the palimpsested stage in sympathy with Weimann's work. But such a reading must also take stock of the problematic emplotments of historical progress and supersession that intertheatricality can presume. This is especially the case with the Henriad's "new histrionicism." As I shall show, Shakespeare's intertheatricality in these plays entails a conception of cultural progress that uncannily resembles a much later, Eurocentric philosophy of world history. To this extent, the Henriad provides the bridge between a religious and a secular conception of supersession grounded in untimely matter—in this case, the matter of the actor's body.

"In Cambyses's Vein"

As many readers have noted, the Henriad's tavern scenes are suffused with self-conscious theatricality. Hal and Falstaff are constantly playacting, turning the Eastcheap tavern into their premodern karaoke-cum-drag bar. Adding to these scenes' performativity is their specification of venue. Although the play-text never explicitly names its tavern the "Boar's Head," it would have been readily recognizable as the watering hole of that name in the Eastcheap parish of St. Michael's, not least because of the pun in *2 Henry 4*: "Doth the old boar feed in the old frank?" (*2H4*, 2.2.133). The Boar's Head was used not only as a tavern but also as a venue for contemporary theatrical performances. The playing companies patronized by the Earl of Oxford and Earl of Worcester performed there often in the 1590s, and when the two joined into one company, they requested that the Lord Mayor grant them the Boar's Head as their playhouse in residence.[22] Hence the tavern scenes neatly undo Weimann's distinction between locus and platea, inasmuch as they present *both* a spatiotemporally circumscribed past *and* a performance space shared by Shakespeare's audience in the present.

The many dramatic and literary forms held up for playful scrutiny in the tavern scenes include morality drama and John Lyly's euphuism. But the only work explicitly name checked is *Cambyses*, Thomas Preston's "Lamentable Tragedy, Mixed Full of Pleasant Mirth," of the 1560s. Why does Falstaff playact in the Persian "Cambyses's vein" (*1H4*, 2.4.385)? Some readers have suggested characterological and thematic parallels between Preston's and Shakespeare's dramas. *Cambyses* sternly chronicles the consequences of its title character's drunkenness and is hence a suitable intertext for the soused Falstaff, whose "give me a cup of sack" (*1H4*, 2.4.384) seems to recall Cambyses's "give it me to drink it off, and see no wine be waste."[23] Preston's Vice character, Ambidexter, also anticipates Falstaff, whom Hal identifies with "that reverend Vice, that grey iniquity" (*1H4*, 2.4.453–54).[24] Yet these readings strike me as too literal minded—or rather, too literary minded. What they cannot account for is that, simply as a *literary* parody, Falstaff's rendition of Cambyses is bafflingly wide of the mark. The distinctively metronomic fourteeners of Preston's play are not reproduced by Sir John, who instead speaks lines written in more up-to-date pentameter.

If Falstaff parodies anything in *Cambyses*, it is not its literary or thematic qualities—such as they are—but its pervasive histrionicism. Preston's play calls for not only an inordinate amount of weeping but also self-commentary on its occurrence. Before his execution by Cambyses, the wicked Judge Sisamnes says to his son Otian: "O childe thou makes mine eyes to run, as rivers doo by streme" (455); Praxaspes and his wife not only weep but also discuss their weeping over the death of their son: "It is even so, my Lord I see, how by him he dooth weep" (575), and "With blubred eyes into mine armes, from earth I wil thee take" (582); and, most crucially, the Queen weeps pitifully when, having heard the story of the three lion cub brothers who refused to kill each other, she recalls Cambyses's cruel murder of his own brother: "These words to hear makes stilling teares, issue from Christal eyes" (1030). Even the Vice weeps at the Queen's death: "A, A, A, A, I cannot chuse but weep for the Queene" (1127). And it is *Cambyses*'s weeping that Falstaff comically replays: "Give me a cup of sack to make my eyes look red, that it may be thought I have wept"; "Weep not sweet Queen, for trickling tears are vain"; "For God's sake my Lords, convey my trustful Queen, / For tears do stop the floodgates of her eyes" (*1H4*, 2.4.384–86, 391, 393–94).[25]

Why Falstaff's comic obsession with the tears of *Cambyses*? Did Shakespeare's all-male company find such theatrical displays of weeping effeminate, and enjoy poking fun at them? Macduff, like many characters, has to apologize for his "woman"-like tears. Revealingly, however, he also associates weeping with playing the "braggart" with his "tongue," as if he were remembering the lachrymose braggadocio of *Cambyses* (*Macbeth*, 4.3.232–33). Thus Macduff's outburst serves to draw attention not just to weeping but also to the histrionic conventions that accompanied its staging. In this, it is typical of Shakespeare's other references to the mechanics of crying: the Page in the Induction of the *Taming of the Shrew* is advised to use an onion to perform wifely tears (Induction 1.120–24), and Katherina herself says of Bianca that her tears are created by putting a "finger in the eye" (1.1.78–9). These scenes provide compelling instances of translucency: the audience sees weeping, but is also clued into the theatrical skill and the materials needed to stage it.[26] At such moments, in other words, Shakespeare's company allows its dramatic characters to become visible as actors who can move in and out of the codes of histrionic performance. We find ourselves in the presence not of heightened emotion, but of self-regarding skill in archaic performance techniques—like a contemporary rock singer at a sound check who cannot resist channeling the histrionic vocal stylings of Elvis, and in a manner that is equal parts parody, homage, and flagrant self-display.

Hence Falstaff's acting "in Cambyses's vein" is far more than just a robust send-up of excessive weeping. It also advertises the self-conscious art of the Shakespearean actor, who simultaneously rehearses *and* distances himself from excessive styles of performance. Throughout the second Henriad, the histrionicism on which such art draws is repeatedly given a local habitation and a name: the orient. As we shall see, Falstaff's turn as the Persian Cambyses is just one of several occasions on which the Henriad codes histrionic excess as oriental. Inasmuch as this tactic works to valorize its actors' "western" prowess, it recalls Edward Said's well-known schematization of the orient as Europe's constitutive other. But as Rumour suggests, the Henriad's "orient" does not just participate within a synchronic logic of *othering*; it is equally cast as the west's point of temporal and geographical *origin*. This logic is apparent in Falstaff's east-west palimpsest. Three discrete but linked "oriental" and "western" layers are implied by his performance of the Persian Cambyses:

1. An orient of *time*, seen as a past style of performance metonymically identified with the over-the-top techniques of English actors who have played eastern despots;
2. An orient of *space*, viewed as a synchronic geographical type of histrionic excess in an eternal present; and

3. A western *space* and *time* of the future that not so much opposes the spatiotemporal orients I have sketched above, as dialectically transcends them under the sign of theatrical self-consciousness, or what I am terming the "new histrionicism."

As this schema suggests, Falstaff's palimpsest hints at a Eurocentric teleology, in which a (theatrical) orient must give rise to a more perfect (theatrical) west. In the Henriad, Cambyses is but the first in a sequence of oriental stage despots who enable this maneuver.

"Not Amurath an Amurath Succeeds"

In a canny reading, Richard Hillman has underlined "the principle of English-Turkish 'shadowing' as a key factor in the Henriad's intertextuality."[27] His test case is Hal's speech upon his ascension to the throne. Hal seeks to reassure his brothers that, rather than the fratricidal king they fear he might become, he will prove a benign monarch:

> This is the English, not the Turkish court;
> Not Amurath an Amurath succeeds,
> But Harry, Harry.
>
> (*2H4*, 5.2.48)

Noting that historically no Amurath ever succeeded another, and that indeed Amurath here has no clear historical referent—the name may refer to Murad I, the Ottoman emperor who died in 1389 and who inflicted enormous cruelty on his son and brother, or anachronistically to Murad III, the Ottoman emperor who died in 1596 and notoriously killed his brother upon his own ascension in 1574—Hillman concludes that "the cultural projection that goes with the name Amurath is effectively detached from historical specificity and released into 'discursive space', to resonate . . . amongst and beyond particular bearers of it."[28] Having liberated "Amurath" from any specific historical figure, Hillman nonetheless rehistoricizes the signifier in relation to sixteenth-century Continental literature, citing a variety of "intertexts" that include Paolo Giovo's and Jacques La Vardin's histories of the Albanian Christian warrior George Scanderbeg's battles with the Ottomans. In the process, he shows how Hal—indeed, the entire second Henriad—is haunted by a series of "Turkish" foils and specular doubles.

Despite Hillman's express interest in the second Henriad's "complex set of intertexts, written and unwritten," he notably omits one set of "unwritten" intertexts, or rather, intertheatrical codes.[29] Overlooked in his reading of Amurath is any consideration of the character as he was performed on the Elizabethan stage. Upon hearing Hal's speech, Shakespeare's original audience may very well have called to mind whatever historical knowledge they possessed of the medieval Murad I and the early modern Murad III. Yet the Amurath with whom Elizabethan playgoers were most familiar was neither of these figures but a generic character from the theater—or rather, a specific theater, the Rose.[30] The earliest instance is the Amurath referred to in George Peele's *Battle of Alcazar*, performed at the Rose in 1589. Peele's character is not based on any historical Amurath or Murad but is instead an entirely conventional oriental despot. Though he is never seen, he is described as "angrie Amurath."[31] And it is as an almost comically over-the-top angry ranter that Amurath takes the stage in other Elizabethan drama. In the popular *Soliman and Perseda* (possibly by Thomas Kyd, and performed in the early 1590s), Amurath is again a generic rather than a historically specific character. Channeling Preston's Cambyses, he is an irascible hothead and fratricide who whips out his sword at the slightest provocation, and meets a suitably violent end at the hands of his other brother, Soliman.[32]

The Amurack, or Amurath, of Robert Greene's *Comicall Historie of Alphonsus, King of Aragon* (c. 1591) is a King of the Turks again based not on any identifiable historical figure but on the recognizably histrionic techniques of the oriental stage despot. He responds to his "prattling" wife, Fausta (who has rejected his plan to marry their daughter Iphigina to Alphonsus), in a ranting fashion that recalls Cambyses's outbursts against his Queen. His outburst is prefaced by a telltale stage direction, "*Amurack rise in a rage from thy chair*":

> What threat'ning words thus thunder in mine ears?
> Or who are they amongst the mortal troops
> That dares presume to use such threats to me?
> The proudest Kings and Kaisers of the land
> Are glad to feed me in my fantasy;
> And shall I suffer, then, each prattling dame
> For to upbraid me in this spiteful sort?[33]

In this speech, and throughout the play, we can hear echoes of another oriental stage despot familiar to playgoers at the Rose: Tamburlaine. Like Marlowe's megalomaniacal atheist, Amurack rails against Mahound (i.e., the Prophet Muhammed), so that "Mahound, provoked by Amurack's discourse . . . Denies to play the Prophet any more" (IV.prologue, 13, 15). Indeed, Greene's imitation of *Tamburlaine* is slavish: it is evident in, among other moments, Amurack's glorification of conquest, invocations of fortune's wheel, and wooing of his war-bride heroine. Yet *Alphonsus* parallels Marlowe's play less in any thematic or linguistic respect than in the histrionicism it calls for. To this extent, we might see Greene's Amurack/Amurath as a reprise of—and a synonym for—the theatrical Tamburlaine effect, an effect generated primarily by excessive bodily techniques and stage properties.

With its opening lines, *Tamburlaine* underscores the inadequacy of anything less than "great and thund'ring speech in a king" (I.1.1.3); and it constantly refers to Tamburlaine's fierce "looks" and body language (I.1.2.56, 3.2.66, II.1.4.76–78, 4.1.173–75, etc.).[34] It is in the testimony of Elizabethan audience members, however, that we can recognize the impact of Tamburlaine's body language. In his *Virigidemiarium* (1597), Joseph Hall satirizes an actor's performance of "the Turkish Tamberlaine"; in the process, Hall furnishes considerable information about the standard theatrical presentation of the character. Tamburlaine speaks loudly, resorting to "huf-cap termes and thundering threats / That his poore hearers hayre quite vpright sets," and he employs melodramatic gesture or "stalking and high-set steps."[35] A pamphlet from 1597 tells of a man who "bent his browes and fetcht his stations vp and downe the rome, with such furious Iesture as if he had been playing Tamberlaine on a stage."[36] Such "furious Iesture" may also have included stamping: in Thomas Dekker's *Satiromastix*, Tucca asks a player: "Doest stampe mad Tamberlaine, does stampe?"[37]

The actor Edward Alleyn became famous as a result of his performances as Tamburlaine, and many of his other star turns—such as the leads in *Tamar Cham* and Greene's *Orlando Furioso*, and Muly Mahomet in Peele's *Battle of Alcazar*—seem to have been custom-made for his Tamburlainian style of "*scenicall* strutting, and furious vociferation."[38] I would argue that the Amuraths we find in plays performed in the 1590s name a loose set of acting conventions associated with Alleyn's Tamburlaine. Even if these Amuraths were not played by Alleyn, they and other characters in the plays I have just mentioned typify the histrionic "oriental" style that had become his hallmark. An exemplary instance is the Turkish mercenary Brusor in *Soliman and Perseda*. Bragging about his past exploits, Brusor claims:

Against the Sophy in three pitched fields,
Under the conduct of great Soliman,
Have I been chief commander of an host,
And put the flint-heart Persians to the sword;
(And) marched (a) conqueror through Asia.
The desert plains of Affricke have I stained
With blood of Moors, and there in three set battles fought;
Along the coasts held by the Portinguze,
Even to the verge of gold-abounding Spain,
Hath Brusor led a valiant troop of Turks.
(1.3.51–60)

Waving his sword in the air and ranting vaingloriously, Brusor emerges as another incarnation of Alleyn's histrionic Tamburlaine.[39] For playwrights in the 1590s, the temptation to imitate or burlesque this histrionic style proved irresistible. Shakespeare arguably succumbed to the temptation in Bottom's ranting disfigurement of a "lofty . . . tyrant"; but he seems also to have remembered the specific details of Brusor's speech when writing the part of Morocco in *The Merchant of Venice*. This Barbary cousin of Brusor likewise swears noisily by his "scimitar / That slew the Sophy and a Persian prince / That won three fields of Sultan" (2.1.25–27). When Morocco is beaten for Portia's hand by the less bombastic and more calculating Bassanio, the Venetian's success is arguably a triumph not only for European wooing skills but also for a different style of acting, less "oriental" than Alleyn's. One arguably sees this very tension in *Othello*, whose title character—having refused in act 1 to wave his sword in stereotypical oriental fashion—lapses back into a primitive histrionicism when he declaims, after killing Desdemona, "Behold, I have a weapon" (5.2.266).

A similar geotheatrical differentiation seems to be at play in *2 Henry 4*. As his dismissive remark about Amurath suggests, Hal pointedly valorizes supposed English moderation over violent oriental excess. But the second Henriad delights in staging Amurath/Tamburlaine's theatricality nonetheless—albeit in displaced or dis-oriented fashion. This histrionicism might be glimpsed in Hotspur's many dazzling tantrums, whose connections to England's feudal past are theatrically underlined by his recognizably older, excessive performance styles. But it surfaces even more unmistakably with the arrival of Pistol in *2 Henry 4*.[40] The ghost of Tamburlaine is conjured by Pistol's drunken declamation about "hollow pampered jades of Asia" (*2H4*, 2.4.141; cf. *Tamburlaine* II.2.3.1). He also channels Muly Mahomet—another oriental despot played by Alleyn at the Rose—from Peele's *Battle of Alcazar* (*2H4*, 2.4.155).[41] As with Falstaff's Cambyses, however, Pistol's east-west palimpsest is composed primarily of intertheatrical rather than strictly intertextual references. His first entrance is prefaced by numerous remarks about his "swaggering," a term that describes not only his quarrelsome disposition but also his bodily techniques—specifically, the "furious vociferation and scenicall strutting" associated with Alleyn's Tamburlaine. These techniques serve a complicated theatrical purpose. Pistol's version of Tamburlaine, again like Falstaff's turn as Cambyses, is not simply an occasion for theatrical parody; it also pays homage to the skill of the Shakespearean actor, who can move in and out of the codes of "oriental" histrionicism with self-conscious "western" versatility. So even as Hal seems to assert an absolute difference between his own techniques and those of Amurath, Pistol's performances ensure that oriental histrionicism is less a dispensed with *other* than a vital, if transfigured, set of techniques in the Lord Chamberlain's Men's repertory.

Something similar happens in *Hamlet*. The Danish prince's advice to the players to avoid "o'erdoing Termagant" and "out-Herod[ing] Herod" (3.2.13–14) may seem to assert a sharp distinction between west and orient so that the latter can be exorcised: not only does Hamlet ridicule two stock oriental characters from the medieval mystery plays, his antipathy to actors who "split the ears of the groundlings" and who "have so strutted and bellowed" (3.2.11, 35) also glances at Alleyn's Tamburlaine or Amurath. Yet Hamlet himself fails to uphold the absolute difference he asserts between genteel acting styles and the barbarous primitivism of past and present oriental stage despots. As Weimann has noted, Hamlet's "plea for a poetics of neoclassical discretion" is upended by his "rehearsal" of "stale" jokes and acting styles, including the archaic ranting of Herod.[42]

Despite his explicit self-differentiation from Amurath in *2 Henry 4*, I would argue that Hal likewise rehearses the very oriental histrionicism he inveighs against. For Weimann, Hamlet's channeling of Herod marks a return to the older, excessive style of acting that characterizes the platea and the "contrariety" of the Vice. Hal's—or rather Harry's—rehearsals of the orient do not so much echo older demotic styles, however, as willfully transform and supersede them. Yet this supersession necessitates not the expulsion of the past but its untimely retention. While Herod is a histrionic model that Hamlet tries desperately to consign to the dustbin of theater history, the character reemerges in *Henry 5* as a vitally active layer of another east-west palimpsest. In his version of Herod, as we shall see, Harry no longer distances himself from Amurath and his over-the-top ilk. Like Falstaff with the tearful Cambyses, Harry instead harnesses the oriental despot's histrionic energies in order to underline his versatile mastery of acting styles.

"Herod's Bloody-Hunting Slaughtermen"

As a child in Stratford, Shakespeare may well have attended a performance of the annual Corpus Christi cycle play in nearby Coventry; the play was discontinued only in 1579, when he was fifteen.[43] If so, he would have seen in the Shearmen and Taylors' pageant of the Slaughter of the Innocents an extraordinary scene of histrionic strutting and bellowing by an oriental tyrant. Having discovered that the three kings have eluded his trap for them, Herod the Great responds with a ferocious outburst: "I stampe! I stare! I loke all abowte!"[44] Herod's tantrum is punctuated by an equally noteworthy stage direction, moreover, one that translates his previous remark into a bravura performance of sustained stamping, staring, and looking all about: "*Here Erode ragis in* the *pagond* and *in the street also*."[45]

Shakespeare stands alone among the major playwrights of the early modern London stage in making repeated reference to Herod. Inasmuch as Herod does make an appearance in the drama of Shakespeare's contemporaries, such as Elizabeth Cary's *Tragedy of Maryam*, the anonymous *Second Maiden's Tragedy*, and *Herod and Antipater*, it is as a historical character lifted from the pages of Josephus's *Of the Antiquities of the Jews*, and unrelated to the pageant Herod. When Shakespeare alludes to Herod, by contrast, it is in almost every instance less the Herod of classical history or of scripture than his histrionic cycle-drama incarnation that informs the reference, whether it is Hamlet's "it out-Herods Herod," or Mistress Page's denunciation of Falstaff as "a Herod of Jewry" who puts on a false "show" (*Merry Wives of Windsor*, 2.1.18, 20).[46] There are also recognizable echoes of the Coventry Herod in other Shakespeare plays. When Petruchio advises Katherine and the wedding guests to "look not big, nor stamp, nor stare" (*Taming of the Shrew*, 3.2.230), it is less his word choice than the implied techniques of over-the-top histrionic performance that recall the Coventry Herod's "I stampe! I stare! I looke all abowte!"[47]

Shakespeare's most complex reference to the cycle-drama Herod appears in the Henriad. In *Henry 5*, Harry warns the besieged citizens of Harfleur that they can soon expect to see

> Your naked infants spitted upon pikes,
> Whiles the mad mothers with their howls confused
> Do break the clouds, as did the wives of Jewry
> At Herod's bloody-hunting slaughtermen.
> (*H5*, 3.3.115–18)

Editors tend to gloss Harry's speech with a reference to the pertinent passage concerning the Slaughter of the Innocents in Matthew (2:13–18). But the dominant detail in Shakespeare's rendition of the episode—the description of the "howls" of upset mothers that "break" the clouds"—arguably derives less from an acquaintance with scripture, which refers in any case only to the single voice of Rachel mourning for her children (2:18), than from a memory of an entertainment such as the Coventry Shearmen and Taylors' pageant. The pageant directs the actors playing the mothers of the slaughtered children to create a hullabaloo of distress: after the children have been murdered, the first soldier asks "Who hard eyuer soche a cry / Of wemen that there chyldur haue lost?" (870–71).

In the Harfleur scene, then, the Hal of *1 Henry 4* has been transformed into a palimpsest, one of whose layers is the Coventry Herod. The relation between the two characters unfolds in what Bryan Reynolds has termed the "subjunctive space" of *as if*.[48] Harry does not have Harfleur's infants put to death; but he can raise the possibility of such a massacre by performing codes of histrionic excessiveness *as if* he were a stage Herod. His, however, is a Herod that can be channeled and discarded at will, as is suggested by his melodramatic yet calculated response to the Dauphin's jest: "for many a thousand widows / Shall this mock mock out of their dear husbands, / Mock mothers from their sons, mock castles down" (*H5*, 1.2.284–86). To some readers, such echoes of Herod might seem of a piece with the Henriad's constant identification of Hal/Harry/Henry with other powerful figures from antiquity, such as Julius Caesar and Alexander the Great, identifications that Hillman sees as exemplary of the Henriad's pervasively typological understanding of history.[49] The subjunctive space in which Harry aligns himself with Herod, however, entails something quite different from a typological relation. This identification is not an instance of the past-oriented "loving likelihood[s]" suggested by Fluellen and the Chorus. It is instead altogether more future oriented, calculating, and, ultimately, triumphal. Harry's Harfleur speech "out-Herods Herod"; but it does so to suggest how Harry's power lies not in Herod-like violence but in the strategic deployment of the histrionic style of the tyrant. In this instance, intertheatricality works to highlight more than the skill of the Shakespearean actor. Harry's theatrical versatility, his self-conscious ability to move in and out of the codes of histrionic performance, seals his success not only on stage but also within the Henriad's narration of England's privileged place in history. Shakespeare's chutzpah in this sequence is to fold the historical success of England back into the histrionic success of his leading players, so that each guarantees the other.

The New Histrionicism, Hegel, and Aufhebung

A recent television ad starts with an actor saying, in a soft voice that gradually crescendos into a roar, "Don't you love commercials where everybody . . . SHOUTS A LOT?" The camera cuts to a stage audience, who scream their assent. The character proceeds to holler his pitch for "Shout" stain remover in the antic manner of 1950s ads (accompanied by a version of the Isley Brothers' hit tune of the fifties, "Shout!"). This ad captures something of the intertheatricality of Shakespeare's company and its relationship to older histrionic playing styles. The difference is that the ad seems to offer little more than the pleasure of recognizing a now archaic code of performance, even if that pleasure is produced in the service of retailing a commodity. Shakespeare, by contrast, presents his histrionic palimpsests as much more than just an opportunity to laugh at old styles. Like Falstaff's performance of Cambyses, Harry's version of Herod demands the rehearsal of a primitive orient to produce a superior west characterized not just by its versatility but also by its sublime self-consciousness. He is no Amurath, but he can play one on (French) television. But while Falstaff's routine only hints at the Eurocentric teleology that narrates the advance from histrionic orient to versatile west, Harry's works *both* within the space of the platea to assert his theater company's superiority on the Elizabethan stage *and* within the representational locus to cement his nation's privileged place in world history. In doing so, the Hal palimpsest not only draws on its "oriental" theatrical past but also gestures towards a "western" philosophical future. And that future's name is Hegel.

In his *Philosophy of History* (1822), Hegel offers an insistently theatrical account of the dialectic of Spirit, arguing that it perfects itself through time and space by taking "the history of the World for its theatre."[50] Hegel's idealist *theatrum mundi*, like Marx's materialist counterpart in the *Communist Manifesto*, enlists Shakespeare to play a key role on its stage. But if Marx is attracted to *Hamlet*'s untimely Ghost and gravediggers, Hegel channels other characters from the play. Speaking about the will required to impose Spirit on the world, Hegel invokes Hamlet's "hue of resolution"—though for the German idealist philosopher this hue is, tellingly, no longer sicklied o'er with the pale cast of thought, for a Hamlet-like self-consciousness is Spirit's very objective.[51] Yet it is less *Hamlet* than the Induction of *2 Henry 4* that arguably provides the theatrical template for Hegel's world history. Just as Rumour plots the "acts commenced on this ball of earth . . . from the orient to the drooping west," so does Hegel narrate the orient as the first "scene" in a global drama that finds its culmination in the west. Echoing Herbert's analogy between the course of history and the westward movement of the sun, Hegel argues: "The Sun—the Light—rises in the East. . . . The History of the World travels from East to West, for Europe is absolutely the end of History."[52]

With its theatrum mundi, *The Philosophy of History* reprises the three layers of the east-west palimpsest which I identified in Falstaff's performance of Cambyses, and which we can now recognize as more aggressively at play in Harry's version of Herod. First, the orient is for Hegel, as it is in the Henriad, a (past) *time* prior to our own, an early scene within a diachronic global drama: "it is the childhood of History" and, like a child, suffers from a surfeit of "unreflected consciousness."[53] Second, the orient is also a theatrical *place* in the present, characterized by its eternal embrace of "*Despotism*": "The East . . . knows only that *One* is Free." Hegel thus situates the orient in synchronic opposition to the German world, which knows "that *All* are free."[54] Hegel's conflation of orient-as-past-time and orient-as-present-place is enabled by his conviction that, even though the east is the first scene of world history, it is also a region incapable of change. He pronounces India, for example, as "a phenomenon antique as well as modern; one which has remained stationary and fixed."[55] Indeed, Hegel sees all of Asia standing outside history in an eternally primitive present: therefore the history of the orient "is, for the most part, really *unhistorical,* for it is only the repetition of the same majestic ruin."[56]

The sterility of oriental repetition underwrites Hegel's commentary on the myth of the self-resurrecting phoenix. This myth, Hegel claims, "is only Asiatic; oriental, not occidental." By contrast, "Spirit—consuming the envelope of its existence—does not merely pass into another envelope, nor rise rejuvenescent from the ashes of its previous form; it comes forth exalted, glorified, a purer spirit."[57] Hegel thus sees the development of Spirit as a process of dialectical transformation rather than one of mere phoenixlike repetition. And here we might recognize the third layer of Falstaff's east-west palimpsest: the potential for "occidental" growth in the future. Hegel's embrace of Spiritual transformation may be couched in the language of universalism, but the geographical-temporal qualifiers in his critique of the phoenix myth betray his Eurocentrist agenda. For true rebirth to take place, and for Spirit to become self-conscious, it must move from the orient, "the region of origination," to the west: "For what is most remarkable in it, this land has not kept for itself, but sent over to Europe. It presents the origination of all religious and political principles, but Europe has been the scene of their development."[58] Hegel imagines the orient less as Europe's *other* than as its immature theatrical *origin*; hence occidental spirit is, fundamentally, oriental Spirit captured, canceled, and transcended—the tripartite dialectical process that Hegel calls "Aufhebung." For Hegel, this process "necessarily implies that the present form of Spirit comprehends within it all earlier steps"; it is in the west, therefore, that the "majestic ruin" of the orient is redeemed.[59] As a result, Hegel's Europe becomes an east-west palimpsest. Far more than Herbert's "Church Militant," however, Hegel's Europe is a palimpsest that insists on the *cancellation* of the oriental past-in-the-present. For Hegel, unlike Herbert, the fantasy of supersession thus disavows its untimeliness, even as it depends on it.

This is the case with Shakespeare's Henriad too, which discloses much the same occidental teleology as Hegel. In Shakespeare's as well as Hegel's theater of history, a bivalently spatial and temporal orient associated with a despotic unself-consciousness must pass on its "majestic ruin" (how else to define the histrionicism of the stage tyrant?) to an occident that dialectically refines it and, under the superior mark of self-consciousness, moves to a position of power on the world stage. The Henriad's east-west palimpsests, in other words, can be interpreted as Hegelian Aufhebung incarnated in the bodily techniques of the Shakespearean actor. That is, if Hegel's philosophy of history depends on even as it disavows the untimely oriental substance of its Spirit, Shakespeare's national history depends on even as it scoffs at the untimely oriental matter of its actors' bodies.

Both the Henriad's intertheatricality and Hegel's dialectic of Spirit instantiate a recognizable poetics of European imperialism. Each licenses—one metaphorically, the other "historically"—an unreciprocal exchange between orient and west: the former is superseded by the latter, which extracts surplus value from it in the form of self-consciousness. Hence the western looting of both temporal and geographical orients can narrate itself as progress. To be sure, the Henriad does not advocate the looting of the orient in the economic guises it had taken by the time Hegel wrote *The Philosophy of History*. The claims the Henriad makes for an occidental prowess based on appropriation and transformation of oriental materials are much more institutionally local: Shakespeare's east-west palimpsests are occasioned not by the future prospect of Levant or East India Company activity in the orient, of course, but by contemporary local competition between London theater companies for playgoers' money. Seen through this end of the critical telescope, the Henriad's intertheatricality is less about English colonial ambitions; it is instead, tautologically but crucially, about the power of Shakespeare's own theater.

Yet as we have also seen, the Henriad crosshatches the local claims its actors make regarding their histrionic versatility with the larger case it makes for England's expansionist ambitions in the shape of a versatile king. And it is here that we might recognize the rhetorical as well as material preconditions for the more blatantly imperialist logic of Hegel's philosophy of world history. Hence when Rumour promises to "unfold / The acts commenced on this ball of earth . . . from the orient to the drooping west," he speaks—at least for us in the twenty-first century—with a "bifold authority" that tweaks Weimann's theorization of early modern performance and points it in a new, anachronistic direction. We can see in Rumour's remark another palimpsest, one that compresses Shakespeare's present less with its histrionic pasts than with its world historical future. For the Elizabethan English vociferation of Shakespearean intertheatricality is irresistibly superinscribed by the Enlightenment German accent of Aufhebung.

But this is to understand the second Henriad's conception of history only as anticipatory and secular—that is, as affirming *avant la lettre* the logic of Hegelian supersession. Typology, however, gestures backward as much as forward; without the Augustinian guarantee that the future is the true meaning and fulfillment of the past, typology—as Kathleen Biddick and Julia

Reinhard Lupton have noted—generates a potentially endless, two-way network of connections between pre- and post-.[60] This much is suggested by the Chorus's comparisons in *Henry 5* between Caesar, Henry, and Essex, whose temporal relations are by no means supersessionary. Is medieval Henry the perfected version of classical Caesar? And the soon-to-be-disgraced Renaissance Essex the perfected version of medieval Henry? Or do the later figures simply refer back to, rather than supersede, the earlier ones? In a similar vein, one might ask: Does the intertheatrical performance of old acting styles simply cancel them? Or can it instead give them a new lease of life? Indeed, the second Henriad's very imbrication in the temporality of supersession reaffirms long-standing religious habits of thought as much as it looks forward to new, secular Enlightenment philosophy.

Shakespeare's second Henriad, then, produces a palimpsest within which we might glimpse the doubly inscribed initials "GH": mediating modern and premodern conceptions of supersessionary geography and history, the plays suggest a superimposition of Georg by George, Hegel by Herbert. One could not find a better illustration of the fundamental untimeliness that underwrites the fantasy of supersession. No matter how much supersessionary time turns its gaze to the future, then, it carries the past with it. And as long as the past remains at work in the matter of the present, it retains an explosive power to speak back, as we shall see in the next part.

PART II

Explosions

Fig. 5. Albrecht Dürer, *The Four Horsemen of the Apocalypse* (c. 1497–98); Rosenwald Collection, image courtesy of the Board of Trustees, National Gallery of Art, Washington, D.C.

A historical materialist approaches a historical subject only where he encounters it as a monad. In this structure he recognizes the sign of a Messianic cessation of happening, or, put differently, a revolutionary chance in the fight for the oppressed past. He takes cognizance of it in order to blast a specific era out of the homogenous course of history—blasting a specific life out of the era or a specific work out of the lifework.

—Walter Benjamin, "Theses on the Philosophy of History"

THOSE WHO SUBSCRIBE to the temporality of supersession respond to polychronicity by reworking the traces of the past-in-the-present as dead or obsolete matter, subordinated to the agency of a progressive present and future. Yet as we have seen with Herbert's "Church Militant" and Shakespeare's Henriad, practitioners of supersessionary time often revivify that which they wish to pronounce dead, thereby granting the supposedly superseded past a new lease of life in the present. Those who practice what I am calling the temporality of explosion seize on this possibility and amplify it. In explosive time, the traces of the past acquire a living agency within, and against, the present. This agency is illuminated by the specific connotations of "explosion" in the time of Shakespeare.

We associate explosion with sudden material disintegration, often accompanied—as OED definition 3 so decorously puts it—"with a loud report under the influence of suddenly developed internal energy." But for Shakespeare's audiences, the word would have called to mind less a bang than a whimper, albeit a noisily dismissive one. It derives from the Latin *explosio*, the noun form of *explaudere*, to clap or hiss a player off stage. In the Renaissance, explosion retained this theatrical sense. But it came to be applied metaphorically in religious discourse, where "explose" meant to dispute a rival doctrine, as when John Foxe writes of certain beliefs that deserve to "be explosed out of all Christian churches."[1] It also, as the OED explains in definition 2 of "exploded," acquired the connotation of being "out of fashion"—that is, untimely. In this section, I understand the temporality of explosion in ways that crosshatch the term's modern and Renaissance senses: it entails the untimely irruption of a past that disputes the present, and with explosive consequences. In this, it resembles at least partially what Shakespeare and his contemporaries would have recognized as the workings of apocalyptic or eschatological time.[2]

In the book of Revelation (a literal Latin translation of "apocalypse," meaning unveiling) the end of days is premised on the reappearance of the past within the present. While visiting the Isle of Patmos, Saint John has a vision of "*one* like unto the Son of man"—a transfigured Christ whose head and hair are "white like wool," and out of whose mouth comes "a sharp two-edged sword" (Revelation 1:13–14, 16). The militant Christ's posthumous return becomes, in Saint John's vision, the occasion for the complete destruction of the sinful present in a series of cosmic calamities, including "stars of heaven [falling] unto the earth, even as a fig tree casteth her untimely figs when she is shaken of a mighty wind" (6:13). This untimeliness is apparent in Christ's description of himself as "the Alpha and the Omega, the first and the last, the beginning and the end" (22:13); he distends temporality, returning from the "first" to explode the present and usher in the "last." Importantly, Saint John imagines this explosion as detonated by volatile matter—specifically, the seven seals that bind the Lamb of God's book. The breaking of each seal produces a rent also in the material world, through which untimely apocalyptic powers irrupt.

Albrecht Dürer's engraving *The Four Horsemen of the Apocalypse* (fig. 5) represents a dramatically distilled illustration of the sequence from the book of Revelation (6:1–8) in which the first four seals are opened to unleash Death, Famine, War, and Pestilence. Brandishing sharp swords as well as a scale of justice, Dürer's horsemen slash open the fabric of the material world and explode into it from some alternate universe. Yet even as the horsemen function as untimely scourges of sin—they are egged on by an angel overhead—the scene might come across as representing not the triumph of a divine plan but rather the irruption of turbulent, uncontrollable forces in the material world. The dynamic volatility of the image in particular suggests less a movement to a singular spiritual end authorized by Christ, who is absent from the scene in any case, than the explosive emergence of something unknown and untimely. What Dürer's engraving produces, in effect, is an eschatological time without a messiah. There is justice in this explosion, the picture seems to say; we just don't know yet what it will lead to.

Dürer's religious fantasy of explosive time finds powerful secular counterparts in modern philosophy. In *Specters of Marx,* Derrida insists on the difference between the ends of teleology and eschatology. For all the echoes of religious thought in Hegel's teleological vision of history, its final stage—

the full self-identity, without contradiction, of Spirit—is different from the end as imagined by eschatology. In its explosive force, Derrida argues, eschatological time does not synthesize but shatters and hence pluralizes. In the process, he tries to imagine, as Dürer does with *The Four Horsemen of the Apocalypse*, eschatological explosions without a messiah. These consist of specters from the past—Marx, Hamlet's father—irrupting into the present, rendering it out of joint in the name of justice, and conjuring the possibility of a radically uncertain future-to-come. Derrida's eschatological time entails neither a Hegelian Aufhebung moving toward a final singularity nor a savior offering a final redemption. Rather, it moves, explosively and without end, toward heterogeneity.[3] In this, Derrida's *Specters of Marx* arguably conjures an additional ghost: Walter Benjamin.

Derrida repeatedly invokes the untimely in *Specters of Marx*. But his eschatological spin on the concept recalls Benjamin rather than Nietzsche. Far more than Nietzsche's, Benjamin's preoccupation with the untimely repeatedly draws on the messianic language of eschatology. It also pays particular heed to the explosive power of objects. Benjamin's work on nineteenth- and early twentieth-century material culture has received considerable critical attention in the current wave of thing studies.[4] But one of his most intriguing meditations on objects concerns the matter of the early modern stage, and it has been largely ignored by scholars of the English Renaissance. In his analysis of seventeenth-century Trauerspiel, or mourning drama, of which he provocatively regarded *Hamlet* as the most exemplary instance, Benjamin argues that the genre is everywhere haunted by the untimely figure of the ruin. The ruined object—which Benjamin sees most embodied in the stage properties of the Trauerspiel—has undergone a hemorrhage of spirit that drains it of its past meaning; it now acquires a new allegorical signification, but in a fashion that also reveals the insufficiency of its present redemption.[5] One might think here, for example, of Yorick's skull, the bony revenant that Hamlet uses to heap scorn on—or "explose"—both past "gibes and gambols" and contemporary "lady's chamber" (5.1.176, 178). Hamlet may redeem the skull of his dead jester as an untimely memento mori; but this is, of course, no final redemption in the theological sense. Rather, Hamlet uses the antique matter of the skull to produce a temporality that, in disputing his present moment, reproduces the explosiveness of eschatology, but without an *eschaton*, or end.

Indeed, Hamlet's treatment of Yorick's skull resembles the "weak messianic" impulse that Benjamin identifies in his "Theses on the Philosophy of History." Like Nietzsche, whose *Untimely Meditations* he quotes in the epigraph to Thesis XII, Benjamin rails against the antiquarian spirit that insists on collecting historical facts simply so that these may be organized in orderly temporal sequence "as things really were."[6] The "Theses" propose instead what we might call an untimely materialist historiography, one that—anticipating Derrida and echoing *Hamlet*—is eschatological even as it lacks the assurance of full messianic redemption. Benjamin's historical materialist "seizes on a memory as it flashes up in a moment of danger" in order to both "wrest tradition away from a conformism that is about to overpower it" and "make the continuum of history explode."[7] The memory flash is like the ruin of Trauerspiel; it is a shard that has been sundered from official history and now presents the possibility for doing and imagining things differently. Blasting this memory from its past context and redeeming it in the present with quasi-eschatological effect, the historical materialist ushers in, if not the messiah, then at least the hope of untimely resistance to his moment of danger. Benjamin thus qualifies historicism's investment in orderly temporal succession, and he does so with a series of metaphors of explosion: the historical materialist "blasts" an oppressed past out of the continuum of history; that past "flashes" up in a moment of danger; it "explodes" the present and opens up the possibility of a new, if uncertain, future.

Benjamin's explosive, eschatological sense of time, together with his larger interest in material culture and ruins, resonates powerfully with two instances of untimely matter in the time of Shakespeare. In the chapters of this section, I consider how John Stow and Shakespeare employ polychronic objects to generate an explosive temporality that differs from that of supersession. Neither version is overtly apocalyptic; but each arguably partakes of a "weak messianic" conception of eschatological time. Both allow past matter to "flash up" in what may be described, after Benjamin, as "a moment of danger"—for the suspiciously Catholic-sympathizing Stow, a period of aggressive Protestant supremacy; for Shakespeare, a climate of fear in the wake of the unsuccessful Gunpowder Plot—and the past each writer evokes shatters the seeming homogeneity of his present. In this section, then, material culture's palimpsests become matériel culture, possessed of an explosive power, even if that explosiveness is often a disputatious whimper rather than an apocalyptic bang.

THREE

The Writing on the Wall

London's Old Jewry and John Stow's Urban Palimpsest

> *The trivial, circumscribed, decaying, and obsolete acquire their own dignity and inviolability through the fact that the preserving and revering soul of the antiquarian man has emigrated into them and there made its home. The history of his city becomes for him the history of himself; he reads its walls, its towered gate, its rules and regulations, its holidays, like an illuminated diary of his youth and in all this he finds again himself, his force, his industry, his joy, his judgment, his folly and vices. . . . Sometimes he even greets the soul of his nation across the long dark centuries of confusion as his own soul; an ability to feel his way back and sense how things were, to detect traces almost extinguished, to read the past quickly and correctly no matter how intricate its palimpsest may be—these are his talents and virtues.*
>
> —Nietzsche, "On the Uses and Disadvantages of History for Life"

WITH HIS THUMBNAIL sketch of the antiquarian, Nietzsche shows how readily civic history can be made to repose in the mundane material relics of urban space. The antiquarian, argues Nietzsche, finds historical riches in "trivial, circumscribed, decaying, and obsolete" things, such as "city . . . walls" and "the towered gate." The heightened attention the antiquarian accords such things anticipates the recent critical fascination with Renaissance material culture, which has itself been dubbed a "new antiquarianism."[1] Yet Nietzsche's sketch admits another element largely missing from work in the field. Despite the scorn he directs at the desire to conserve every trivial thing, he praises the antiquarian's "ability to feel his way back and sense how things were, to detect traces almost extinguished, to read the past quickly and correctly no matter how intricate its palimpsest may be." Here Nietzsche hints at what scholarship on material culture often elides: that the object is not a temporally singular entity but rather polychronic, multiply inscribed through and by time. Tellingly, the metaphor Nietzsche employs for this multiple inscription is the palimpsest, which recognizes the temporal excess and thus the untimely potential of the antiquarian's seemingly trivial things.

Nietzsche's caricature of the antiquarian historian was not composed with John Stow in mind. But it uncannily captures the spirit of the sixteenth-century London antiquary's most famous project—his *Survey of London* (1598, revised 1603).[2] In this extraordinary work of urban chorography, the nostalgically minded Stow anticipates Nietzsche by treating his beloved London, which had changed so dramatically since his pre-Reformation childhood, "like an illuminated diary of his youth." In the process, Stow does more than simply map London's geography and plot its history. Instead, his *Survey* discovers the city's past *in* its physical features. That past is not, for Stow, a synchronic totality quarantined from his present; nor is it even a linear sequence of moments that diachronically evolves into the now. Rather, it anachronistically resides in the living city as legible matter, as (in Nietzsche's words) "traces almost extinguished." For Stow as for Nietzsche's antiquarian, the city is a polychronic palimpsest: everywhere he looks, he sees the manifold traces of the past writ, and rewrit, large. And he does so by focusing on precisely those trivial things that Nietzsche regards as the antiquarian's chief fetishes, the city walls and the towered gate. Stow reads, quite literally, the writing on the wall—more specifically, the wall of one of its crumbling towered gates, Ludgate—and he finds in that writing the untimely traces of London's medieval Jewry.

As I shall demonstrate, Stow attends to these traces partly to document a superseded past: Jewish matter provides him with a typologically coded "then" supplanted by the Christian "now." Yet the polychronic elements of Stow's London do not always resolve themselves into a temporality of supersession. Nietzsche notes that the antiquarian "finds . . . himself" in the mundane details of the past, and this applies very much to Stow. His identification with London's antique matter results at times in a different intuition of temporality, one in which the past is less canceled by the present than set to work in and against it. In this, he can be seen as a practical theorist of the temporality of explosion. Like Walter Benjamin's historical materialist, for whom a memory of the past "flashes up in a moment of danger," Stow seizes on past matter in ways that fracture his present.[3] And he too apprehends the past in a moment of danger. With the Protestant ascendancy, any strong attachment to pre-Reformation objects—relics, church plaques, even books—could attract official attention and censure. Partly because his antiquarian collections included old Catholic texts, Stow was suspected of Papist sympathies, and he had at least one discomforting run-in with the authorities on that score. Their suspicions were not without justification. In *The Survey*, as we shall see, Stow uses the past not to celebrate but to put pressure on London's post-Reformation identity. And although much of his energy is devoted to identifying and retrieving materials that might be associated with London's Catholic past, he also finds in untimely Jewish matter matériel with which to explode the time of his Protestant present. In his simultaneous reproduction and refusal of supersession, then, Stow underscores the multitemporality of London as urban palimpsest.

The Time of the Urban Palimpsest

"Urban palimpsest" is a phrase whose time seems to have come in literary, cultural, and architectural studies. In recent years, there has been a wave of scholarship that reads individual cities—Delhi, Tokyo, Mexico City, Barcelona, Istanbul, Johannesburg—for the traces they disclose of multiple historical moments.[4] As the author of one such reading of Havana remarks, "Every city is an urban palimpsest, a used parchment covered with the fragmentary scrawls of its own past."[5] This insight affirms Freud's well-known fascination, expressed in *Civilization and Its Discontents* (1930), with Rome's polychronicity: "A modern visitor to Rome . . . will see Aurelian's wall virtually unchanged, save for a few gaps. Here and there he will find stretches of the Servian wall that have been revealed by excavations. . . . One need hardly add that all these remnants of ancient Rome appear as scattered fragments in the jumble of the great city that has grown up in recent centuries, since the Renaissance. True, much of the old is still there, but buried under modern buildings. This is how the past survives in historic places like Rome."[6] Freud's version of Rome, which provides him with an analogy for the memory traces buried in the unconscious, might suggest that the past is merely a positive entity awaiting exhumation. Yet this would be to overlook the extent to which the urban palimpsest not only contains but also reworks the past in the present. The metaphor of the palimpsest is useful in suggesting the polychronicity of any city; but we might think also about the different ways in which it can be used also to conceive the city's temporality. After all, an intuition of the city's polychronicity can be enlisted to produce a variety of temporal effects.[7] How, then, is the past not just found but actively created within and by the matter of the urban palimpsest? And what temporalities can that matter be made to materialize?

One approach to these questions is modeled by Andreas Huyssen. In his study *Present Pasts: Urban Palimpsests and the Politics of Memory*, Huyssen treats such modern urban spaces as Berlin, Buenos Aires, and New York as dynamic sites for the refashioning of matter as memory. He implicitly universalizes the figure of the urban palimpsest inasmuch as he recognizes the polychronicity of any city: "A palimpsest implies voids, illegibilities, and erasures, but it also offers a richness of traces and memories, restorations, and new constructions that will mark the city as lived space."[8] Nevertheless, Huyssen is interested chiefly in the urban palimpsest as a uniquely modern, or even postmodern, problematic. With its many museums and monuments, the modern western city materializes what he regards as the hypertrophy of memory characteristic of the late twentieth century. This is partly symptomatic, he argues, of a collective response to the traumas of our age, particularly the Holocaust.[9] Yet, Huyssen observes, this proliferation of memory is fraught with peril, inasmuch as it is also implicated in the detemporalizing logic of global capitalism. As he points out, "the paradox is that memory discourses themselves partake in the detemporalizing process that characterizes a culture of consumption and obsolescence. Memory as re-presentation, as making present, is always in danger of collapsing the constitutive tension between past and present, especially when the imagined past is sucked into the timeless present of the all-pervasive virtual space of consumer culture."[10] Far from safeguarding the difference between now and then, memory discourses can expand the empire of the present.

To resist consumer culture's detemporalized virtual space, or what he calls its "cyber-amnesia," Huyssen draws—albeit critically—on trauma theory. The therapeutic process of working through trauma, of selectively remembering the ghosts of the past in order to bury them and secure movement into the future, provides a model for exorcizing the specter of temporal nondifferentiation.[11] But whereas trauma theory focuses on individual practices of remembering and forgetting, Huyssen embraces the potential of collective memory discourses. The urban palimpsest, he argues, should rework the past to "remember the future," not through wholesale forgetting (as Nietzsche had advocated) but through creative engagement with historical memory.[12] He sees such an engagement in the emerging cityscape of Berlin. The fall of the Wall has led to struggles over historical memory in its many major projects of urban reconstruction; these include not only the fractured "voids of Berlin"—empty spaces that suggest the erasure of memory—but also its seemingly antithetical museums, which seek to mark a "new global Berlin as capital of the twenty-first century."[13] With the emphasis Huyssen places on remembering the future through selective memory practices, one may detect in his urban palimpsest a version of the logic of supersession. It is less overtly teleological or unilinear than its religious counterpart, but the rudiments are the same: producing the past is an act of temporal distancing that enables and secures futurity.

A somewhat different temporality of the urban palimpsest emerges in Walter Benjamin's writing. At times Benjamin uses archaeological metaphors redolent of Freud to represent the polychronicity of the city: "Memory," writes Benjamin, "is the medium of past experience, just as the earth is the medium in which dead cities lie buried."[14] But elsewhere he employs other metaphors of temporality. In 1919, Benjamin first read Baudelaire's *Artificial Paradises,* one of whose concluding sections is entitled "The Palimpsest." Baudelaire seems to have influenced his perception of Paris in *The Arcades Project* as a multilayered memory-scape, in which the rubbish of the past awaits and is redeemed by the flâneur (or city stroller) in the present.[15] Yet this redemption is not supersessionary, at least in the sense of ushering in a more complete future that replaces the past. Rather, the flâneur redeems past matter to pluralize and destabilize the city as it is now. Benjamin notes how

> Paris is built over a system of caverns from which the din of Métro and railroad mounts to the surface, and in which every passing omnibus or truck sets up a prolonged echo. And this great technological system of tunnels and thoroughfares interconnects with the ancient vaults, the lime quarries, the grottoes and catacombs which, since the early Middle Ages, have time and again been reentered and traversed. Even today, for the price of two francs, one can buy a ticket

> of admission to this most nocturnal Paris, so much less expensive and less hazardous than the Paris of the upper world. The Middle Ages saw it differently. Sources tell us that there were clever persons who, now and again, after exacting a considerable sum and a vow of silence, undertook to guide their fellow citizens underground and show them the Devil in his infernal majesty.[16]

This is the city apprehended not as a static map but—in the words of Philip Kuberski—as "a complex mnemonic device which undermines the palpable evidence of stone and steel: beneath one's feet and behind one's gaze another city, unconscious, ancient and modern, and included in the mythic and historical cycles of death and rebirth, suddenly comes to light."[17] Yet what "comes to light"—the conventional Enlightenment metaphor adapted here, in Kuberski's psychoanalytic reading, to represent the return of the repressed—is not simply the past as it was. Rather, the encounter with Paris's memory traces allows the flâneur to unearth alternative temporalities within the present cityscape, and to explode the empty homogeneous time of official history.

Huyssen's and Benjamin's urban palimpsests have certain features in common. Each goes beyond mere recognition of the city's polychronicity by insisting that its palimpsested matter can generate specific temporal effects. And each also underscores how the urban palimpsest creates rather than simply discovers the past. But whereas Huyssen's urban palimpsest is implicated in the temporality of supersession, with its guaranteed movement into a secure future, Benjamin's suggests—like the weak messianic eschatology of his "Theses on the Philosophy of History"—a temporality of explosion, with its radical critique of the now.[18] As I shall argue, the different temporalities of both Huyssen's and Benjamin's urban palimpsests speak to the London of John Stow's *Survey*.

Stow reproduces certain aspects of supersessionary temporality; and he does so in ways that, like Huyssen, both respond to historical trauma and lament the challenges to memory posed by capitalist modernization. Also like Huyssen, Stow discloses the past to be less a positive entity than a set of competing narratives produced by selective memory and misprision. But the London of Stow's *Survey* is equally redolent of Benjamin's urban palimpsest. Indeed, for all the obvious differences between the relatively cheerful English antiquary and the melancholic German Jewish philosopher, Stow is in some ways Benjamin's doppelgänger. Both see the city less as a static grid than as a dynamic, heterogeneous space, best apprehended even as it is transformed by those who walk its streets. Just as the flâneur Benjamin is mesmerized by the mundane physical details of Paris and Berlin, so too is the perambulatory Stow entranced by the physical minutiae of his London. And like Benjamin, Stow is particularly attracted to the critical power of ruins and fragments.

Stow's extended walking tours through London are in many ways a response to the dislocations of the Reformation. He lingers on formerly Catholic sites, whose old monuments embody collective memories at risk of being erased. But London's walls and towers provide him with more neutral civic spaces in which he can subtly engage the problem of a superseded religion and its material remainders in the present. The city walls of Stow's London, like the Parisian underground of Benjamin's flâneur, contain the secret traces of another buried city and time: just as the Métro tunnels palimpsest the echo of modern technology with the forgotten thrum of an old satanic presence ("the Devil in his infernal majesty"), so do Elizabethan London's walls open up to reveal the ruins of a forgotten religious past. And like Benjamin's flâneur, Stow uses the sudden irruption of this old time to dispute the modernizing time of his present.

The Time of Stow's Hebrew Characters

Describing the repair of London's crumbling Ludgate wall—a civic project undertaken in 1586—Stow relates a remarkable discovery. As workmen toiled to restore a structure that commemorated King Lud, the supposed pagan founder of the city, they found instead the remains of another, unexpected religious past: "When the same gate was taken downe, to bee newe buylded, there was founde couched within the wal thereof, a stone taken from one of the Jewes houses, wherein was grauen in Hebrew caracters, these wordes following. חך מצב חר משח בן הרב ר יצחק."[19] Confronted with this writing on the wall, Stow was evidently at something of a loss. He transcribed the inscription as best as he could; but he was no Hebrew scholar, and his characters do not quite make sense. One word (משח) is the name Moshe; another (יצחק) is Yitzhak. Yet other words (especially the cluster at the end of the inscription, חך מצב חר) are more cryptic.[20] Still, Stow got it more right than subsequent seventeenth-century editions of the *Survey* did; these reproduce the Hebrew inscription with increasing ineptitude, rendering it ever more incoherent.[21] Antony Bale has speculated that Stow personally supervised the typesetting of the characters in the 1598 edition, taking advantage of the recent import of movable Hebrew typefaces from Italy. Bale proposes that this special care represents a sympathetic attitude on Stow's part to Jews.[22] Whether or not this is the case, Stow was evidently concerned to reproduce the Hebrew characters of Ludgate wall with maximum accuracy.

There are arguably several desires at play in Stow's painstaking reproduction of the Hebrew inscription. One can recognize in it an antiquarian longing for historical verisimilitude and transparency, a wish to render empirical data accurately in order that the past may become literally *legible*. Yet Stow proceeds to make sense of the inscription in an odd way. To gloss the Hebrew, he reverts to a language other than English: "חך מצב חר משח בן הרב ר יצהק. *Haec est statio Rabbi Mosis filii insignis Rabbi Isaac*; which is to say, this is the Station, or Ward of *Rabby Moses*, the sonne of the honorable *Rabby Isaac*, and had beene fixed vppon the front of one of the Jewes house as a note, or signe that such a one dwelled there."[23] Stow here does not so much translate the Hebrew as supplement it with a Latin tag that he then translates into English. *Statio* he renders as "station or ward"; this leads him to the conclusion that the inscription had been affixed to a Jewish rabbi's house whose materials were looted and reworked by the barons, during their war with King John in 1215, for the purpose of civic improvement. Stow was evidently quite taken with this deduction. He remarks no fewer than four times in the *Survey* that the barons, after laying waste to the Old Jewry, undertook the repair of the city walls with stones from the houses of London's Jews.[24]

Why did Stow furnish the Latin gloss and avoid translating the Hebrew directly into English? Maybe the Latin was part of the original inscription, though his text insists that the stone "was ingrauen in Hebrewe Caracters." Maybe, not knowing Hebrew, Stow obtained the Latin translation from another antiquary. But in producing his trilingual text, Stow plotted a familiar religious as well as linguistic path: the dissemination of the Word from the Hebrew of Moses, via its Catholic reworking in Latin, to its vernacular redemption in the English of Anglican liturgy. We may thus be tempted to see in Stow's translation a supersessionary religious history, a Protestant *translatio verbi dei*: each language successively becomes the vessel of the Word of God by claiming for itself an authority that draws on even as it replaces that of an earlier holy tongue. This process of verbal translation also parallels the material translation Stow records of "stones taken from the Jewes broken houses," in which private Jewish matter is appropriated and transformed for civic

Catholic welfare before resurfacing as crumbling matter in the Protestant present.

Both types of translation resonate with Kathleen Biddick's study of how early Christian historiography was informed by the logic of supersession, according to which the Old Testament past was preserved in "new" Christian legal, liturgical, and linguistic structures precisely so that it may be canceled.[25] This logic, as we have seen, looms in George Herbert's ambivalent adaptation of typology in *The Temple*. For Herbert, the dead letter of the Jewish past, often figured as Moses' graven stone tablets, is superseded by the living gospel of the Christian present, written on the true believer's heart. And in Stow's discovery of a stone inscribed with the name of Moshe, or Moses, we might see the reproduction of a Christian set piece in which stony, dead Jewish matter is superseded by a living city of God bound to a new covenant.

Yet the logic of supersession doesn't quite do justice to Stow's sense of history, which is (as we shall see) both nontriumphal and curiously non-Protestant. Nor does it fully explain Stow's diligent labor in recording the original inscription. One might maintain, with Bruno Latour, that the antiquarian mania of collecting and conserving is predicated on the assumption of an absolute break with the past: "Historians reconstitute the past, detail by detail, all the more carefully inasmuch as it has been swallowed up forever."[26] But such an intuition of loss needn't imply only a temporality of supersession. Stow's painstaking reproduction of the cryptic Hebrew as well as the more familiar Latin indicates, I would argue, another impulse at play, one that exceeds any simple wish for historical conservation. Stow evidently savors his encounter with a past materialized as an inscrutable inscription in and on the present, an inscription whose mystery is not fully erased by its translation into Latin or English, let alone its relocation inside the Ludgate wall. And he clearly wants his readers to experience something of the strangeness of that encounter. I shall argue that Stow seeks not just to conserve a lost past divided from his moment but also to make the matter of the present—especially Ludgate, proud symbol of the city's origin and identity—heterogeneous and not fully coincident with itself, either culturally or temporally. In other words, Stow wants to produce in his readers an effect of the untimely. And this desire shapes his distinctive adaptation of the genre of chorography.

Ptolemy distinguished chorography from geography on the basis of scale: where geography maps the globe, chorography describes counties, cities, and other smaller divisions.[27] In his treatise on geography, Nathanael Carpenter develops Ptolemy's distinction using England as a specific illustration:

> The *Geographer*, who willing to delineate out any part of the Earth, (as for example, our Realme of *England*) he would describe it as an Iland, encompassed round with the sea, & figured in a triangular forme, only expressing the principall and greater parts of it. But the *Chorographer* vndertaking the description of some speciall and smaller part of *England*; as for example, the City of *Oxford*, descends much more particularly to matters of small quantity and note: such as are the Churches, Colledges, Halls, Streets, Springs; giuing to each of them their due accidents, colours, lineaments, and proportion, as farre forth as Art can imitate Nature. Neither in this kind of description needs there any consideration of the places adioyning, or the generall draught of the whole Iland.[28]

In Carpenter's analysis, the English geographer exhibits a drive to synthesize, producing a singular ideality such as an "Iland" or "our Realme of *England*." By contrast, even as the English chorographer describes a smaller singularity such as "the City of *Oxford*," his impulse is to atomize and pluralize. Fastening onto a million things within the city, he splits and multiplies his object. This splitting and multiplication is just as apparent in his chorographical understanding of time. The geographer seeks to map a global space in a singular moment; by contrast, the chorographer, as Howard Marchitello notes, describes "topography not exclusively as it exists in the present moment, but as it has existed historically."[29] If the geographer sees the wood, then, the chorographer sees the trees—and not just the trees but also the polychronic record of their transformations inscribed in their rings.

The pluralizing impulse is evident in much English Renaissance chorography, from William Camden's magisterial *Britannia* (1586) to Michael Drayton's chorographical poem *Poly-Olbion* (1622).[30] And it is apparent everywhere in Stow's *Survey of London*, which cannot really be said to "map" the city so much as to polychronize and hypertextualize it. With Stow, a walk down the street becomes an exercise in deferral worthy of *Tristram Shandy*: every detail he encounters serves as a mnemonic for multiple historical detours. Stow thus transforms London from the synchronic grid captured by cartographers into a polychronic assemblage of multiple moments in time.[31] Even though he often relates the history of a building, monument, or other object in chronological sequence, his polychronic instincts repeatedly resist the narration of time, and hence of London's history, as a unilinear progression from "old" to "new." On the first page of the *Survey*, for example, Stow pointedly complicates the supersessionary time informing a popular theory of London's origin. He considers the then widespread suggestion that Trinobant—London's former name—is derived from "Troy Nova," or New Troy, and that the city was founded as a replacement for the older Troy by Brutus, a descendant of Aeneas. Such a supersessionary fantasy, Stow opines (quoting Livy), is motivated by a dubious desire "*to make the first foundation of Cities more honourable, more sacred, and as it were of greater maiestie.*"[32] Indeed, Stow refuses to countenance any one myth of "first foundation" and instead recounts several tales of London's beginning; in this way, he reads difference and multiplicity into the city's very moment of origin.

This impulse is evident in his account of Ludgate. Stow begins his description of London's physical features with the structure, a monument that itself commemorated the city's beginning.[33] Supposedly named for London's mythical founder King Lud, Ludgate was invested with an extraordinary symbolic power: the traditional point of exit from the city in monarchs' coronation processions from London to Westminster, it represented a portal connecting, in a collective fantasy of civic and national time, past to future and old to new.[34] When Stow wrote his *Survey*, of course, that time had acquired a decidedly Protestant telos. Although Puritan iconoclasts under Edward VI destroyed the image of Lud that had stood atop the gate since the Middle Ages, a new statue of Lud and his sons, dressed in military gear, was installed in the reign of Elizabeth on the gate's east side (fig. 6). But the city leaders added an extra touch to the renovated structure: they also erected a triumphal statue of Elizabeth on the gate's west side outside the city (fig. 7). As one left the city for Westminster, then, the image of Elizabeth doubled and replaced that of Lud. Ludgate thus materialized a supersessionary, Protestant vision of English history. It recast the perhaps mythical warrior king who had defended England against its antique Roman invaders as a nationalist *figura* of the Protestant Queen of England, vigilantly protecting the nation from its Roman Catholic aggressors.

Yet in Stow's *Survey*, something strange happens to this vision of Ludgate. The structure loses its status as monument both to singular civic origin and to supersessionary Protestant time; instead, it becomes narratively and culturally hybrid. Stow repeats Geoffrey of Monmouth's and Raphael Holinshed's patriotic accounts of Lud, including the story of his building of Lon-

Fig. 6. Statues of King Lud and his two sons, formerly on the east side of Ludgate, now in St. Dunstan-in-the-West Church, London; photograph by the author.

don. But Stow proceeds to question whether Lud had anything to do with the gate, observing that the "name, as *Ludsgate*, or *Fludsgate*, hath beene of late some question among the learned."[35] It is in this context that Stow enthusiastically reveals within Ludgate the trace of an unexpected Jewish past, placed there by its medieval Catholic renovators. In the process, Stow provides the most illuminating illustration of what one might dub his untimely materialism—that is, his intuition not only that London is a dynamic space that bears the polychronic traces of reworking, reusing, and rewriting, but also that its identity in the present stands to be transformed by those traces. And as Stow's fascination with the Hebrew characters in Ludgate's wall makes clear, the most untimely traces he finds are those that derive from London's Old Jewry.

The Time of Old Jewry

As its name suggests, Old Jewry implies not simply a location but also a temporality. The street in London, EC2, that now bears the name was known

Fig. 7. Statue of Queen Elizabeth, formerly on the west side of Ludgate, now in St. Dunstan-in-the-West Church, London; photograph by the author.

before the fourteenth century as Colechurch Street; the consensus has long been that it was renamed "Old Jewry" only after the watershed year of 1290, in which all the Jews of England—according to Stow, a total of 15,060, though some medieval historians have recently claimed the true number to be closer to three thousand—were banished from the realm at the decree of Edward I.[36] Not surprisingly, the street's name has been read as a monument to this historical rupture: Old Jewry is customarily assumed to be where the Jews lived until their expulsion from London and England.

The "Old" of Old Jewry may, however, be of less cataclysmic provenance. In a preexpulsion Latin document that outlines the limits of the parish of St. Stephen's, there is a reference to "veteri Judaismo," or Old Jewry. This suggests that Jews had once lived in the street before moving elsewhere in the city.[37] Records listing Jewish-owned properties at the time of the expulsion indicate that the City's community had migrated from Colechurch Street to residences in the streets adjacent to it and the open-air marketplace in Cheapside: in particular, Catte Street, to the immediate north of Colechurch Street; Bassinghall Street, off Catte Street to the north, and the location of Bakewell Hall, later Gresham College; Ironmonger Lane, one block to the west of Colechurch Street; Milk Street, two blocks to the west of Ironmonger Lane; and the northeast end of Wood Street, one block farther to the west.[38] This larger district came to be referred to in civic documents as "in Iudaismo," or "in Jewry." But it was not a walled-off ghetto like its Venetian counterpart. Although the City Assizes of 1276–77 and 1277–78 stipulate that "no one shall hire houses from Jews, nor demise the same to them for them to live in outside the limits of the Jewry," London's Jews lived "in Iudaismo" side by side with Christian neighbors.[39]

Thus if the "Old" of Old Jewry is a vexed and slippery term, so equally is "Jewry." London's medieval Jewry—a term that refers diversely to a community, a street, and a district—was not a static place but, in Michel de Certeau's sense, a space, constantly morphing, transformed by practice.[40] A good many of these practices were the product of hostility to Jews, whether by the Crown, the church, or the public at large. The first Jews in London possibly came from Rouen with William the Conqueror, and until the expulsion the community remained the King's possessions—granted certain liberties and protections, but also subject to frequent taxes and tallage. The Jews' dubious legal status meant that they were often barred from inheriting property; many Jewish-owned residences were escheated to Christians, often at the arbitrary discretion of the King.[41] The church also took an active part in the dispossessions. Buildings on the street of Old Jewry were repeatedly converted for Christian use long before 1290: both St. Olave's Church and St. Mary Colechurch, on the west side of the street, were once synagogues, as was a third building on the northeast side that was converted in the 1250s into a monastery for the Friars of the Sackcloth. This was but a prelude to the general closures of 1283, when the archbishop of Canterbury, John Peckham, ordered that all synagogues in the diocese of London be destroyed.[42] Public violence also transformed the shape of the city's Jewry. Mob attacks, such as those after the coronation of Richard I on September 3, 1189, and the infamous massacre of four hundred London Jews on April 5, 1264, led many of the London community to seek residences elsewhere in England or to leave the country altogether.[43]

Not all the Jewish migrations within medieval London were simply the result of discrimination and violence. London Jews worked as merchants and also in the city's growing credit agency market, which proved to be a highly lucrative profession in the thirteenth century.[44] The prosperity of many of the community members enabled them to buy expensive houses in the Cheapside district, where intense commercial activity gave property a high market value. The area known as "in Iudaismo" boasted numerous fine synagogues and private houses. It was particularly reputed for its lavish stone buildings, many of which were built, owned, and inhabited by Jews. At the time of the expulsion, the enormous stone house on Catte Street owned by Antera, widow of Vives, was assessed at an annual rental of 12 pounds 17 shillings, an exorbitant sum for the late thirteenth century.[45] And although escheats may have alienated Jewish property into Christian hands, much Christian property—including property that had formerly been Jewish—was also acquired by wealthy Jews. In 1228, for example, Elias, son of Benedict le Eveske, bought back from John de Gyse the stone house that had formerly belonged to Moses Bugi in the parish of St. Olave's.[46]

The impossibility of pinning down London's medieval Jewry to a single, unchanging location is amplified by the fact that there were two other areas in the city and its suburbs temporarily inhabited by or associated with Jews. Next to Aldgate in the east of the city was the so-called Poor Jewry; and in the Cripplegate ward outside the city walls, just south of the Barbican, were the Jewin Gardens, the cemetery that, until 1177, served as the English Jewish population's sole place of burial.[47] Yet subsequent to the expulsion, the "Old" of Old Jewry worked to ossify its noun and make the phrase designate a singular Jewish place, people, and time, all of which were defined by their irrevocable pastness. We might sense in the history of the street's name, then, something akin to the workings of Christian supersessionary time as theorized by Biddick: the Old Jewry demarcated not just a place but also a past time from which London's Christian present could temporally distinguish itself.

Indeed, it was Old Jewry not as a dynamic, hybrid space but as a static, singular place—legible only under the mark of its own supersession—that exerted a fascination on early modern Londoners' imaginations. Even three hundred years after the expulsion, Londoners had a keen sense of the past occupants of the Old Jewry and the historical rupture that had made it "Old." In *The Unfortunate Traveler* (1595), Thomas Nashe imagined the dissolution of Rome's Jewish community in a fashion that superimposed the London street onto an Italian setting: "All fore-skinne clippers, whether male or female, belonging to the old Iurie, should depart and auoid vpon pain of hanging, within twentie daies."[48] And Nashe's nemesis Garbiel Harvey, bridling at the possibility that Jews might be officially readmitted to England, wrote that "I am beholding to the old Jewry, but have no great fancy to a new."[49]

Despite their legendary enmity, then, Harvey and Nashe seem to have agreed in styling London's Jewry as irredeemably "Old." By contrast, other writers fantasized the ghosts of London's Jewish past returning to haunt the present Christian residents of the Old Jewry.[50] Crucial scenes in Ben Jonson's London-located revision of *Every Man in His Humor* take place in the street, especially in one building: the Windmill Tavern. The Windmill was a famous watering hole and horse-rental location. But it was also, as Jonson's good friend John Stow notes, once a synagogue.[51] At one crucial moment in *Every Man in His Humor*, the street and the building's past leak into the present of Jonson's play. The rakish Wellbred, resident at the Windmill, writes a letter to his good friend Ned Knowell, asking him: "Hast thou forsworn all thy friends i' the Old Jewry? Or dost thou think us all Jews that inhabit there, yet? If thou dost, come over, and but see our frippery; change an old shirt for a whole smock with us. Do not conceive that antipathy between us and Hogsden, as was between Jews and hogs' flesh."[52] Wellbred's letter tantalizingly poses the possibility of Old Jewry's residents still being Jewish, only to discount it through his use of the past tense: the Jewish "antipathy" to pork "was," not "is."[53] In Jonson's fantasy, then, the "Jewishness" of Old Jewry is confined to symbolic resonances of the past—specters that work in the interest of supersessionary time, because as fantastical revenants their very impossibility ensures the Christianity of the present. By contrast, as his account of the Ludgate wall shows, Stow is fascinated by material Jewish remnants that have survived into his time. As a result, he conceives the temporality of London's Old Jewry somewhat differently from Nashe, Harvey, and Jonson.

The Time of Stow's Jewish Buildings

We now know that Renaissance London was by no means a non-Jewish city. Cultural historians and literary critics from C. J. Sisson and Cecil Roth to Roger Prior and James Shapiro have recognized how the Tudor and Stuart city boasted a sizable, if concealed, Jewish community, consisting mostly of Marrano immigrants from Portugal and Spain. Spanish Inquisition records indicate that a visitor to England in 1605 saw London Jews celebrating Passover.[54] Indeed, Antony Bale has proposed that contact with living Jews may have been what led Stow to record the inscription on the Ludgate wall. But Stow makes no reference to Tudor Jews or *conversos* such as Dr. Roderigo Lopez, the Queen's Portuguese physician who had attracted considerable public attention when he was tried and executed just five years before the first edition of the *Survey*.[55] Instead, Stow follows Nashe, Harvey, and Jonson in regarding Jews as the very stuff of history, of a seemingly unequivocal past. In the first edition of 1598, he discusses numerous episodes from Anglo-Jewish history, including the barons' looting of London Jews' property in 1215 and the hanging of Norwich Jews in 1241 for their part in the crucifixion of a young Christian boy.[56] If Stow was fascinated by England's Jewish past in his first edition of the *Survey*, he had developed a full-blown obsession by the time of the revised and supplemented 1603 edition, to which he added four new pages on Anglo-Jewish history from the Conquest to the expulsion. In these pages, Stow, like Nashe, Harvey, and Jonson, makes Old Jewry a synecdoche for an entire religion and people apprehended under the mark of belatedness: the Jews who dwelt there appear in his narrative as always already vanished, such as one "Benomy Mittun," who had been the owner of a house deeded by Henry III to Semane the crossbowman, and one "Moses of Canterbury" whose house in St. Olave's parish had been escheated to a Christian.[57]

Thus the time of the Jews is, for Stow, pluperfect passive—they are not has-beens, but *had*-beens, always already absent because irrevocably past. Yet their material relics acquire a curious presence in the *Survey*. We might call this tendency Stow's Neutron Bomb historiography: the people are vaporized, but the buildings remain. In fact, the buildings do not just remain—they acquire marvelously picaresque lives that span from the twelfth century to the early seventeenth. Stow repeatedly identifies old Jewish structures that have assumed new identities: the synagogue at Threadneedle Street in the

Broad Street Ward that has become St. Anthony's Hospital; a Jewish stone house at the northeast side of Ironmonger's Lane that is now the King's "Wardrobe"; and, perhaps most tellingly, a Jew's house, forfeited to Henry III, that was either converted into or replaced by a *Domus Conversorium* for Jewish converts to Christianity.[58] (In a fitting irony that Stow may have appreciated, this Domus Conversorium was itself converted, once there were no more Jews to convert, into the Public Record Office.)

As these instances suggest, the hints of supersessionary time are everywhere in Stow's lives of formerly Jewish buildings. If the Domus Conversorium houses converted Jewish souls, Stow's Old Jewry houses converted buildings. He pauses for two pages to recount the conversion history of the Windmill Tavern. Once a synagogue, it "was defaced by the Cittizens of London, after that they had slaine 700 Iewes, and spoyled the residue of their goods." Shortly thereafter, the building was alienated to "a new order of Fryers, called *de poenitentia Iesu* or *Fratres de sacca*, because they were appareled in sackecloth." In the fourteenth century, Stow continues, the building passed into the possession of Robert Fitzwalter, who owned a mansion—later the Grocer's Hall—adjoining it. Later it was owned by Robert Large, Lord Mayor of London, and Hugh Clopton, a mercer, also Lord Mayor in 1492. Noting the building's current purpose, Stow wryly notes: "And thus much for this house, sometime the Iewes Synagogue, since a house of Fryers, then a Noble Mans house, after that a Marchauntes house, wherein Mayoralties haue beene kept, and now a Wine Tauerne."[59] "Thus much for this house": the phrase smacks of supersessionary time, with its simultaneous recognition and distancing, through conversion, of a Jewish past.

But Stow's description of the life of "this house" offers an altogether more complex encoding of temporality than my discussion above might suggest. In tracing the different phases of the house's usage, Stow does not privilege its Christian forms. If anything, he hints at the logic of supersession only slyly to mock it: the Jewish synagogue has not been redeemed but profaned by its Christian conversion, which has reduced it to a mere tavern. Indeed, if Stow were writing now, he might argue that this profanation has continued into our own present. The synagogue-cum-tavern has long disappeared, but it is memorialized on a building at the northeast end of Old Jewry with a plaque that reads: "The Great Synagogue Stood Near This Site Until 1272." The present occupants of the building are, perhaps appropriately, a finance company called Liquid Capital—a strikingly literal illustration of Marx and

Engels's claim that, in the age of capital, "All that is solid melts into air, all that is holy is profaned."[60]

Stow of course is no proto-Marxist. He repeatedly criticizes the impact of commerce on London, but only because he fears that selfish entrepreneurship and rapid urban growth will erase old traditions of collective memory.[61] Similarly, his implicit critique of supersessionary logic—that material conversion does not always yield a superior Christianity, and sometimes works to "melt" and "profane" Christian and Jewish matter alike—is sponsored not by political radicalism but by religious conservatism. As Ian W. Archer and others have observed, Stow's historiography strongly suggests a Catholic bent.[62] His contemporaries suspected as much. Stow was reported in 1569 to the Queen's Council, quite possibly by his estranged brother Thomas, for having many "dangerous books of superstition" in his possession. After Stow's house had been searched, Bishop Grindal announced that "his bokes declare him to be a great favourer of papistrye."[63] Officially, that was the end of the matter. It is tempting, however, to see Stow taking a revenge of sorts on his Protestant adversaries some thirty years later: in the *Survey*, he meticulously records all the names inscribed on Catholic-era monuments and church plaques, but he pointedly omits the names on new monuments. Indeed, the diarist John Manningham reported in 1603 that Stow claimed "those men have been the defacers of the monuments of others, and so worthy to be deprived of that memory whereof they have injuriously robbed others."[64]

Stow's aversion to Protestant practices of iconoclasm bespeaks an attitude reminiscent of Nietzsche's antiquarian. The trivial objects of civic history need to be retrieved in all their dynamic, palimpsest-like complexity; what is most profane for Stow, therefore, is less the transformation of matter than the erasure of memory. Saving the past's material traces from extinction is Stow's cause. He wages this battle by two means: critique of iconoclastic destruction, and recovery of forgotten histories. Thus he singles out for scorn "one Vicker," who "for couetnousnes" melted down brass plaques fixed on graves, "which he conuerted into coyned siluer"; for Stow, the vicar's chief crime was that he "left no memory of such as had beene buried vnder them."[65] The imperative to recover memory prompts Stow's list of Catholic bodies buried beneath a glass factory in Hart Street that was once a "Fryers hall."[66] But he is equally willing to recover the relics of a surprisingly wide variety of non-Protestant practices and peoples: not just Catholic but also pagan, as exemplified by his cheerful accounts of the remains of the city's

Roman inhabitants and the bones and teeth of prehistoric giants that he had seen seventy years earlier in his childhood.[67]

The Time of Stow's Historiography

Such nostalgia, as Archer aptly characterizes it, entails a fascinating contradiction. Stow looks to find threads of historical continuity that link the past to the present; but that search is predicated on a sense of discontinuity, on a fear that the present no longer contains the past and that the past is in danger of receding forever from memory. Lawrence Manley has noted how Stow's assertion of historical continuity in London's rites and traditions paradoxically performs its own historical break, projecting onto the past an integrated social order now under attack from the amnesiac iconoclasm and acquisitive individualism of the Reformation.[68] And Andrew Griffin has similarly found in Stow's historiography a tension between continuity and rupture: "It figures the past as both radically distant from the present and surprisingly close to it, as absolutely foreign to the present and as something to which the present relates intimately."[69] One might develop Manley's and Griffin's insights to think about what happens to the matter of the past in the *Survey*; the more Stow finds past matter in the present—a seeming proof of historical continuity—the more it appears under the mark of iconoclasm and forgetting—a seeming proof of historical rupture. A dialectic of legibility and inscrutability emerges from this contradiction. Stow reads past matter as a source of civic tradition that lends meaning to the present; yet because he also fears its mnemonic power to be receding, it becomes mere writing, ciphers robbed of spirit just as Stow's Jewish buildings are robbed of people. But as the sole material remainder of the past, that writing must be preserved at all costs.

This contradiction between continuity and rupture is what most distinguishes Stow's recording of the Hebrew characters in the Ludgate wall. On the one hand, Stow praises the barons' recycling of old Jewish matter to maintain London's traditional walls and gates, which accords with his strong sense of civic responsibility and charity. But he also expresses discomfort with the barons' willingness to erase the city's Jewish past. He sees the barons as motivated by a greed at odds with their ostensible charity: their goal, he claims, was simply to "fill their owne purses," for when they "broke into the Iews houses," they "rifeled their coffers."[70] Hence in Stow's reading, the matter of Old Jewry is subjected to both triumphal supersession and lamentable erasure. But in the palimpsest that is the Ludgate wall, Stow recognizes not just the acts of Protestant-like defacement that have produced the structure but also the untimely irruption that makes the illegible religious matter of the past available to, and disruptive of, the present. Despite his longing for the continuities of a traditional, ritual time that would lend meaning to the present, and despite his intuition of a ruptured time that has divorced the past from the now, there is also the hint in Stow's narrative of a third temporality: a time in which the ruined past explodes into the present and critiques it. With this explosive temporality, Stow does to the writing on the wall something quite different from what had been done to it by the barons.

As we have seen, Stow relies on a Latin translation to make sense of the Hebrew inscription. But the original Hebrew, if we can deduce it correctly from his *Survey*, is "מצבח ר משח בן הרב ר יצהק," or "matzevat r[abbi] Moshe ben harav r[abbi] Yitzhak": the "matzevat" of Rabbi Moshe, son of Rabbi Yitzhak. The word "מצבח," or "matzevat," interests me here. It corresponds to what Stow records as "מצב" and renders in Latin as "statio," station or ward; but its nominative form, "matzeva," means "monument" or "gravestone." In all likelihood, what Stow saw in 1586 was the remainder not of a house but of an old gravestone—presumably from the Jewin Garden cemetery—that the barons had looted in 1215. Indeed, the gravestone may have been that of Rabbi Moshe ben Itzhak, one of the greatest writers of medieval London Jewry.[71] If so, the historical event that Stow misreads as a looting of a private Jewish house entails a more transparently supersessionary logic. Consecrated matter was taken by the barons from Jewish holy ground, reworked, preserved yet canceled. The remnants of Old Jewry—or at least of the Jewish cemetery—became part of the fabric of the Christian city; the sacred Jewish past was retained, but only so that it could be desecrated.

This act of supersessionary desecration uncannily anticipates a recent historical phenomenon. In his documentary *Shtetl* (1996), filmmaker Marian Marzynski accompanies Nathan Kaplan, a seventy-year-old Jewish man from Chicago, to Bransk, a small Polish shtetl in eastern Poland.[72] Though it was once a lively Jewish village where Kaplan's family had lived, there are now virtually no traces of its prewar Jewish past. While in Bransk, Marzynski and Kaplan meet Zbyszek, a young Polish antiquarian—the John Stow figure of the film—who has devoted several years to collecting relics that memorialize the shtetl's Jewish history. The trio search in vain for Jewish physical structures in the village. Finally, they find gravestones bearing Hebrew characters, but not in any consecrated ground. Instead, the gravestones are, like the eponymous letter in Poe's *Purloined Letter*, invisible by being fully visible: they have been transformed into paving stones for the town footpaths. Bransk provides a signal instance of the supersessionary desecrations that characterize the cityscapes of European Christian culture. Whether it is the incorporation of old pagan temple bricks and their inscriptions into the walls of Pisa Cathedral, the conversion of Islamic minarets into bell towers in Andalusia, or the relocation of Jewish tombstones to London's city walls or modern Polish city footpaths, the matter of "old" religious structures has been repeatedly recycled and spectacularly profaned in "new" urban sites.

But that is not the kind of relation to the past modeled by either Stow's treatment of the crumbling Ludgate wall or Marzynski's attention to the gravestones. Both Tudor English antiquarian and modern Polish filmmaker record an act of supersession—the conversion of Jewish matter into a Christian civic structure. Yet both frame the spectacle of a stone inscribed with Hebrew characters to suggest an unusual way in which, to paraphrase *Hamlet*, the imagination can trace the dust of the past in the matter of the present. Both Stow and Marzynski seek less to subordinate the Jewish past within a triumphal Christian epoch, whether by actual supersession or by direct translation, than to allow that past to speak back in its disruptive strangeness. In *Shtetl*, Marzynski unearths one of the gravestones, which he pointedly presents as an untimely object (fig. 8). In the image I have reproduced here, it is striking what is and isn't translated by the subtitle. Marzynski's command to the people who raise the stone, spoken in Polish, is rendered into English: "Bring it [i.e., the gravestone] into the light." But the writing on the stone that comes to "light"—we might recall here the antique, temporally heterodox matter that "comes to light" in Philip Kuberski's analysis of Benjamin's Paris—escapes translation. By refusing conversion into the film's universal gold standard of English, the Hebrew inscriptions on the Bransk gravestone remain out of joint with the now.[73] Indeed, the untranslated residue of the past-in-the-present might serve as a powerful synonym for the untimely; for if supersession seeks to plot timely progression, it is by means of translating the old into a new, universal master language that makes the past intelligible only in the terms of the present.

In the *Survey*, Stow quietly resists the direct translation of London's Jewish past into the master language of the Anglo-Protestant vernacular. And he does so partly by allowing the Hebrew inscription in Ludgate's wall a degree of autonomy, glossing it first in Latin rather than translating it directly

Fig. 8. Image from *Shtetl*, directed by Marian Marzynski (Frontline, 1996).

into English. Of course the past that Stow retrieves, as his Latin mistranslation of "מצב" as "station" makes clear, is a misprision. Yet even as he reworks the matter of London's Jewish past, that past helps him rework his present. In the process, Stow does not transform London into a New Jerusalem, the Protestant supersessionary sequel to and cancellation of an Old Jewry.[74] Rather, like the mnemonic matter in Benjamin's urban palimpsest, his treatment of Ludgate's Hebrew characters creates a faultline in the now through which the past resurfaces as an untimely disturbance, one that pluralizes London both culturally and temporally. The barons may have rebuilt Ludgate in 1215 to secure the city's future, an act of urban maintenance in line with Stow's sense of civic responsibility. But their violent destruction of Jewish memory is of a piece with the more recent wave of Protestant iconoclasm and amnesia that Stow so clearly reviles. Stow, then, does not redeem Ludgate's Hebrew inscription in solidarity with London's living Jews, as Antony Bale has suggested he does. Instead, we might see him submitting to another, unexpected solidarity. He mourns the loss of old Catholic materials that have been obliterated by the Protestant Reformation; and this leads him to feel sympathy not for Jews, living or dead, but for Jewish stones that have likewise been defaced. Hence the irruption of a forgotten thirteenth-century Hebrew inscription into Stow's present, whether in the crumbling matter of Ludgate in 1586 or in the text of the *Survey* in 1598 and 1603, also disputes the time of Protestant London and its willful erasure of the pre-Reformation past.

Here we might see Stow's Anglo-Jewish historiography as somewhat analogous to the French traveler Jean de Léry's Brazilian ethnography, at least as analyzed by Michel de Certeau. Confronted with the strangeness of the New World during his 1556 visit to Brazil, de Léry performed what de Certeau sees as an exercise in colonialist epistemology, translating the space of the other into a systematic ethnography of Indian culture, complete with glossary. Yet this project foundered on the untranslatable song of the Tupinamba Indians, whose sound both horrified and "ravished" de Léry with its beauty. As de Certeau points out, not only did the song remain stubbornly other to de Léry, it also opened up a space of alterity within himself as the supposedly knowing subject, a space of presymbolic bodily pleasure, or *jouissance*.[75] Something similar happens with Stow who, despite the drive to omniscience of his antiquarian chorography, discovers an alterity in the Hebrew characters that in turns limns an otherness within him and the time within which he is writing.

But this is not the privatized otherness of the jouissance that de Certeau attributes to de Léry. Rather, it is a more political self-estrangement, one that is illuminated by Nietzsche's remark about the antiquarian's identity with his city. If, for the antiquarian, "the history of his city becomes for him the history of himself" and "he reads its walls, its towered gate, its rules and regulations, its holidays, like an illuminated diary of his youth and in all this he finds again himself," Stow's discovery of the Hebrew is equally a discovery of linguistic, cultural, and religious alterity within the projected self of his beloved London. Perhaps this alterity affords Stow a jouissance of sorts, albeit a jouissance of a more collective stripe: his city is, happily for him and those he speaks for, not the homogeneous New Jerusalem his former antagonists have made it out to be. Shakespeare, as we shall see in the next chapter, likewise explodes the homogeneous time of Protestantism by locating a temporal alterity within his own moment of danger. He does so with actual explosives. Stow, by contrast, resorts to more subtle munitions. Yes, Stow's *Survey* imagines a London curiously devoid of its living Jews. But by producing the city as an urban palimpsest riddled with the cryptic traces of Jewish matter, Stow quietly says to the city's Protestant authorities: it's time to read the writing on the wall.

FOUR

The Smell of Gunpowder

Macbeth and the Palimpsests of Olfaction

> MERCURY. *Peace, good squib, go out.*
> CRITES. *And stink, he bids you.*
> —Ben Jonson, *Cynthia's Revels*

DID THE SHAKESPEAREAN stage stink?

The Jonsonian theater certainly did. In the prologue to *Bartholomew Fair*, the Scrivener complains that the Hope Theatre—where Jonson's play was first performed in 1614—is "as dirty as Smithfield, and as stinking every whit."[1] Such a description may confirm the worst suspicions of modern readers, who all too easily imagine the early modern playhouse—in an age before deodorant, daily baths, and air conditioning—to have been a malodorous cesspit of the great unwashed, populated by reeking groundlings against whom the only available protection was the plague-palliating nosegay or pomander. But while Jonson may refer here to the space of the theater as a whole, he also knew something of the bad odors that could be produced specifically on the stage. Among the early modern theater's most dazzling special effects were two fireworks mentioned by the Caroline playwright Richard Lovelace in his epilogue to *The Scholars*: "rosin-lightning flash" and "squibs."[2] Low-tech these fireworks may have been, but they packed an explosive theatrical punch. Rosin powder was thrown at candle flames to produce flares; squibs, famously called for in the stage directions to *Doctor*

Faustus, were employed to produce flashes and loud bangs.[3] Because of their visual and acoustic impact, it is easy to overlook how both effects also stank—especially the squib, which became a virtual synonym for bad odor, as the epigraph from Jonson's *Cynthia's Revels* suggests. Like all gunpowder products, the squib combined foul-smelling ingredients—sulfurous brimstone, coal, and saltpeter—that reeked all the more when detonated. In his 1588 manual on the manufacture of explosives, Peter Whithorne writes that the saltpeter of gunpowder "is made of the dunge of beasts . . . and aboue all other, of the same that commeth of hogges, the most and best is gotten."[4] If saltpeter's fecal origins were not enough, gunpowder's customary mode of preparation only served to amplify its malodorousness: Whithorne explains that its ingredients "must be compounded with the oile of egges, and put . . . under hot dung for a moneth."[5] Little wonder, then, that Jonson's Crites insists in *Cynthia's Revels* on the squib's "stink."

Squibs, perhaps in tandem with rosin powder, were almost certainly used at the beginning of *Macbeth* to produce the effect of its famous stage direction: "*Thunder and lightning*" (1.1.0). The controlled detonation of fireworks would have helped create not only the necessary sound and light effects for the opening scene but also the poor air quality described in the three witches' bizarre incantation, "Hover through the fog and filthy air" (1.1.12).[6] In its first performances, then, the play most likely began not just with a bang but with a stink, one that would have persisted through the first scene as the fireworks' thick smoke wafted across the stage and into the audience. Even in the open-air Globe, the smell would have been strong; if performed indoors at court for King James, it would have been stifling. Given the squib's dungy provenance, its stench might have lent an extra olfactory charge to Lady Macbeth's invocation of the "dunnest smoke of Hell" (1.5.49).[7]

This chapter, then, considers what may seem like a familiar subject in *Macbeth* criticism: gunpowder. It does so less to cast light on the infamous Gunpowder Plot, however, than to ponder the ways in which the smelly materials of early modern theatrical performance got to work on their audiences or, for the purposes of this chapter, their olfactors. In the process, I consider how the smell of *Macbeth*'s "thunder and lightning" was as theatrically important as its visual and acoustic impact, and the ways in which playgoers' responses to the odor of the squibs were not just physiologically conditioned but also implicated within larger cultural syntaxes of olfaction and memory. But I do not seek to explain the smell of *Macbeth* simply according to the cultural poetics of its historical moment. Indeed, I am interested in how the play's smells put pressure on the very notion of a self-identical moment as the irreducible ground zero of historical interpretation. For I locate in smell a polychronicity that, in the specific instance of Shakespeare's play, generates an explosive temporality through which the past is made to act upon, and shatter the self-identity of, the present. I shall argue that, like the spectacle in Stow's *Survey* of the Hebrew writing on Ludgate's wall, Shakespeare's stinking squibs allowed a supposedly superseded religious past to intervene in and pluralize the Protestant moment of the play's first performance. In my reading, therefore, Shakespeare's gunpowder again turns the material culture of the Renaissance stage into matériel culture: untimely matter with explosive effects not just in physical space but also in time.

Smell and the Time of Historical Phenomenology

What, then, does it mean to experience *Macbeth* not just with one's eyes and ears but also with one's nose? Thus posed, my question places this chapter in dialogue with the new critical movement that Bruce R. Smith has termed "historical phenomenology." In a series of important studies, Smith and scholars such as Wes Folkerth have attempted to move beyond a purely textual approach to Shakespeare's plays by insisting on the embodied experiences of those who saw and, in particular, *heard* them. This new perspective entails a mediation of the social and the natural, the cultural and the physiological. As Smith has explained, "historical phenomenology" seeks to combine "a modern scientific understanding of the 'hardware' of human hearing with attention to the historical 'software' of early modern culture."[8]

In *The Acoustic World of Early Modern England*, Smith reconstructs the experience of sound in Shakespeare's culture. He catalogues a rich medley of acoustic elements—including urban sounds such as bells and street criers, and rustic noises such as farm animals' cries—but he pays particular attention to the sounds of the stage. In his historical-phenomenological analysis, the staging of thunder and lightning was an important component of early modern playgoers' experience of Shakespeare's plays. *The Tempest*'s opening stage direction—"*A tempestuous noise of Thunder and Lightning heard*"—is, according to Smith, "the last and most concentrated in a series of attention-focusing noises, clamors, and tumults" that also includes the opening stage direction of *Macbeth*. For Smith, the sound of thunder and lightning significantly shapes the "auditory fields" of both plays, as well as the way in which audiences respond to them.[9]

A historical-phenomenological analysis of *Macbeth*'s thunder and lightning need not be confined just to the fireworks' acoustic dimension. There have been many studies of how early modern spectators may have responded to the visual effects of *Macbeth*—the mysterious dagger that Macbeth sees in 2.1; the joint-stool on which Banquo's ghost appears in 3.4; the mirror held up by the last king in the procession of Banquo's royal descendants conjured up by the witches in 4.1.[10] Moreover, in a play so obsessed with sight and its potential dangers (as suggested by Macduff's "destroy your sight / With a new Gorgon" [2.3.68–69] or the Witches' "Show his eyes and grieve his heart" [4.1.126]), it is only fitting that its spectacles should have begun with a burst of retina-searing pyrotechnics.[11] But the powerful stink of *Macbeth*'s fireworks also calls for a theorization of the scene's, and the play's, smellscapes.

So far, smell has been absent from historical-phenomenological studies of *Macbeth* or Shakespeare's stage. There are many reasons for this omission. Olfaction—at least in the wake of Freud—has been subject to a pervasive cultural and, until recently, critical undervaluation: while sight has been linked since the nineteenth century to reason and civilization, smell has frequently been regarded as the province of the primitive.[12] As a result there has often been a whiff of the scandalous in studies of smell, which have tended to treat the topic as a subset of scatology.[13] There is the additional practical difficulty of unearthing historical evidence of smells; these are less accessible than sounds, which can often be recovered by extrapolating from printed texts. What, one might ask, would constitute an archive of smell? Our language also constrains us. We have a complex, differentiated array of terms for colors and phonemes, yet have no such terminology for the spectrum of odors. The words we use to represent smell tend to be not nominal but comparative—an object smells *like* something. Smell, therefore, has a tendency to slide referentially.

It also slides temporally: as Proust repeatedly attested, smell can trigger memory.[14] Mallarmé, picking up his abandoned pipe, expressed amazement at how its odors sent him back in time to another country: "Amazed and touched, I was breathing the smells of the past winter which came back to me. I had not touched my faithful friend since my return to France, and London, the London I had experienced all by myself in the past year, came back to me."[15] Shakespeare likewise remarks on the time-traveling effects of smell in Sonnet 5, where he observes that perfume is not simply an object in the present:

> Then, were not summer's distillation left,
> A liquid prisoner pent in walls of glass,
> Beauty's effect with beauty were bereft,
> Nor it nor no remembrance what it was. . . .
> (5.9–12)

Smell can conjure up for "remembrance" an otherwise inaccessible past experience and make it crash into the present with exceptional vividness. As neuroscientists have come to realize, the part of the brain that processes olfactory experiences is located in the cortical nucleus of the amygdala, which is also involved in the consolidation of memory. From a neurological as well as an experiential perspective, then, smell and memory are metonymically associated with each other.[16]

The referential and temporal slipperiness of smell equally illuminates a potential problem in historical phenomenology—its express goal of translating sensory experience into meaningful information within and about a single historical "moment." In an important study, Wes Folkerth seeks to identify what Shakespeare's sounds "would have meant, and how their meanings would have been received by the people who heard and understood them in specific contexts, with early modern ears."[17] Folkerth's analysis has two related agendas: sensory perception is converted into the perception of sense, which in turn permits the articulation of a systematic, cultural grammar of sound. Smith does something similar when he speaks of "the boundaries of the auditory field . . . established in the cacophony" that opens a play like *Macbeth*. "Cacophony"—an incoherent noise—resolves itself into an "auditory field" with coherent "boundaries."[18] Like all spatial metaphors, the "auditory field" implies a synchronic mode of analysis, in which the terrain of a single historical moment is mapped. But smell's slipperiness resists any such mapping.

Macbeth is a play that repeatedly smudges the boundaries dividing the present "moment" from other times, as evidenced in Lady Macbeth's remark, "Thy letters have transported me beyond / This ignorant present, and I feel now / The future in the instant" (1.5.56–58).[19] Indeed, the coherence of linear time is repeatedly fractured in the play, as suggested by Macbeth's insistence that his future—like that of Walter Benjamin's angel of history—is not ahead of, but "behind" him (1.3.115).[20] This is the play in which Shakespeare most dabbles in the untimely. *Macbeth* uses the word twice: in the first instance, Macduff explains the effects of "boundless intemperance," which leads to "the untimely emptying of the happy throne / And fall of many kings" (4.3.67–69); and in the second, he describes how he was "from his mother's womb / Untimely ripp'd" (5.10.15–16). Both instances play off the common sense meaning of "untimely" as premature.[21] Yet elsewhere *Macbeth* generates an effect of the untimely that is altogether closer to Nietzsche's "unzeitgemässe" and Benjamin's "moment of danger," inasmuch as it involves an explosive memory of the past that shatters the present.[22] This explosive untimeliness is most apparent in the stage effect that introduces the play's first scene. As I shall show, *Macbeth*'s squibs not only produce a polychronic compression of diverse moments in time; they also suggest how the past can critique the present. In this, they demand a different governing metaphor from the synchronic "auditory field" of the historical-phenomenological project.

The metaphor I propose instead is, once again, the palimpsest.[23] In contrast to the synchronic "field" of historical phenomenology, the palimpsest necessitates that we read transtemporally. It is a particularly useful metaphor for smell as well: both the literary palimpsest and the memory-inducing odor involve a compression of different times, of multiple "fields," into one space. The polychronicity of smell, however, is in one respect different from that of the palimpsest. The latter comprises polychronic traces contained inside the object. By contrast, the centrifugal nature of smell—its propensity to smell *like* something else, and hence to evoke the past by metonymic association—locates its polychronicity ambivalently inside and outside the object. Whereas a transtemporal plurality of materials is visible or audible *within* (say) a collage that mixes contemporary and old printed matter or a new hip-hop song that samples old sound recordings, smell tends to generate polychronic experiences, present and past, that branch *outside* its object and into the smeller.

Thus if the textual or sonic palimpsest is a polychronic object experienced by the subject, the olfactory palimpsest is the subject's polychronic experience of an object—an experience that significantly expands the definition of materiality. Much recent scholarship on so-called material culture has tended to equate materiality with the physicality of objects.[24] But we might do well to remember Marx's criticism of those "materialist" philosophers who limit their understanding of materiality only to the form of the object, and thus neglect the equally material "human sensuous activity" that interacts with, transforms, and is transformed by the object.[25] Similarly, the materiality of smell is not quite synonymous with the object; it embraces the subjective olfactory experience of the object, an experience that also reworks that object. This confusion is embodied in the very word "smell," which as a noun tends to refer to an object but as a verb can refer to the practice of both subject (in its transitive form: "I smell the coffee") and object (in its intransitive form: "the coffee smells"). The subjective reworking of the olfactory object, I shall argue, is what would have happened to the squibs detonated in the earliest performances of *Macbeth*, most likely in the spring of 1606.[26] Playgoers could have supplied, by olfactory association, a variety of phenomenological receptive horizons—among them, the contemporary Gunpowder Plot, but also memories of older theatrical and religious experiences. Each of these memories transformed *Macbeth*'s fireworks into something else, something unstuck in time. So if synchronic analysis maps the "field" of a single moment, and diachronic analysis traces a progression over time, *Macbeth* calls for a polychronic analysis, one sensitive to the explosive temporality generated by its smelly squibs.

Stygian Odors: The Stench of the Political Present

Because the sulfurous odor of *Macbeth*'s fireworks was every bit as strong as their bright flash and loud crackle, Renaissance audiences would have begun their experience of the play with a keen awareness of the smell of gunpowder. This must have been a highly charged encounter in the wake of then-recent events. The play, presumably written and staged in the months after the discovery of the Gunpowder Plot of Guy Fawkes and his Catholic co-conspirators, is clearly attuned to the scandal's most publicly discussed details: the horror unleashed by a supposedly loyal subject who seeks to kill a king, and the treasonous role of equivocation. As Garry Wills has noted, the play even echoes certain keywords from the scandal—the "blow" about which one of the conspirators had secretly warned a relative who planned to attend the Houses of Parliament on November 5, and the "vault" underneath the Houses of Parliament in which Fawkes had stored thirty kegs of gunpowder.[27] For an audience member attuned to these words in the wake of the scandal, it would have been hard not to be subliminally reminded of the plot by Macbeth's remarks, immediately before the murder of Duncan, "that this blow / Might be the be-all and the end-all" (1.7.4–5), or immediately after it, that "the mere lees / Is left this vault to brag of" (2.3.93–94).

One of the most famous phrases in *Macbeth* may have likewise conjured for some audience members—not least King James—the specter of the Gunpowder Plot. In the first of ten annual sermons before the King on November 5, 1605, Lancelot Andrewes observed that, despite their intentions, the plotters had failed to make the day over to diabolical disorder, for it remains God's day: "Be they fair or foul, glad or sad (as the poet calleth Him) the great *Diespater*, 'the Father of days' hath made them both."[28] Shakespeare likewise yokes "fair" and "foul" in the witches' and Macbeth's first appearances (1.1.11, 1.3.38), albeit with far less assurance of providential delivery than Andrewes's sermon. Even though the plot is never alluded to directly, then, its presence is everywhere in the play, like a pervasive odor.

Or rather, less *like* an odor than *in the form* of an odor. The smell of the King's Men's fireworks may well have been a ruse designed to evoke the plot subliminally, as it almost certainly was in another play performed by the company in the same year: Barnabe Barnes's *The Devil's Charter*. The play contains many echoes of *Macbeth*. Its characters equivocate, and its Lady Macbeth–like anti-heroine—the evil Lucretia—speaks of Arabian perfume, is afflicted by spots, and is observed by a physician who cannot cure her. But it is the play's use of fireworks that most connects *The Devil's Charter* not just to *Macbeth* but also to the Gunpowder Plot. The play cannot stop detonating squibs—it does so on at least five occasions—and the stage directions make explicit that these are meant to *smell*: "the Monke draweth to a chair on midst of the stage which hee circleth, and before it an other Circle, into which (after semblance of reading with exorcismes) appeare exhalations of lightning and sulphurous smoke in midst whereof a divill in most ugly shape."[29] After one such "exhalation" of "sulphurous smoke," a devil ascends, claiming that he has been "sent from the foggy lake of fearefull *Stix*."[30] With this line, *The Devil's Charter* alludes unmistakably to the Gunpowder Plot. In his speech to Parliament immediately after the plot's disovery, James anticipated Barnes's devil in identifying the sulfurous exhalations of the plotters' gunpowder with the stench of "lake of fearefull Styx": "So the earth as it were opened, should haue sent forth of the bottome of the *Stygian* lake such sulphured smoke, furious flames, and fearefull thunder, as should haue by their diabolicall *Domesday* destroyed and defaced, in the twinckling of an eye, not onely our present liuing Princes and people, but euen our insensible Monuments reserued for future ages."[31]

As James's remark suggests, the Gunpowder Plot prompted imaginings of eschatological time—a "diabolicall *Domesday*" that would have usurped the end of the world as prophesized in Revelation. And if the sulfurous smell of gunpowder evoked for James the prospect of apocalypse, *Macbeth*'s squibs may have likewise provided the olfactory prelude to its characters' powerful experiences, after Duncan's murder, of apocalyptic time. "By th'clock 'tis day," remarks Ross, "And yet dark night strangles the travelling lamp" (2.4.6–7); "A falcon," adds the Old Man, "Was by a mousing owl hawked at and killed" (2.4.12–13). These inversions of cosmic and animal order are characteristic of the upside-down nightmare world of medieval apocalyptic prophecy, a world presided over by Satan.[32] As I shall show later, Shakespeare arguably used the smell of gunpowder to produce other experiences of eschatological time in *Macbeth*, albeit ones that suggest less medieval apocalyptic prophecy than the "weak messianic" explosions of Benjamin's "Theses on the Philosophy of History." Yet if Benjamin's is an eschatological temporality without Christ or devil, *Macbeth*'s explosions retain a connection to Satan; after all, the odor of sulfur in Shakespeare's time—and indeed in our own, if Hugo Chávez's notorious remark about George W. Bush's "smell of sulfur" is any indication[33]—was a stinking sign of diabolical activity.

When James made his pronouncements after the revelation of the plot, the sulfurous smell of gunpowder had long been linked to Satan and hell. Despite gunpowder's Chinese origin, European myth attributed its invention first to the devil (a canard reiterated by Edward Coke in the wake of the plot) and then, in Protestant England, to an evil yet apocryphal German friar named Bartold Schwarz.[34] English references to gunpowder's provenance repeatedly invoke its devilish inventor. Jonson lambasted the friar "Who from the Divels-Arse did Guns beget"; Thomas Dekker described the cannons of war as "Hells hot Sulpherous throats," pausing to "curse that sulphurous wit, / Whose black inuention, first gaue fire to it."[35] All these remarks suggest that playgoers could have easily reacted to the smell of *Macbeth*'s fireworks in ways that reinforced James's linking of the "sulphured smoke" of hell to the gunpowder used by Guy Fawkes. But the memories potentially triggered by the diabolical stink of *Macbeth*'s fireworks were by no means confined to recent political events. They may also have pointed further back in time, to earlier theatrical experiences.

The association between bad smells and hell had been exploited on the English stage since the Corpus Christi drama. The annual play presented by the Chester Cooks, for example, included a Hell Mouth that emitted smoke and what was evidently a hideous stench.[36] As gunpowder manufacturing technologies became more widespread throughout England in the fifteenth and sixteenth centuries, theatrical performances increasingly resorted to cheap fireworks as a foul-scented stage effect with which to conjure up the illusion of the satanic. Records of guild entertainments in Coventry list numerous expenditures on gunpowder; and in *The Castle of Perseverance*, the stage directions call for the devil Belial to sport spark-spouting gunpowder "pypys" in his hands, ears, and arse.[37] As this scatological image suggests, the flaming arses of stage devils in late medieval drama drew heavily on traditions of carnivalesque representation that differ from King James's apocalyptic post-plot pronouncements. Even after the Reformation banished representations of the sacred from the stage, cheeky firework-toting devils remained a recurrent feature of the public playhouses. The stage directions for plays from Marlowe's *Doctor Faustus* ("Mephostopholis with fireworks") to Thomas Heywood's *Silver Age* ("the Devils appear at every corner of the stage with several fireworks . . . fireworks all over the house") and Robert Tailor's *The Hog Hath Lost His Pearl* ("A flash of fire, and LIGHTFOOT ascends like a spirit") suggest a profusion of gunpowder-reeking devils whose sulfurous odor probably provoked holiday excitement rather than political outrage.[38]

In other words, the dungy stink at the beginning of *Macbeth* may have made its olfactors remember not just the recent Gunpowder Plot and its supposedly Stygian agents but also a festive countertradition of representing the demonic that had its roots in popular old Catholic entertainments. The play thus superimposed current political events upon archaic theatrical practice—a polychronic palimpsest paralleling that of the Porter in act 2, who simultaneously evokes the "equivocators" of the Gunpowder Plot and the stock porter of Hell-gate from medieval mystery drama.[39] In both cases, *Macbeth* invited playgoers to contemplate "real" horror in the present yet distance themselves from it by recalling the play's festive antecedents. But the temporal indeterminacy prompted by the play's fireworks was not the only way in which *Macbeth* used smell to make confusion's masterpiece.

Confusing the Nose of the King

> *I understood that my work must, if it was to have any value, acquire a moral dimension; that the only important divisions were the infinitely subtle gradations of good and evil smells. Having realized the crucial*

> *nature of morality, having sniffed out that smells could be sacred or profane, I invented, in the isolation of my scooter-trips, the science of nasal ethics.*
>
> —Salman Rushdie, *Midnight's Children*[40]

As King James's remarks about the Gunpowder Plot's relation to the sulfurous smoke of hell and "diabolical domesday" suggest, the official representation of threats to the realm easily marshaled the language of olfaction. Indeed, James had already resorted to this very strategy before the plot. In his infamous 1604 attack on tobacco and the dangers it posed to the nation, he had called smoking "hateful to the nose," and proceeded to compare—in language that uncannily anticipates his response to the plot—"the black stinking fume" of tobacco to "the horrible stygian smoke of the pit that is bottomless."[41] In William Drummond's poem on the five senses, the King's nose was likewise singled out as the means whereby the nation's troubled subjects might be protected from devilish machinations:

> Give him the feeling of their woes
> And then noe doubt his royall nose
> Will quickly smell, those Rascalles forth
> Whose black deedes, have eclipst his worth.[42]

Likewise, the "black deedes" of the Gunpowder Plot were understood to have been foiled by the King's nose. The official story was that James had cracked the code in an intercepted letter that warned of a "blow" in the forthcoming November 5 session of Parliament.[43] But a ballad composed shortly thereafter attributed the success of James's sleuthing to his literally smelling out the plot:

> . . . our King he went to the Parliament
> to meet his Noble Peers-a;
> But if he had knowne
> where he should have been blown,
> He durst not have gon for his Eares-a.
>
> Then, "Powder I smell," quothe our gracious King
> (now our King was an excellent smeller);
> And lowder and lowder,

quoth the King, "I smell powder";
And downe he run into the Cellar.[44]

This last example draws more on festive than on demonological traditions of representation. But like James's *Counterblast to Tobacco* and Drummond's poem on the senses, the ballad fantasizes an absolutist nasal ethics—to adapt Salman Rushdie's felicitous phrase—according to which the King's nose is valorized as the organ uniquely equipped to tell the difference between fair and foul morality.

This ethics is perhaps not surprising in a culture where both virtue and sin were repeatedly coded olfactorily. Catholics had long distinguished between the odor of sanctity emitted by saints and priests and the putrid stench of moral corruption. The Reformation may have shaken belief in the physical odor of sanctity, but the opposition between the sweet scent of sanctity and the stink of sin persisted in Protestant writing in a fashion that was only ambivalently metaphorical. In his poem "The Banquet," George Herbert asks whether the "sweetnesse in the bread" of the Eucharist can "subdue the smell of sinne." He discounts the possibility that there can be any physical deodorant strong enough to perform such a task: "Doubtlesse, neither starre nor flower / Hath the power / Such a sweetnesse to impart." Rather, "Onely God, who gives perfumes, / Flesh assumes, / And with it perfumes my heart."[45] This spiritual perfume affirms a perhaps typically Protestant understanding of the Eucharist, according to which the physical matter of the Communion wafer no longer has power over the spirit, let alone the nose; perfume comes directly from God to the Christian heart. Even as Herbert shifts the odor of sanctity outside the realm of physical olfaction, however, he arguably strands the "smell of sinne" in the realm of the premetaphorical and the material, where it strikes the nostrils rather than the heart.

Likewise, Shakespeare has a tendency to register sin olfactorily. Hence Claudius's "offence is rank! it smells to heaven" (*Hamlet*, 3.3.36), and Emilia not only "thinks upon" but also "smell[s]" Iago's "villainy" (*Othello*, 5.2.198). The opposition is most poignantly illustrated in Lady Macbeth's remark that "Here's the smell of the blood still. All the perfumes of Arabia will not sweeten this little hand" (5.1.42–43). The "smell of the blood" may be imperceptible to audiences, but it is certainly not just a metaphor to Lady Macbeth. Bad smell is in all these instances an index of inner moral truth—a connection that may be glimpsed also in the dual olfactory and ontological meanings of the word "essence" in early modern English. In its entry for "essence," the

OED notes how its divergent meanings of "that which constitutes the being of a thing" (definition 7) and "a fragrant essence; a perfume, a scent" (definition 10) were both in use by the early seventeenth century.[46]

Yet olfaction in *Macbeth* is hardly a reliable means of ascertaining virtue or sin. In marked contrast to James's supposedly preternatural ability to sniff out essences, it is significant that the saintly King Duncan fails utterly as an olfactory arbiter. Just as he cannot read the signs of treason on the first or the second Thane of Cawdor's countenance—"there's no art / To find the mind's construction in the face" (1.4.11–12)—so he fails to smell the evil lurking in Macbeth's castle:

> KING
> This castle hath a pleasant seat. The air
> Nimbly and sweetly recommends itself
> Unto our gentle senses.
>
> BANQUO
> This guest of summer,
> The temple-haunting martlet, does approve
> By his loved mansionry that the heaven's breath
> Smells wooingly here. . . .
> . . . I haue observ'd
> The air is delicate.
> (1.6.1–6, 9–10)

Duncan is not, in the words of the ballad about King James and the Gunpowder Plot, "an excellent smeller." His discovery of heaven's breath in the castle where Lady Macbeth has just wished "the dunnest smoke of hell" (1.5.49) is decidedly odd, and perhaps all the more so given that castles were traditionally associated with the stench of gunpowder. As Ulrich von Hutten noted in 1518, castles were built "not for pleasure but for defense, surrounded by moats and trenches, cramped within, burdened with . . . dark buildings for bombards and stores of pitch and sulfur. . . . Everywhere the disagreeable odor of powder dominates."[47] And in the playhouses where the King's Men performed *Macbeth*, "the disagreeable odor of powder" may well have been perceptible during the first scenes set in Macbeth's castle—act 1, scenes 4, 5, and 6—if the sulfurous odor of the squibs detonated at the beginning not just of act 1, scene 1, but also of act 1, scene 3, had not yet dissipated.[48]

Yet the play doesn't ask us to believe that Macbeth's castle really *does* stink, or that its true essence should have been sniffed out by a more gifted smeller. Rather, Duncan's mis-olfaction underlines how easily foul blurs into fair, and vice versa, in this relentlessly equivocal play. It also provides a reminder that *Macbeth*'s inversions, confusions, and palimpsests are not simply semiotic problems—they are also integral aspects of the experience of smell. In Thomas Tomkis's university play *Lingua: Or the Combat of the Tongue, and the Five Senses for Superiority* (1607), Phantastes tells Olfactus, the sense of smell, that "of all the Senses, your obiects haue the worst luck, they are always iarring with their contraries; for none can weare Ciuet, but they are suspected of a proper badde sent."[49] In other words, a good smell is no longer a reliable sign of a good essence; foul odors might be masked by the fair. Perfume in particular had become a growing source of suspicion.[50] Indeed, Shakespeare may have had the smell of perfume partly in mind when, in language redolent of *Macbeth*, he accused modern women of "Fairing the foul with art's false borrow'd face" (Sonnet 127.6); developing the theme, he praises his Dark Lady, whose breath "reeks" (130.8) without any cosmetic scent. Similarly, some writers welcomed the unadorned honesty of gunpowder's sulfurous odor when compared to what perfume might hide: "Musk and civet have too long stifled us," says the captain in James Shirley's *The Doubtful Heir*, "there's no recovery without the smell of gunpowder."[51]

Macbeth, then, is a play mired in olfactory confusion—whether the temporal confusion of contemporary politics and archaic stagecraft prompted by the smell of the play's fireworks, or the ontological confusion of fair and foul prompted by Duncan and Banquo's apprehension of Macbeth's hellish castle as a haven for "heaven's breath." Performed in part for a King who supposedly derived certainty from the essences he smelled, we might ask of *Macbeth*: Why is the play so alert to the temporal and moral slippages induced by smell? Indeed, why problematize the absolutist nasal ethics that Drummond and popular ballads associated with James? I would argue that these conundrums resonate with a relatively recent historical development that has had important implications for the cultural history of smell: the Protestant abolition of incense from churches.

"Smoke, like Incense": The Missing Scent of Sanctity

In Tomkis's *Lingua*, Olfactus describes his services to the body. He claims to minister odors to the brain that

. . . clense your heads, and make your fantasie
To refine wit, and sharpen inuention
And strengthen memory, from whence it came,
That old deoution, incense did ordaine
To make mans spirits more apt for things diuine.[52]

In this passage, Tomkis connects the unusual mnemonic power of smell to the effects of Catholic incense. As Montaigne remarked in his essay on smells, "the use of incense and perfumes in churches (so ancient and so universally received in all nations and religions), was intended to cheer us, and to rouse and purify the senses, the better to fit us for contemplation."[53] The odor of incense thus both signified divine presence and provided a memory of the state of mind befitting religious devotion. Yet even as *Lingua* presents incense as a spur *to* memory, it was by 1605 (the year of *Lingua*'s first performance) equally an object *of* memory, as its use had been substantially curtailed by the Protestant Reformation. Although no official edict banning incense was issued, the burning of incense in churches was progressively discontinued during Elizabeth's reign. Celebrating this change, John Bale sneered at the Catholics with whom he identified the ritual: "They will be no more at cost to have the air beaten and idols perfumed with their censers at principal feasts."[54]

Incense came increasingly to be seen as a stage effect of a now superseded theatricality—be it the theatricality of Catholic church ritual or of religious entertainments. William Lambarde, reflecting in 1570 on a spectacular pre-Reformation Whitsuntide celebration at Saint Paul's Cathedral in London, remembered above all the smell of incense:

> In the Dayes of ceremonial religion, . . . [I] once saw at *Poules* Churche in *London*, at a Feast of *Whitsuntyde*; wheare the comynge downe of the *Holy Gost* was set for by a white Pigion, that was let to fly out of a Hole, that yet is to be sene in the midst of the Roofe of the greate Ile, and by a longe Censer, which descendinge out of the same Place almost to the verie Grounde, was swinged up and downe at such a Lengthe, that it reached with th'one Swepe almost to the West Gate of the Churche, and with the other to the Quyre Staires of the same; breathinge out over the whole Churche and Companie a most pleasant Perfume of such swete Thinges as burned thearin.[55]

The nostalgic tone of this passage only underscores the extent of the Reformation's break with the "Dayes of ceremonial religion." Yet even though Lambarde remembered the "most pleasant Perfume" of the Censer with wistful longing, the Protestant antipathy to the smell of incense grew in the century after the Reformation: an anonymous 1623 sermon against the "perill of Idolatrie" inveighs against the specific dangers of rituals that involve "incense, and odours."[56]

The abolition of censing in the English churches was aided and abetted by a widespread pathologization of olfaction. In his *Essayes upon the Five Senses*, Richard Brathwait observed that smell "is an occasion of more danger to the body than benefit, in that it receives crude and unwholesome vapours, foggie and corrupt exhalations, being subject to any infection."[57] Coupling the pathologization of smell with a partisan reinterpretation of Galenic physiology—for Galen, "to smell" was to take a substance into the brain[58]—Protestant English writers transformed the once beneficent odor of incense into brain poison. Hence in his poem on the five senses, Drummond prays that

When Myrrhe, and frankinsence is throwne
And altars built to Gods unknowne,
Oh lett my Soveraigne never smell
Such damned perfumes, fitt for hell.
Let not such scent, his nostrilles stayne,
From Smelles, that poison canne the Brayne.[59]

Likewise Isabella employs the sweet fumes of incense to poison Livia in Thomas Middleton's *Women Beware Women*.[60] For Middleton and Drummond, then, the formerly fair had been transformed into the lethally foul.

But if Middleton and Drummond fantasize scenarios in which the unequivocally sweet smell of incense conceals its poisonous essence, Shakespeare goes even further in *Titus Andronicus*, where Lucius refers to Alarbus's burning flesh "whose smoke, like incense, doth perfume the sky" (1.1.145). Lucius's remark, despite the play's explicitly pagan setting, might seem designed to travesty Catholic ritual: the sacrifice of Alarbus smudges the olfactory boundary between the fair and the foul, blurring the difference between the sweet-scented odor of incense and the acrid stench of burnt human flesh. It is unlikely that this episode was accompanied in performance by a smelly stage effect such as a squib. Nevertheless, the scene undermines any univocal Catholic association of incense's odor with divine presence by overlaying it with the olfactory trace of something altogether more unsettling. It is a confusion that in some ways anticipates *Macbeth*'s presentation of a king for whom "heaven's breath / Smells wooingly" amid scenes reeking of diabolical gunpowder.

Yet *Titus Andronicus*'s dubious "smoke, like incense" is no doctrinaire debunking of Catholic ritual. Rather, I see it as a symptom of a widespread sense of confusion and loss generated by the abolition of censing and the pathologization of smell. With the removal of incense from the churches, English men and women came to inhabit a new olfactory universe in which sweet smells no longer suggested the presence of the divine. Of course, all representations of God—visual as well as olfactory—had been expunged not just from the churches but also from the playhouses. This transformation has been thoroughly studied with respect to the visual and verbal conventions of the early modern theater. But its impact needs to be understood also in relation to rituals of smell. The departure of God's sweet-scented presence from the sphere of dramatic representation is evident in those few plays that called for the burning of incense. The King's Men resorted to censing on at least two occasions. In Ben Jonson's *Sejanus His Fall*, performed by the company in 1603, stage directions describe a scene of worship in which a priest "after censing about the altar placeth his censer thereon."[61] And in Shakespeare and Fletcher's *Two Noble Kinsmen*, performed ten years later, a stage direction requests the conveyance of "incense and sweet odours" to an "altar" (5.3.s.d.). These scenes might seem to offer Catholic representations of the sacred, and indeed, Jonson was still a practicing Catholic when he wrote *Sejanus*. Yet in both instances, incense is an olfactory mnemonic not for God but for pagan deities—Fortune in *Sejanus*, Diana in *Two Noble Kinsmen*. As Gary Taylor has argued, to read these plays "as allegories of Catholicism requires us to ignore their paganism, to act as though the signifier was transparent, and therefore irrelevant."[62] The King's Men could burn incense as well as explode squibs; but the smell of incense in their plays was commandeered for self-consciously theatrical, and fictional, paganisms. To this extent, the plays exemplify Stephen Greenblatt's famous argument about how the Reformation emptied out the rituals of the church and, by turning them into forms of theater, made them available for appropriation by the playhouses.[63]

The ambivalent emptying out of Christian olfactory ritual in *Titus Andronicus*, *Sejanus*, and *The Two Noble Kinsmen* finds a far darker corollary in *Macbeth*. Like Herbert's "Banquet," in which the "smell of sinne" lingers in the nostrils while Christ's "perfume" has become literally immaterial, *Macbeth* shows that, after the Reformation, all that remained for the nose in religious representation was the foulness of the diabolical. Hence the stench of the play's squibs may have prompted associations with the scent of Catholic churches not because firework and censer smelled alike but because they had, in a prior olfactory episteme, presumed each other: the odor of holy scented-sticks was the missing valence in a formerly widespread olfactory binary of sweet and sulfurous. It is this binary that *Macbeth* so comprehensively undoes by collapsing the fair into the foul—or by making of the fair a desirable but ineffectual absence, as with Lady Macbeth's longed-for "perfumes of Arabia." It's hard not to see in this reference an exoticization, or a literal re-orientation, of the Roman Catholic past, as a result of which God's sweet smell has become an unobtainable eastern commodity.

Lady Macbeth's re-orientation of the Catholic odor of sanctity bears comparison with an episode in Luís Vaz de Camões's Portuguese epic *Os Lusíadas* (1572). Bacchus, who supports the Moors in their constant struggles with the Portuguese fleet of Vasco da Gama as it makes its historic voyage to India, tricks two of da Gama's men by luring them to a counterfeit Christian altar on which he has scattered "the sweetest incense / Of Arabia."[64] As in *Macbeth*, the suggestion of divine odor is placed under erasure by the invocation of "Arabia"—which, in the Moor-bashing *Os Lusíadas*, means shading the godly scent of incense into something Islamic and hence demonic. But for the Catholic Camões, counterfeit Arabian incense would still have presumed true Christian incense back home in Portugal. For Shakespeare's audience, by contrast, there could be no doubling back from godless Arabian perfume to a divine presence assured by English incense. Lady Macbeth's invocation of missing "perfumes of Arabia," then, doubly banishes the Catholic odor of sanctity: she expels it to a temporal as well as geographical orient, where it cannot help but retroactively lose its virtue.

The disappearance of godly odors from the English Protestant sensorium, and their usurpation by a whiff of oriental hell, is underscored by *Macbeth*'s one clear allusion to another travel narrative about Portuguese India. The text to which it alludes is not Portuguese, however, but English. Describing his 1583 voyage to Goa, the London merchant Ralph Fitch wrote that he embarked "in a ship of London called the *Tiger*, wherein we went for Tripoli in Syria; and from thence we took the way for Aleppo."[65] A scrambled version of this line appears in the third scene of *Macbeth*, when the Witches refer to a "sailor's wife" whose "husband's to Aleppo gone, master o'th'Tiger" (1.3.3, 6). What prompted Shakespeare to reproduce this detail from Fitch's travel narrative, and to assign it to the Witches, is unclear. But it may not be a coincidence that after arriving in Aleppo, Fitch journeyed east on "the way to Persia, Turkey, and Arabia." His oriental itinerary led him neither to Arabian perfume nor to incense, however, but instead—just outside Babylon—to "a mouth that doth continually throw forth against the air boiling pitch with filthy smoke." Of this "filthy" wonder, he observed: "The Moors say that it is the mouth of Hell."[66] It is tempting to speculate that Shakespeare, writing an exchange between characters who supposedly frequent "the pit of Acheron" (3.5.15), remembered the *Tiger*'s journey to Aleppo precisely because that journey, at least in Fitch's narrative, led inexorably to the stink of sulfur.

Fitch's more recognizably Protestant olfactory world, reeking of hell and bereft of godly perfume, is *Macbeth*'s. Lady Macbeth looks to the east, and to the past, for the fragrant odor of sanctity, but she finds instead only the sinful "smell of blood." Indeed, not just divine scents but holy rituals of any kind are strikingly absent from the play. Although Nevill Coghill has argued that an earlier version of *Macbeth* staged Edward healing scrofula, the playtext as we have inherited it—including the alterations by Thomas Middleton—is suffused with a sense of *deus absconditus*.[67] As a result, it reeks also of *bonus olfactus absconditus*. Yet the striking absence of fair smells in *Macbeth*, underscored by the pungent stink of its squibs, may have provided audiences with a reminder not just of England's Catholic past but also of a lost temporality associated with ritual olfaction. Sweet scents in the church brought eternity into living time; foul stenches in the theater, however, could only highlight a profound absence in the symbolic order: "nothing is / But what is not" (1.3.140–41). In performances of *Macbeth*, then, the smell of gunpowder could have done far more than evoke the recent Plot and a tangled web of theatrical associations with hell. For some playgoers, it may also have enabled a simultaneous longing for an older, now forbidden religious culture of the senses that offered more succor than the new religion could provide.

The antitheatricalists were certainly onto something when they discerned in the pansensuality of the public playhouses echoes of the Catholic Church.[68] What they failed to recognize, however, is that the theater did not and could not spell a straightforward return to the sensory world of the old faith. A play like *Macbeth* derives much of its power from its polychronic ambivalence: it powerfully evokes the scented rituals of the past, but that evocation less recovers the past than fractures the present. In short, the foul smell of gunpowder unleashed by *Macbeth* is temporally double, evoking a past-in-the-present. Such doubling is not surprising in a play that thematizes equivocation, "paltering" with its playgoers as much as its characters "in a double sense" (5.8.20). But the temporal doubling of the squib's odor suggests neither a playful plurality of interpretation (the carnivalesque perspective of the punning Porter) nor a diabolical duplicity (King James's perspective on the language of traitors, Catholics, and witches).[69] Rather, it is intimately connected to the palimpsest-like nature of smell itself, to its uncanny power to evoke multiple memories and associations from across a broad spectrum of time.

The odor of gunpowder in *Macbeth*, I have speculated here, might have prompted memories of contemporary political scandal, archaic stagecraft, and the suppressed religion that linked the two. But this list is by no means comprehensive. The stink of *Macbeth*'s squibs must have also provoked audience experiences that are simply too culturally elusive or quirkily subjective to be readily legible to us now. More attention by future Shakespeare scholars to the historical phenomenology of theatrical odors might help to recover some of these other memories and associations. But the particular challenge posed by the smell of *Macbeth* is less one of maximizing the recovery of Renaissance playgoers' responses than of recognizing the extent to which the vagaries of matter, time, and memory on the Shakespearean stage—and within material culture in general—demand special, and necessarily incomplete, practices of interpretation. Satisfyingly total as historical phenomenology's panoptic mappings of "moments" and sensory "fields" may seem to be, we might do well also to embrace the more speculative mode of polychronic reading I have begun to sketch here. In particular, this kind of reading can make us more sensitive to the temporalities produced by the untimely stage matter of Shakespeare's plays.

Macbeth uses gunpowder to explode the temporal partitions between past and present, and thereby blast open the "empty homogeneous time" of Shakespeare's Protestant moment. To read *Macbeth* in this way is to move away from our familiar modes of historicist interpretation. It resists turning the play into either a synchronic reflection of contemporary political scandal or a marker of diachronic transition between two different epochs, in which Catholic belief and ritual are apprehended solely under the mark of their supersession by Protestantism. Instead, my reading fastens on the play's recognition that the Catholic past is less divided from the Protestant moment than all too present within it—and with potentially explosive consequences.

One explosive consequence—the Gunpowder Plot's intended outcome—was never to happen. But a second consequence—audience recognition, even disputation, of something missing in the olfactory spectrum of the "new" religious dispensation emblematized by King James and his crime-busting nose—was one possible effect of *Macbeth*. Like Benjamin's historical materialist, who "seizes on a memory as it flashes up in a moment of danger" in order to explode the empty homogeneous time of the present, Shakespeare and the King's Men used their squibs as temporal explosives, transforming stage materials into untimely matériel that shattered the olfactory coordinates of Protestant time.

In the end, though, time in *Macbeth* is not simply explosive. As only befits a play so obsessed with doubleness, its untimely temporality can never be characterized in the singular. Ross remarks after the death of Duncan, "By th'clock, 'tis day,/ And yet dark night strangles the travelling lamp" (2.4.6–7). This day that is night, like the fair that is foul, suggests the explosive, upside-down world of apocalyptic prophesy—a world that, as we have seen, lurks in the smell of *Macbeth*'s gunpowder. But Ross's remark hints also at another temporality. The day-and-night world described by Ross is distinguished by a double time: in it, two seemingly different and even opposing moments are conjoined. Here the conjunction is deadly, with one of its elements strangling the other. But what if this monstrous conjunction did not entail a struggle to the death? What if its elements peaceably conversed? How might we imagine a time of conjunction in which, like a bearded witch, the two-in-one makes partners of supposed opposites and, in doing so, opens up the possibility of unexpected futures? It is to this possibility that I turn in the next part.

PART III

Conjunctions

Fig. 9. Henry Peacham, sketch of *Titus Andronicus* in performance, c. 1595; courtesy of the Marquess of Bath, Longleat House, Warminster, Wiltshire, United Kingdom.

It is not only the Bedouins and the !Kung who mix up transistors and traditional behaviours, plastic buckets and animal skin vessels. What country could not be called a "land of contrasts"? We have all reached the point of mixing up times.

—Bruno Latour, *We Have Never Been Modern*

How might we characterize the relation between the temporality of conjunction and those of supersession and explosion? They are in one crucial respect similar: all are materialized by palimpsest-like entities that conjoin multiple times. What distinguishes the temporality of conjunction, however, is its distribution of agency within the palimpsested object. Whereas the practitioners of supersession treat only the present as active and the past as dead or obsolete matter, and whereas the proponents of explosion grant agency primarily to the live traces of the past that dispute and shatter the present, those who practice the temporality of conjunction recognize the combined activity of all its polychronic components.[1]

Perhaps the most compelling advocate for the temporality of conjunction and polychronic agency is the actor-network theorist Bruno Latour. In *We Have Never Been Modern*, Latour argues that the fantasy of modernizing time, in which the present progresses from a primitive past toward an improved future, is enabled by a mapping of the supposedly insurmountable split between subject and object onto a sharp partition between now and then. This twin separation concentrates agency in one pole of each opposition at the expense of the other. In the process, modernity disavows hybrid actants—what Latour calls "quasi-objects"—that blur the boundaries between subject and object or present and past. The quasi-object (e.g., a greenhouse gas that is equally a natural and a cultural event, or Latour's toolbox that is both antique and modern) mixes up "different periods, ontologies or genres."[2] Because these multiple ingredients are all active, the quasi-object demands to be seen not as a singular entity but rather as an "actor network"—or, to use Gilles Deleuze and Félix Guattari's better known term, a rhizome. In botany, the rhizome is a sprawling, subterranean plant system—the potato tuber is the most familiar specimen—without a singular root; it functions by establishing connections between multiple nodes. For Deleuze and Guattari, the rhizome is a suggestive metaphor for any symbiotic system comprising supposedly disparate elements that act in concert. In their discussion, a wasp and an orchid constitute a rhizome, as do a human and her viruses. Deleuze and Guattari use the rhizome primarily as a figure with which to critique hierarchy and identity: unlike "arborescent" models of development such as the family tree, the rhizome's connections are horizontal rather than vertical, and presume a dispersed heterogeneity.[3] But the rhizome's difference from other plant forms is suggestive also for understandings of temporality and agency.

Indeed, the three temporalities I discuss in this book might each be profitably compared to a different model of plant life. The temporality of supersession is figured by Hegel's arborescent model of historical progress in *The Philosophy of History*: "It may be said of Universal History, that it is the exhibition of Spirit in the process of working out the knowledge of that which it is potentially. And as the germ bears in itself the whole nature of the tree, and the taste and form of its fruits, so do the first traces of Spirit virtually contain the whole of that History."[4] Like supersessionary time, Hegel's tree follows a singular course from origin to end. The germinal matter of the tree's beginning predicts its fulfillment in the future; and the growing tree at each stage of its development retains its past forms in the material residue of its rings. Agency is thus located only in the tree's present life, which builds on the matter of the past simply to ensure progress into the future.

The temporality of explosion invites a rather different model of plant life. In a critique of nineteenth-century historicism that draws heavily on Benjamin's "Theses on the Philosophy of History," Dipesh Chakrabarty argues for the critical power of what he calls "subaltern pasts," polychronic events that have been suppressed by the dominant historiographical narratives of modernization. These subaltern pasts, like Benjamin's vision of the oppressed past that "flashes up" in a present "moment of danger," generate "a disjuncture of the present with itself."[5] Chakrabarty characterizes the subaltern past as a *shomoy-granthi*—Bengali for "time-knot," a term that suggests a whorl in a tree or a joint in a stick of bamboo. Whereas Hegel styles history as a seed that grows straightforwardly into a tree, the shomoy-granthi is both an organic part of a growing plant and violates its supposedly normal course of development.[6] Chakrabarty's critique of historicism thus resonates with Deleuze and Guattari's critique of the arborescent model. Yet the shomoy-granthi still presumes a singular plant, even if its agency is transferred from the Hegelian principle of purposeful progression to a Benjaminian principle of heterodox disruption.

By contrast, the temporality of conjunction suggests the multiple, symbiotic agency of the rhizome. The various components of Deleuze and Guattari's rhizomes, like those of Latour's actor networks, can combine active elements from different times. But—as Latour argues—such networks are disavowed by a modernity that, insisting on its purification of linear, chronological time, displaces the specter of its own polychronicity onto "premodern" cultures, such as "the Bedouins and the !Kung who mix up transistors and traditional behaviours, plastic buckets and animal skin vessels."[7] As a result, it is perhaps easier to recognize the rhizome in the time of Shakespeare—or, perhaps more accurately, to recognize the time of Shakespeare in the rhizome. Consider Henry Peacham's famous illustration, dating from the mid-1590s, of a scene from a performance of *Titus Andronicus* (fig. 9). In it, Tamora, Queen of the Goths, pleads for mercy from Titus, the Roman general who has defeated her in war.[8] The characters' costumes and hand properties are a fascinatingly polychronic mélange. Titus, standing in the center of the drawing, wears a "classical" toga and laurel wreath; Tamora, to his right, seems to be clad in more "early modern" gear (including a crown), as are the halberd-clutching Roman guards on the left and Tamora's kneeling sons, Demetrius and Chiron, each of whom sports English doublet and hose. But the most strikingly polychronic figure is the character on the right—Tamora's lover, Aaron the Moor—who wears both Elizabethan clothes and classical headgear.

Peacham's drawing materializes the rhizomatic temporality of conjunction to a tee. And it does so less because it collates elements from "classical" and "early modern" times than because it renders each of those times plural and active, without subordinating one to the other. In the drawing, both past and present are temporally out of joint. Titus's toga is at odds with the play's Elizabethan moment of production, while the early modern gear jars with the classical time of the play. As a result, neither Roman past nor English present is a self-identical time. Rather, both are polychronic actor networks: a past-in-the-present, a present-in-the-past. Yet they also work in conjunction with one another to synthesize a visually distinctive and memorable playworld. Indeed, many modern cinematic and stage adaptations of Shakespeare's play have reproduced the polychronicity of Peacham's drawing. Julie Taymor's film *Titus* (2000), for example, combines visual elements (costumes, buildings) from classical Rome and fascist Italy in a way that is particularly redolent of Peacham. As Jonathan Bate has remarked of Peacham's drawing, "There could be no better precedent for modern productions which are determinedly eclectic in their dress, combining modern and ancient, the present as well as the past."[9]

At this point, however, a potentially serious objection suggests itself. In moving from orderly tree to disruptive shomoy-granthi to synthesizing rhizome, the relations I have sketched between the temporalities of supersession, explosion, and conjunction may seem uncannily close to the supersessionary logic of Hegelian Aufhebung. Indeed, a quick perusal of this book's tripartite structure might lead the reader to ask: Is supersession this book's thesis, explosion its antithesis, and conjunction its synthesis? In trying to un-think the dialectical teleology of supersession, then, have I simply reproduced it?

Conjunction *is* a synthesis of sorts. But it is a synthesis very different from Hegel's. Indeed, my account of conjunction draws to a large extent on Michel Serres's counter-Hegelian theorization of synthesis as a proximation rather than a transcendence of supposedly disparate elements: this synthesis performs not a Hegelian erasure of difference but rather an embrace of alterity.[10] Put in more rhetorical terms, Serres's synthesis operates in the anti-identitarian mode of metonymy, whereas Hegelian synthesis operates in the identitarian mode of metaphor. Metaphor asserts an identity between two different elements that transcends the difference between them; metonymy makes no such claim and instead presumes nearness rather than identity as the elements' principle of relation. If there is an echo of Hegelian Aufhebung in my tripartite distinction between supersession, explosion, and conjunction, then, it should be heard as a parodic and even untimely echo, inasmuch as my "final" temporality embodies a synthesis that refuses singularity, that opens up to heterogeneity, and (importantly) that does not supersede the previous two temporalities. Instead—like the Archimedes Palimpsest—the untimely matter of this book allows for the simultaneous articulation of multiple temporalities. Conjunction may *differ* from supersession and explosion; but it does not *cancel* or *transcend* them, as the matter I examine in the following two chapters makes clear.

This section considers two ways in which the temporality of conjunction is materialized by Renaissance theorists of untimely objects. In Chapter 5, it is legible in Margaret Cavendish's vitalist account of matter as a palimpsest, each of whose inscriptions are in touch with otherness. If Cavendish sees all matter as conjunctive, Chapter 6 reads the temporality of conjunction in the actions performed on, with, and by one untimely object: the handkerchief in *Othello*. The two chapters also show how the Renaissance treatment of conjunction might enter into conversation with more recent theorizations of polychronic matter—the feminine materiality of Hélène Cixous's *écriture féminine*, the crumpled topology of Michel Serres's neo-Lucretian physics. Hence the matter of Renaissance conjunction can be conjoined, in untimely fashion, with that of our own time. But perhaps such untimeliness is also very much timely. For, as Latour notes, "We have all reached the point of mixing up times."

FIVE

Touching Matters

Margaret Cavendish's and Hélène Cixous's Palimpsested Bodies

> *Cleopatra [is] infinite intelligence, completely applied to making life, to making love, to make: to invent, to create, from one emotion to draw out ten thousand forms of beauty, from one joy ten thousand games.*
>
> —Hélène Cixous, "Sorties"

> *As for* Cleopatra, *I wonder she should be so Infamous for a Whore, since she was constant to those Men she had taken. . . . If they say true Love can dissemble, they may as well say Truth is no Truth, and Love is no Love: but the Lover delivers his whole Soul to the Beloved. Some say she was Proud and Ambitious, because she loved those had most Power: She was a Great Person her self, and born to have Power, therefore it was natural to her to love Power.*
>
> —Margaret Cavendish, *The World's Olio*

Two women, from different times, from different worlds, touch in one body—albeit a body that is not one but multiple, palimpsested, polychronic. The scene? It, too, is multiple. Paris, 1975: the Algerian-French feminist Hélène Cixous brushes up against the Egyptian queen Cleopatra in the heterogeneous, intertextual body of Cixous's écriture féminine. Antwerp, 1655: the exiled English writer Margaret Cavendish, Duchess of Newcastle, rubs shoulders with Cleopatra in Cavendish's labyrinthine gallery of the mind where, in her words, "so many creatures be, / Like many Commonwealths."[1] Washington, D.C., 2008: Cixous joins with Cavendish in extolling the "infinite variety" of Cleopatra, or at least does so within the somewhat more finite variety of this chapter.

My two epigraphs may seem to set up a circuit of identification that plays out as a transhistorical syllogism. Cixous is Cleopatra (North African queens both, celebrating female fecundity); Cavendish is Cleopatra (aristocratic women both, loving female power); therefore Cixous is Cavendish. It is precisely these assertions of identity that I want to resist, however, not least because Cixous and Cavendish also resist them. In Cixous's "Sorties," Cleopatra is not possessed of a singular identity but is rather a protean male-woman whose sex is not one: "the feisty queen, to whom everything is becoming—scolding, laughing, crying—at every instant another face, at each breath a passion, flesh struggling with a desire for more love, more life, more pleasure, at every moment, the queen with ten tongues; she spoke them all."[2] Cixous claims not only to love Cleopatra but also to love *like* Cleopatra, embracing the other within herself. This embrace, which Cixous calls "Other-Love," models plurality as an alternative to patriarchal fantasies of singular identity.[3] Cavendish's interest in Cleopatra also chafes against singularity. Like Cixous, Cavendish is drawn to Cleopatra as a figure of a particular kind of love—one where the Lover delivers his or her "whole Soul" to the Beloved. This is no fantasy of union or merger: rather, it bespeaks Cavendish's recurrent interest in the movement of souls from body to body, so that—at least in love—the body becomes multiple, populated by two or more souls. The love that Cavendish describes thus aspires not to singular identity but rather to a conjunction of differences: a literally touching relation between parts of an irreducibly plural self. As Sara Ahmed notes in a discussion of the queer plurality of the hand, "What touches is touched, and yet 'the toucher' and 'the touched' do not ever reach each other; they do not merge to become one."[4]

In this chapter, I tease out the touching relations between Cixous and Cavendish. Like Ahmed's discussion of the hand, my account of these relations does not perform a merger or union. The two women may touch, but they cannot be made to speak in one voice: in addition to their different historical, cultural, and linguistic accents, it is impossible to reconcile Cavendish's royalism with Cixous's radical democratism, or Cavendish's pleasures of the rational soul with Cixous's jouissance of the flesh. Yet, just as they both join with Cleopatra, so can they be invited to talk with each other. What particularly interests me is how their touching relations can be illuminated by their different theories of matter as itself embodying a touching relationality. Both Cixous and Cavendish understand all matter not just to touch otherness—other bodies, other times—but also to contain within itself the trace of that otherness. This shared emphasis on tactility informs the interest each woman displays in reworking matter. Like Marx, Cixous and Cavendish insist on the material "sensuous activity" that interacts with, transforms, and is transformed by the physical object.[5] As we saw in the preceding chapter, smell facilitates such transformations; touch does too.

The sense most engaged in studies of Renaissance material culture, however, has been sight. Early modern objects tend to be described as they present themselves to the spectator or reader; they are frequently reproduced in photographs or period-piece illustrations. Both tendencies encourage us to apprehend the object as if it were separated from us by the glass screen of a museum display case. This separation allows us to satisfy our voyeuristic curiosity all the while respecting an appropriate distance—temporal as much as spatial—that not only preserves the object from a tactile encounter that might change it but also reifies it as a singular physical entity, preserved as a period piece in a frozen time capsule.

By contrast, touch—like smell—implies a more direct interaction with an object, one that makes the object inescapably plural. In *Touching Feeling*, Eve Kosofsky Sedgwick builds on Renu Bora's distinction between "texture" with one *x* and "texxture" with two *x*'s to underscore the effect—the visible supplement denoted by that extra *x*—of touch on the object: "A brick or a metalwork pot that still bears the scars and uneven sheen of its making would exemplify texxture in this sense."[6] "Texxture" is a particularly apt term for the matter theorized by both Cixous and Cavendish. Each sees touching matter as always joined by and containing within itself a supplement or other—like the extra *x* in "texxture"—that makes it multiple. Because Cixous and Cavendish repeatedly resort to metaphors of (re)writing to figure the inscription of that supplementary other, their theorizations of matter irresistibly lead to the palimpsest. But their palimpsests do not seek to perform the work of supersession by writing over previous inscriptions to press the claim of a new and improved truth. Nor do their palimpsests perform the work of explosion by resurrecting a forgotten lifeworld to dispute their current ones. Rather, they operate primarily in the mode of conjunction, bringing together disparate elements and placing them in conversation with one another. That is, they turn "texts" into "texxts" within which both old and new inscriptions are simultaneously legible and mutually transformed. We might characterize these conjunctive palimpsests as networks of dialogic tactility, networks that allow their various inscriptions to engage in touching intercourse.[7]

As Sedgwick notes, touching implies a relation not only of contiguity but also of erotic affect: "A particular intimacy seems to subsist between textures and feelings."[8] That is why I have started this chapter with two epigraphs about love, both of which may initially seem a world away from questions of matter and the untimely. Yet it is precisely the erotic and affective dimensions of touching that allow both Cixous and Cavendish to imagine a matter that not only embraces otherness but also constellates into unexpected and even queer assemblages across time. As Sara Ahmed says of touch in relation to queer orientations and conventional genealogies, "Touch . . . opens bodies to some bodies and not others. Queer orientations are those that put within reach bodies that have been made unreachable by the lines of conventional genealogy. Queer orientations might be those that don't line up, which by seeing the world 'slantwise' allow other objects to come into view. It is no accident that queer orientations have been described by Foucault and others as orientations that follow a diagonal line, which cut across 'slantwise' the vertical and horizontal lines of conventional genealogy."[9] Ahmed's analysis sheds light on how Cixous's and Cavendish's theorizations of touching matter presume a "slantwise" historiography. If queer orientations imply erotic pairings that deviate from the horizontal or spatial lines of genealogy (i.e., from normative male-female couplings and their offspring), they can equally disrupt genealogy's vertical or historical lines of lineal succession and suggest alternative modes of temporal relation. A queer historiography grounded in slantwise touches makes unexpected hookups across space and time, allowing past, present, and future anachronistically to conjoin and transform each other. Little wonder, then, that Carolyn Dinshaw has termed the principle behind her own anachronistic historiography in *Getting Medieval*—within which a gay Jewish man of the late twentieth century and a married Christian woman of the fifteenth century can enter into intercourse—the "queer touch."[10]

By theorizing a matter that allows times chronologically remote from each other to touch, Cixous and Cavendish offer a suggestive alternative to a historicism wedded to the reflex of what Jonathan Goldberg and Madhavi Menon have dubbed "heterotemporality"—that is, the assumption of an absolute temporal difference between past and present.[11] Cixous's and Cavendish's dialogic tactility ask that we rethink difference in a historical as much as a materialist framework. If the other is not opposed to but in touch with me, then a dialogic approach to the other of the past might seek less to quarantine it from, than palimpsest it within, the present. When read together, therefore, Cixous's and Cavendish's writings clear space for a historiography grounded not in period integrity and incommensurable historical difference but in the polychronic temporality of conjunction. Cixous and Cavendish each articulate fantasies of touching matters, in both senses of that phrase. These fantasies, materialized in their theories of matter and love, prompt both women to touch not only other cultures but also other times. In this chapter, then, Cixous and Cavendish are fellow travelers, undoing the bar of historical difference in and between their writing.

Cixous and the Matter of Metonymy

Two women, from different times, from different worlds, touch in one body—albeit a body that is not one but multiple, palimpsested, polychronic. In her essay "The Laugh of the Medusa" (1974), Cixous touches upon the snake-haired Gorgon of classical myth within the boundlessness of the female body: "We're stormy, and that which is ours breaks loose from us without our fearing any debilitation. Our glances, our smiles, are spent; laughs exude from all our mouths; our blood flows and we extend ourselves without ever reaching an end."[12] Five years later, in her *Vivre l'orange* (1979), Cixous meets the Brazilian writer Clarice Lispector within the multiplicity of "orange," to celebrate Lispector's ability to write about objects in ways that respect their material and semiotic plurality—as suggested by the polysemy of her title's "orange," which is indeterminately fruit and color, noun and adjective.[13]

Cixous's transition between these different affinities, from laughing with the Medusa to savoring the orange with Lispector, parallels the history of Renaissance studies' engagement with the "material" in the last quarter of a century. If Cixous's stormy, laughing female body resonates with the carnivalesque laughter of Mikhail Bakhtin's grotesque body and its material stratum—paradigms of the body that were popular in the 1980s, but for many now might seem hopelessly dated—her later turn to objects anticipates the more fashionable fascination with material culture of recent years.[14] These affinities suggest rich points of departure for dialogue between French feminism and Renaissance studies on the question of materiality. Yet they also suggest a significant difference. That difference, for me, concerns Cixous's conception of matter. Throughout her work, matter possesses a textual and tactile dimension that has been largely absent from the more positivist analyses of bodies and things in Renaissance studies.

This may seem like a rather surprising claim. After all, Cixous's "Laugh of the Medusa" and its sister essay/rewriting, "Sorties," have become infamous for their supposed biological essentialism. "Woman must write her body," Cixous commands in "Sorties."[15] Her imperative has been understandably slighted as a naïve reversal, a valorization of feminine corporeality over masculine logos. But this critique, I would argue, has misunderstood the very phrase "writing the body." The participle does not presume the ontological priority of the noun; rather, the body is materialized for Cixous in and by writing. Écriture féminine is a rewriting and displacement of the western patriarchal text of the body. In its phallocentrism, this text works to articulate not only sexual difference between a male body centered in one organ and a female body marked by that organ's lack but also metaphysical difference between an active, "convex" Form and a passive, "concave" Matter. This second difference gets recast, at least in Cixous's reading of Mallarmé, as a distinction between father and son that completely banishes—or "buries"—the woman and her body.[16] Hence she is simultaneously inside and outside the phallocentric text. But it is precisely this bipositionality that lends the buried female body a power to undermine phallocentrism by enabling "a transformation of each one's relationship to his or her body (and to the other body)."[17] For this buried female is not just the singular other to the self-same. In standing *both* inside *and* outside the economy of phallocentrism, she discloses the factitiousness of a singular identity that opposes rather than includes the other. "That doesn't mean," writes Cixous, that "she is undifferentiated magma; it means that she doesn't create a monarchy of her body or her desire. Let masculine sexuality gravitate around the penis, engendering this centralized body (political anatomy) under the party dictatorship."[18] Cixous here does not so much reclaim a female body prior to language as rewrite the patriarchal text of that body, diverting the agency of inscription from the "centralized . . . party dictatorship" to a nonidentitarian (because plural) "she" who "doesn't create a monarchy." This "she" creates a new body-text, "the vast, material, organic, sensuous universe we are." Her "material" thus resembles what Deleuze and Guattari, writing some years after Cixous's essay, call a Body without Organs: a rhizomatic mode of relationality in touch with otherness and hence irreducibly multiple.[19]

It is in literature that Cixous finds this "other" body and the "other" in the body.[20] That explains her title, "The Laugh of the Medusa," as well as her extended digressions in "Sorties" through the works of Homer, Kleist, and Shakespeare. But Cixous does not so much reread this patriarchal canon as rewrite it. And her rewritings of each male writer further undermine her supposed biological essentialism. In her account, the feminine "writing of the body" that undoes the phallocentric text has already been performed by "that being-of-a-thousand beings called Shakespeare"; his plays are scenes of endless becoming-other, where "man turns back into woman, woman into man."[21] For Cixous, *Antony and Cleopatra* exemplifies écriture féminine inasmuch as that play writes the body by writing the other into the body. If Antony (dressed in Cleopatra's clothes) and Cleopatra (wearing his sword Phillippan) embody how "man turns back into woman, woman into man," that chiasmus exemplifies Cixous's feminist dialogics, where seeming opposites cross over, find common ground, and enlarge that ground.

This chiasmic strategy characterizes her own relation with Shakespeare, who bears the traces of Cixous even as her text bears the traces of Shakespeare. In the English version of "Sorties," Shakespeare is never quoted as such; his words have either been translated back into English from Cixous's French translation, or are paraphrased in her poetic reworkings of the play. Similarly, Shakespeare haunts Cixous's own words in her many intertextual allusions to *Hamlet* and *Macbeth*.[22] The inscription of the feminine body thus amounts to a dialogic touching up of Cixous's writing with Shakespeare's and Shakespeare's with Cixous's: each is the *x*-factor that transforms the other text into a palimpsested "texxt." As Ann Rosalind Jones has noted, Cixous's écriture féminine is "a conscious response to socioliterary realities, rather than . . . an overflow of one woman's unmediated communication with her body . . . [her] work shows that a resistance to culture is always built, at first, of bits and pieces of that culture, however they are disassembled, criticized, and transcended."[23] But if Jones's concluding remark evokes the ghost of Hegelian Aufhebung, in which difference is transcended by a singular identity without remainder, Cixous's palimpsests insist on an irreducible plurality: for her writing chiasmically locates herself in the other and the other in herself.

The somewhat vexed term that she gives this chiasmic relation is "bisexuality." Cixous has drawn criticism for the heterosexual matrix of her conception of bisexuality, which can seem like a Platonic "wholeness" that leaves no room for anything beside the binary of male and female.[24] But this exclusivity is nonetheless what Cixous sets out to question. Importantly, she distinguishes between two types of bisexuality: the first is "a fantasy of a complete being, which replaces the fear of castration and veils sexual difference insofar as this is perceived as the mark of a mythical separation . . . Ovid's Hermaphrodite, less bisexual than asexual, not made up of two genders but of two halves. Hence, a fantasy of unity."[25] By contrast, "the *other bisexuality*" is "the location within oneself of the presence of both sexes, evident and insistent in different ways according to the individual, the nonexclusion of difference or of a sex, and starting with this 'permission' one gives oneself, the multiplication of the effects of desire's inscription on every part of the body and the other body."[26] Cixous's reference to "both sexes" still works to naturalize a totalizing binary system of male and female; but her "other bisexuality" offers a glimpse of a nonbinary logic predicated not on the closed specular economy of the phallus and its lack but on an expansive tactile economy that connects each "part of the body" to its neighbors, without beginning or end.[27]

We might characterize this redefinition of bisexuality in more textual terms: it is, in effect, an endorsement of metonymy over metaphor. Cixous's dialogic bisexuality is embodied not in identity between two different elements but in relations of touching proximity. To this extent, Cixous echoes Luce Irigaray, whose "The Sex That Is Not One" proposes a model of textual pleasure based not on the metaphorical operation of singular identification but rather on the metonymic register of contiguity. For Irigaray, the latter is exemplified by the two lips of the female genitalia, which touch rather than identify. Their contiguity models the plurality not only of woman's sexual pleasure but also of her speech: "What she says is never identical with anything, moreover; rather, it is contiguous. *It touches (upon)*."[28] A more textual version of this touching contiguity—materialized in "desire's inscription on every part of the body and the other body"—also informs Cixous's dialogics. Écriture féminine, then, is a feminist theory of metonymy that has implications for not only the (re)inscription of matter but also the formation of new relations in love, in writing, in political action—and across time. In this, Cixous "touches (upon)" not just Irigaray but also that "being-of-a-thousand beings" called Margaret Cavendish.

Joining Cavendish

Two women, from different times, from different worlds, touch in one body—albeit a body that is not one but multiple, palimpsested, polychronic.

Throughout her writing, Cavendish imagines the meetings of two souls in one corporeal location. In her story "The Propagating Souls" from *Natures Pictures* (1664), she relates how the souls of two lovers, after death, become permanently bonded in a celestial body: "These Souls being fruitfull, they left many of their issues, called Meteors, which are shining Lights like Stars."[29] Likewise, at the beginning of *CCXI Sociable Letters* (1664), she writes to an unspecified friend that "my mind and thoughts live always with you, although my person is at a distance from you; insomuch, as, if Souls dies not as Bodies do, my Soul will attend you when my Body lies in the grave; and when we are both dead, we may hope to have a Conversation of Souls, where yours and mine will be doubly united, first in Life, and then in Death."[30] If Cavendish fantasizes the souls of Platonic lovers becoming "united" within the body of the cosmos or the body of an individual, it is a union that nonetheless preserves the dialogic capacity of the other so that a "Conversation of Souls" might take place.

Such a conversation is in many ways the governing conceit of *The Blazing World* (1666). Cavendish's remarkable novella portrays the migrations and transmigrations of a nameless young woman, kidnapped by a lustful merchant and transported to another world that joins her own at its north pole. This new world is populated by hybrid creatures—bear-men, fox-men, bird-men, satyrs, and so on—who take her to meet their Emperor. So impressed is he by Cavendish's heroine that he makes her Empress, and grants her unlimited power. She sets up an academy of knowledge, where she is advised by invisible yet material spirits. Much of her curiosity about the natural world concerns the possibility of conversation between souls: "She asked again, whether souls did choose bodies? They answered, that Platonics believed, the souls of lovers lived in the bodies of their beloved."[31] The spirits also speak of a woman from another world, the Duchess of Newcastle (that is, Margaret Cavendish), who will assist her in the project of writing a "Jewish Cabbala." The Duchess's soul transmigrates to the Empress's world, and vice versa; the two become firm friends, even platonic lovers. When they tour England, the Duchess and the Empress enter the Duke's body: "And then the Duke had three souls in one body; and had there been but some such souls more, the Duke would have been like the Grand Signor in his seraglio, only it would have been a platonic seraglio."[32] The final act in this proliferating, quasi-erotic drama of platonic transmigration comes when the Empress realizes that war has been declared against her country of origin in her native world. She seeks counsel from the Duchess: "The Duchess told the Empress, that it was requisite that Her Majesty should go her self in body as well as in soul; but, I, said she, can only wait on your Majesty after a spiritual manner, that is, with my soul. Your soul, said the Empress, shall live with my soul, in my body; for I shall only desire your counsel and advice."[33] And, several interruptions notwithstanding, the two women cohabit happily ever after.

Thus the relationship between Cavendish and the Empress resembles Cixous's chiasmic inscriptions of "Other-Love": the Empress inhabits Cavendish as a creature of her literary imagination, even as (within the story) Cavendish's soul inhabits the Empress's body. In all Cavendish's literary transmigrations, her souls do not merge but join together in relations based on a touching affinity. Indeed, metonymic "joining" is Cavendish's characteristic mode of relationality. Referring to the simultaneous publication of her *Observations on Experimental Philosophy* and *The Blazing World* in one book—two souls in one body?—Cavendish argues that "I join a work of fancy to my serious philosophical contemplations."[34] This joining is thematized also within *The Blazing World*. When she says in her introduction that "I added this piece of fancy to my philosophical observations, and joined them as two worlds at the ends of their poles," she anticipates the mode of interglobal transmigration that begins the novella: "They were not only driven to the very end or point of the Pole of that world, but even to another Pole of another world, which joined close to it."[35] Joining characterizes not just the relations between Cavendish's worlds but also the properties of the Blazing World itself. It is populated by fantastical creatures whose transspecies hybridity assumes a conjunction rather than a purification of disparate elements. And in times of crisis, the World's ships are also metonymically "joined": "In a great tempest they would join their ships in battle array . . . for their ships were so ingeniously contrived, that they could fasten them together as close as a honey-comb without waste of place; and being thus united, no wind nor waves were able to separate them."[36] The rhizomatic figure of the honeycomb typifies the joinings of the Blazing World: for the honeycomb is an open-ended, decentralized assemblage that presumes a transspecies network of agency—that is, bees and flowers.

This joining together of disparate elements in contiguous "honeycomb" relations is crucial also to Cavendish's conception of the self, which she views not as unitary and irreducible but as comprised of myriad "worlds." "By creating a world within yourself," the spirits tell the Empress, "you may enjoy all both in whole and in parts, without control or opposition, and may make what world you please, and alter it when you please, and enjoy as much pleasure and delight as a world can afford you."[37] As Geraldine Wagner has noted, the creation of worlds within the self is a leitmotif throughout Cavendish's writing.[38] In her preface to *Natures Pictures*, Cavendish remarks that "in my Brain a large Room I had built, / Most curious furnisht, and as richly gilt, / Fill'd with my Lord, his Children and the rest / Of my near Friends."[39] And in one of the dedicatory poems to her *CCXI Sociable Letters*, we read:

> This Lady only her self she Writes,
> And all her Letters to her self Indites;
> For in her self so many creatures be,
> Like many Commonwealths, yet all Agree.[40]

Of course, the idea of worlds-within-worlds is a staple topos of the time. It features, for example, in the analogical cosmology of microcosm (or body) and macrocosm (or universe) that pervades Renaissance European medical and political writing, from Paracelsus to Hobbes.[41] But no matter how much the royalist Cavendish may have been influenced by the macrocosmic model of the sovereign body expounded in *Leviathan*, her fantasies of "many Commonwealths" within her do not assume a Hobbesian *corpus politicum* composed of irreducible parts.[42] Despite her avowed desire for a singular identity modeled on imperial sovereignty—she famously asserts in the introduction to *The Blazing World* that "though I cannot be *Henry* the Fifth, or *Charles* the Second, yet I endeavour to be *Margaret* the *First*"—Cavendish's singular self is infinitely self-dividing.[43] Through her letter-writing and her novellas she repeatedly pluralizes herself, finding the other within herself and herself within the other, as suggested by the many "Conversations of Souls" that she imagines.

This embrace of the plural is evident everywhere in her work. "English is a compounded Language," she argues, "mithredated of many ingredients . . . so, if I speak the English that is spoken in this age, I must use such words as belongs to other Nations, being mixed therein."[44] Mixture is equally the basis of Cavendish's theory of literary invention. When the Empress's soul tours England with the Duchess, she takes great interest in the theaters of London, about which the Duchess observes that "all or most of their plays were taken out of old stories, but yet they had new actions, which being joined to old stories, together with the addition of new prologues, scenes, music and dancing, made new plays."[45] Cavendish's fascination with linguistic joinings and mixtures extends to her experiments in genre. As we have seen, the fictional *Blazing World* is daringly joined with her scientific treatise *Observations on Experimental Philosophy*. Even *The Blazing World* is itself a self-conscious exercise in mixed genres: Cavendish tells the reader that "the first part is *romancical*, the second *philosophical*, and the third is merely fancy, or (as I may call it) *fantastical*."[46] Likewise, in the introduction to *Natures Picture*, she claims that "though my work is of Comicall, Tragicall, Poeticall, Philosophicall, Romancicall, Historicall and Morall discourses, yet I could not place them so exactly into severall Books, or parts as I would, but am forced to mix them one amongst another."[47] Here she redeems Peter Quince's much-maligned gallimaufry of "tragical mirth, merry and tragicall, tedious and brief" (*Midsummer Night's Dream*, 5.1.57), making mixture and contradiction, rather than singularity, the organizing principle of her invention.

Cavendish's fantasies of metonymic touching, infinite self-subdivision, and linguistic mixing are more than just feats of the imagination. Even though Virginia Woolf slighted Cavendish's writing, there has been a tendency to regard Cavendish as a kind of proto-Woolf, making a "room of her own" in an entirely privatized imagination.[48] This idealist view is questionable on two counts. As I have argued, there is a persistently dialogic strain throughout Cavendish's writing that qualifies her solipsism; she does not just subdivide internally but also finds traces of the other in herself, and vice versa. Just as importantly, moreover, Cavendish's fantasies of mixture and plurality are interarticulated with a thoroughly materialist cosmology. Tellingly, her characterization of English as a "compounded language . . . mithredated of many ingredients" invokes a popular medical substance, mithridate, whose supposed efficacy depended on its nonsingularity: it conventionally contained up to sixty-five different substances.[49] Cavendish's feats of the imagination are thus, like Cixous's acts of feminine writing, equally feats of matter. And, also like Cixous, she conceives of matter as irreducibly plural.

Cavendish Matters

It is difficult to pin down Cavendish's theory of matter. Throughout her writing, she continually reworks her understanding of the natural world. But refashioning is itself integral to her conception of matter. She asserts in *The World's Olio* that

> Nature hath not onely made Bodies changeable, but Minds; so to have a Constant Mind, is to be Unnatural; for our Body changeth from the first beginning to the last end, every minute adds or takes away: so by Nature, we should change every Minute, since Nature hath made nothing to stand at a stay, but to alter as fast as Time runs; wherefore it is Natural to be in one Mind one minute, and in another the next; and yet Men think the Mind Immortal. But the Changes of Nature are like the Sleights of a Juggler, we see many several Shapes, but still but one Matter.[50]

Here we see how Cavendish, even as she seems to respect the body/mind distinction, also destabilizes it; the mind is just as prone to the protean flux of nature as is the body—indeed, she sees in both "but one Matter," a "Matter" so universal that she elsewhere insists on the materiality even of the soul.[51] This theory of universal "Matter" is stated yet more succinctly in her *Philosophical Letters* (1664), where she claims that "the Ground of my Philosophy . . . is Infinite Matter."[52] But what exactly is this "Infinite Matter" that Cavendish sees as the basic foundational principle of the universe, and what are its properties?

Cavendish's materialism deviates from both the Aristotelian cosmology of the four elements and the mechanistic philosophy that is customarily narrated as replacing it. She rejects the irreducibility of the elements in *Poems, and Phancies* (1664): "The several *Elements* are all of one *Matter*."[53] One might think that her "Infinite Matter" would have a greater affinity with the materialism of Epicurus and Lucretius, for whom all compounds are composed of the basic building blocks of matter—atoms.[54] And indeed, Cavendish early on embraced the idea of atoms. In *Poems, and Phancies*, for example, she not only asserts that the universe is composed of small atoms of various shapes, sizes, and motions, she also compares herself to an "unsettled *Atom*."[55] Yet in her later writings, she comprehensively rejects atoms:

> I conceive Nature to be an Infinite body, bulk or magnitude, which by its own self-motion is divided into infinite parts, not single or individable parts, but parts of one continued body . . . it is impossible to have single parts in Nature, that is parts which are individeable in themselves, as Atomes; and may subsist single, or by themselves, precised or separated from all other parts; for although there are perfect and whole figures in Nature, yet are they nothing

> else but parts of Nature, which consist of a composition of other parts, and their figures make them discernable from other parts or figures of Nature.[56]

As this shows, Cavendish's later theory of matter is corporeal, infinitely divisible, and self-moving. In this, she departs from the then dominant mechanistic philosophy of Hobbes. She instead embraces the vitalist theory of matter, a heady brew of Paracelsan cosmology and new science.[57] Paracelsus had proposed that the universe was a self-contained economy within which each part had its own animating soul; for William Harvey and others, this animism provided a necessary corrective to the mechanistic, spiritless physical universe of Descartes, Hobbes, and the atomists, for whom the causes of motion could never be immanent within any material body. Like Harvey, Cavendish sought to restore agency to matter, making it rational and capable of choice. Hence for Cavendish, a billiard ball will move when hit by a cue or another ball, not because it is reacting to an outside force but because it *chooses* to move.[58]

Cavendish's conversion from atomism to vitalism was an unlikely development on two counts. First, the vitalist "moment" had long passed by the time Cavendish came to embrace it in 1663, having run its course in the interregnum; and, second, Cavendish's royalist politics were at odds with the radical liberalism of other vitalists, such as Milton. Yet, as John Rogers has suggested, vitalism appealed to Cavendish inasmuch as it allowed her to articulate a feminist materialism.[59] Hobbes's theory of mechanistic matter was masculinist, proposing an external male cause that engenders motion, reducing matter to passive feminine effect. By contrast, Cavendish makes her matter self-moving—that is, she propounds a principle of active femininity. If this very notion is, by the standards of her day, hermaphroditic, she pluralizes it yet further by insisting that all matter consists of inseparable rational, sensitive, and inanimate parts. The rational guides the inanimate, and is thus matter's agentic component. Hence Cavendish in effect dispenses with a primum mobile, as well as the masculinist theory of active form that is pervasive in western metaphysics from Plato to Hobbes.[60]

Cavendish's understanding of corporeal matter is not the same as Cixous's. In contrast to the psychosexual convulsions of Cixous's anarchic female body, Cavendish's body of nature is orderly in its organization and its movements. If Cixous's flesh is "explosion, diffusion, effervescence, abundance,"[61] Cavendish's dutifully heeds the choices of its rational components. Catherine

Gallagher has noted that Cavendish's royalist belief in sovereign government paradoxically underwrites her feminism.[62] But in Cavendish's version of vitalism, sovereignty is devolved from an absolute monarch to self-ruling matter, thereby suggesting unexpected common ground not just between theories of matter and politics but also between royalism and liberalism. Despite this residue of hierarchical thinking, Cavendish anticipates Cixous in making her corporeal matter the template for a tactile economy of unending otherness. Not only is Cavendish's matter dividable into animate and inanimate parts; it is also dividable into infinite worlds. In her poem "Of Many *Worlds* in This *World*," she asserts:

> Just like as in a *Nest of Boxes* round,
> *Degrees* of *Sizes* in each *Box* are found;
> So in this *World* may many other be,
> Thinner and less, and less still by degree;
> Although they are not subject to our *Sense*,
> A *World* may be no bigger than *Two-pence*.[63]

And in the lines that follows, she goes on to reflect on how a woman's earring may contain "millions of atoms," and hence countless worlds; in which case "ladies well may wear / A world of worlds, as pendants in each ear." In this vision, as in her fantasies of the self, worlds lurk within worlds; there is always otherness nested within any seeming whole. The gendered connotation of Cavendish's "*Nest of Boxes*" is highly suggestive, resonating as it does with Irigaray's discussion of the womblike *chora* in Plato.[64] But whereas Plato seeks to exclude the chora from his distinction between matter and form, the "nest" is for Cavendish the enabling maternal figure for a tactile matter that embraces, rather than excludes, the other.

Cavendish herself insists that the refusal of worlds within worlds is a masculinist stance. In a passage that beautifully illuminates the gender politics of her materialism, she questions the accomplishments of those men—including her namesake Thomas Cavendish—credited with circumnavigating the world: "It is said, that *Drake* and *Cavendish* went around the World, and others, because they set out of one place, and went till they came to the same place again, without turning: But yet, in my conceit, it doth not prove they went round the whole World; for suppose there should be a round Circle of a large Extent, and within this Circle many other Circles, and likewise without, so that it if one of these inward or outward circles be compas'd, shall we say it was the Circumference Circle, when it may be it [*sic*] was the Center Circle?" To which Cavendish wryly adds the observation: "Surely the World is bigger than Mens Compas, or Embracing."[65] It is perhaps typical of Cavendish that, when calling to mind the figure of the globe, she thinks of it not as a monad circumscribed by a singular surface but rather as an endless, contiguous series of circles or orbs, nesting within each other like Russian dolls.

Like Cixous's corporeal matter, Cavendish's global matter is textual, and in a variety of senses. We might remember that "textum" in Latin is a weaving or a joining together. For Cavendish, matter is textual in just this way: no matter can be in and of itself but rather must bear the trace of something else with which it is joined. This underwrites her conviction that, contra Aristotle, "there is no such thing as simple bodies in Nature; for if Nature her self consists of a commixture of animate and inanimate Matter, no part can be called simple, as having a composition of the same parts."[66] Her conviction is evident also in the materialist cosmology of *The Blazing World*, where "parts do only assist and join with parts, either in the dissolution or production of other parts and creatures."[67] Nothing is irreducible and individuated, which is why atoms are for her nonsensical; rather, everything is metonymically related to everything else, within the endlessly morphing—yet rational—body of nature.

Despite her insistence on the flux of matter, Cavendish insists that there cannot be anything truly new: all "innovations" are just reconfigurations—or, like mithridate, recompoundings—of extant matter. In the process, she repeatedly resorts to images of writing and rewriting to figure matter's transformations. We might recall what she has to say about new plays as rewritings of old stories. Likewise, the "new world" of *The Blazing World* is a self-conscious rewriting of old worlds. The invisible yet material spirits advise the Empress to write a "Jewish Cabbala" with any of the souls of natural philosophers from antiquity ("Aristotle, Pythagoras, Plato, Epicurus or the like") or modern times ("Galileo, Gassendus, Descartes, Helmont, Hobbes, H. More, etc."). The proposal to (re)write a "Jewish Cabbala" is in marked contrast to the supersessionary overwriting of Jewish stone tablets in Herbert's *Temple* and the explosive use of Hebrew writing in Stow's *Survey of London*. Cavendish's Jewish Cabbala implies a different temporality—conjunction with an antique yet living Jewishness that, rather than serving as western tradition's obsolete past or exploding it from within, nests inside and reanimates it. This dialogic relation with antique Jewish mysticism also informs the Renaissance

Hermetic writings of Giovanni Pico della Mirandola and Giordano Bruno.[68] But whereas Pico's and Bruno's interest in the Cabbala is born of a will to arrive at absolute truth, Cavendish's seems shaped more by a desire to form slantwise partnerships across space, culture, and time—a desire grounded in Cavendish's vitalist materialism.

The Blazing World's most slantwise partnership is forged when the (fictional) Empress resolves to cowrite her Jewish Cabbala not with any male philosopher, past or present, but with the (real-life) Duchess of Newcastle, Margaret Cavendish herself. This unusual relationship leads them each to write "celestial worlds" of the imagination, one of which ends up being the text of *The Blazing World*.[69] But like Cixous's écriture féminine, Cavendish's dialogic writing experiment does not produce a female space completely exterior to male philosophy. She instead rewrites Aristotle's matter, Van Helmont's vitalism, and Hobbes's organicism to articulate her own feminist materialism. Likewise in her *Observations*, she devotes an entire book to male philosophers, whose principles she adapts even as she vigorously disputes them.

Hence Cavendish's *writing* of matter thematizes her *theory* of matter: both entail a compounding of self and other, a production of figures that seem to possess singular integrity yet are palimpsested—or "nested"—mixtures. Rogers rightly notes the gendering of matter as feminine within the vitalist tradition, and for Cavendish this may have been one of the tradition's most appealing features.[70] But her matter is more than any one univocal gender can hope to define. It is "compounded," in Cavendish's words, "bisexual," in Cixous's, or, to use another term, favored by Bruno Latour, "hybrid." And, like Latour's polytemporal hybrids (recall his simultaneously modern and antique toolbox, or his characterization of his genes, some of which are "500 million years old, others 3 million, others 100,000 years"), Cavendish's compounded matter is resolutely polychronic, epitomizing the temporality of conjunction.[71]

The Polychronic Matter of History

In *We Have Never Been Modern*, Latour critiques the unilinear conception of time that underwrites modern history. "Modernization," he argues, "consists in continually exiting from an obscure age that mingled the needs of society with scientific truth, in order to enter into a new age that will finally distinguish clearly what belongs to atemporal nature and what comes from humans."[72] In Latour's analysis, modernity distinguishes its knowledge systems from those of premodernity on the basis of a supposedly progressive separation and purification of subject and object. As a result, premodern alchemy, astrology, and vitalist philosophy become impure knowledge systems, whose entities—evil planets, magical stones, rational particles—are endowed with powers that blur the boundary between subject and object, human and thing, culture and nature. Modernity's ontological separation of subject and object is paralleled by a temporal separation of now from then: in contrast to the purified self-identity of modernity's now, premodern cultures are polychronic, exemplified by those Bedouins and !Kung who (as we have seen earlier) "mix up transistors and traditional behaviours, plastic buckets and animal-skin vessels."[73] But according to Latour, the modernizing project of ontological and temporal purification has always been impossible—which is why, in his words, "we have never been modern." It is less that we are still "premodern," which would be to imagine ourselves in relation to a progressive chronology. Rather, our knowledge systems are ineluctably hybrid, full of "quasi-objects" (greenhouse gases, strains of HIV) that are neither purely natural nor purely cultural; and these quasi-objects are polychronic, combining elements from many times.[74]

Robert Boyle's air pump is, for Latour, the material object that both inaugurates modern history and discloses its impossibility. The pump was a hybrid, a machine that revealed the natural law of the vacuum and flouted the political law of the king's absolute sovereignty by being man-made yet operating independent of his jurisdiction. As such, it engendered two very different discourses that have come to be seen as incompatible—scientific description of fact in which objects are agents, and social contextualization of phenomena in which humans are prime movers.[75] In 1667, Boyle demonstrated his air pump at the Royal Society in London. Margaret Cavendish was present for the demonstration, the first woman ever admitted by the institution. It is nice to think that at the very moment in Latour's account that history supposedly slides into History—that is, at the instant when the modernizing project of disciplinary and temporal purification supposedly begins—Cavendish, a committed exemplar of hybridity and polychronicity, should have been in attendance.[76] Just as Irigaray reads the maternal chora back into Plato's inscription of masculine matter and form, so we might read Cavendish back into the modern purifications of politics and science, subjects and objects, modernity and premodernity. Irrupting into the scene of Boyle's demonstration, then, is another history, or rather, in Cixous's words, an "other history"—a history that, in its dialogic embrace of the other, offers an alternative to the modernizing history critiqued by Latour.[77] This is not a history that seeks to trace a diachronic progression through different epochs. Rather, it insists on unexpected conversations between diverse agents across time.

Cavendish was not keen on history as a genre. In "The Anchorite," she criticizes historians as inevitably partial and given to detraction in chronicling the lives of bad men. But elsewhere she offers a suggestive defense: history, she claims, is "brown and lovely."[78] In light of her portrait of Cleopatra, it is tempting to speculate that she was thinking of the Egyptian queen. Cavendish's "brown and lovely" history, in which she joins herself to Cleopatra, is perhaps reminiscent of Nietzsche's monumental history, which allows modern men to identify with figures from the past.[79] Yet Cavendish's is a historiography based not on identification but on "brown and lovely" contact with women from the past, the "Other-Love" advocated by Cixous.[80] Indeed, Cavendish would have understood the erotics of Cixous's Other-Love. In calling history "brown," Cavendish resorts to a common seventeenth-century colloquialism for sexually desiring: Simon Eyre lustfully addresses his wife as "my brown queen of periwigs" in Thomas Dekker's *Shoemaker's Holiday*.[81] A historiography oriented toward Other-Love offers an alternative to historicist paradigms within which past and present are violently partitioned, whether by the Aufhebung of Hegelian Spirit or the rupture of the Foucauldian epistemic break. Instead of insisting on the difference and distance of the past, Other-Love seeks out slantwise temporal relations within which supposedly remote points in time suddenly become touchingly close.[82]

These slantwise relations are exemplified by Cixous's and Cavendish's uncannily similar dialogues with Shakespeare. Even as they each dispute canonical male history—Cixous with her critique of phallocentrism, Cavendish with her critique of male circumnavigators—they nonetheless express an affinity with Shakespeare, particularly his creation of Cleopatra. For Cixous, Shakespeare is a "man of a thousand beings," each of whom nests in his and her fertile imaginations; as a result, those thousand beings cannot be confined to any one period. For Cavendish, Shakespeare is likewise the conduit through which she gains access to souls supposedly divided from him by sex and from her by time. As she remarks of Shakespeare, in terms that anticipate Cixous's, "one would think he had been Metamorphosed from a Man to a Woman, for who could describe Cleopatra better than he hath done?"[83]

Cavendish's fantasy of Shakespeare-as-Cleopatra performs a conjunction not only of different genders but also of different times. And her Cixous-like perception of Shakespeare's metamorphic transformation into a woman invites the additional conjunction of seventeenth-century English royalist and twentieth-century Algerian French feminist. Two women, from different times, from different worlds, touch in one body—albeit a Shakespearean body that is not one but multiple, palimpsested, polychronic.

Cixous's and Cavendish's historiographies, grounded in their readings of Shakespeare as much as in their theories of touching matter, do not simply entail contact between two singular bodies from different times. The contact they imagine instead presumes a temporal otherness always already inscribed within each body. Both theorize an irreducible polychronicity in writing and matter, a past-in-the-present and a present-in-the-past. It is notable that for both Cixous and Cavendish, the Shakespearean past-in-the-present takes an oriental form—one that supplements the Jewish Cabbala rewritten by the Empress and the Duchess in *The Blazing World.* Within their palimpsests, Cixous and Cavendish place themselves in touch with the Egyptian Cleopatra, who becomes part of, but not the same as, them. The self-exoticizing dimension of their Cleopatran palimpsests resonates with the soubriquet Cavendish acquired as "the Queen of Sheba."[84] This nickname says much about Cavendish's carefully cultivated outlandishness; but it may also give some readers pause. Cixous's and Cavendish's self-orientalizations arguably anticipate the tendency in the imperialist imagination of nineteenth-century Europe to reify the east as a seductive and feminine space irrevocably divided from male western rationality. But it is too easy to dismiss Cixous's and Cavendish's self-exoticizations simply as orientalist fantasies. For, as Said notes, orientalism's fundamental gambit is to insist on irreducible difference between west and east. By contrast, the dialogic matter theorized by Cixous and Cavendish demands that we think against and beyond the difference that informs any binary economy. *All* matter, for them, is self-exoticizing, inasmuch as it is always marked by the trace of an "other," temporal as much as sexual or cultural.

The transtemporal relations I have sketched within and between the two women confirm Latour's insistence that every actor network "brings together elements from all times."[85] Like Latour, Cixous and Cavendish insist on the polychronic properties of writing and matter. In this, they are hardly singular. Indeed, one of the greatest gifts that feminism continues to offer, whether to historical study in general or to early modern studies in particular, is its commitment to a conjunctive sensibility. That is, it presumes conversation—but not identity—between women (and, for that matter, men) across time. This sensibility has been increasingly disguised or disallowed in the name of situating the past within its historical moment. The dialogue between Cixous and Cavendish, however, suggests that it is time for both feminism and Renaissance studies to question time—at least the purified, linear time of historicism—and to imagine a temporality grounded in the queer touch that conjoins past and present.

Cixous's and Cavendish's relations with Shakespeare's North African queen materialize, in Irigaray's words, a sex that is not one; their relations also materialize, in Biddick's words, a temporality that is not one. We might be especially interested, therefore, in the temporal disturbances and conjunctions that accompany another of Shakespeare's African characters, in a play that has been famously slighted for its so-called "Double Time." I shall touch (upon) this play, and its untimely matter, in the next chapter.

SIX

Crumpled Handkerchiefs

William Shakespeare's and Michel Serres's Palimpsested Time

We must obey the time.
—William Shakespeare, *Othello*, 1.3.301

. . . *Some other time.*
—William Shakespeare, *Othello*, 3.3.55

Othello has long been regarded as afflicted by a temporal anomaly in need of correction. Cracking the infamous "double time" conundrum—do the events of the play take place over a day and a half or over a much longer duration?—was a favorite parlor game of Shakespeareans for more than a century, and the temptation to straighten out the play's story into an orderly, linear succession of events remains irresistible to many readers.[1] In this chapter, by contrast, I consider how the play refuses linear temporality. Rather than a singular progression that can be geometrically plotted, time in *Othello* is a dynamic field whose contours keep shifting, bringing into startling and anachronistic proximity supposedly distant and disparate moments. So if some of the play's critics have sought to heed Othello's injunction to "obey the time" by making its events march in lockstep with a unilinear chronology, I instead follow his advice, to Desdemona, to find "some other time" —not another moment in time but, rather, another understanding of temporality altogether.

This other temporality is materialized in *Othello*'s most untimely stage property: the handkerchief. It is untimely inasmuch as it keeps moving from hand to hand at the wrong time, and with disastrous effects. Desdemona inadvertently drops it when it is least in her interest to do so; Emilia picks it up and gives it to Iago, wrongly believing he wants it for himself when he hopes to plant it on Cassio; Cassio gives it to Bianca, mistakenly thinking that she will happily "take out the work" (4.1.148), that is, have its embroidered pattern copied; Bianca throws it back at Cassio as "some minx's token" (4.1.147) that suggests his infidelity to her; a jealous Othello misconstrues its sudden appearance as proof of Cassio's relationship with Desdemona. But if the handkerchief is untimely in its movements from character to character, it is even more untimely in its polychronicity. As we shall see, it is simultaneously antique Egyptian token and disposable European trifle, old pagan fetish and New Testament instrument of healing, obsolete emblem of true love and present marker of promiscuity. By quilting together old and new, pre- and post-, past and present—just as the play (at least in Iago's imagination) knots "old black ram" and "young ewe" into the infamous "beast with two backs" (1.1.88–89, 116)—the handkerchief hints at how *Othello* refuses temporal as much as racial purity. Rather, the play, like the handkerchief, trades in an impure, preposterous temporality that we might call crumpled time.

Explaining his topological understanding of time, Michel Serres resorts to a metaphor that has a serendipitous relevance to *Othello*:

> If you take a handkerchief and spread it out in order to iron it, you can see in it certain fixed distances and proximities. . . . Then take the same handkerchief and crumple it, by putting it in your pocket. Two distant points suddenly are close, even superimposed. If, further, you tear it in certain places, two points that were close can become very distant. . . . As we experience time—as much in our inner sense as externally in nature, as much as *le temps* of history as *le temps* of weather—it resembles this crumpled version much more than the flat, overly simplified one.[2]

In this chapter, I read Othello's napkin in proximity to Serres's handkerchief. Both help illuminate the crumpled time of Shakespeare's play, in which supposedly discrete points—different historical "moments" but also temporally coded distinctions of religion, race, and sexuality—are repeatedly made to be "suddenly . . . close, even superimposed." Though in their racial and religious guises such superimpositions unleash within the play the fear of miscegenation and Venetians "turning Turk," they are equally flashpoints for critique and the possibility of "some other time." Indeed, *Othello*'s handkerchief suggests how polychronic matter can activate a heterodox temporality of conjunction, one that disregards the entrenched partitions and distances informing the geometric lines of chronological time.

To this extent, *Othello*'s handkerchief is reminiscent of the palimpsested matter theorized by Cixous and Cavendish. Like the latter, the handkerchief operates in a metonymic mode, bringing supposedly distant entities into contiguous relation. In doing so it also suggests the erotics of joining that, as we have seen, is the hallmark of both Cixous's and Cavendish's materialisms. The handkerchief touches, in reality and in imagination, several characters' hands and faces, and thus conjoins disparate bodies in networks of sexual association. But more important, like Cixous's and Cavendish's dialogic matter, it erotically conjoins elements from different times. Like the actors' bodies and the theatrical squibs that I have examined in the second Henriad and *Macbeth*, *Othello*'s handkerchief shows how the matter of the Shakespearean stage is implicated in complex networks of agency that connect past and present in multiple ways. In this, it allows us to expand our understanding not just of material culture but also of temporality. So, too, does Serres's handkerchief.

Crumpling Time

> *The space* between*—that of conjunctions, the interdisciplinary ground—is still very much unexplored.*
>
> —Serres, *Conversations on Science, Culture, and Time*[3]

In chapter 5, I presented Hélène Cixous as Margaret Cavendish's twentieth-century traveling companion. But in terms of sheer eclecticism, the polymath Cavendish's closest counterpart in the modern French academy may be Michel Serres, the maverick philosopher who trained as a mathematician, teaches the history of science, and writes about classical literature and medieval religion in the allusive style of a poet-troubador. His books include studies of Zola, Jules Verne, and Hergé; Lucretius, Leibniz, and Carpaccio; geometry, the senses, and angelology. This brief list suggests how Serres's written work, like Cavendish's, moves relentlessly and insistently across traditional disciplinary and generic boundaries. If there is a common thread linking his disparate writings, it is this commitment to movement across partitions. Serres everywhere longs for synthesis—though not in its Hegelian sense of progression toward an end goal. For Serres as for Cavendish, synthesis instead implies an endless invention that produces unexpected combinations and conjunctions.[4]

Serres's disciplinary promiscuity is coupled with an almost dizzying rapidity of movement across temporal periods. Describing the experience of reading Serres, Bruno Latour marvels that "in the space of one paragraph, . . . we find ourselves with the Romans then with Jules Verne then with the Indo-Europeans then, suddenly, launched in the Challenger rocket, before ending up on a bank of the Garonne river. . . . you have a time machine that gives you this amazing freedom of movement."[5] This high-speed time travel is of a piece with Serres's drive for rapprochement between supposedly separate and even opposed elements. Hence he often conjoins the distant past and the present in surprising ways. Serres has, for example, scandalized some intellectual historians by reading Lucretius' poem *De rerum natura*, written in the first century A.D., as nothing less than "a treatise on physics."[6] Justifying his conjunction of classical poet and modern scientific discipline, Serres refutes the chronological view of time as linear and entailing stable, quantifiable periods and temporal distances. The assumption that "the past is bygone and the present authentic" additionally possesses for Serres a problematic quasi-religious component: "It supposes that between long-lost times and the new era there is some advent, some birth of a new time."[7] Serres turns instead to a variety of liquid metaphors—a river with turbulent eddies that flows upstream as well as down, a percolation whereby one flux passes through a filter but another does not—to suggest ways in which the seemingly distant past and present may come into unexpected contact.[8]

These liquid metaphors are consistent with Serres's reading of Lucretius as not just a poet of the atom but also a scientist of fluid mechanics. Historians of science may think of fluid mechanics as a modern knowledge system that has superseded Newtonian solid-state physics. But Serres insists that "Mediterranean antiquity had water shortages and, thus, thought only of fluids."[9] What particularly attracts Serres to Lucretius is his insistence on turbulence, the deviations or swerves in the fall of atoms which he calls the *clinamen*, and which resist the rigid, linear trains of cause and effect. Therefore Serres not only teases out parallels between Lucretius and modern chaos theory; he also advances a conception of fluid time that is thoroughly Lucretian, inasmuch as it resists the straight and narrow lines of chronology and allows for untimely swerves and divagations: "There is in Lucretius a global theory of turbulence, which can make that time [i.e., nonlinear fluid time] really understandable."[10]

Serres's commitment to dynamic fluidity may suggest an affinity with the imaginative world of *Othello*, which has to navigate turbulent waters not just metaphorically but also literally in the transition from its first to its second act. Having miraculously survived the storm at sea that sank the invading Turkish fleet, Othello reaches port in Cyprus and announces his arrival with a speech that recalls the Lucretian turbulence not just of fluids but also of love:

> If after every tempest come such calms,
> May the winds blow till they have wakened death,
> And let the labouring barque climb hills of seas
> Olympus-high, and duck again as low
> As hell's from heaven.
> (2.1.182–86)

But what is most striking about Othello's speech is not the liquid dynamism of its images, or any sense that the world is in a constant state of flux. Shakespeare expresses this view more forcefully with Antony's meditation on how his identity is as changeable as a cloud and "indistinct / As water is in water" (*Antony and Cleopatra*, 4.15.10–11).[11] By contrast, Othello's speech works through a proximation of two distant and opposed topological points: it insists that the "high" and "heaven" are unexpectedly contiguous with, and even occupy the same time as, the "low" and "hell." Such a conjunction of opposites, as we shall see, is typical of the play. It is typical also of Serres.

In this context, it is all the more notable that Serres's most graphic and extended metaphor of time is one not of liquid turbulence but of sudden, unexpected topological conjunction. After discussing the ways in which Lucretius can help him imagine a nonsequential time in which supposedly distant points touch, Serres proposes that it "can be schematized by a kind of crumpling, a multiple, foldable diversity."[12] He then turns to the extended set piece of the folded handkerchief in order to theorize a palimpsested temporality of conjunction. Serres argues that the spatial properties of the handkerchief illuminate the tension between time conceived geometrically and time conceived topologically:

> Classical time is related to geometry, having nothing to do with space, as Bergson pointed out all too briefly, but with metrics. On the contrary, take your inspiration from topology, and perhaps you will discover the rigidity of those proximities and distances you find arbitrary. And their sim*pli*city, in the literal sense of the word *pli* [fold]: it's simply the difference between topology (the handkerchief is folded, crumpled, shredded) and geometry (the same fabric is ironed out flat). . . . Admittedly, we need the latter for measurements, but why extrapolate from it a general theory of time? *People usually confuse time and the measurement of time*, which is a metrical reading on a straight line.[13]

Serres's caveat applies to readings of *Othello*. Critics of double time in the play have confused temporality and the measurement of time; for no matter how useful chronology may be in ironing out *Othello*'s events into a credible sequence, it inevitably neglects how the play repeatedly crumples and palimpsests time.

Serres's crumpled handkerchief illustrates a topological theory not simply of palimpsested time, however, but also of critical activity. Inasmuch as the crumpling of the handkerchief serves as Serres's metaphor for the forging of nonlinear connections between past and present, it foregrounds how the temporality of conjunction is generated by a creative act that couples critic and historical materials. As with Walter Benjamin's explosive recoveries of the past in present moments of danger, Serres's crumpling of the past into the folds of the present is an act of strategic proximation—it requires the artful labor of the critic, a labor that goes beyond mere empirical description of things as they really are or were. Serres thus allows us to recognize how our critical activities *create* the past and the present, less in the sense of making them up than of persistently transforming the web of relations that tether the past to us—and us to it. We less obey the time, then, than make the time.

The critic crumples time; but, as Serres points out, these crumplings are never *just* the invention of the critic—they are equally enabled by the contours of the handkerchief that she crumples.[14] Yet this formulation raises the question of agency. Throughout his writing, Serres imagines a "messenger"—in his early work he dubs it Hermes, and later an "angel"—who functions as a fleet-footed agent of rapprochement between seeming opposites, whether disciplinary or temporal.[15] Shakespeare would have understood. Indeed, he stages such an agent in the mercurial Puck, who puts a girdle around the earth in forty minutes and communicates between the diverse realms of human and fairy, aristocrat and yokel, classical Athenian and contemporary English artisan.[16] Yet in the case of Serres's handkerchief the agent of rapprochement is a thing. And likewise in *Othello*, the handkerchief as much as any human subject mediates between different worlds. Indeed, fold Serres's twentieth-century handkerchief and—voilà—it becomes Othello's seventeenth-century one. But what does it mean for a thing to mediate between different times? What does this tell us about its matter? And how, more fundamentally, can a handkerchief be an agent?

What's the Matter? Or, How to Do Things with a Handkerchief

> *You were an actor with your handkerchief.*
>
> —Ben Jonson, *Volpone,* 2.3.40

Of a play that obsessively asks "What is the matter?" (indeed, no fewer than twenty times),[17] it is perhaps only appropriate to ask: What is the matter of *Othello*'s most significant hand property, the handkerchief? This "napkin," we are told, is a small white cloth, embellished with a spotted strawberry pattern that may or may not be the mummified remains of Egyptian virgins' hearts. To reduce the matter of the handkerchief to its physical form or substance, however, is to repeat a misprision of the "material" that has arguably been a feature of much recent scholarship on material culture.[18] Indeed, if we follow Aristotle's classic distinction between form as actuality and matter as *dynameos*, or potentiality, we might regard what has been called "material" culture as "formal" culture. As Marx notes in his "Theses on Feuerbach," however, those materialists who attend only to the object's form ignore the equally material dimensions of praxis and transformation. Matter is for Marx, as for Aristotle, not simple physicality but rather dynamic material worked—or reworked—by subjects in their "sensuous" interactions with objects over time.[19]

This perception fits the dynamic matter of *Othello*'s handkerchief. The napkin is associated throughout the play with work, both as reified product (the "work" or pattern in the handkerchief that Cassio admires and asks Bianca to copy) and as labor in action (the work done on it by various agents, from the putative Egyptian sibyl who imbrued it with the dye of mummified maiden hearts, to Othello's parents who bequeathed it to their son as an heirloom that will govern his lot in love, to Iago who transforms a supposed sinecure of fidelity into "ocular proof" [3.3.365] of its opposite). Work is not only done on and to the handkerchief, however; it is seemingly done also by the handkerchief itself, as when Iago—having employed mention of it to induce a seizure in Othello—remarks, "Work on, my medicine, work!" (4.1.41). In its many complex associations with work, then, the matter of the handkerchief raises questions about the nature and extent of agency.[20]

Marx's understanding of matter locates agency at only one pole of the opposition between subject and object. As he makes clear in his essay on the commodity form in *Capital*, he regards the attribution of agency to objects as the hallmark of fetishism.[21] For Marx, the very idea of agentic objects surrenders not just to a category confusion but also to anachronism by lending credence to a superseded or primitive system of magical belief associated in Europe with pagan Africans. On this score, Marx was preempted by Thomas Rymer and his notoriously bilious reading of *Othello*. In his *Short View of Tragedy* (1693), Rymer railed against the undue importance that Othello, and *Othello*, attribute to a mere object: "So much ado, so much stress, so much passion and repetition about an Handkerchief? Why was not this call'd the Tragedy of the Handkerchief? What can be more absurd?" Echoing Emilia's denunciation of the handkerchief as a "trifle" (5.2.235), Rymer asserts that it "is so remote a trifle, no Booby, on this side Mauritania, cou'd make any consequence of it."[22] Rymer's division between south and north, Africa and Europe, carries with it also an implied temporal divide between a primitive and a rational understanding of objects: only a pagan African can be expected to make so much "consequence of," that is, attribute causative power to, a mere thing; Shakespeare and his audiences should not be so anachronistically foolish.[23] This conception of agency persists in much modern criticism of the play. Even as they disavow Rymer's racism, many of *Othello*'s modern readers see the whole point of the handkerchief as its insignificance: it is simply a blank screen onto which the play's characters project and reify their fantasies.[24]

Yet Rymer's response to the play recognizes the power that *Othello* bestows on the handkerchief. Rather than offering a demystification of the fetishistic attribution of agency to an object, the play is, as Rymer says, a "Tragedy of a Handkerchief," dominated by an object that behaves like a subject. Stagings of *Othello* have often confirmed this tendency. As (the appropriately named) Julia Hankey notes of Sam Mendes's 1997 National Theatre production, in which the handkerchief was left on stage during the intermission, Othello's napkin seemed to be "challenging one of us to pick it up and prevent a tragedy."[25] And for some critics, the handkerchief is indeed a magical agent. The best instance is Robert Heilman, whose entire book *Magic in the Web* is devoted to the conceit of the handkerchief's magical power: far from being only a "trivial object," it is for Heilman a "talisman" that has "the dramatic role of leading us in to the crowning statement in the play of love."[26] Indeed, the ascription of magical power to the napkin is now a deeply engrained habit in literary criticism, as is shown by its repeated characterization as the "fatal handkerchief" that inflicts mortal harm on Othello and Desdemona, or by its use as the active subject of a medley of verbs (the handkerchief makes, causes, leads, and so on).[27]

But *Othello*'s suggestion that a handkerchief might acquire a humanlike agency has never quite shrugged off the aura of the absurd, as is evidenced by a long history of responses to the play that range from Rymer's outrage to Monty-Pythonesque silliness. A Web site devoted to tricks with a handkerchief instructs its browsers on how to fold a figure called the Orator; and it does so in a way that, even as it suggests Serres's crumpled handkerchief, explicitly invokes *Othello*:

> To "make up" the Orator, tie a common knot in corner A of the handkerchief. . . . Fit the knot on the forefinger of left hand, . . . draw the sides B and C over the thumb and middle finger to form the arms, and our Orator stands forth . . . ready to entertain his audience. If, now, the speech of Othello, beginning, "Most potent, grave, and reverend seigniors," or, indeed, any sounding remarks, be given, accompanied with appropriate gestures of its arms and solemn nods of its head, the ludicrous effect of the Orator will cause great fun and many a merry laugh.[28]

This set of instructions not only surreally transforms a handkerchief into an Orator, an object into a subject. By invoking the opening lines of Othello's self-defense before the Venetian court (1.3.76), it also reduces the title character of Shakespeare's tragedy to the title character of Rymer's "Tragedy of a Handkerchief." For all its delicious absurdity, the Orator registers in pitch-perfect fashion the discomforting challenge the play poses to conventional understandings of agency, and hence to tragedy. After all, Othello's self-defense amounts to an artful argument that he has had no agency in his relationship with Desdemona—that *she* picked him up (as if he were simply a handkerchief?), rather than vice versa. And Desdemona herself proceeds to adopt this strategy: rather than "confess that she was half the wooer," as Brabanzio asks (1.3.175), she characterizes her desire for Othello as a "duty" (1.3.185), a mechanical necessity rather than an active choice. The court scene thus only adds to the sense of an upside-down world in which a mere napkin perversely has more agency than its tragic handlers.

Discomfort with the handkerchief's agency arguably suffuses even those readings of *Othello* that insist on it. One symptom of this discomfort is a pronounced and disproportionate tendency to focus on the *meaning* rather than the *matter* of the handkerchief: Heilman, for instance, argues that the handkerchief "guides us beyond the literal object into the symbolization of love."[29] This has the effect of transforming the napkin from magical textile into marvelous text that, while more than mere trifle, falls short of out-and-out supernatural talisman. It is rather a fetish in a Freudian sense, a substitute for a phantasmatic whole—in this case, a redemptive love—that the handkerchief's beholders both in and out of the play project onto it, whether through symbolization or narrative. And if the handkerchief is the bearer of meaning, it is because its handlers and/or readers have made it so. Subjects are thus reinstated as agents—or, rather, as literary critics hungry for sense. The handkerchief, a blank surface inscribed with uncertain Egyptian emblems, is transmuted into a cryptic Rosetta stone that promises a treasure of meaning to the artful decoder, a meaning that nonetheless derives from the decoder. Just as the napkin of *A Lover's Complaint* is covered with "conceited characters" onto which its love-afflicted owner projects and reads her own story, so do the strawberries embroidered on Othello's handkerchief provide the play's critics, desirous for meaning, with suggestive reading material that provides opportunities for them to exercise their critical agency.[30]

Psychoanalytic critics once glossed the strawberries as a sign of Othello's mother's nipple or of phallic power; more recently, they have interpreted it also as a signifier of menstrual blood and the threat of maternity.[31] Historically minded readers have pointed out that in the Renaissance strawberries signified virtue, while hypocritical virtue was often emblematized by a strawberry plant with an adder hiding beneath it.[32] Feminist critics have noted that Iago's description of the handkerchief as "spotted"—a term that suggests not only a moral blemish but also syphilitic infection—transforms the strawberries, at least in Othello's mind, into symbols of women's always already fallen nature.[33] And readers over the past three decades have been particularly influenced by Lynda E. Boose's interpretation of the strawberries as simultaneously an early modern emblem of virginity and a homologue to the bloodstains on publicly displayed matrimonial sheets—a convention that, with *Othello*'s climax, finds a grisly analogue in the stage bed's sheets, which bear the bloody traces not of consummated nuptials but of murder and suicide.[34]

These ingenious displays of critical endeavor supplement the creative interpretive activity to which the handkerchief is subjected in the play itself. In act 3, Othello tells Desdemona how

That handkerchief
Did an Egyptian to my mother give.
She was a charmer, and could almost read
The thoughts of people. She told her, while she kept it
'Twould make her amiable, and subdue my father
Entirely to her love; but if she lost it,
Or made a gift of it, my father's eye
Should hold her loathed, and his spirits should hunt
After new fancies.
(3.4.53–61)

The handkerchief's magical power, Othello claims, derives not only from its provenance in an exotic feminine world of mothers and magical charmers but also from the unusual composition of its matter:

A sibyl that had numbered in the world
The sun to course two hundred compasses
In her prophetic fury sewed the work.
The worms were hallowed that did breed the silk,
And it was dyed in mummy, which the skilful
Conserved of maidens' hearts.
(3.4.68–73)

Despite these elaborate accounts of how the handkerchief came to his mother—via an Egyptian charmer—from a sibyl-weaver, Othello later claims it to be "an antique token / My father gave my mother" (5.2.223–24).[35] With the competing and conflicting stories the play's characters and critics read into it, the handkerchief emerges less as a fetish than as a palimpsest, a writing surface upon which multiple signs and narratives are inscribed and erased.

I am rather drawn to the idea of the handkerchief as a palimpsest, for reasons I explain below. But if we see this palimpsest as simply a text to be interpreted, even if that meaning is multivalent, we cannot adequately address the problems of matter and agency that it raises.[36] To regard the handkerchief as a bearer of meaningful marks that transcend its dangerous matter is to repeat a problem thematized in the play. Throughout *Othello*, the image of the written page serves as the basis of the social or symbolic order; yet the multiple marks on the page, rather than guaranteeing the fabric of the social, can spoil it by collapsing back into the grimy materiality they would supersede. "Was this fair paper, this most goodly book," asks Othello of the supposedly fallen Desdemona, "Made to write 'whore' upon?" (4.2.73–74).[37] Similarly, the handkerchief is begrimed with the traces of many narratives that, rather than supplying a plenitude of meaning, unravel the social even as they promise it. In this, the handkerchief underscores how its accumulated dirt signifies both cultural decorum (i.e., the polite evacuation of bodily fluids into its folds) and the abject persistence of that which threatens and is supposedly excluded from the social.

Rather than focusing simply on what the handkerchief might *mean*, therefore, we should think also about what the handkerchief *does*—or more specifically, what is done with the handkerchief, and what couldn't be done without it. A useful starting point for this shift of emphasis is suggested by a line from Ben Jonson's *Volpone*, in a sequence that has itself been read as a comic reworking of the handkerchief subplot in *Othello*.[38] Celia, locked in her house by her jealous old husband Corvino, spies Volpone, disguised as a mountebank, addressing a crowd beneath her window. When he asks for a handkerchief from the audience, Celia throws hers down to him. Corvino, convinced that the gesture betrays her wayward sexual desires, reprimands Celia with the intriguing remark that I have quoted as the epigraph to this section: "You were an actor with your handkerchief." Corvino's accusation insists that Celia needs a stage property to do what she did—that she has become an actor in a drama of cuckoldry only with the help of an accessory that, from another Venetian play, we already associate with the specter of sexual infidelity. In the process, the syntax of the line also works to give star cobilling to the handkerchief, suggesting that Celia and Handkerchief are a sinister double act, a vaudeville duo performing at Corvino's expense.

This double act necessitates expanding our understanding of agency, and moving beyond binaries of agentic subject and passive object as well as the "category confusion" of the magical fetish. Rather than understand the handkerchief as either magical or passive, we might instead explain its relation to agency with recourse to Bruno Latour's theory of mediation and the actor network. For Latour, mediation does not entail, as it is customarily understood to do, an intermediary medium of transmission between two preexisting entities such as subject and object. Rather, mediation materializes networks of agency comprising multiple actants (whether humans, animals, things, or knowledge systems), which collectively produce something different from what any of their components can do alone.[39] From this vantage point, Serres's crumpled handkerchief is but one actant in a mediated actor network. It is not a lone object, nor can it generate points of topological connection between its folds or pleats by itself. It can only be crumpled by the action of the handkerchief crumpler, with whom it forms a network. But in turn it too is an actor, contributing to the collective agency of its mediation with the crumpler, who could not do what he does without it.

Othello's handkerchief enters into a diverse array of actor networks: Desdemona and handkerchief is, if only for Othello, a network performing matrimonial chastity and honor; Iago and handkerchief is a network that induces a seizure in Othello; Bianca and handkerchief, spied by Othello and egged on by Iago, is a network performing "ocular proof" of Desdemona's guilt (3.3.365). There are other, more mundane networks into which the handkerchief enters: it is used to bandage an aching head (3.3.289–90) and "wipe [a] beard" (3.4.440), or blow a nose, clean an ear, and wipe a mouth ("nose, ears, and lips" [4.1.39–40]). Peter Stallybrass has been one of the few readers of *Othello* attentive to how the meaning of the handkerchief cannot be extricated from the bodily actions it performs: it is a powerful signifier of dirtiness and promiscuity precisely because of its close association with the body's apertures and their effluvia.[40] We should be wary, however, of subordinating what is *done* with the handkerchief to the question of what it ultimately *means*. There are too many networks within which it acts for its meaning ever to settle. As the handkerchief binds together different people—Othello's mother and father, Othello and Desdemona, Emilia and Iago, Cassio and Bianca, Cassio and Desdemona, Othello and Iago—it simultaneously stitches and unstitches its meanings. "It is not words that shakes me thus," insists Othello as he falls prey to Iago's subliminal linking of the handkerchief to Desdemona's sexual infidelity (4.1.38–39). Nevertheless, Othello does respond here to the handkerchief as if it were indeed "words," albeit of a special kind. For the handkerchief is, within the syntax of the play's actor networks, less a meaningful noun than a free-floating part of speech. It is a thing turned into a conjunction: an and-kerchief. And as a conjunction, it serves to bind together not only different meanings and different people but also different times.

Preposterous Time

In *Shakespeare from the Margins*, Patricia Parker exfoliates the meanings of the "preposterous" in Shakespeare's writing in general and in *Othello* in particular.[41] The word appears twice in the play, both times in connection with perverse sexuality: Brabantio thinks it impossible "for nature so preposterously to err" (1.3.62) while speculating about how Othello could have induced Desdemona to fall in love with him, and Iago, in conversation with Roderigo, claims that without the exercise of reason over lust, "the blood and baseness of our natures would conduct us to most preposterous conclusions" (1.3.323–24). As Parker rightly notes, the preposterous disrupts linear time: the term is etymologically derived from "prae" (before) and "posterior" (after), and thus implies the act of putting afterward what should be temporally as well as socially prior. Indeed, *Othello* is a play that pivots on the disruption of social sequences: the "old gradation," Iago complains, has been forgotten (1.1.36). In Parker's discussion, preposterous temporality is a synonym for inversion—for putting the cart before the horse, Cassio before Iago, the general's wife before the general.[42] But the preposterous disruption of "first before, then after" need not take only the equally linear form of "first after, then before." It can also materialize as a coevalization of "before and after" that imagines, in the words of Kathleen Biddick, a temporality that is not one.[43] This double time takes the form not of a sequence, or even an inverted sequence, but rather a proximation and superimposition of supposedly disparate temporal points, as materialized by Serres's crumpled handkerchief.

This other preposterous time abides by the conjunctive antilogic of "both . . . and," of *coincidentia oppositorum* rather than the identitarian and sequential logic of "either . . . or" or "first . . . then." *Othello* is riddled with such conjunctions. The play famously yokes the opposing generic traits of comedy and tragedy.[44] But its coincidentia oppositorum extend crucially also to realms of human identity: to sexuality—strawberries that suggest both virginity and sexual activity, Othello's "I think my wife be honest, and think she is not" (3.3.386); to race—the coupling of old black ram and young white ewe in the beast of two backs, the Othello "who is more fair than black" (1.3.288), the "black weed" Desdemona "Who art so lovely fair" (4.2.67–88); and to religion—Christians who are damned as Turks, Othello who in his final speech is simultaneously "circumcised dog" (5.2.354) and defender of Christian honor.

These contradictory identities are all temporally coded. Marital fidelity is a thing of the past and promiscuity is current ("the hearts of old gave hands, and our new heraldry is hands, not hearts" [3.4.44–45]); black is "old" and white is "young"; Christianity is recent and "circumcised dogs" are superseded (no matter that Islam comes historically after Christianity). The very conditions of *Othello*'s performance in the open-air Globe reinforce the sense of a temporal coincidentia oppositorum. Much of the play emphatically takes place at nighttime—Othello and Desdemona's moonlit elopement, Iago and Roderigo's interruption of Brabanzio's sleep, the Venetian council's special late meeting, Iago and Cassio's drunken after-hours celebration, Desdemona's bedtime murder, Othello's suicide—yet *Othello* would have been performed at the Globe in the light of day. This required from its audience less a suspension of disbelief than a willingness to abide with contradiction, temporal as much as conceptual. A preposterous double time, then, is the condition of the play not only as read but also in its original conditions of performance.[45]

Those who have wanted to solve *Othello*'s double-time conundrum have sought to impose on the play an orderly logic of "pre" followed by, rather than coeval with, "post." They thus see time as a unilinear absolute with which the characters must march in lockstep: as Othello says, "We must obey the time" (1.3.298). Othello's initial obedience to unilinear temporality is supposedly illustrated in his own progression from pagan slave to free Christian. In a brilliant reading, Julia Reinhard Lupton has recognized the play's immersion in the Pauline typological imaginary, with its insistence on a Jewish "before" superseded by a Christian "after." As she notes, however, the play unsettles the unidirectional temporality of this supersession. Under Iago's influence, Othello undergoes a preposterous typological reversion that sees him not only "*paganized*—made exotic, savage, barbarian," but also "*Islamicized and Judaized*, brought back into contact with a law that should have been dissolved by the rite of baptism."[46] For many readers, however, Othello's final speech supposedly corrects any such lapse by having his inner Christian vanquish and supersede both his inner Turk and his base "Indian" or "Iudean" (5.2.346). Thus does the play supposedly expel the specter not just of religious hybridity but also of a preposterous temporality in which "before" and "after" are simultaneous. Othello and the play obey the time again.

But are hybridity and preposterous time simply specters that the play conjures so that they may be exorcised? In a richly suggestive essay, Bruce Boehrer has noted how *Othello* offers two discourses of the hybrid. One is Iago's. His is a phobic discourse that registers miscegenation as a monstrous bestial and even interspecies act, as instanced in his remark to Brabanzio that "you'll have your daughter covered with a Barbary horse" (1.1.113). But if Iago excoriates hybridity as an antisocial pollution that must be expunged, Othello—at least in Boehrer's analysis—welcomes hybridity as a symbiotic principle of communion and reciprocal transformation in the manner of a Deleuzian rhizome. Hence whereas "Iago exists to keep the self—and selfhood—intact," Boehrer sees Othello as embodying "the impulse to commune, to unite, to extend and escape the self in ways that ultimately entail a rewriting and eventually an unwriting of personal identity." Boehrer acknowledges that the play's monstrous and symbiotic hybrids alike conflate not only disparate "places and people" but also "disparate times"; he doesn't, however, delve into the latter possibility.[47] Yet Iago's phobic response to hybridity is arguably an example of what Johannes Fabian, in *Time of the Other*, characterizes as anthropology's denial of coevalness.[48] Iago's hybrids are temporally coded in such a way as to make them preposterous anachronisms—the "beast with two backs" is, after all, both "old black ram" and "young white ewe" (1.1.116, 88–89)—that should not be allowed to couple. In this, Iago is arguably not only the play's anthropologist but also its historicist, seeking even more than Othello does to obey the time by keeping old and young, then and now, chastely separated.

Othello's may be, as Boehrer suggests, a utopian rhetoric of temporal as well as interpersonal communion. One might counter, however, that the hybrids imagined by Othello are less utopian than dystopian: after all, he is one of the play's most insistent mouthpieces for the fear of Christians turning Turk.[49] And even if his relationship with Desdemona represents an unconventional yoking of temporally disparate categories of race as well as age, he anxiously registers it as a potentially volatile and perverse disjunction. But the real work of dissolving the distance between disparate temporal points in the play is performed not by Othello in particular or even by subjects in general. Rather, it happens with and around the handkerchief—or, more precisely, with and around the and-kerchief networks that work to couple temporally coded differences of religion and race.

What may initially seem to be merely a fashionable European trifle increasingly acquires the semblance of an antique African fetish, or *fetisso*.[50] The Dutch travel writer Peter Marees writes scornfully in 1600 about how Africans not only attribute magical power to their "fetissos," which he dismisses as mere "toyes and trifles," but also give them food and drink.[51] So when Emilia—who also refers to the handkerchief as a "trifle"—tells us that Desdemona "so loves the token . . . that she reserves it evermore about her / To kiss and talk to" (3.3.297, 299–300), the handkerchief doubles as both Venetian love bauble and African idol. Other and-kerchief networks in the play conjoin different African and European elements. Othello tells Desdemona that his mother acquired the handkerchief from "an Egyptian charmer"; but his tale of the sibyl who wove the handkerchief in a "prophetic fury" also channels the "furor profetico" of Ariosto's Cassandra in *Orlando Furioso*.[52] And the attention Iago draws to the handkerchief's red spots evokes what was regarded simultaneously as a superseded Jewish, a modern Greek, and an exotic African custom. Robert Burton remarks in *The Anatomy of Melancholy* that "in some parts of *Greece* at this day, like those olde *Iewes*, they will not beleeue their wiues are honest, *nisi pannum menstruatum prima nocte videant*"—unless they see on the first night a blood-stained cloth.[53] Yet the spots recall also a passage in Leo Africanus's *Geographical Historie of Africa*, a text that we know Shakespeare drew on when writing *Othello*. Leo recounts that on wedding nights in Fez, "a certaine woman standeth before the bride-chamber doore, expecting till the bridegroome hauing defloured his bride reacheth her a napkin stained with blood, which napkin she carrieth incontinent and sheweth to the guestes, proclaiming with a lowd voice, that the bride was euer till that time an vnspotted and pure virgin."[54]

If the handkerchief is thus tethered to the practices of antique cultures and religions, it is also redolent of the new covenant of Christianity; when Desdemona seeks to cure Othello's headache by "binding" his "forehead" with the handkerchief, Shakespeare's audiences could have subliminally associated it also with the words of Acts 19:11–12, in which "God wrought special miracles by the hands of Paul: so that from his body were brought unto the sick handkerchiefs or aprons, and the diseases departed from them." The handkerchief's Christian powers, however, readily devolve into superseded Catholic trumpery. By calling the napkin a "trifle," Emilia resorts to a term associated not only with frivolous fashionable items but also with Protestant denunciations of Catholic "idols" such as saints' relics.[55] In the English translation of John Calvin's *Treatise of Reliques*, objects of Catholic worship—"bones, shyrtes, girdles and other lyke baggage"—are repeatedly characterized as idolatrous "trifles" that substitute fetishistically for a missing spiritual presence: "Let vs begynne then at Jesus Christe, of whome because they could not saye that they had the naturall body . . . they haue gathered in stede therof thousands of other trifles, to supplye this want."[56] Like Serres's handkerchief, then, Othello's napkin participates in multiple networks that crumple time, superimposing seemingly distant points so as to make what is elsewhere distinguished as "old" and "new" preposterously close and coeval.

One could doubtless write an orderly diachronic biography of the handkerchief not unlike Othello's own story of his life: its passage from Africa to Europe, from pagan to Christian ownership, from noble exemplar of love to begrimed embarrassment.[57] But inasmuch as it enters the and-kerchief networks I have described here, it plots not a linear geometric sequence but a dynamic topology, in which supposedly secure points become mobile vectors in seismic shifts that superimpose past and present. To this extent, the handkerchief is a palimpsest. The very idea of the palimpsest involves an element of the preposterous: it disregards temporal sequence by conjoining upon one writing surface the inscriptions of past and present. But the palimpsest is not simply a complex text awaiting decoding, even though that is certainly one of the actions that can be performed with it. It is, more accurately, an assemblage of polychronic agents, including writers, readers, and materials. The palimpsest is, like Serres's crumpled handkerchief, an object produced in and contributing to an actor network. And in its unexpected temporal conjunctions, that network revokes Othello's mandate to "obey the time."

The and-kerchief network, whether Shakespeare's or Serres's, exemplifies this disobedient temporality. And that is what makes the material of both handkerchiefs a powerful rejoinder to the work of temporal partition being performed in our current moment. The Bush administration's "war on terror" has rhetorically presumed a community of modern nations temporally divided from backward religious and political cultures, be these a "medieval" Islam in need of (Protestant?) "reformation" or an "Old" Europe superseded by "New" converts to America's allegedly democratizing mission. The political costs of temporally distancing cultures—of putting them "in the waiting room of history"—have been laid bare by postcolonial theorists and writers such as Dipesh Chakrabarty.[58] In an important critique of the supersessionary temporality of modernization—which locates global cultures at different points on a progressive trajectory of development with Europe necessarily at its cutting edge—Chakrabarty argues for the critical potential of what he calls "subaltern pasts." These are not past subaltern agents such as nineteenth-century Indian factory workers or peasants. Rather, they are pasts that are themselves subaltern, suppressed by the dominant historiographical narratives of modernization. But such pasts are not simply bygone history: they conjoin with the present, suggesting for Chakrabarty a "possibility for our own lives and for what we define as our present." Subaltern pasts thus usher into our moment "a plurality of times existing together, a disjuncture of the present with itself."[59] This models a crumpled, polychronic temporality in which neither is the past dead nor the future unborn: indeed, Chakrabarty distinguishes suggestively between the singular "future that 'will be'" of linear historicist temporality and the plural "futures that already 'are'" of subaltern historiography.[60]

The task of thinking across and beyond the temporal partitions that subtly inform notions of racial and religious identity is thus a timely one. Shakespeare's and Serres's handkerchiefs aid in such a task, however, by being untimely. They are untimely not only in the preposterous superimpositions that characterize the networks into which they enter but also in the challenge they present to our time—in the sense of both our historical moment and our modern conception of linear temporality. Othello's handkerchief may be regarded by Cassio and others as a fashionable accessory; but in the actor networks for which I have enlisted it here, it is decidedly unfashionable. The German word for unfashionable, *unzeitgemässe*, also happens to be the term that Nietzsche's translators have rendered as "untimely." Indeed, Nietzsche could be speaking of *Othello*'s and-kerchief networks when he defines what is unzeitgemässe as the traces of the past that should be seen as "acting counter to our time and thereby acting on our time."[61] Untimely matter in the time of Shakespeare, then, is not just the stuff of Renaissance wonder cabinets. It enters into actor networks with us in the present. And in doing so, it allows us to realize that "some other time" is not necessarily long ago, nor even awaiting us in the future. It is here now, if we only learn to recognize its folds.

CODA

Dis-Orientations

Eastern Nonstandard Time

UNTIMELY MATTER IN the time of Shakespeare challenges the fantasy of the self-identical moment or period, of the sovereign moment-state divided from its temporal neighbors. It materializes instead a temporality that is not one. Yet in all the instances I have examined in this book, untimely matter remains potentially in thrall to what we might call Eastern Standard Time: the presumption that the orient, where the sun rises, is the location of the past. The physical traces in the western present of orientalized pasts—engraved Mosaic tablets, the bodily techniques of Asian stage despots, a Hebrew gravestone, a Catholic odor of sanctity associated with perfumes of Arabia, a recycled Jewish Cabbala, a handkerchief's Egyptian embroidery—temporally divide matter from itself, transforming it into an oriental-occidental palimpsest. But that temporal self-division becomes legible precisely because of the Eastern Standard Time that characterizes, in each case, the past as oriental and the oriental as past. The primal scene of material culture's temporal self-division, as we saw in chapter 1, takes place on Mount Sinai. Yet in its very primacy, that scene insists again on the geographical self-identity, relative to the west, of the orient as origin. Thus it is perhaps appropriate to conclude this book by returning to the vicinity of that scene, Egypt, to think about the ways in which untimely matter can also dis-orient the supposedly unitary origin of Eastern Standard Time and trouble the persistent equation of the orient and past.

One such dis-orientation is performed by Amitav Ghosh's extraordinary exercise in postcolonial ethnography, *In an Antique Land* (1992).[1] This "history in the guise of a traveler's tale," as the book is subtitled, arose from the anthropological fieldwork Ghosh undertook as a Ph.D. student during the 1980s in Egypt—an "antique land" not just because of its association with ancient civilization but also because of its contemporary rural inhabitants' supposed exclusion from modernity. As he recounts his interactions with Egyptian villagers, Ghosh simultaneously tells the story of another pair of travelers to Egypt in the twelfth century: a Tunisian Jew, Abraham Ben Yiju, and his Indian slave and business associate, Bomma. Ghosh painstakingly pieces together their peregrinations from a paper trail of letters that had until the late nineteenth century been housed in a synagogue in Fustat, now part of Cairo. Ben Yiju—a devout Jew, son of a rabbi, and brother to merchants in Sicily—migrated from Tunisia to Cairo, and later to Aden and Mangalore in India's Malabar Coast, where he lived for twenty years, fathered two children, and met Bomma. Even as Ben Yiju identified as a Jew, he spoke and wrote in Arabic, was well versed in Sufi traditions of mysticism, and married a Hindu. *In an Antique Land* thus dramatizes a world of movements across cultural and religious boundaries that we have come to regard as insuperable. Looking for contemporary traces of the transcultural affinities and border crossings that he finds in the paper trail of Ben Yiju and Bomma, Ghosh visits the Egyptian shrine of Sidi Abu Hasira, a medieval Muslim saint who was also a Jewish rabbi. He is detained at the site by authorities who cannot understand why an Indian should be interested in the shrine. As Ghosh is interviewed by a suspicious official, he has a gloomy revelation: "But then it struck me, suddenly, that there was nothing I could point to within his world that might give credence to my story—the remains of those small, indistinguishable, intertwined histories, Indian and Egyptian, Muslim and Jewish, Hindu and Muslim, had been partitioned long ago."[2]

Ghosh's metaphor of partition evokes his native India and the East Pakistan he lived in as a child, as well as the violent cartographical divisions of British colonialism and superpower imperialism. His use of the partition metaphor is not just spatial, however. It is also temporal. Speaking of "the borders that were to divide Palestine" in the 1940s, Ghosh notes that they had "already been drawn, through time rather than territory, to allocate a choice of Histories."[3] This temporal partition, between supposedly antique cultures of the orient and supposedly developed western ones, is the enabling fantasy of the supersessionary temporality that Ghosh calls History with a capital *H*. As alternatives to History, Ghosh seeks to retrieve histories with a lowercase *h*, which he sees as nonlinear networks characterized by hybridity and polychronicity. For, as he says, "it was precisely the absoluteness of time and the discreteness of epochs that I always had trouble in imagining."[4]

In an Antique Land's temporal border crossings are everywhere materialized by physical things. For Ghosh, the objects of Egypt and India are repeatedly out of time. These "antique" lands teem with commodities that represent a widely coveted modernity—color television sets, motorbikes, hypodermic syringes, a diesel water pump.[5] But if such objects represent a future-in-the-present, *In an Antique Land* is full also of uncanny objects that represent a past-in-the-present—the crumbling shrines of Muslim saints, Egyptian folk medicines dismissed as fossils, the ruins of old cities such as Fustat in Cairo ("the last skeletal remains of the city whose markets once traded in the best the world could offer").[6] The polychronicity of all these things, however, is camouflaged by the partition that History erects between oriental antiquity and western modernity—a partition that requires any object to assume single temporal citizenship in one moment-state, either as relic (of the past) or as talisman (of the future).

Yet not all objects in *In an Antique Land* submit so readily to History's geotemporal partitions. One of the most resonant material presences in the narrative—an untimely space to which Ghosh's imagination repeatedly returns—is the old synagogue of Fustat's *geniza*. From this Hebrew word, Ghosh spins a web of unexpected transcultural and transtemporal connections. He speculates that *geniza* is related to the Persian *ganj*, meaning treasure; the latter term survives in modern Indian place names that are themselves hybrid survivals from the British Raj. (Dharamsala, the Indian town that is the seat of the Dalai Lama's Tibetan government in exile, is adjacent to a village called McLeod Ganj.) These etymological associations mirror the web of transcultural and transtemporal connections materialized within the geniza as a physical space. In orthodox Jewish tradition, a geniza is a storehouse for written documents containing the name of God, which it is unlawful to erase or destroy. A treasure trove of papers pertaining to Egyptian Jewry was deposited in the geniza at Fustat during the more than eight centuries of its existence. The papers, looted by Europeans in the nineteenth century, have subsequently resurfaced in archives in Russia, England, and the United States, where they have been catalogued according to the punctual dates of historical chronology. In the Fustat synagogue geniza, however, there was no filing system. Papers were stored willy-nilly, with no temporal order;

materials from the twelfth and the nineteenth centuries nestled in close proximity.

For Ghosh, the geniza's former contents serve not just as the primary archive for his recovery of Ben Yiju's and Bomma's story but also as a figure for the polychronicity of history with a small *h*. The temporality of that polychronicity, however, is complex. In a manner reminiscent of Jewish matter and writing throughout this book, the geniza's dispersed papers are multitemporal. Like the Hebrew characters of Stow's *Survey*, they are explosive, disputing the assumptions of the present. Like the Empress and Duchess's Jewish Cabbala in Cavendish's *Blazing World*, they are conjunctive, inasmuch as Ghosh uses them to perform dialogues between past and present, orient and occident, that model the possibility of conversation across, and against, partition. Yet like the Mosaic tablets of Herbert's *Temple*, they are superseded, having been looted and desecrated by the agents of European empire.

It would seem, then, that Ghosh's geniza abides by Eastern Standard Time. For all its multitemporality, it is an oriental past; only the dead letters of its papers remain, eastern relics preserved in western archives. The geniza itself is an object of nostalgia with which Ghosh upholds even as he laments the fact of temporal partition—it is his Paradise Lost, exiled forever to the past. As such, it reinscribes the fantasy of the orient as origin, divided from the western now. Ghosh thus cleaves to the familiar geographical poles of supersessionary time, even if he articulates that time more in the register of mourning than of triumph. Indeed, Kathleen Biddick sees the ghost of supersession as haunting *In an Antique Land*. In a powerful critique, Biddick argues that Ghosh's fantasy of a medieval Golden Age in which Jews and Arabs are defined by affinity rather than partition is troubled by the shadow of slavery. By anxiously insisting that Bomma's status as "slave" is not the demeaning property category of American history but rather the ennobling condition of Sufi poetry, which figures the worshipper as a slave to God, Ghosh elides the "pervasive evidence for a large-scale, not so easily domesticated, institutionalized slavery in the military-bureaucratic sectors of the Geniza world."[7] As Biddick notes, the Arabic word for slave, *saqlabi*, served as a common synonym for "eunuch." Yet Ghosh cuts this figure of cutting from his narrative in order to lend a phantasmatic plenitude both to Bomma (whom we are not permitted to think of as castrated) and to his medieval Golden Age (which we are not permitted to think of as marred by an oppressive and violent slave-holding culture). This tactic, Biddick argues, parallels the supersessionary excision of the circumcised Jew to produce the "universal" polity of Christendom.

Biddick is right to detect within Ghosh's silences around slavery the hint of supersession. And the supersessionary temporality that such silences license is arguably reinforced by Ghosh's production of a medieval Golden Age that serves as a lost oriental origin partitioned from the western modernity that has violently replaced it. Yet this reinscription of Eastern Standard Time cannot completely cancel the work of dis-orientation that the geniza also performs. For Ghosh's supposedly oriental origin proves hard to pinpoint not just in linear time but also in geographical space: its documents "come to Fustat from the far corners of the known world."[8] Indeed, Ben Yiju's correspondence from Aden and Mangalore was once housed next to nineteenth-century wedding papers from Bombay, antique African biblical parchments, and twelfth-century letters from Sicily. Ghosh's geniza papers may open up to the "other time" repeatedly materialized by Shakespeare's untimely matter—be it the supersessionary actor's bodies in the Henriad, the explosive squibs of *Macbeth*, or the conjunctive napkin of *Othello*. But more explicitly than Shakespeare's untimely matter, the geniza papers also trouble Eastern Standard Time. Of European as well as Asian and African provenance, they materialize pasts that are not singularly oriental.

The geniza papers are thus marked as much by geographical plurality as by polychronicity. In the process, they hint at circuits of globalization different from those we now associate with capitalism. If capitalism presumes a global system in which all commodities are translated into the homogenizing master language of exchange value, the global networks of the geniza allow for the endless proliferation of alterities that can communicate with but are not fully translatable into each other. Following the example of the geniza papers, then, we might try to globalize or dis-orient the oriental pasts materialized by Shakespeare's untimely matter. After all, the obsolete histrionics of his Asian stage despots are the work of English actors in Shakespeare's past as much as his present. Likewise, the odor of Lady Macbeth's lost Arabian perfume communicates with that of lost English incense; and the strawberry pattern on Othello's handkerchief suggests not just the mummy of antique Egyptian virgins but also the nuptial blood-spots of antique European bedsheets. The actor networks into which all these stage materials enter thus unsettle the geographical singularity of their pasts as much as they refuse the temporal singularity of their presents. Shakespeare's "oriental" pasts cannot be exclusively oriental, just as his presents cannot be temporally self-identical.

Untimely matter in the time of Shakespeare thus embodies, to use Dipesh Chakrabarty's words, "the plurality that inheres in the 'now,' the lack of totality, the constant fragmentariness, that constitutes one's present." This plurality, Chakrabarty adds, is suppressed by those who compulsively deploy "the historicist or ethnographic mode of viewing that involves the use of a sense of anachronism in order to convert objects, institutions and practices with which we have lived relations into relics of other times."[9] Or, we might, add, into relics of other places and cultures. But Shakespeare's untimely stage materials, like the geniza papers, are far more than mute fossils of dead civilizations. They enter into clamorous, global networks of agency in their pasts—and in our presents. These global networks, moreover, are not necessarily those of capitalism or superpower imperialism. If Eastern Standard Time (or EST) is the time of Washington, D.C., and hence the time of American imperial power, Shakespeare's stage materials, like the geniza papers, allow us to produce something we might call Eastern Nonstandard Time: that is, they help confound the fantasy that insists on treating the orient and the past as synonyms partitioned from the west. And in our war-addled time, such untimely dis-orientations couldn't be timelier.

NOTES

All references to Shakespeare's plays are to *The Norton Shakespeare.*

INTRODUCTION. PALIMPSESTED TIME

Note to epigraph: Serres with Latour, *Conversations on Science, Culture, and Time*, 60.

1. For studies of the early modern wonder cabinet, see Mullaney, "Strange Things, Gross Terms, Curious Customs"; Impey and Macgregor, *The Origins of Museums*; Agamben, "The Cabinet of Wonder," *The Man Without Content*; and Swann, *Curiosities and Texts.*

2. As Douglas Bruster notes in an important essay about the new work on Renaissance material culture ("The New Materialism in Early Modern Studies," in *Shakespeare and the Question of Culture*), the anthology or edited collection has become the favored genre for scholarship in the field. See de Grazia, Quilligan, and Stallybrass (eds.), *Subject and Object in Renaissance Culture*, which includes essays on a variety of early modern objects, including feathers, textiles, and Communion wafers; Fumerton and Hunt (eds.), *Renaissance Culture and the Everyday*, whose back-cover blurb boasts an even more extensive catalogue of items such as "mirrors, books, horses, everyday speech, money, laundry baskets, graffiti, embroidery, and food preparation"; Orlin (ed.), *Material London, ca. 1600*, whose essays examine various aspects of material culture in London, including the fashion for brightly colored clothes, Irish mantles, and yellow starch; and Harris and Korda (eds.), *Staged Properties in Early Modern English Drama*, which examines stage properties ranging from false beards to domestic furnishings.

3. The fascination with "things" is not a phenomenon confined to scholarship on Renaissance material culture. It is apparent in most other periods of literary and cultural studies, as is evidenced by the titles of recent edited collections about material culture from pre- to postmodernity, such as Daston (ed.), *Things That Talk,* and Brown (ed.), *Things.* A notable exception to the elision of time in the study of objects is Ahmed, *Queer Phenomenology.*

4. The term was coined by Patricia Fumerton in her introduction to Fumerton and

Hunt (eds.), *Renaissance Culture and the Everyday*, 3. I critique it in "The New New Historicism's *Wunderkammer* of Objects."

5. Jameson, *The Political Unconscious*, 1.

6. The *longue durée* approach, popularized by the Annales school of French history, is most clearly elaborated in the work of Fernand Braudel: see in particular his essay "History and the Social Sciences." Recently there has been a trend toward microhistoricization—that is, contextualizing literature within temporal units as small as single year. The best illustration of this approach is Shapiro, *1599*.

7. Fumerton, "Introduction," in Fumerton and Hunt (eds.), *Renaissance Culture and the Everyday*, 1–17, esp. 6; and Wall, *Staging Domesticity*, i.

8. Latour, *We Have Never Been Modern*, 75.

9. For studies of the institutional transmigration of property, after the Reformation, from the monasteries to the commercial playhouses, see Greenblatt, "Shakespeare and the Exorcists," in *Shakespearean Negotiations*, esp. 112–13, and Stallybrass, "Worn Worlds," esp. 312. On the Roman traces inscribed in early modern London's city walls and gates, especially Ludgate, see Harris, "Ludgate Time."

10. These conceptions of time are examined in closer detail in my studies of the second Henriad (chapter 2), *Macbeth* (chapter 4), and *Othello* (chapter 6). Key work on Shakespearean conceptions of time includes Quinones, *The Renaissance Discovery of Time*; Waller, *The Strong Necessity of Time*; Sypher, *The Ethic of Time*; and Fletcher, *Time, Space and Motion in the Age of Shakespeare*.

11. Compare Deleuze, *The Fold*, whose first section is called "The Pleats of Matter" (3–13).

12. Even so-called presentism, a movement currently garnering attention in Shakespeare studies for its challenge to historicist orthodoxy, has tended to reify the present and the past as temporally discrete, if mutually implicated, entities. For the most clear exposition of presentism as a critical method in Shakespeare studies, see Grady and Hawkes (eds.), *Presentist Shakespeares*.

13. According to the table of Papias, 47 atoms of time = 1 ounce; 8 ounces of time = 1 ostent, i.e., 1 minute. See Papias, *Grammaticus clarus an. 1053*. I discuss George Herbert's adaptation of this concept of the atom in the last section of Chapter 2.

14. Bruster, *Shakespeare and the Question of Culture*, 191. For other Marxist-inflected critiques of the "materialism" of studies of early modern material culture, see Sinfield, "*Poetaster*, the Author, and the Perils of Cultural Production"; and Hawkes, "Materialism and Reification in Renaissance Studies."

15. A notable exception to this trend is the Marxist-inflected work on early modern clothes and textiles by Peter Stallybrass, one of the pioneers of object studies, and Ann Rosalind Jones. See Stallybrass, "Marx's Coat"; Stallybrass, "Worn Worlds"; Jones and Stallybrass, "'Rugges of London and the Diuell's Band'"; Stallybrass and Jones, "Fetishizing the Glove in Renaissance Europe"; and Jones and Stallybrass, *Renaissance Clothing and the Materials of Memory*. For a collection of essays that explores the tensions between cultural materialism and material culture, see Perry (ed.), *Material Culture and Cultural Materialisms in the Middle Ages and the Renaissance*.

16. Bruster, *Shakespeare and the Question of Culture*, 203.

17. Speaking of the "critical fetishism that pervades the new materialism," Bruster notes that it "is a fetishism that, in replacing large with small and the intangible with what is capable of being touched or held, threatens to restrict the new materialism's usefulness as cultural and historical explanation"; *Shakespeare and the Question of Culture*, 204.

18. Brown, *A Sense of Things*; see also his essay "The Tyranny of Things (Trivia in Karl Marx and Mark Twain)." The tendency to dematerialize the fetish by converting it into a sign that points to a lack in the subject has a long critical history: see, for example, Baudrillard's essay "Fetishism and Ideology," in *For a Critique of the Political Economy of the Sign*, 88–101. For Freud's classic account, see "Fetishism." On the fetishistic nature of the Thing, see Lacan, *Le Séminaire VII*; and Žižek, *The Sublime Object of Ideology*.

19. Marx, "The Fetishism of Commodities and the Secret Thereof," 319–29.

20. Hawkes, "Materialism and Reification in Early Modern Studies," 118. Examples of essays whose titles explicitly invoke the "life" of early modern things include Bruster, "The Dramatic Life of Objects in the Early Modern Theatre"; and Sutton, "Porous Memory and the Cognitive Life of Things."

21. On the culturally hybrid, early modern provenance of the discourse of the fetish, see William Pietz's series of essays in *Res*: "The Problem of the Fetish, I"; "The Problem of the Fetish, II"; and "The Problem of the Fetish, IIIa." For a classic anthropological study of the anachronism of the African fetish, see Nassau, "The Philosophy of Fetishism." For a study of the nineteenth-century European interest in fetishism and its "primitive" African provenance, see Masuzawa, "Troubles with Materiality."

22. On the *hijab* and its vexed status as the western emblem of Islam's premodernity, see Yegenoglu, *Colonial Fantasies*, esp. chaps. 2 and 5; and El Gundi, *Veil*. For a discussion of the recalcitrant temporality of the veil, see Davis, "Time Behind the Veil." On the recent use of "medieval" as a rhetorical device with which to make other cultures temporally distant or regressive, see Holsinger, *Neomedievalism, Neoconservatism, and the War on Terror*.

23. Serres with Latour, *Conversations*, 45.

24. Shapin, "What Else Is New?" esp. 144. Shapin offers this assessment in the context of a description of the matter of his kitchen: "I'm writing in the kitchen, surrounded by technology. There is a cordless phone, a microwave oven, and a high-end refrigerator, and I'm working on a laptop. Nearby is a gas range, a French cast-iron enameled casserole, and a ceramic teapot. Drawers to my left hold cutlery—some modern Chinese-made stainless steel, some Georgian sterling silver. In front of me is a wooden book-stand, made for me by a talented friend and festooned with Post-it reminders of things to do (a method I prefer to my digital calendar). I'm sitting on a semi-antique wooden chair, though when my back is hurting I tend to switch to a new, expensive ergonomic contraption." Revealingly, Shapin characterizes the multitemporal nature of his kitchen objects as "a technological palimpsest" (144). Another compelling study of the polychronic simultaneity rather than unilinear progression of technology is de Landa's *Thousand Years of Nonlinear History*.

25. For a useful overview of critical approaches to modern material culture, see Dant, *Material Culture in the Social World.* The scholarly turn to objects has even attracted attention from the mainstream U.S. press; see Eakins, "Screwdriver Scholars and Pencil Punditry." For an excellent theoretical meditation on the temporality of matter, see Lyotard, *The Inhuman*, 8–21.

26. Marx, "Theses on Feuerbach," 400. For a theoretically sophisticated meditation on the temporality of matter implied by Marx's response to Feuerbach, see Butler, *Bodies That Matter*, where she notes that Marx conceived of matter "as a principle of *transformation*, presuming and inducing a future" (31).

27. Aristotle, *De anima*, 2:555.

28. Derrida, *Of Grammatology*, 60.

29. In her account of New World travel literature, Fuller draws on a broadly deconstructive understanding of materiality as a deferred presence; see Fuller, "Ralegh's Fugitive Gold," esp. 238n19. Goldberg's studies of "writing matter" have moved from an explicitly Derridean investment in cultural graphology to a fascination with Lucretius (via Michel Serres); see Goldberg, *Writing Matter*, "Writing Shakespearean Matter Again," and "Lucy Hutchinson Writing Matter."

30. Ryle, *Collected Papers*, esp. "Thinking and Reflecting," 2:465–79, and "The Thinking of Thoughts: What Is 'Le Penseur' Doing?" 2:480–86; and Geertz, *The Interpretation of Cultures*, passim. For a particularly useful overview and critique of thick description in early modern studies, see Bruster, "Deep Focus," esp. 31–38.

31. See Ferguson, "Feathers and Flies"; and Helgerson, "The Buck Basket, the Witch and the Queen of Fairies."

32. Appadurai, "Introduction," esp. 11, 47, 34. See also Kopytoff, "The Cultural Biography of Things."

33. See, for example, Olson, Reilly, and Shepherd (eds.), *The Biography of the Object in Late Medieval and Renaissance Italy*, whose essays draw explicitly on Appadurai and Kopytoff in examining a range of objects in late medieval and Renaissance Italy: sculpture, table glassware, jewelry, miraculous painted images, choir screens, chapels, and antiquities.

34. For an extended application of Appadurai's and Kopytoff's theorizations of the social life of things to the early modern stage property, see the contributions to Harris and Korda (eds.), *Staged Properties in Early Modern English Drama*, as well as the introductory essay, "Towards a Materialist Account of Stage Properties," esp. 18.

35. Compare Fredric Jameson's argument, concerning the supposed tension between synchronic and diachronic interpretation, that "individual period formulations always secretly imply or project narratives or 'stories'—narrative representations—of the historical sequence in which such individual periods take their place and from which they derive their significance"; *The Political Unconscious*, 28.

36. Stallybrass, "Worn Worlds," 312.

37. On theatrical garments and their haunting by their religious pasts, see Stallybrass, "Worn Worlds"; on the "haunted" costume worn by the ghost of Hamlet's father, see Jones and Stallybrass, *Renaissance Clothing and the Materials of Memory*, esp. 245.

38. Biddick, *The Typological Imaginary*, 1.

39. Jameson, *The Political Unconscious*, 1.

40. Jameson, *The Political Unconscious*, 151. I have discussed the polychronic aspects of Jameson's exoskeleton metaphor elsewhere: see Harris, "(Po)X Marks the Spot."

41. See Nietzsche, *Untimely Meditations.*

42. As Daniel Brezeale notes, a book by August Berger that Nietzsche borrowed from the University of Basel library in January 1872 just before he started work on his first *Untimely Meditation*—his polemic against Daniel Strauss—"is entitled *Die Idee des Realgymnasium für Freunde und Berforder hoherer und zeitgemässer Jugendbildung dargstellt*, that is, 'The Idea of a Practical/Technical High School [there is no real English equivalent for the German term *Realgymnasium*], Expounded for Friends and Supporters of Higher and Up-To-Date [*zeitgemässer*] Secondary Education.' It seems quite likely that Nietzsche's use of *Unzeitgemässe* in his series was intended at least in part *ironically*, as a parody of the quite common use of the term *zeitgemäss* that he had most recently encountered in Berger's title"; in Nietzsche, *Untimely Meditations*, xlv.

43. Nietzsche, *Untimely Meditations*, 60.

44. For their critique of *chronos* (and their embrace of *aeon*), see Deleuze and Guattari, *A Thousand Plateaus*, 260–65. Deleuze and Guattari relate their conception of the untimely to Foucault's notion of the "Actual," which they see as the horizon of becoming, or that which explodes the reified presence of the present. Deleuze and Guattari, *What Is Philosophy?* 112–14.

45. Grosz, *The Nick of Time*, 117.

46. Derrida, *Specters of Marx*, e.g., 63. For a powerful critique by an early modernist of Derrida's reading of both Marx and *Hamlet*, see Halpern, "An Impure History of Ghosts."

47. The phrase is, of course, part of the title of Francis Fukuyama's notorious book, *The End of History and the Last Man*. Much of Derrida's *Specters of Marx* is a critique of Fukuyama; see esp. 70–95.

48. Derrida, *Specters of Marx*, 21–23.

49. OED, "joint," sb. 2.

50. Sidney, *The Countess of Pembroke's Arcadia*, 237.

51. *Hamlet*, 5.1.187–89. For a suggestive discussion of temporality that begins with an analysis of the corporeal metaphor implied by Hamlet's "time out of joint," see Freeman, "Queer Temporalities."

52. For a discussion of recent paleographic studies of the Archimedes Palimpsest, see Miller, "Reading Between the Lines." The palimpsest also contains the only known original Greek version of another work by Archimedes on infinity, fourteen pages of commentaries on Aristotle's treatise on the logic of categorization, and ten pages of speeches by the fourth-century B.C. Athenian orator Hyperides.

53. 1 Corinthians 1:17–19. On Saint Paul's rejection of Greek philosophy as well as Jewish law, see Badiou, *Saint Paul*, 43. Badiou claims that it was not Paul but Saint John who reappropriated *logos* for Christian theology.

54. Compare Jeffrey J. Cohen who, in a discussion of temporality in medieval studies, has theorized how the present "might encounter within itself the sedimented past, thence to erupt with the intensity of an unanticipated future"; *Medieval Identity Machines*, 1–34, esp. 7.

55. For the theory of the actor network, see Latour, *We Have Never Been Modern*, passim; Latour, *Reassembling the Social*; and Law and Hassard (eds.), *Actor Network Theory and After*. Other work in Renaissance studies that builds on actor-network theory includes Charnes, "We Were Never Early Modern," a revised version of which appears in her *Hamlet's Heirs*, chap. 4; and Yates, "Accidental Shakespeare." Yates here develops and moves beyond his insightful account of early modern objects in his earlier monograph, *Error, Misuse, Failure: Object Lessons from the English Renaissance*.

56. See Genette, *Palimpsests*; Bornstein and Williams (eds.), *Palimpsest*; and Zabus, *The African Palimpsest*.

57. Thus described, the palimpsest both resonates with and differs from Freud's famous "mystic writing pad," the child's writing tablet from which notes can be magically removed by the simple ruse of lifting a sheet of semitransparent paper that covers a block of dark wax beneath it; see "A Note Upon the 'Mystic Writing-Pad.'" For Freud, the pad entails simultaneous processes of permanent inscription (the multiple impressions left on the block of wax) and erasure (the lifting of the sheet). The notable similarity between palimpsest and pad is that both are complex metaphors of overwriting on one surface. Obviously Freud uses the pad to describe a problem of the *subject* (the relations between perception and consciousness), while I use the palimpsest to get at a problem of the *object* (the relations between materiality, temporality, and agency). Still, I am struck by how—*pace* Derrida's redaction of Freud—both metaphors are not simply graphological; they also involve some kind of material remainder that interacts with, and is transformed by, the inscriptions on it. See Derrida, "Freud and the Scene of Writing."

58. Duffy, *Marking the Hours*.

59. Peter Stallybrass, private correspondence with the author. I thank Peter for drawing my attention to this magnificent text, housed at Smith College.

60. Peter Stallybrass, "Publication Circuit in Early Modern Europe." I am grateful to Peter for sharing his unpublished work with me.

61. Of course, studies of the early modern body's physiology, particularly those of its humors and passions, have constituted one of the most dynamic sites of discourse about early modern "matter." The most prominent scholar in this regard is Gail Kern Paster, who in a series of studies has traced the relations between early modern discourses of matter, corporeality, and gender; see, e.g., *The Body Embarrassed* and *Humoring the Body*, esp. 39. See also Parker, *Shakespeare from the Margins*, 254.

62. I derive the phrase "practical theory" from Henry S. Turner, who considers practical theories of "plotting" space in *The Renaissance Stage*.

63. On the links between musical tempo and temporality in Shakespeare, especially *The Tempest*, see Peterson, *Time, Tide, and Tempest*, esp. chaps. 1, 5.

64. Chakrabarty, *Provincializing Europe*, 112. For useful discussions of the problems

of the "early modern" as a period designation, see Starn, "The Early Modern Muddle"; Bruster, "Shakespeare and the End of History"; and de Grazia, "The Modern Divide." Queer theory has provided some of the most useful interventions in problems of period terminology: see Goldberg and Menon, "Queering History," and Freccero, *Queer/Early/Modern.*

65. Said, *Orientalism*, 8.

66. Said leaves the question of temporality more or less untouched in *Orientalism.* Instead time appears in his book not as an ideological effect complicit with orientalism but as an absolute chronology by which to measure its historical development. Kathleen Biddick offers both a celebration of Said's book and a critique of its silence on temporality in her illuminating article "Coming out of Exile."

67. Chakrabarty, *Provincializing Europe*, 8; Fabian, *Time and the Other*, 32; Latour, *We Have Never Been Modern*, 72.

68. In its first definition of "oriental," for which it lists the earliest instance of the word (in Chaucer), the OED conflates its spatial and temporal properties: "Belonging to, or situated in, that part or region in which the sun rises." Cf. the OED definition of "occidental," 1.

69. Kruger, *The Spectral Jew.* For a reading of *The Merchant of Venice* that exemplifies how the Jew is the privileged Christian metonymy for the superseded past, see Heschel, "From Jesus to Shylock."

70. See Greenblatt, *Shakespearean Negotiations*, 1.

PART I. SUPERSESSIONS

Note to epigraph: Hegel, *Phenomenology of Spirit*, ¶188, 114–15.

1. For a classic discussion of the typological temporalities of Christian figura and littera, see Auerbach, "Figura."

2. Biddick, *The Typological Imaginary*, 13–18.

3. In this, Biddick's interpretation of supersessionary time is uncannily close to Lee Edelman's polemical argument about futurity and the specter of the queer; see Edelman, *No Future.* In a brilliant riposte to the heteronormative fetishization of the child as the figure of reproductive futurity, Edelman notes how this figure is perversely dependent on the queer—or what he calls, punning on Lacan's and Žižek's accounts of the *sinthome* as the drive that sustains the fantasy of identity, the "sinthomosexual." The sinthomosexual is so named not just because his desires are symptomatic of the death drive that opposes reproductive futurity but also because the repeated violence committed against him in the name of futurity is symptomatic of the disavowed repetition compulsion at the heart of heteronormative sociality. For Biddick, who like Edelman insists on the *jouissance* that drives fantasy, the Jew rather than the queer is the antisocial sinthome sustaining the Catholic fantasy of supersession; the repeated, violent "cutting" of the Jew from the present betrays the kernel of compulsive pleasure hidden in that fantasy.

CHAPTER I. READING MATTER

1. The winning caption, submitted by Alex Wellen, was printed with the cartoon in the *New Yorker*, September 18, 2006, on the back page.

2. In the "Wolf Man" case, Freud uses the expression "primal scene" to refer to the sight of sexual relations between the parents, as observed, constructed, and/or fantasized by the child and interpreted by the child as a scene of violence; it has a shaping influence on the child's subsequent relation to sexuality. Importantly, the primal scene is, in a sense, not primal; even as it generates a future (in the shape of the child's development), it simultaneously produces a past (a prior set of libidinal cathexes screened by the scene). See "From the History of an Infantile Neurosis." I appropriate the expression here to refer to Exodus's stone tablets and altars as a fantasy of primacy that simultaneously produces a pre- and a post- time of matter.

3. For a discussion of the death drive and its foreclosure of futurity in the context of queer theory, see Edelman, *No Future.*

4. My thoughts on consequence are, again, shaped by queer theory; see especially Jagose, *Inconsequence.*

5. For a discussion of the material status of the communion wafer in the Eucharist controversy of the Protestant Reformation, see Greenblatt, "The Mousetrap." On the ways in which the modern suspicion of objects has its discursive roots in a Protestant demonization of Catholic investments in materiality, see Stallybrass, "The Value of Culture and the Disavowal of Things."

6. Herbert, "The Sinner," line 14, in *The English Poems of George Herbert,* 59. All further references to *The Temple* are cited in the text.

7. Goldberg, *Voice Terminal Echo,* 115.

8. Lampe, "The Reasonableness of Typology," 13.

9. Auerbach, "Figura," 29–53, 51.

10. Auerbach, "Figura," 51.

11. See Benjamin, "Theses on the Philosophy of History," in *Illuminations*, 253–64; and Derrida, *Specters of Marx.* I discuss Benjamin's and Derrida's conceptions of temporality and futurity in more detail in part II.

12. Jameson, *The Political Unconscious,* 29. For a discussion of the religious subtext of Jameson's thought, see Brown, "The Dark Wood of Postmodernity."

13. Jameson, *The Political Unconscious*, 28.

14. Jameson, *The Political Unconscious*, 296.

15. See Badiou, *Saint Paul*; and Agamben, *The Time That Remains.*

16. Lupton, *Afterlives of the Saints,* and *Citizen-Saints.*

17. Biddick, *The Typological Imaginary.*

18. Fish, *The Living Temple*, 1.

19. Although Fish situates Herbert within a specifically Reformation tradition of catechizing, he also sees in Herbert's sense of religious history the pre-Protestant influence of Augustine's *De catechizandis rudibus*; see Fish, *The Living Temple*, 147–50.

20. For an excellent discussion of Herbert's recent critical fortunes, see Kneidel, "Herbert and Exactness."

21. Strier, *Love Known*, 149. Strier offers a fiercely Protestant reworking of Louis Martz's earlier Anglo-Catholic Herbert, who retreats from the institutions of the world to the solace of private spiritual exercises associated with the Counter-Reformation; see Martz, *The Poetry of Meditation*. Strier's radically dematerializing Protestant Herbert finds counterparts in Shuger, *Habits of Thought in the English Renaissance*, and Hodgkins, *Authority, Church, and Society in George Herbert*. Both Shuger and Hodgkins similarly identify Herbert's emphasis on inwardness with a movement away from ecclesiastical structures: see Shuger, 106, and Hodgkins, 174–75. In her influential reading of Herbert's specifically Protestant adaptation of typology, *Protestant Poetics and the Seventeenth-Century Religious Lyric*, Barbara Kiefer Lewalski makes much of Herbert's distinction between Solomon's Old Testament temple and its signs of physical labor with the new, ineffable temple "not made with hands (Acts 7:47–8)" (309); this anticipates Strier's vision of a Herbert who not only chooses individual over institutional devotion but also has to repudiate any contaminating trace of materiality in his temple of the heart.

22. Schoenfeldt, *Prayer and Power*, 273. See also Schoenfeldt's chapter on Herbert and digestion in his *Early Modern Bodies and Selves*, 96–130.

23. Malcolmson, *Heart-Work*, 1. See also her *George Herbert*.

24. Fish, *Living Temple*, 5.

25. Ferrar, "The Printers to the Reader," in Herbert, *The English Poems of George Herbert*, 31.

26. Walton, *Life of Mr. George Herbert*, 116.

27. Walton, *Life of Mr. George Herbert*, 48.

28. Indeed, Strier expressly advances his view of the Unworldly Herbert *in spite of* the poet's substantial church-restoring enterprises: as he says, "Despite his care for the physical structure at Bemerton, Herbert felt some of the impulses that led to Quakerism"; *Love Known*, 150.

29. Herbert, *The Latin Poetry of George Herbert*, 40–41.

30. As a result, Fish's two Herberts uncannily parallel two Fishes—the Fish of *The Living Temple* for whom certainty is the telos, and the Fish of *Self-Consuming Artifacts*, for whom uncertainty is the desired outcome.

31. Malcolmson, *Heart-Work*, 121.

32. Schoenfeldt, *Prayer and Power*, 17. Cf. Schoenfeldt's analysis of Herbert's obsession with food, where he argues that edible matter "traces . . . the inner contours of the devotional subject"; *Bodies and Selves*, 96.

33. In *The English Works of George Herbert*, the argument of which he proceeded to summarize in *Formative Types in English Poetry* , 15–31, George Herbert Palmer split Herbert's life into four phases that trace a progression from the material world to the spiritual (un)world: Education (1593–1619), Hesitation (the eight years of his Oratorship), Crisis (anguished uncertainty about his vocation after his mother's death in 1627), and Consecration (his priesthood, 1630–33).

34. Tuve, *A Reading of George Herbert*, esp. 27–29, 112–13; Summers, *George Herbert*, esp. 123–46.

35. See Walker, "The Architechtonics of George Herbert's *The Temple.*" Stanley Stewart, in "Time and *The Temple,*" rejects the view of *spatial* progression from matter to spirit that informs Walker's analogy with the Hebraic temple. But Stewart still abides by a dematerializing hermeneutic inasmuch as he reads *The Temple* as enacting a *temporal* progression from worldly to spiritual engagement: it "moves in time from an earlier state of unpreparedness to a later one of preparedness" (98).

36. As Amy M. Charles observes in her biography of Herbert, "it would be a mistake to regard Bemerton as in any sense a retreat from the problems of the world"; Charles, *A Life of George Herbert*, 157. See also Targoff, *Common Prayer*, 97–98, and Malcolmson, *Heart-Work*, 26–45.

37. Herbert, *A Priest to the Temple, Or, The Country Parson His Character, and Rule of Holy Life*, in *The Country Parson, The Temple*, 69.

38. Annabel M. Endicott [Patterson] argues that the pessimistic chronicle and prophecy of world history that is "The Church Militant" does not accord with the expectation of a movement to lasting peace and grace implied by Walker's analogy with the Hebraic temple; see "The Structure of George Herbert's *Temple*: A Reconsideration." Fish asserts that for Herbert, "rest and closure are unavailable except in some premature and therefore dangerous assumption that God's building is already finished"; *Living Temple*, 155. And in *God's Courtier* Marion White Singleton argues that the structure of *The Temple* is "relational" rather than architectural and that "The Church-porch" and "The Church Militant" act as inadequate frames for the attempt of "God's courtier . . . to make himself into a Temple" (163).

39. Easily the best reader to date of Herbert's matter is Michael Schoenfeldt; in *Bodies and Selves*, he attends illuminatingly to the recalcitrant omnipresence of food and physiology in Herbert's accounts of spirituality (96–130). However, he pays little attention to nonedible matter, and even less to the matter of typology and signification.

40. For a discussion of Herbert's attitude to dung, see Nelson, "Death, Dung, the Devil, and Worldly Delights." Schoenfeldt's discussion of Herbert and food in *Bodies and Selves*, 96–130, tellingly bypasses dung, a material remainder of digestion that cannot be recuperated for the spiritual self.

41. Herbert, *Country Parson*, 58. Here Herbert shows a greater tolerance for the language of artisanal labor than elsewhere in his writings; as Malcolmson notes, he is often disdainful of labor as a polluting "curse." See *Heart-Work*, 124.

42. *Outlandish Proverbs, Selected* (London, 1640), sig. A4. On the attribution of the *Outlandish Proverbs* to Herbert, see Charles, *A Life of George Herbert*, 196–97.

43. Herbert, *Country Parson*, 88.

44. Herbert, *Country Parson*, 84.

45. Todd, *The Opacity of Signs*, 11. While Todd focuses specifically on how Augustine's theory of signs shapes much of *The Temple*, other critics have seen a wide variety of Augustinian influences on Herbert. Arnold Stein, in *George Herbert's Lyrics*, notes Her-

bert's familiarity with the rhetorical principles outlined in Augustine's *De doctrina Christiana*, as does Michael P. Gallagher in "Rhetoric, Style, and George Herbert." Stanley Fish argues for Herbert's debt to Augustine's catechistic view of history in *The Living Temple* (147–50). And in *Protestant Poetics*, Barbara Lewalski situates Herbert in a more narrowly Protestant tradition, but she recognizes the debts of that tradition to Augustine's distinction between Law and Grace in *De spiritu et littera* (114).

46. Augustine, *On Christian Doctrine*, 3.9.13. For a sustained discussion of how early modern writers understood idolatry as a perversion of divine signification and teleology, see David Hawkes, *Idols of the Marketplace.*

47. Walton, *Life of Mr. George Herbert*, 29–30.

48. Shakespeare, Sonnet 130, in *The Norton Shakespeare*, l. 6.

49. For a discussion of Shakespeare's sonnets as engaged in a fetishistic troubling of Augustinian signification, see Freinkel, *Reading Shakespeare's Will*, 203–33. Freinkel applies her argument to Sonnet 20 in her essay "The Shakespearean Fetish."

50. Herbert uses the "rose" to such ends in *The Temple*, where it serves as a figure for the Church as the antitype prefigured by "the rose of Sharon" in the Song of Solomon (2:1); see "Church-rents and schisms" (150, l. 1) and "The Rose" (182).

51. In *The Temple*, Herbert typologically associates the "ink" of the Christian heart with the blood of Christ's sacrifice: "Since bloud is fittest, Lord, to write / Thy sorrows in, and bloudie fight; / My heart hath store, write there, where in / One box doth lie both ink and sinne" (59, ll. 21–24). "Ink" perhaps has a vestige of this typological significance in the sixteen-year-old Herbert's sonnet.

52. As my language here suggests, Herbert's treatment of Augustine's theory of signs is illuminated by Jacques Lacan's distinction between the metaphorical operation that crosses over from signifier to signified and the metonymical operation that sends language sliding from signifier to signifier. Though his ostensible sources for this distinction are Roman Jakobson and Sigmund Freud, in "The Agency of the Letter in the Unconscious" Lacan tellingly frames his argument with an ironic reference to Saint Paul (2 Cor. 3:6) that speaks also to Augustine's condemnation (see Lacan's n. 31) of those who "follow the letter" rather than the "spirit" of the sign: "Of course, as it is said, the letter killeth while the spirit giveth life. . . . Even so, the pretensions of the spirit would remain unassailable if the letter had not shown us that it produces all the effects of truth in man without involving the spirit at all"; "The Agency of the Letter in the Unconscious," 158.

53. Compare Jonathan Goldberg's reading of Herbert's compulsive retextualization of logos: "Christ is the way, the door: the dead letter kept in circulation and kept from arrival at anything more or less than endless supplementation"; *Voice Terminal Echo*, 123.

54. Augustine, *On Christian Doctrine*, 1.2.2. I have cited Todd's translation in *Opacity of Signs*, 23. Augustine makes the remark in the context of his distinction between verbal signs and nonverbal things; he does concede, however, that things are ultimately signs of God.

55. Hawkes, "Exchange Value and Empiricism in the Poetry of George Herbert," esp. 83. See also Hawkes, *Idols of the Marketplace*, 122–33. The "Jewish" poems have largely

escaped extended critical scrutiny; critical discussions often relegate them to footnotes that lament their lack of distinction. In a footnote on "Self-condemnation," for example, Strier confirms Stein's observation in *George Herbert's Lyrics*, 89, about " 'the lesser passions' not moving Herbert to distinguished expression"; *Love Known*, 12n21.

56. Lewalski, *Protestant Poetics and the Seventeenth-Century Religious Lyric*, 114. See also Preus, *From Shadow to Promise*, 16–21; and Froehlich, "The State of Biblical Hermeneutics at the Beginning of the Fifteenth Century."

57. See "The Bunch of Grapes" (140, ll. 24–28), "The Sinner" (59, ll. 13–14), "Aaron" (179, ll. 1–5, 16–20), "Sion" (120, ll. 1–2, 12–13).

58. The conceit can be found also in Herbert's Latin poetry; in "Homo, Statua," he writes: "Sum, quis nescit, Imago Dei, sed saxea certe" (I am, stupid, the Image of God but Surely rock); *The Latin Poetry of George Herbert*, 80–81.

59. On the visual effects of Herbert's pattern poems, see Westerweel, *Patterns and Patterning.*

60. Critics have noted the tension in "The Altar" between the claims it makes for the poet's artful skill and for God's shaping grace. Many have subsumed the former to the latter: Malcolmson argues that the poem asserts itself to be a "[divinely] authorized work of [human] artfulness like the building of Solomon's Temple" (*Heart-Work*, 85). Schoenfeldt sees the poem as aspiring "to show God's power by relinquishing all claim for its artful shape to the provenance of God" (*Prayer and Power*, 162), yet he asserts that it ultimately blurs the distinction between Herbert's and God's craft (167). Strier, by contrast, argues that "Herbert could hardly be confusing or equating his art with God's" (*Love Known*, 193).

61. Dryden, *MacFlecknoe*, 8.

62. Tuve, *A Reading of George Herbert*, 104.

63. Tuve, *A Reading of George Herbert*, 32–33. See also Sandler, " 'Solomon Vbique Regnet,' " whose otherwise adept reading of Herbert's typological reworking of the Old Testament temple follows Tuve in speaking a of a homogeneously Christian New Covenant.

64. Biddick, *The Typological Imaginary*, 3, 16. Julia Reinhard Lupton's brilliant discussion of how typology shapes Renaissance periodization also draws on a largely Catholic tradition of iconography: see *Afterlives of the Saints*, 3–39.

65. Badiou reads Saint Paul as the revolutionary antiphilosopher of the Christ-event—i.e., the Incarnation (*Saint Paul*, 31). Hence for all his avowed atheism, Badiou's sense of the event implies a recognizably Catholic conception of history.

66. Lewalski, *Protestant Poetics*, 128. Strier also considers Protestant revisions of typology, but less for their transformations of temporality than for how they prefigure the regenerate individual as well as Christ; see *Love Known*, 152.

67. For discussions of the extraordinarily intricate web of typological and intertextual references evoked by Herbert's cluster of grapes, see Tuve, *A Reading of George Herbert*, 112–13; Summers, *George Herbert*, 127; Lewalski, *Protestant Poetics*, 312–13; and Bloch, *Spelling the Word*, 145.

68. Lewalski, *Protestant Poetics*, 313.

69. For a similar discussion of the graphological metaphors Herbert repeatedly uses throughout *The Temple*, and the ways in which these trouble the opposition Saint Paul draws in 2 Corinthians 3:6 ("The letter killeth, but the spirit giveth life"), see Goldberg, "The Dead Letter: Herbert's Other Voices," in *Voice Terminal Echo*, 101–23.

70. Tuve, *A Reading of George Herbert*, 196.

71. Goldberg, *Voice Terminal Echo*, 123.

72. See OED, "Easter," sb. 1. "Eostre" is related also to the Sanskrit "usra," meaning dawn.

73. Stewart argues in "Time and *The Temple*" that "the placement of ['Church Militant'] is a hieroglyphic of a temporal relation. . . . The voice in 'Church Militant' does not sound with the wonderfully intense tones of a soul in agony precisely because it belongs to one who exists apart from time; and time is the defining feature of a world in which change and anxiety exist" (105). In *Protestant Poetics*, Lewalski concentrates on the temple's function as "an overarching typological symbol," with the three sections of Herbert's work presenting "various dimensions of the New Covenant Church"; in this schema, " 'The Church Militant' shifts from a spatial to a temporal scheme to present a third dimension of the Christian Church on earth—its public, visible form" (289). And Kathleen Lynch, in "*The Temple*," argues that "we need to counterbalance our notions of progress throughout *The Temple* with a sense of the graphic impact of Herbert's three-part structure," with "The Church-porch" and "The Church Militant" constituting "side panels" to the center panel of "The Church" (142, 144).

74. In the "B," or Bodleian, manuscript there is one blank flyleaf; in the "W," or Williams, manuscript there are five.

75. For both Annabel Endicott and Lee Ann Johnson, the blank leaves that separate "The Church" from "The Church Militant," as well as the extra flourishes in "W" and the "Finis" at the end of "The Church" in both manuscripts, suggest that "The Church Militant" is a separate effort and has no place in *The Temple*; see Endicott, "The Structure of George Herbert's *The Temple*," and Johnson, "The Relationship of 'The Church Militant' to *The Temple*."

76. Herbert (ed. Hutchinson), *The Works of George Herbert*, 476. Amy L. Charles lends strong support to Hutchinson's dating of the poem as "early": "Its affinities with Donne's *Second Anniversarie* (1612), the tone of its references to Spain, and it sanguine prophecy of the spread of religion to America all suggest an early date," *Life of George Herbert*, 82.

77. A number of readers have attempted to provide historical context for the American reference in "The Church Militant." Malcolmson dwells on the Herbert family's interests in the Virginia Company in *Heart-Work* (198–202) and *George Herbert* (22), as does Jeffrey P. Powers-Beck in *Writing the Flesh*, 190–221. But some readers have suggested other American contexts that need not date the poem to the early 1620s. Hawkes rightly notes Herbert's awareness of how the influx of gold from the New World has created an economic crisis, which connects to mercantile arguments made throughout the late six-

teenth and early seventeenth centuries; "Exchange Value and Empiricism in the Work of George Herbert," 81. When Nicholas Ferrar tried to publish *The Temple*, it was briefly held up by the censors because of the lines in "The Church Militant" about America; as Dwight Levang has noted, the Puritan preacher Samuel Ward was imprisoned only two years later for uttering remarks almost identical to the lines that caused such trouble—which suggests that the lines had a currency in 1633 disregarded by readers who wish to date the poem as "early." See Levang, "George Herbert's 'The Church Militant' and the Chances of History."

78. Such a reading, of course, ignores the heavy eroticization of the meal on offer in "Love (III)", not to mention the obvious corporeality involved in eating.

79. Lynch, "*The Temple*," 149.

80. It is a reference that evidently appealed to one of his seventeenth-century admirers. In his biographical note on Herbert from 1652, Barnaby Oley wrote in terms that recall the opening lines of "The Church Militant": "I hope no man will think . . . that I give him leave to *construe my words Mathematically*, as if there was not an atome, or hair of a good man, or man of God in our Church"; "A Prefatory View of the Life of Mr Geo. Herbert," prefixed to Herbert's *Remains* , reprinted in Patrides (ed.), *George Herbert*, 75.

81. According to the table of Papias, 47 atoms of time = 1 ounce; 8 ounces of time = 1 ostent, i.e., 1 minute. See Papias, *Grammaticus clarus an. 1053*.

82. The first English translation of *De rerum natura* was Lucy Hutchinson's (then) unpublished version of the 1650s; the first published English translation was Thomas Creech's 1682 edition, and the first English treatise on atomism was Walter Charleton's *Physiologia Epicuro-Gassendo-Charletoniana* (1654). But Lucretius was available to Latin-literate English readers as early as the sixteenth century in editions published in Paris and Antwerp, such as Denys Lambinus's text, which was accompanied by a substantial commentary and went into four editions between 1564 and 1583. On the history of Lucretian thought in early modern England, see Stones, "The Atomic View of Matter in the XVth, XVIth, and XVIIth Centuries"; Kargon, *Atomism in England from Hariot to Newton*; Lezra, *Unspeakable Subjects*, 15–31; and Harris, "Atomic Shakespeare."

83. Hutchinson (trans.), *Lucretius: De rerum natura*, 25.

84. Lucretius, *De rerum natura*, 2.1119–20, 1124–25; in Hutchinson (trans.), *Lucretius: De rerum natura*, 82.

85. Lucretius, *De rerum natura*, 2.215–17; in Hutchinson (trans.), *Lucretius: De rerum natura*, 61.

86. Serres, *Hermes*, 99.

87. I have discussed elsewhere how spices, as commodities in an age of mercantile commerce, became especially associated with transnational movement from the orient to Europe. See Harris, *Sick Economies*, 120–28.

88. For a powerful reading of Herbert's nonprogressive conception of history, see Goldberg, "Herbert's 'Decay' and the Articulation of History."

89. It should be remarked that, elsewhere in *The Temple*, it is grace rather than Sin that seems to provide the equivalent of the Lucretian swerve or declension. In his cryptic

poem "Coloss. 3.3," Herbert argues that "*Life* hath with the sun a double motion." This first motion, he argues, is "straight"; the second is "*Hid* and doth obliquely bend" (100, ll. 1–3). One motion follows the necessity of nature; the other is a contingent choice to embrace God. This double motion once again uncannily recalls Lucretius's materialism, in which atoms too have a double motion—straight down, as dictated by the physics of the fall, but also "obliquely bending" thanks to their resistant declensions. "The Church Militant," by contrast, presents the movement of the Church as following the solar path of necessity, while the movement of Sin is what "obliquely bends" that path.

90. I discuss the etymological origin of "taint" in *The Merchant of Venice* in *Sick Economies*, 77.

91. See, e.g., Edmund Spenser, *The Faerie Queene*, book 1, canto 2; and Thomas Dekker, *The Whore of Babylon*, in *The Dramatic Works of Thomas Dekker*, vol. 2, passim. Likewise, Peter Pett's poem "Time's Journey to Seeke His Daughter Truth" (1599) presents Spain as a Whore of Babylon who, with Rome's blessing, attacks England; see Iwasaki, "*Veritas Filia Temporis* and Shakespeare." On the trope of the Whore of Babylon, see Dolan, *Whores of Babylon*.

92. Malcolmson, *Heart-Work*, 203; but see also her qualification of this position, 263n44.

93. Hawkes, "Exchange Value and Empiricism in the Poetry of George Herbert," 81.

94. For a related discussion of how medieval writers viewed Judaism under the mark of a spectrality that haunts Christianity in the (paradoxical) shape of an embodied materiality, see Kruger, *The Spectral Jew*.

CHAPTER 2. PERFORMING HISTORY

1. See, for example, Michael Hattaway's introduction to his edited collection *The Cambridge Companion to Shakespeare's History Plays*: "'There is figures in all things' (*Henry V*, 4.7.30): stage-Plantagenets could signify individuals contemporary with Shakespeare. In the Chorus to Act V of *Henry V* Shakespeare explicitly compares Henry's triumphant return from Agincourt to a wished-for return for Robert Devereux, Earl of Essex who, at the time of the play's composition, was in Ireland dealing with the Tyrone rebellion" (16); noting Elizabethan authority's suspicion of history plays, Hattaway goes on to discuss the "widespread habit of scrutinizing the past for analogues of the present, a habit of mind that derives from typological reading of the Bible" (19). For a discussion of typological thought in the second Henriad, including Fluellen's linking of Harry to Alexander the Great, see Hillman, *Intertextuality and Romance in Renaissance Drama*, 26–57.

2. Greenblatt, "Invisible Bullets," in *Shakespearean Negotiations*, 21–65.

3. See, for example, Hillman, *Intertextuality and Romance in Renaissance Drama*, which I discuss in more detail below.

4. Barthes, *S/Z*, 21. Indeed, some critics have suggested that for all its promise of

playful dialogue between texts, intertextuality is little more than traditional source study: see Culler, *The Pursuit of Signs*, 118.

5. See Zumthor, "Le carrefour des rhétoriqueurs," esp. 336; Bloom, *The Anxiety of Influence*; and Kristeva, *Semeiotikè*, esp. 262.

6. See Aristotle, "De anima," 555; and Marx, "Theses on Feuerbach," 400.

7. On nostalgia in the Henriad, see Charnes, "Reading for the Wormholes."

8. After being "discovered" in Britain and the United States in the 1980s, Weimann's work is currently receiving renewed attention as an alternative to the mainstream and arguably attenuated materialism of new historicism. See Drakakis, "Discourse and Authority"; and Reynolds and West (eds.), *Rematerializing Shakespeare*, whose essays, dedicated to Weimann, build on his heterodox materialism and theories of theatrical authority and representation.

9. Partly to resist the subversion/containment paradigm advanced by Stephen Greenblatt in "Invisible Bullets," cultural materialists spoke of "dissident" practices: see, for example, Sinfield, *Faultlines*.

10. Weimann, *Shakespeare and the Popular Tradition*, 73–85. I appropriate Mikhail Bakhtin's term "chronotope" here; although he applies it specifically to the form of the novel, it remains a useful tool with which to illuminate different epistemological and theatrical formations of space and time. See Bakhtin, *The Dialogic Imagination*.

11. Weimann, *Shakespeare and the Popular Tradition*, 79.

12. Preston, *King Cambises*, line 744. All further references are cited in the text.

13. Weimann, *Author's Pen and Actor's Voice*, 82.

14. Weimann, *Author's Pen and Actor's Voice*, 85.

15. "Bifold authority," the words employed by Troilus to describe the split between his conviction of Cressida's fidelity and the new testimony of his senses (*Troilus and Cressida*, 5.2.144), has become Weimann's catchphrase to describe the divided forms of authority on the medieval and Tudor stages. See, for example, Weimann, "Bifold Authority in Shakespeare's Theatre."

16. In the quarto text of *2 Henry 4* (1600), one of Falstaff's speech prefixes in act 1, scene 2 is rendered as "Old." instead of "Falst."; and in *1 Henry 4*, Prince Hal calls Falstaff "my old lad of the castle" (1.2.42). See Goldberg, "The Commodity of Names." For an extended (and somewhat unconvincing) discussion of supposed points of historical connection between the Cobham-Oldcastles and the second Henriad, see Scoufos, *Shakespeare's Typological Satire*.

17. I would add that this is perhaps typical of how Weimann's understanding of the intertheatrical palimpsest is sometimes wistfully oriented toward a golden past of folk drama. For example, Weimann claims that Shakespeare's aesthetic of disfigurement "does not go as far as the mainstream of folklore had gone," implying that the Elizabethan theater stands at the twilight of a vital demotic tradition; Weimann, *Author's Pen and Actor's Voice*, 88.

18. See Berger, *Imaginary Audition*.

19. Hedrick and Reynolds, "'A Little Touch of Harry in the Night,'" esp. 171.

20. Hopkin, Ingman, and Reynolds, "Nudge, Nudge, Wink, Wink, Know What I Mean, Know What I Mean?" esp. 161.

21. Here my discussion of the palimpsested nature of Shakespearean performance recalls Luke Wilson's observation, "Where mimesis gives way to representation—where the actor speaks out from inside his character—character thins out and agency becomes palimpsestic, revealing agency-for-another lurking behind agency-for-oneself, the player and playwright speaking out of the mouth of the character"; see *Theaters of Intention*, 177.

22. The new company's letter to the Lord Mayor, written in March 1602, is reprinted in Pollard (ed.), *Shakespeare's Theater*, 326. For studies of the history of the Boar's Head, see Sisson, *The Boar's Head Theatre*; and Berry, *The Boar's Head Playhouse.*

23. Johnson, *A Critical Edition of Thomas Preston's* Cambises, line 530. All further references to the play are from this edition, and cited in the text.

24. And like Ambidexter, Falstaff does a comic turn as a *miles gloriosus*. See Weimann, *Shakespeare and the Popular Tradition*, 124.

25. Indeed, at the level of textual style, Falstaff's remarks recall not the clumsy fourteeners of Cambyses, but the language of drama contemporary with *1 Henry 4*. For example, Falstaff's reference to "tears" that "stop the floodgates of her eyes" potentially alludes to *Soliman and Perseda*, 4.1.94–95: "How can mine eyes dart forth a pleasant look, / When they are stopped with floods of flowing tears?" But even this parody of writerly style seems to be prompted by familiarity less with a playscript than with a memorably histrionic technique of acting.

26. For a discussion of the performance of tears in Shakespeare, see Cohen, *More Power to You*, 7–18.

27. Hillman, *Intertextuality and Romance in Renaissance Drama*, 38.

28. Hillman, *Intertextuality and Romance in Renaissance Drama*, 27.

29. Hillman, *Intertextuality and Romance in Renaissance Drama*, 38.

30. Of the plays I consider here, Peele's *Battle of Alcazar* and both parts of Marlowe's *Tamburlaine* were performed by the Admiral's Men at the Rose; the production details of *Soliman and Perseda* and Greene's *Alphonsus* are not clear, though Philip Henslowe's 1598 inventory of the Admiral's Men's stage properties includes an "owld Mahametes head" that corresponds to the most spectacular stage effect, in 4.1, of Greene's play; see Foakes and Rickert (eds.), *Henslowe's Diary*, 319.

31. Peele, *The Battell of Alcazar, Fought in Barbarie, Betweene Sebastian King of Portugall, and Abdelmec King of Marocco*, sig. D4.

32. *Soliman and Perseda*, 1.5.77–80.

33. Greene, *The Comicall Historie of Alphonsus, King of Aragon*, 3.2.179–85.

34. All references are to Marlowe, *Tamburlaine Parts One and Two.*

35. Hall, *The Collected Poems of Joseph Hall, Bishop of Exeter and Norwich*, 14–15.

36. E. S., *The Discovery of the Knights of the Post*, sig. C2v. For this and other references, I am indebted to Richard Levin's painstaking survey of contemporary responses to Tamburlaine, "Contemporary Perception of Marlowe's *Tamburlaine.*"

37. Dekker, *Satiromastix*,4.3.169; in Dekker, *The Dramatic Works of Thomas Dekker*, 1:364.

38. Ben Jonson, *Timber; Or Discoveries*, in Jonson, *Ben Jonson*, 12 vols. (Oxford: Clarendon Press, 1947), 7:587. On Edward Alleyn's distinctive acting style, see Armstrong, "Shakespeare and the Acting of Edward Alleyn," and Andrew Gurr's convincing critique of Armstrong, "Who Strutted and Bellowed?" On Alleyn's career, see Hosking, *The Life and Times of Edward Alleyn.*

39. Indeed, Tamburlaine's sword seems to have been a vital component of his histrionic onstage effect. In the first part of *Tamburlaine*, he dramatically moves from his past life as a shepherd to his new role as "terror to the world" when he sheds his shepherd's "weeds," declaiming: "This complete armour and this curtle-axe / Are adjuncts more beseeming Tamburlaine" (1.2.41, 42–43).

40. When the two parts of *Henry 4* are performed in repertory, Pistol can easily be played by the same actor who plays Hotspur, thereby linking the two characters and their histrionicism. This was the case in the 2004 Washington, D.C., Shakespeare Theatre repertory productions, directed by Bill Alexander, of *Part 1* and *Part 2*.

41. When Pistol tells Mistress Quickly "feed and be fat, my fair Calipolis," audiences may have recognized the allusion to the scene in *The Battle of Alcazar* where Muly Mahomet offers his starving wife the raw flesh of a lion.

42. Weimann, *Author's Pen and Actor's Voice*, 24.

43. For records of performance of the Coventry Corpus Christi play, particularly its staging of the Herod sequences, see Ingram (ed.), *Records of Early English Drama.*

44. "Pageant of the Shearmen and Taylors," in Craig (ed.), *Two Coventry Corpus Christi Plays*, l. 779.

45. "Pageant of the Shearmen and Taylors," l. 783.

46. For discussions of the shared features of and difference between Herod's various dramatic incarnations in the Corpus Christi cycle drama, see Parker, "The Reputation of Herod in Early English Literature"; Hussey, "How Many Herods in the Middle English Drama?"; Weimann, *Shakespeare and the Popular Tradition in the Theater*, 65–72; Skey, "Herod the Great in Medieval European Drama"; Staines, "To Out-Herod Herod"; Bushnell, *Tragedies of Tyrants;* Stevens, "Herod as Carnival King in the Medieval Biblical Drama"; and Coletti, "Re-Reading the Story of Herod in the Middle English Innocents Plays."

47. I discuss the links between the Coventry Herod and Shakespearean styles of acting in my essay "'Look not Big, nor Stamp, nor Stare.'"

48. See Reynolds, *Performing Transversally*, 4–5, 120.

49. Hillman, *Intertextuality and Romance in Renaissance Drama*, 57.

50. Hegel, *The Philosophy of History*, 54.

51. Hegel, *The Philosophy of History*, 24. Hegel turns once again to *Hamlet* at the end of his *Philosophy of History*, borrowing the language of the play to describe the 2,500-year trajectory of his study: "Well said old mole. Cans't work in the earth so fast?" For further discussion of the mole's importance to Marx's materialism as well as Hegel's idealism, see Stallybrass, "'Well Grubbed, Old Mole'"; and de Grazia, "Teleology, Delay, and the *Old Mole*."

52. Hegel, *The Philosophy of History*, 103.

53. Hegel, *The Philosophy of History*, 99.

54. Hegel, *The Philosophy of History*, 104.

55. Hegel, *The Philosophy of History*, 139.

56. Hegel, *The Philosophy of History*, 106.

57. Hegel, *The Philosophy of History*, 73. For a discussion of the trope of the phoenix in Shakespeare's history plays, see Menon, *Wanton Words*, 165.

58. Hegel, *The Philosophy of History*, 99, 101.

59. Hegel, The *Philosophy of History*, 79.

60. Biddick, *The Typological Imaginary*, 1–21; and Lupton, *Afterlives of the Saints*, 3–39.

PART II. EXPLOSIONS

Note to epigraph: Benjamin, "Theses on the Philosophy of History," in *Illuminations*, 263.

1. Foxe, *Actes and Monuments of These Latter and Perilous Dayes*, 2:25.

2. For a useful survey of English apocalyptic thought in the sixteenth and seventeenth centuries, see Patrides and Wittreich (eds.), *The Apocalypse in English Renaissance Thought and Literature.*

3. Derrida, *Specters of Marx*, e.g. 37, 90.

4. As Bill Brown has noted, Benjamin understood the history *in* things diversely: as a material residue (Benjamin, *Moscow Diary*, 123); as the impression of social life recorded on their surfaces ("On Some Motifs in Baudelaire," *Illuminations*, 155–200); as the record of the subject's formation in modernity ("The Work of Art in the Age of Mechanical Reproduction," *Illuminations*, 236); and as the trace of a collective and unconscious utopian longing ("Paris, Capital of the Nineteenth Century," *Reflections*, 148). See Brown, "How to Do Things with Things (A Toy Story)." But Benjamin's most extensive meditations on nineteenth- and twentieth-century material culture come in *The Arcades Project*, where he examines fashionable items and numerous other objects in the arcades and the broader cityscape of nineteenth-century Paris; and *Berlin Childhood Around 1900*, in which he often focuses on remembered objects—socks, a sewing box, a desk—from his childhood. I discuss *The Arcades Project* in more detail in Chapter 3.

5. Benjamin, *The Origins of German Tragic Drama*, 132–33. For an excellent discussion of the untimely power of the ruin in early modern writing, see Griffiths, "The Sonnet in Ruins."

6. Benjamin, *Illuminations*, 255. Benjamin quotes from Nietzsche's "Of the Use and Abuse of History" at the beginning of Thesis XII: "We need history, but not the way a spoiled loafer in the garden of knowledge needs it" (*Illuminations*, 260).

7. Benjamin, *Illuminations*, 255, 261.

CHAPTER 3. THE WRITING ON THE WALL

Note to epigraph: Nietzsche, "On the Uses and Disadvantages of History for Life," 93.

1. Grady, *Shakespeare's Universal Wolf*, 24.

2. Stow's *Suruey of London* was first published in 1598; it was reissued in 1603 with substantial additions. After his death, the *Survey* was repeatedly updated in the seventeenth and eighteenth centuries by antiquarians such as John Strype. In its textual history, then, the *Survey* is itself much like the London described by Stow—a palimpsest subject to constant reinscription, emendation, and erasure.

3. Benjamin, "Theses on the Philosophy of History," in *Illuminations*, 255.

4. On Delhi, see Dalrymple, *City of Djinns*, whose abiding conceit is of a "city disjointed in time, a city whose different ages lay suspended side by side as in aspic" (9); on Tokyo, see Hidenobu, *Tokyo*, in which the author, armed with old maps, wanders through Tokyo's lanes and alleys and discovers that its lots, despite repeated annihilation by earthquake, fire, and war, are still shaped by land use patterns from its earliest settlement; on Mexico City, see Davilla, "Mexico City as Urban Palimpsest in Salvador Novo's *Nueva Grandeza Mexicana*," which considers how Novo treats the city as a palimpsest composed of past, present, and even future textual, spatial, and cultural layers based on architecture, literary history, and personal recollections; on Barcelona, see Barril and Vivas, *Barcelona*, which reads the city as a cosmopolitan site of rewriting in which all visitors, from Roman legions to modern immigrants, leave their mark on the city's construction materials; on Istanbul, see Gür, "Spatialisation of Power/Knowledge/Discourse," which reads the Sultanahmet district in Istanbul as an urban palimpsest whose archival structure has been made through discursive representations, each constructed on the preceding one; on Johannesburg, see Graham, "Memory, Memorialization and the Transformation of Johannesburg," which considers the transformations of South Africa's cityscapes in the wake of apartheid, including Constitution Hill in Johannesburg, where the Old Fort—a prison predating the Anglo-Boer War used to house political prisoners during apartheid—has been transformed into the site of the new Constitutional Court Building.

5. See Denis, "Treasure City."

6. Freud, *Civilization and Its Discontents*, 8.

7. For a fascinating reading of Shanghai that regards the city's past not as a positive entity that survives in the present but rather as a continuously produced and reproduced range of discursive effects, see Schaeffer, "Shadow Photographs, Ruins and Shanghai's Projected Past."

8. Huyssen, *Present Pasts*, 84. Yet even as Huyssen invokes (re)writing as a metaphor for urban space, he is oddly nervous about doing so. "My focus on reading palimpsests," he assures his readers, "is not some imperialism of *écriture*"; rather, he claims that his concern is "to respect the fundamental materiality and formal traditions of the different media of memory" at work in the urban palimpsest (7).

9. Huyssen, *Present Pasts*, 7. Huyssen notes how civic memory practices have been altered by globalization and the politics of Holocaust commemoration, which "attaches

itself like a floating signifier to historically very different situations" (99); this has affected the design of Latin American monuments, memorials, artworks, marked sites, and a "memory park" in Buenos Aires that commemorate the violence of regimes from the 1970s and 1980s.

10. Huyssen, *Present Pasts*, 10.

11. Nietzsche discusses the importance of forgetting in "On the Uses and Disadvantages of History for Life," 60–64. The major works of trauma theory, and the emphasis they place on working through and/or moving forward, are Caruth, *Unclaimed Experience*, and LaCapra, *Writing History, Writing Trauma.* Huyssen discusses, in order to distance himself from, trauma theory on 127 and 172n26.

12. Huyssen, *Present Pasts*, 29.

13. Huyssen, *Present Pasts*, 30, 84.

14. Cited by Howard Eiland, "Translator's Foreword," in Benjamin, *Berlin Childhood Around 1900*, xii. On Benjamin and the city, see Gilloch, *Myth and Metropolis.*

15. Writing of memory, Baudelaire asks: "What is the human brain, if not an immense and natural palimpsest? Such a palimpsest is my brain; such is yours too, reader. Everlasting layers of ideas, images, and feelings have fallen upon your brain as softly as light. Each succession has seemed to bury all that went before. And yet, in reality, no layer has perished"; see Baudelaire, *Artificial Paradises*, 147.

16. Benjamin, *The Arcades Project*, 85.

17. Kuberski, *The Persistence of Memory*, 18–19.

18. Huyssen's analysis of memory politics moves toward a renunciation of linear temporality in favor of multiple kinds of time experienced at the intersection between the individual and the social: language and literature, space and architecture, politics and art. Indeed, he elsewhere considers Benjamin's embrace of heterodox urban temporalities in "Modernist Miniatures." Yet Huyssen still insists on an absolute distinction between past, present, and future that "good" memory practices observe in order to progress from the traumatic event (*Present Pasts*, 112).

19. Stow, *A Survey of London, by John Stow*, 1:38.

20. In all likelihood, based on the Latin translation, the inscription was "matzevat rabbi moshe ben harav rabbi yitzhak," which means (literally) "monument of Rabbi Moshe son of Rabbi Yitzhak." I am assuming that what Stow records as "מצב חר" should be "מצבת ר." Hebrew has two related forms for rabbi: (a) "rav" or "harav" (הרב) with definite article "ha" (ה), denoting the occupation with all its gravitas; and (b) "rabbee," as title, abbreviated in writing to "r" [ר]. Note the duplication in relation to Yitzhak of "harav" and "rabbi." The one part of Stow's inscription that remains inscrutable to me is the concluding (or in Hebrew, beginning) word, "חך." It may in fact not be a word but, like the use of "ר" for "rabbee," a pair of initials denoting a phrase. Perhaps Stow has mistranscribed the "ך" (or kof), and it should instead read "ו" (or vav). With Hebrew's tendency to pair adjectives for reinforcement, the possibilities are endless: it could be, for example, "hagadol v'hanechbad" ("the great and honored"). I am grateful to Stella Harris for assistance with my translation, and for further speculations.

21. In the 1633 edition, for instance, the inscription is rendered "חך מצבחר משחבן הרבר ןצחה"; Stow, *Survey of London . . . Begunne first by the paines and industry of Iohn Stovv, in the yeere 1598*, 37.

22. Bale, "Stow's Medievalism and Antique Judaism in Early Modern London," esp. 79–80.

23. Stow, *Survey of London*, 1:38.

24. Stow observes that "I reade that in the year 1215. the 6. of king *Iohn*, the Barons entering the City by *Ealdgate*, first tooke assurance of the Citizens, then brake into the Jewes houses, searched their coffers to fill their owne purses, and after with great diligence repaired the walles and gates of the Citie, with stones taken from the Jewes broken houses" (1:9); and that "the Barons broke into the Iews houses, rifeled their coffers, and with the stone of their houses repaired the gates and walles of London" (1:279). He gives more specific information about the repairs' location in two other passages: early in the *Survey*, he claims that "*Robert Fitzwater, Giffrey Magnauile* Earle of Essex, and the Earle of Glocester, chiefe leaders of the armie, applied all diligence to repaire the Gates and walles of this Cities, with the stone taken from the Jewes broken houses, namely, *Aeldgate* being the most ruinous, (which had giuen them an easie entrie) they repaired" (1:29–30); though he specifies Aldgate here, he later focuses his attention on Ludgate: "I reade, as I tolde you, that in the yeare 1215. the 17. of king *Iohn*, the Barons of the Realme, being in armes against the king, entred this Citie, and spoyled the Jewes houses, which being done, *Robert Fitzwater*, and *Geffre de Mangna villa*, Earle of Essex, and the Earle of Gloucester, chiefe leaders of the Armie, applied all diligence to repayre the gates and wals of this Citie, with the stones of the Jewes broken houses, especially (as it seemeth) they then repaired or rather new builded Ludgate" (1:38).

25. See Biddick, *The Typological Imaginary*, esp. chap. 1.

26. Latour, *We Have Never Been Modern*, 69.

27. Ptolemy's *Geography*, written in the second century A.D., was translated at Vicenza in 1475 and thence in many editions, with considerable impact on the practice of chorography in Britain. See Evans, *A History of the Society of Antiquaries*, 2. For discussions of English Renaissance chorography, see Helgerson, "The Land Speaks"; Mendyk, "Early British Chorography"; Marchitello, "Political Maps"; Klein, *Maps and the Writing of Space in Early Modern England and Ireland*, esp. 137–48.

28. Carpenter, *Geographie Delineated Forth in Two Bookes, Containing the Sphericall and Topicall Parts Thereof*, 1:2.

29. Marchitello, *Narrative and Meaning in Early Modern Europe*, 78.

30. See William Camden, *Britannia* (London, 1586), published in Latin, and translated into English by Philemon Holland as *Britain, Or a Chorographicall Description of the Most Flourishing Kingdomes, England, Scotland, and Ireland*; and Drayton, *Poly-Olbion.* Although the English Renaissance chorographers were influenced by Ptolemy's *Geography*, there was a strong native tradition of chorographical description in medieval England prior to Ptolemy's translation, as exemplified by William Fitzstephen's twelfth-century description of London, of which Stow made considerable use.

31. For a reading of Stow's "mapping" of London, and the overlaps and tensions between chorographical and cartographical understandings of space, see Adrian, "Itineraries, Perambulations, and Surveys," esp. 39–44.

32. Stow, *Survey of London*, 1:1.

33. For more on the temporalities of Ludgate as both civic monument and debtors' prison, see Harris, "Ludgate Time."

34. Manley, *Literature and Culture in Early Modern London*, 226. For Anne Boleyn's coronation in 1533, for example, Ludgate was "costly and sumptuously garnished with gold, colours, and azure"; Elizabeth's precoronation approach to Ludgate was announced by the playing of music at the site. See Withington, *English Pageantry*, 1:184, 202.

35. "King *Lud* (as the foresaid *Giffrey* of *Monmouth* noteth) afterward, not only repaired this Cittie, but also increased the same with faire buildings, Towers and walles, and after his owne name called it *Caire-Lud*, as *Luds* towne, and the strong gate which he builded in the west part of the Cittie, he likewise for his owne honour named *Ludgate*"; Stow, *Survey of London*, 1:1.

36. See, for example, Stacy, "The Conversion of Jews to Christianity in Thirteenth-Century England," esp. 269n38.

37. Jacobs, "The London Jewry, 1290," esp. 34. As one historian notes, however, "Etymologically the identification of the *vicus judeorum* with Old Jewry is not as straightforward as might be assumed. The term 'Old Jewry' came into use only after the 1290 expulsion. It occurs first in the *Calendar of Wills proved and enrolled in the Court of Hustings* as *la Olde Iuwerie* in 1327–8, and as *la Elde Jurie* in 1336. Here 'old' means 'former' or 'late' "; Hillaby, "The London Jewry," 5.

38. See Jacobs, "The London Jewry," 36.

39. *Calendar of Letter-Books Preserved among the Archives of the Corporation of the City of London at the Guildhall*, 219.

40. De Certeau, *The Practice of Everyday Life*, 91–130.

41. Hillaby, "London," esp. 98.

42. As Hillaby remarks, "The statute of Jewry of 1253 enacted that 'there will be no synagogues save in those places wherein they were in the time of the lord King John'; full worship itself became difficult since it was further enacted that Jews must 'in their synagogues, one and all, worship in subdued tones . . . so that Christians hear it not' "; "London," 100.

43. Hillaby, "London," 135–36, 144.

44. See Mundill, "Anglo-Jewry Under Edward I."

45. On medieval mob attacks against London Jews, see Jacobs, "The London Jewry," 20; and Hillaby, "London," 149–50.

46. Hillaby, "London," 99.

47. On Poor Jewry, see Stow, *Survey of London*, 1:149; on Jewin Garden, see 1:301.

48. Nashe, *The Unfortunate Traveller*, in *The Complete Works of Thomas Nashe*, 2:307.

49. Harvey, *Pierce's Supererogation or A New Praise of the Old Ass*, 51–52.

50. For a discussion of the medieval figuration of the Jew as a spectral ghost—albeit a ghost who is unacceptably material and embodied in relation to the Christians who have superseded him—see Kruger, *The Spectral Jew.*

51. Stow, *Survey of London*, 1:277–78. See also Jonson, *Every Man in His Humor*, 1.1.173. The original version of the play, printed in the Quarto of 1601, has an Italian setting; the references to London's Old Jewry appear first in the 1616 Folio edition, which relocates the play in England.

52. Jonson, *Every Man in His Humor*, 1.1.151–56.

53. The possibility of a Jewish present is raised again by Jonson in the character of Kitely, who is referred to as "the rich merchant i'the Old Jewry" (1.1.137–38). He assumes distinctive "Jewish" qualities according to the codes of the 1590s London stage: a miserly moneymaker, Kitely has adopted a son whom he has named "Cash"—an echo, perhaps, of the two theatrical Jewish fathers who utter variations on "my daughter, my ducats" in *The Merchant of Venice* and *The Jew of Malta.* And like Shylock and Barabas, Kitely compulsively invests in "jewels" and measures the qualities of humans by the "carat" (2.1.14, 3.2.22). Once again, however, Jonson raises the specter of a Jewish present only to exorcise it: we are assured of the non-Jewishness of merchant and adopted son whom, Kitely declares, was baptized as a Christian (2.1.20).

54. On Tudor London's Jewish or crypto-Jewish communities, see Sisson, "A Colony of Jews in Shakespeare's London"; Roth, "The Middle Period of Anglo-Jewish History (1290–1655) Reconsidered"; Prior, "A Second Jewish Community in Tudor London"; Shapiro, *Shakespeare and the Jews*, 62–88.

55. For a particularly thoughtful revisiting of the Dr. Lopez affair that places new attention on the vicissitudes of his Portuguese as well as his Jewish identity, see Campos, "Jews, Spaniards, and Portingales."

56. Perhaps most revealing is Stow's discussion of Bakewell Hall in Basinghall Street: "That this house hath been a Temple or Iewish Sinagogue (as some haue fantasied) I allow not, seeing that it had no such forme of roundness, or other likenesse" (1:286). Stow is most likely wrong about its provenance; evidence indicates that it had indeed been once used as a synagogue. But this remark indicates that his fascination with London's Jewish past was not entirely his own, and that there was indeed a tradition of speculation about whether or not certain buildings had once been Jewish, based on (mistaken) assumptions about the universally circular structure of synagogues.

57. Stow, *Survey of London*, 1:279, 1:280, 2:335.

58. Stow, *Survey of London*, 1:280, 2:42–43.

59. Stow, *Survey of London*, 1:277–78.

60. Marx and Engels, "The Communist Manifesto," 476.

61. See Howard, "Competing Ideologies of Commerce in Thomas Heywood's *If You Know Not Me You Know Nobody, Part II*," esp. 169.

62. Archer, "The Nostalgia of John Stow," esp. 29. See also Beer, "John Stow and the English Reformation, 1547–1559"; Kastan, "Opening Gates and Stopping Hedges"; and Collinson, "John Stow and Nostalgic Antiquarianism."

63. Stow, *Survey of London*, xvi–xvii.

64. Manningham, *Diary of John Manningham, of the Middle Temple*, 103.

65. Stow, *Survey of London*, 2:75. The rogue in question was Meredith Hamner, vicar of St. Leonard's from 1581 to 1592; see 2:369.

66. Stow, *Survey of London*, 1:148.

67. Stow, *Survey of London*, 1:152, 1:275. Stow does speculate, however, that that the giant's "shanke bone" might come from an "Oliphant," and the tooth from a "monstrous fish" (1:275).

68. Manley, "Of Sites and Rites," esp. 51.

69. Griffin, "Preserving and Reserving the Past in Stow's *Survey of London*."

70. Stow, *Survey of London*, 1:9, 1:279.

71. Jacobs observes that "there can be little doubt that this was the tombstone of R. Moses b. Isaac, the author of the 'Sepher Hassoham,' the most considerable literary production of English Jews before the expulsion"; see "The London Jewry, 1290," 35.

72. *Shtetl*, dir. Marian Marzynski (Frontline/Marz Associates, 1996).

73. Compare Dipesh Chakrabarty's discussion of colonial translation, which sees it as modeled on "the generalized exchange of commodities, which always needs the mediation of a universal, homogenizing middle term"; *Provincializing Europe*, 85.

74. On the motif of the New Jerusalem in Renaissance English Protestant thought, see Haller, *The Rise of Puritanism, or the Way to the New Jerusalem as Set Forth in Pulpit and Press from Thomas Cartwright to John Lilburne and John Milton, 1570–1643*.

75. See de Certeau, "Ethno-graphy: Speech or the Space of the Other: Jean de Léry," in *The Writing of History*, 209–43. On the "ravishing song" of the Tupinamba Indians, see Jean de Léry, *History of a Voyage to Brazil*, 141, 144.

CHAPTER 4. THE SMELL OF GUNPOWDER

Note to epigraph: Jonson, *Cynthia's Revels*, in *The Complete Plays of Ben Jonson*, 2:83, ll. 115–16.

1. Jonson, *Bartholomew Fair*, Induction 154. Jonson has a vivid olfactory imagination; not only does he rail against bad smells in plays like *Cynthia's Revels* and *Bartholomew Fair*, he also sought to produce sweet odors in court masques, such as *Chloridia*, which calls for a personation of Rain to sprinkle the room with "sweet water"; see *Ben Jonson: Selected Masques*, 311. See also Nagler, "Towards the Smell of Mortality," esp. 48.

2. Gurr, *The Shakespearean Stage*, 221.

3. Marlowe, *Doctor Faustus*, 169 (3.2.28); the stage direction is found in the A-text (see note to 3.2.28. s.d.). See also Dessen and Thomson, *A Dictionary of Stage Directions in English Drama 1580–1642*, s.v. "squib."

4. Whithorne, *Certaine Waies*, fol. 24.

5. Whithorne, *Certaine Waies*, fol. 46.

6. The conventional wisdom has been that thunder was produced on stage by rolling a cannon ball on the floor, as Ben Jonson alludes to with the "roul'd bullet" in the

prologue to *Every Man in His Humor*, line 18. Significantly, though, this "bullet" is an afterthought to the "nimble squibbe" he refers to in the previous line, which suggests that the two practices may have been used in tandem.

7. Andrew Gurr notes that "fireworks or rosin for lightning flashes were available at the amphitheatres but unpopular at the halls because of the stink"; see Gurr, "*The Tempest*'s Tempest at Blackfriars," esp. 95.

8. Smith, "Introduction," esp. 22–23.

9. Smith, *The Acoustic World of Early Modern England*, 276.

10. See Coddon, "'Unreal Mockery'"; Calderwood, *Shakespearean Metadrama*, 12–14; and Goldberg, "Speculations."

11. For a study of theatrical lighting and illumination in the original performances, see Graves, *Lighting the Shakespearean Stage, 1567–1642*. For a thorough study of theatrical lightning and other special effects, see Butterworth, *Theatre of Fire*.

12. See Classen, Howes, and Synnott, *Aroma*; Jenner, "Civilization and Deodorization?"; and Rindisbacher, *The Smell of Books*. In *Civilization and Its Discontents* (see *The Standard Edition of the Complete Psychological Works of Sigmund Freud*, 21:99–107), Freud provides what has been arguably the most influential account of the devaluing of smell over the centuries; he roots this transition in evolutionary biology, arguing that as primitive humans began walking upright, they could no longer smell themselves or their potential mates; hence the sense of smell became devalued and erotic stimulation became more a function of vision.

13. See, for example, Corbin, *The Foul and the Fragrant*; and Laporte, *History of Shit*.

14. For an insightful discussion of the relations between smell and memory in Proust, see Fuss, *The Sense of an Interior*, 151–212.

15. Rindisbacher, *The Smell of Books*, 158.

16. Scientific studies of the proximity within the amygdala of synapses connected to olfaction and memory include Herz and Engen, "Odor Memory"; and Buchanan, Tranel, and Adolphs, "A Specific Role for the Human Amygdala in Olfactory Memory." For an important discussion of recent neuroscientific understandings of olfaction and memory, and how these might help frame research on early modern experiences of smell, see Dugan, "The Ephemeral History of Perfume," introduction.

17. Folkerth, *The Sound of Shakespeare*, 8. Folkerth pays attention also to another "soundscape" that would have contributed to early modern playgoers' experiences of *Macbeth*: the ominous sound of hautboys, or shawms, that begin 1.6 and 1.7 (108).

18. Smith, *The Acoustic World of Early Modern England*, 276.

19. The play's unusual disruptions of time have attracted much critical attention; see, for example, Driver, "The Uses of Time"; Nakatani, "Expressions of Time in *Macbeth*,"; Abiteboul, "La temporalité dans *Macbeth*,"; and Berry, "Reversing History." For a discussion of how *Macbeth* problematizes the conventional linear—and lineal—temporality of succession, see Goldberg, "Speculations."

20. My thoughts here are influenced by Joseph Campana. In a brilliant and as yet unpublished essay, "The Bloody Babe and the Crowned Child: Killing Time in *Macbeth*,"

presented at the 2007 Shakespeare Association of America seminar "Shakespeare and the Question of Time," Campana notes how both *Macbeth* and Walter Benjamin deform *chronos*, or numerable, linear time, and embrace *kairos*, or the contraction and cessation of sequential time.

21. Shakespeare uses the word "untimely" on nineteen occasions. In every case it is to suggest a supposedly premature occurrence. More often than not, it is death that is untimely: the corpse of Richard II is carried off the stage in an "untimely bier" (5.6.52), Richard III's enemies are "untimely smothered in their dusky graves" (4.4.70), death is supposed to lie on Juliet like an "untimely frost" (4.4.55), the dead Romeo and Paris "untimely lay" (5.3.257), and the terminal line of Oswald, slain by Edgar, is "O, untimely death!" (*King Lear* [Conflated Text], 4.6.255). Yet this prematurity is also notably associated with birth, with an interruption that ushers in an unexpected and even monstrous future. Not only is Macduff from his "mother's womb / Untimely ripped"; Lady Anne also wishes that any child of Richard of Gloucester be "abortive . . . / Prodigious, and untimely brought to light" (1.2.21–22), so that it may frighten its mother. The untimely has a monstrous power in its refusal of "proper" time; moreover, it is perceived to have an almost supernatural agency, a power to do work on the time by virtue of its not being of the time.

22. Benjamin, "Theses on the Philosophy of History," in *Illuminations*, 255.

23. Indeed, Folkerth himself resorts suggestively to the metaphor of the palimpsest. In a suggestive analysis of the 1888 sound recording of Henry Irving performing the opening soliloquy of *Richard III*, Folkerth writes that "the recording of the opening speech of *Richard III* . . . is a deceptively complex historical artifact. While listening to Irving speak, you are not only listening *to* a particular historical event, you are listening *through* history as well. What sounds like obtrusive background noise is actually layer upon audible layer of acoustic technology, a sonic palimpsest of different temporalities" (*The Sound of Shakespeare*, 6). The recording is a "sonic palimpsest," Folkerth explains, because what we listen to is not just the whirr of the wax cylinder that recorded Irving's voice but also the hiss of the audiotape onto which that recording was later transferred, and the graininess of resolution obtained when the tape was converted to a digital file.

24. I have written elsewhere on this tendency. See Harris, "The New New Historicism's *Wunderkammer* of Objects"; and "Shakespeare's Hair."

25. Marx, "Theses on Feuerbach," 143.

26. *Macbeth*'s date of composition and early performance history remain speculative. The earliest date of which we have a record of performance is 1611, but the play is usually regarded as having been written and first performed in 1606. This is largely because of the Porter's joking reference to "an equivocator" (2.3.8), which most editors regard as an allusion to the recently executed Jesuit priest, Father Henry Garnet, who had written a treatise defending equivocation for persecuted Catholics. For a discussion of the play's date of composition and first performance, see Stephen Greenblatt's introduction to *Macbeth* in Shakespeare, *The Norton Shakespeare*, 2555–56.

27. William B. Barlow, quoted in Wills, *Witches and Jesuits*, 21. Compare "the mere

lees / Is left this vault to brag of" (*Macbeth*, 2.3.91–92) and "but this blow / Might be the be-all and the end-all" (1.7.4–5).

28. Andrewes, *Ninety-Six Sermons*, 4:207. Rebecca Lemon, in "Scaffolds of Treason in *Macbeth*," notes other texts that, in the immediate wake of the Gunpowder Plot, use the formula of "fair and foul"; see 33–35.

29. Barnes, *The Devil's Charter*, 43.

30. Barnes, *The Devil's Charter*, 120.

31. James I, *His Maiesties Speech in this Last Session of Parliament*, sig. E3v.

32. Shakespeare employs the logic of inversion with his parody of apocalyptic prophesy in *King Lear*, where the Fool predicts a time "When priests are more in word than matter, / When brewers mar their malt with water; / when nobles are their tailors' tutors," and so forth (3.2.79–81). The genre's most famous instance is the medieval "Merlin's Prophecy," which appeared in many guises; see Coote, "Merlin, Erceldoune, Nixon."

33. Addressing the United Nations on September 21, 2006, a day after U.S. president George W. Bush had spoken to the assembly, Venezuelan president Hugo Chávez notoriously remarked that "the devil came here yesterday, and it smells of sulfur still today." See "Chavez: Bush 'devil'; US 'on the way down,'" CNN.com International, http://edition.cnn.com/2006/WORLD/americas/09/20/chavez.un/index.html, posted 21 September 2006 (accessed 26 October 2007).

34. Hale, *Renaissance War Studies*, 392.

35. Jonson, "The Vnderwood," in Jonson, *Ben Jonson*, 8:212, l. 202; and Dekker, *The Artillery Garden*, sigs. C1v, D1v.

36. See Mills (ed.), *The Chester Mystery Cycle*, 302–3. I am grateful to Kurt Schreyer for this reference.

37. See Ingram (ed.), *Records of Early English Drama*, 326–27, 339, 341, 347, 159, 368–69, 374, 378, 391, 473–74, 477; and *The Castle of Perseverance*, 1. On devils and fireworks, see Paxson, "Theorizing the Mysteries' End in England, the Artificial Demonic, and the Sixteenth-Century Witch-Craze"; and Palmer, "The Inhabitants of Hell." For a thorough survey of representations of the devil on the English stage, see Cox, *The Devil and the Sacred in English Drama, 1350–1642*.

38. Marlowe, *Doctor Faustus*, A-text, 2.1.151 s.d.; Heywood, *The Silver Age*, in *Heywood's Dramatic Works*, 3:121; and Tailor, *The Hog Hath Lost His Pearl*, 5.1.47 s.d. See also Dessen and Thompson, *Dictionary of Stage Directions*, s.v. "fire."

39. For a discussion of the medieval echoes in this scene, see Wickham, "Hell-Castle and its Door-Keeper."

40. See Rushdie, *Midnight's Children*, 380.

41. James I, *A Counter-blaste to Tobacco*, sig. C4v.

42. Drummond, *Quinque Sensus*. The poem is printed in slightly different form, under the title of "For the Kinge," in Drummond, *The Poetical Works of William Drummond of Hawthornden*, 2:296–99.

43. James's father had perished from gunpowder burns, and, suspecting that the letter's "blow" might refer to a similar threat, James ordered a search of the Houses of

Parliament vaults, where the kegs—and Fawkes—were found. See Wills, *Witches and Jesuits*, 23–34.

44. "Of Catesby Faux and Garnet," fols. 125–25v. A transcription of this ballad, which matches my own, is available online at http://www.bcpl.net/~cbladey/guy/html/song.html (accessed 26 October 2007).

45. Herbert, *The English Poems of George Herbert*, 185–86 (ll. 13, 5, 19–21, 22–24).

46. In its entry for "essence," the OED notes how its divergent meanings of "that which constitutes the being of a thing" (definition 7) and "a fragrant essence; a perfume, a scent" (definition 10) were both in use by the early seventeenth century. The movement of the word from ontological to olfactory spheres was in large part enabled by the sixteenth-century Swiss physician Paracelsus, who applied the term to "solutions containing the volatile elements or 'essential oil' to which the perfume, flavour, or therapeutic virtues of the substance are due"; see OED, s.v. "essence," 9a.

47. Duby and Braunstein, "Toward Intimacy," esp. 539.

48. See Floyd-Wilson, "English Epicures and Scottish Witches," esp. 142.

49. Tomkis, *Lingua*, sig. H4.

50. See Nagler, "Towards the Smell of Mortality."

51. Shirley, *The Doubtful Heir*, sig. B1.

52. Tomkis, *Lingua*, sig. I1.

53. Montaigne, *The Complete Essays*, 352–54, esp. 353–54.

54. Cited in Atchley, *A History of the Use of Incense in Divine Worship*, 351. Atchley's book is a rich compendium of information about the history of incense and censing from the ancients to the nineteenth century.

55. William Lambarde, *A Topographical Dictionary*; quoted in Warton, *History of English Poetry from the Twelfth to the Close of the Sixteenth Century* 2:221–24. I am grateful to Kurt Schreyer for this reference.

56. In *Certaine Sermons*, 71.

57. Brathwait, *Essayes upon the Five Senses*, fol. 72.

58. See Palmer, "In Bad Odour." See also Galen, *On Anatomical Procedures*, 186, 195; and Eastwood, "Galen on the Elements of Olfactory Sensation."

59. Drummond, *Quinque Sensus*.

60. Middleton, *Women Beware Women*, 5.2.14.

61. Jonson, *Complete Works*, 4.5.177.

62. Taylor, "Divine [ ]sences," esp. 26.

63. Greenblatt, *Shakespearean Negotiations*, 119.

64. De Camões, *The Lusíads*, 27.

65. Fitch, "The Voyage of Mr Ralph Fitch Merchant of London," 252.

66. Fitch, "The Voyage of Mr Ralph Fitch Merchant of London," 253.

67. Coghill, "*Macbeth* at the Globe, 1606–1616 (?)."

68. In their complaints about the theater, the so-called antitheatricalists chafed obsessively against the playhouses' supposedly decadent sensuality. Henry Crosse, for example, fumed that in the theater "every sense [is] busied"; Crosse, *Virtue's Commonwealth*, sigs. Q2–Q2v.

69. The best discussion of doubleness and inversion in *Macbeth* remains Stallybrass, "*Macbeth* and Witchcraft."

PART III. CONJUNCTIONS

Note to epigraph: Latour, *We Have Never Been Modern*, 74–75.

1. The temporality of conjunction is both redolent of and subtly at odds with the view of time that informs the critical movement in Shakespeare studies called presentism. Critics identified with this movement have drawn on a loose ensemble of cultural materialist, poststructuralist, and Frankfurt School theory to read Shakespeare in relation not just to his time but also to our own. They thus instinctively deploy a version of the temporality of conjunction by assuming that the matter of the past is always already inflected by our own historical situatedness. But even as presentists have challenged the positivist tendencies of a historicism that would seek to describe Shakespeare's moment as it really was, they have often regarded the "present" and the "past" as temporally discrete, albeit related, entities. For the most clear exposition of presentism as a critical method in Shakespeare studies, see Grady and Hawkes (eds.), *Presentist Shakespeares*.

2. Latour, *We Have Never Been Modern*, 73.

3. Deleuze and Guattari, *A Thousand Plateaus*, esp. 2:4–13.

4. Hegel, *The Philosophy of History*, 17–18.

5. Chakrabarty, *Provincializing Europe*, 109; compare Benjamin, "Theses on the Philosophy of History," in *Illuminations*, 255.

6. Chakrabarty, *Provincializing Europe*, 112.

7. Latour, *We Have Never Been Modern*, 74. We might thus compare Latour's critique of modern time to Chakrabarty's account of how subaltern pasts are dismissed as premodern by historicism because of their hybrid translations of political and religious agency; see *Provincializing Europe*, esp. 72–96.

8. The scene seems to correspond to 1.1.104–20, in which Tamora pleads for her son's life. The text of this speech is reproduced beneath the illustration.

9. Jonathan Bate, "Introduction," 43. For a discussion of Julie Taymor's *Titus* that speculates on the film's debts to Peacham's drawing, see Walker, "'Now Is a Time to Storm.'"

10. In response to Latour's observation that for Serres the "classical virtue of philosophy continues to be the synthesis," Serres remarks: "Yes, I'm racing toward a synthesis. No doubt it will be unexpected in relation to the totals and subtotals that can be arrived at now. Why? Because no doubt it will be made more through comparativism than by sequential linking, more through Hermes's swift travels than by deduction or solid construction." And in the same interview, Serres says that "Hegel's error was . . . in claiming that contradiction produces time." See Serres with Latour, *Conversations on Science, Culture, and Time*, 73, 51.

CHAPTER 5. TOUCHING MATTERS

Note to epigraphs: Cixous, "Sorties," 126; Cavendish, *The World's Olio*, 131–32.

1. Cavendish, *CCXI Sociable Letters*, sig. d.
2. Cixous, "Sorties," 123.
3. Cixous, "Sorties," 99.
4. Ahmed, *Queer Phenomenology*, 106.
5. Marx, "Theses on Feuerbach," 143.
6. Sedgwick, *Touching Feeling*, 14.
7. In using the term "dialogic," I am of course glancing at the increasingly neglected work of Mikhail Bakhtin. On Bakhtin's dialogics, see Bakhtin, *Rabelais and His World* and *The Dialogic Imagination*; also Volosinov, *Marxism and the Philosophy of Language.* For affinities between Bakhtin and feminist dialogics, see Bauer and McKinstry (eds.), *Feminism, Bakhtin, and the Dialogic.*
8. Sedgwick, *Touching Feeling*, 17.
9. Ahmed, *Queer Phenomenology*, 107.
10. Dinshaw, *Getting Medieval*, passim. Dinshaw's book is interested in queer identifications that work across temporal boundaries and identitarian differences: for example, Robert Glück's novel *Margery Kempe*, an imaginative work in which a San Francisco gay man in 1994 identifies passionately and mystically with Margery in much the same way that Margery herself identified with Christ and the Virgin Mary.
11. Goldberg and Menon, "Queering History," esp. 1611.
12. Cixous, "Laugh of the Medusa."
13. Cixous, *Vivre l'orange.*
14. In the grotesque body of early modern carnival, writes Bakhtin, "the stress is laid on those parts of the body that are open to the outside world, that is, the parts through the world enters the body or emerges from it, or through which the body itself goes out to meet the world" (*Rabelais and His World*, 26). With her insistence that the woman's body is multiple, overflowing, and becoming, Cixous complements Bakhtin's theory of the grotesque and underscores its largely suppressed gendered dimensions. Some influential studies of the early modern body have employed Bakhtin's grotesque paradigm to tease out constructions of gender—see, for example, Stallybrass, "Patriarchal Territories"; and Paster, *The Body Embarrassed.*
15. Cixous, "Sorties," 94. To give just one example of this reputation, an anthology of literary theory often used in the undergraduate English classroom identifies Cixous's feminism as exemplifying "one strand of essentialist theory"; see Rivkin and Ryan (eds.), *Literary Theory*, 767. See also the powerful criticisms of Cixous voiced by Jones, "Writing the Body"; Moi, *Textual/Sexual Politics*; and Spivak, *In Other Worlds.* So when Cixous writes of Woman that "her libido is cosmic, just as her unconscious is worldwide: her writing also can only go on and on, without ever inscribing or distinguishing contours . . . I am spacious singing Flesh" ("Sorties," 88), most if not all early modern scholars are likely to share Ann Rosalind Jones's reservations about "the concept of *féminité* as a

bundle of Everywoman's psychosexual characteristics: it flattens out the lived differences among women" (Jones, "Writing the Body," 365).

16. Cixous, "Sorties," 63, 65.

17. Cixous, "Sorties," 83.

18. Cixous, "Sorties," 87.

19. Cixous, "Sorties," 83. Compare Deleuze and Guattari, *A Thousand Plateaus*, which models the earth as a body without organs: "This body without organs is permeated by unformed, unstable matters, by flows in all directions, by free intensities or nomadic singularities, by mad or transitory particles" (40).

20. Spivak complains in *In Other Worlds* (149) that Cixous has an attenuated understanding of writing; whereas Derrida sees it as *différance*, the principle of differentiation and deferral, Spivak claims that Cixous regards it simply as literary writing. But I believe she ignores the extent to which Cixous understands literature as a particularly dialogic province of différance.

21. Cixous, "Sorties," 98.

22. See, for example, Cixous's remarks about woman's desire: "What does she want? To sleep, perchance to dream" ("Sorties," 67); or about the return of the hitherto repressed active female principle: "They, the feminine ones, are coming back from far away, from forever, from 'outside,' from the heaths where witches stay alive" ("Sorties," 69).

23. Jones, "Writing the Body," 367.

24. Spivak also notes of Cixous that "in much of her argument for 'bisexuality,' she is sometimes reminiscent of the Freud who silenced female psychoanalysts by calling them as good as men. The question of the political or historical and indeed ideological differential that irreducibly separates the male from the female critic of phallocentrism is not asked" (Spivak, *In Other Worlds*, 146–47).

25. Cixous, "Sorties," 84.

26. Cixous, "Sorties," 85.

27. The economy of the neighbor has become an important issue in so-called political theology; see Žižek, Santner, and Reinhard, *The Neighbor*.

28. Irigaray, "The Sex That Is Not One."

29. Cavendish, *Natures Pictures Drawn by Fancies Pencil to the Life*, 133.

30. Cavendish, *CCXI Sociable Letters*, 2.

31. Cavendish, *Blazing World*, 175.

32. Cavendish, *Blazing World*, 194.

33. Cavendish, *Blazing World*, 206.

34. Cavendish, *Blazing World*, 123.

35. Cavendish, *Blazing World*, 124, 126.

36. Cavendish, *Blazing World*, 129.

37. Cavendish, *Blazing World*, 185.

38. Wagner, "Romancing Multiplicity." However, Wagner is more inclined to see synthesis than dialogics in Cavendish's writing—a tendency apparent in her argument that *The Blazing World* is a romance, her conviction that Cavendish's transmigrations of

the soul constitute a merger or union, and her assessment that Cavendish's theory of matter entails "oneness" (1, 20, 24).

39. Cavendish, *Natures Pictures*, sig. A2.

40. Cavendish, *CCXI Sociable Letters*, sig. d.

41. For studies of early modern analogical cosmology, see Barkan, *Nature's Work of Art*; and Foucault, *The Order of Things*, chap. 1.

42. For a useful study of the organicism of Hobbes's *Leviathan*, see Pye, "The Sovereign, the Theater, and the Kingdome of Darknesse." On Cavendish's intellectual relations with Hobbes, see Hutton, "In Dialogue with Thomas Hobbes."

43. Cavendish, *Blazing World*, 124.

44. Cavendish, *Natures Pictures*, sig. C6. In some respect, Cavendish's intuition about the dialogic properties of language resembles Volosinov's dialogic theory of language: "Each and every word expresses the 'one' in relation to the 'other.' I give myself verbal shape from another's point of view," Volosinov, *Marxism and the Philosophy of Language*, 86. Compare Schwab, "Irigarayan Dialogism," esp. 58.

45. Cavendish, *Blazing World*, 192.

46. Cavendish, *Blazing World*, 124.

47. Cavendish, *Natures Pictures*, sig. C4.

48. Woolf complained that Cavendish's "philosophies are futile, and her plays intolerable, and her verses mostly dull"; see Woolf, *The Common Reader*, 77. For the view that Cavendish's writing strategy anticipates Woolf's, see Rogers, *The Matter of Revolution*: "She was herself deeply invested (*pace* Virginia Woolf) in building a philosophical 'Cottage' of her own" (200).

49. One recipe for mithridate is given by Celsus: "Costmary 1·66 grams, sweet flag 20 grams, hypericum, gum, sagapenum, acacia juice, Illyrian iris, cardamom, 8 grams each, anise 12 grams, Gallic nard, gentian root and dried rose-leaves, 16 grams each, poppy-tears and parsley, 17 grams each, casia, saxifrage, darnel, long pepper, 20·66 grams each, storax 21 grams, castoreum, frankincense, hypocistis juice, myrrh and opopanax, 24 grams each, malabathrum leaves 24 grams, flower of round rush, turpentine-resin, galbanum, Cretan carrot seeds, 24·66 grams each, nard and opobalsam, 25 grams each, shepherd's purse 25 grams, rhubarb root 28 grams, saffron, ginger, cinnamon, 29 grams each"; Celsus, *De medicina*, 2:57.

50. Cavendish, *The World's Olio*, 162.

51. See, for example, "Of the Rational Soul of Man": "Of all the opinions concerning the Natural Soul of Man, I like that best which affirms the Soul to be a self-moving substance; but yet I will add a *Material* self-moving substance"; Cavendish, *Observations upon Experimental Philosophy*, 2:45.

52. Cavendish, *Philosophical Letters*, 5.

53. Cavendish, *Poems, and Phancies*, 44.

54. See chapter 1, note 82.

55. Cavendish, *Poems, and Phancies*, sig. b4. For a discussion of Cavendish's relation to atomism, and how the latter might illuminate her outlandish conjunction with the Earl of Newcastle, see Goldberg, "Margaret Cavendish, Scribe."

56. Cavendish, *Observations upon Experimental Philosophy*, 1:135, 136–37.

57. On seventeenth-century versions of vitalism, see Wheeler, *Vitalism*; Rogers, *Matter of Revolution*; Pagel, *William Harvey's Biological Ideas*, 251–77; and Yolton, *Thinking Matter*, 1–26. For Cavendish's relationship to vitalism, see Stevenson, "The Mechanist-Vitalist Soul of Margaret Cavendish."

58. See Rogers, *Matter of Revolution*, 191–92. One might compare Cavendish's critique of mechanistic causality to Fredric Jameson's in *The Political Unconscious*, 23–25, which also invokes the billiard-ball model of cause and effect. But Cavendish embraces neither the Leibnizian expressive causality nor the Althusserian structural causality that Jameson poses as the alternatives to Cartesian mechanism—unless one sees her theory of the rational parts of matter as a voluntarist model of expressive causality.

59. Rogers, *Matter of Revolution*, 201. On the gender politics of Cavendish's experimental science, see Keller, "Producing Petty Gods." For a countervailing view that understands Cavendish's theory of matter as decidedly not feminist, see Boyle, "Margaret Cavendish's Nonfeminist Natural Philosophy."

60. Although Cavendish repeatedly professes her faith in God, she seems to do so with a measure of anxiety born of the logical consequences of her self-moving, vitalist nature, which has no need of a masculine, transcendent power. It is perhaps not surprising, therefore, that Rogers sees Cavendish as the most likely target of the Cambridge Platonist Ralph Cudworth's denunciation, in 1678, of "hylozoic atheism" (Rogers, *Matter of Revolution*, 194).

61. Cixous, "Sorties," 91.

62. See Gallagher, "Embracing the Absolute." For qualifications of Gallagher's influential thesis, see Sherman, "Trembling Texts," which argues for Cavendish's sense of her historical agency rather than subjection; and Trubowitz, "The Reenchantment of Utopia and the Female Monarchical Self," which argues for Cavendish's sense of other-connectedness.

63. Cavendish, *Poems, and Phancies*, 54.

64. In Irigaray's reading of Plato's *Timaeus*, the distinction between matter and form is enabled by even as it excludes the chora, the feminized receptacle on which phallic form impresses itself to produce matter. See Irigaray, *Speculum of the Other Woman*, 243.

65. Cavendish, *The World's Olio*, 174.

66. Cavendish, *Observations upon Experimental Philosophy*, 3:37–38.

67. Cavendish, *Blazing World*, 153.

68. On the Renaissance Hermetic tradition and its relation to the Cabbala, see Yates, *Giordano Bruno and the Hermetic Tradition*, esp. 84–114 and 257–74.

69. Cavendish, *Blazing World*, 181, 188.

70. In "A Science Turned Upside Down," Lisa T. Sarasohn argues that "the substance of her philosophy and its exposition justified a revolution in the interpretation of the traditional female role" (290). Rogers does acknowledge, however, that the masculine is encoded in Cavendish's theory of matter as the inanimate parts that are subservient to the rational female parts (Rogers, *Matter of Revolution*, 201–2).

71. Latour, *We Have Never Been Modern*, 75.

72. Latour, *We Have Never Been Modern*, 69.

73. Latour, *We Have Never Been Modern*, 69.

74. On the "quasi-object," see Latour, *We Have Never Been Modern*, 51–55.

75. See Latour, *We Have Never Been Modern*, 15–32. Latour's analysis of Boyle's air pump draws largely on Shapin and Schaffer's *Leviathan and the Air-Pump*, which focuses on the differences between Hobbes's political and Boyle's scientific interpretations of the pump. Latour points out that Shapin and Schaffer themselves perform the purification characteristic of modern history by insisting ultimately on a political gold standard for interpretation, rather than allowing the proliferation of hybrids that characterize Boyle's and Hobbes's standoff: "Boyle is not simply creating a scientific discourse while Hobbes is doing the same thing for politics; Boyle is creating a political discourse from which politics is to be excluded, while Hobbes is imagining a scientific politics from which experimental science has to be excluded" (Latour, *We Have Never Been Modern*, 27).

76. For an account of this episode, see Mintz, "The Duchess of Newcastle's Visit to the Royal Society."

77. Cixous, "Sorties," 83.

78. Cavendish, *Natures Pictures*, 355; *The World's Olio*, 7.

79. In his essay "On the Uses and Disadvantages of History for Life," Nietzsche writes that monumental history "is the belief in the solidarity and continuity of the greatness of all ages and a protest against the passing away of generations and the transitoriness of things." But he also complains: "How much of the past would have to be overlooked if was to produce that mighty effect, how violently what is individual in it would have to be forced into a universal mould with all its sharp corners and hard outlines broken up in the interest of conformity!" (69).

80. Cavendish's affinities are often qualified, however, by her competitive desire for fame. She observes in *Natures Pictures*, "I have not read much History to inform me of the past Ages, indeed I dare not examin the former times, for fear I should meet with such of my Sex, that have out-done all the glory I can aime at, or hope to attaine" (sig. c1)—a position somewhat at odds with her portrait of Cleopatra.

81. Dekker, *The Shoemaker's Holiday*, 17.27–28.

82. This is a far cry from the metonymic mode of history that Hayden White attributes to Marx, which is largely a synchronic determinism redolent of Hobbesian mechanism. According to White in *Metahistory*, Marx's dialectical view of history is enabled by a mechanistic materialism whereby the Base determines Superstructure through "a succession of distinctive means of production and the modes of their relationships, a succession that is governed by strict causal laws"; this "cause-effect" relationship White sees as "Metonymical" (286).ter

83. Cavendish, *CCXI Sociable Letters*, 130.

84. In September 1668, Thomas Povey wrote to a friend about his travels in the northern countries, expressing excitement about his visit "to see the Queen of Sheba and her more considerable Prince, the Duke of Newcastle"; *Calendar of State Papers, Domestic*

Series, November 1667 to September 1668, 602. For a discussion of this soubriquet, see Crawford, "'Pleaders, Atturneys, Petitioners and the like.'"

85. Latour, *We Have Never Been Modern*, 75.

CHAPTER 6. CRUMPLED HANDKERCHIEFS

1. The "double time" theory—that the events of *Othello* take place *both* in dizzyingly rapid succession *and* over an extended duration that would allow more time for Othello to suspect Cassio of adultery with Desdemona, Bianca to accuse Cassio of neglecting her, and Iago to pester Emilia a "hundred times" for the handkerchief—was first outlined by John Wilson in *Blackwood's Magazine* (November 1849, April and May 1850), but it was given its classic formulation by A. C. Bradley in "The Duration of the Action in *Othello*" in his *Shakespearean Tragedy*, published in 1905 (423–29). As early as the seventeenth century, however, Thomas Rymer complained in *A Short View of Tragedy* of the inconsistencies in the play's time scheme (123). For useful summaries of the double-time problem, see E. A. J. Honigmann's introduction to the third Arden edition of *Othello*, 68–74, and Michael Neill's introduction to the Oxford Shakespeare edition of *Othello*, 33–76. Even recent criticism of the play has shown a tendency to straighten out the play's temporalities by attempting to "solve" the problem: see Bradshaw, *Misrepresentations*, 148–68; and Sohmer, "The 'Double Time' Crux in *Othello* Solved."

2. Serres with Latour, *Conversations*,60.

3. Serres and Latour, *Conversations*, 70.

4. "Cross-breeding—that's my cultural idea. Black and white, science and humanities, monotheism and polytheism," Serres and Latour, *Conversations*, 28.

5. Serres and Latour, *Conversations*, 43–44.

6. Serres, *Hermes*, 98. See also Serres, *The Birth of Physics*.

7. Serres and Latour, *Conversations*, 48.

8. Serres and Latour, *Conversations*, 58.

9. Serres and Latour, *Conversations*, 47.

10. Serres and Latour, *Conversations*, 59.

11. Readers have noted in Antony's speech an Ovidian if not a Lucretian understanding of transformation. For a Serres-like study of how Ovid's metamorphic cosmology is indeed a "physics" whose traces can be read in English Renaissance drama, see Poole, "The Devil's in the Archive." For a reading of *Othello* attentive to its sustained images of fluidity, see Hopkins, *Shakespeare on the Edge*, 87–114.

12. Serres and Latour, *Conversations*, 59.

13. Serres and Latour, *Conversations*, 60–61.

14. Serres and Latour, *Conversations*, 61.

15. See Serres, "Le messager"; *Hermes*; and *Angels*.

16. For a brilliant discussion of *A Midsummer Night's Dream* and Puck that draws in part on Serres, see Turner, *Shakespeare's Double Helix*.

17. 1.1.83, 1.2.38, 1.3.58, 2.3.150, 2.3.163, 2.3.176, 2.3.193, 2.3.251, 3.4.159, 4.1.50, 4.2.114,

5.1.50, 5.1.75, 5.1.111 (twice), 5.2.47, 5.2.105, 5.2.168, 5.2.171, 5.2.259. See Shaw, "'What Is the Matter?'"

18. I have written about the tendency to equate the "material" of "material culture" with physical form in "The New New Historicism's *Wunderkammer* of Objects"; and "Shakespeare's Hair."

19. Marx, "Theses on Feuerbach," 400.

20. The question of the handkerchief and "work" has been considered extensively in Marxist criticism of the play, particularly that which engages feminist questions. Dympna Callaghan, for example, sees the handkerchief as a magical commodity fetish from which women's work has been erased; see "Looking Well to Linens." See also Korda, "The Tragedy of the Handkerchief," in *Shakespeare's Domestic Economies*, 111–58.

21. Marx, "The Fetishism of the Commodities and the Secret Thereof," 319–29. For some Marxists, the recent wave of scholarship on material culture performs precisely this fetishistic operation: David Hawkes has criticized what he sees as a tendency in such scholarship for "things [to] abandon their objective nature altogether, and actually become subjective agents." As this assessment makes clear, Hawkes regards agency as a synonym for subjecthood—and to think otherwise is, for him, to submit to laughable superstition: "The name for the belief that certain objects [are agents] is magic." See Hawkes, "Materialism and Reification in Early Modern Studies," esp. 118.

22. Rymer, *A Short View of Tragedy*, 159.

23. For related analyses that explain Othello's obsessive belief in the handkerchief by reference to his African background, see Feldman, "Othello's Obsessions"; and Mudford, "*Othello* and the 'Tragedy of Situation.'" Despite scant evidence that Shakespeare had any knowledge of archaic Ethiopian religious tradition, Fernand Balsperger argued that the handkerchief was an Ethiopian fetish or amulet. See Baldensperger, "Was Othello an Ethiopian?"

24. As Lynda E. Boose notes in her influential essay "Othello's Handkerchief," a significant number of scholars have regarded the handkerchief's essence as residing in its actual insignificance: see Fiedler, *The Stranger in Shakespeare*, 149; Stockholder, "Egregiously an Ass," esp. 265; and Alexander, "Thomas Rymer and *Othello*," esp. 75. In "Impertinent Trifling," Harry Berger, Jr., considers how the insignificant napkin achieves a rich psychological existence of its own. The most compelling instance of this strain of criticism is provided by Marxist readings of the handkerchief. Paul Yachnin argues that the handkerchief is a reification of wonder crucial to the late Elizabethan playhouse; see "Wonder-effects."

25. Hankey, *Shakespeare in Production*, 207. See Martin Butler's review of this production in the *Independent*, 21 September 1997, and also Michael Neill's introduction to *Othello*, 98.

26. Heilman, *Magic in the Web*, esp. 211–14.

27. Anna Jameson referred to the "fatal handkerchief" in 1832; see her *Shakespeare's Heroines*, 176. The phrase has subsequently become a commonplace in literary criticism. See, for example, Andrews, "Honest Othello," esp. 273. Even a Marxist critic, denouncing

what he regards as Dympna Callaghan's misunderstanding of agency and commodity fetishism in her reading of the play, refers to the "fatal handkerchief"; see Egan, review of Jean E. Howard and Scott Cutler Shershow (eds.), *Marxist Shakespeares.*

28. "Made with a Handkerchief: The Orator," http://www.20kweb.com/orator.html, July 25, 2007.

29. Heilman, *Magic in the* Web, 211–12.

30. *A Lover's Complaint*, in Shakespeare, *The Norton Shakespeare*, l. 16. The strawberries are Shakespeare's innovation; the handkerchief in his source, Giovanni Battista Giraldi Cinthio's *Gli Hecathommithi,* is simply embroidered "alla moresca": "The Lady often took with her a handkerchief—a gift from the Moor—which was most delicately embroidered in the Moorish fashion"; Cinthio, *Gli Hecatommithi*, Third Decade, Seventh Novella, trans. Bruno Ferraro, in Neill's introduction to *Othello*, 439.

31. Martin Waugh in "*Othello*, the Tragedy of Iago," in Faber (ed.), *The Design Within*, tries to interpret the symbol of the handkerchief around which the tragedy resolves as a fetish, the child's substitute for the breast (166). In "Iago, the Paranoiac," also in Faber, Gordon Ross Smith suggests as an alternative that "since breast and penis symbols are often interchangeable . . . the strawberries might equally or better have been penis symbols, or even actual representations of the glands, enwreathed in 'curious' hair-like leaves (176). Jean Jofen synthesizes these views in "The Case of the Strawberry Handkerchief." For a reading of the strawberries as evoking menstrual blood, see Snow, "Sexual Violence and the Male Order of Things in *Othello*," esp. 392.

32. See Ross, "The Meaning of Strawberries in Shakespeare."

33. See Newman, "'And wash the Ethiop white,'" esp. 156. For a discussion of the syphilitic meanings of "spotted," see Harris, "(Po)X Marks the Spot."

34. Boose offers her theory of the link between the strawberries and the matrimonial sheets in "Othello's Handkerchief"; it has since informed powerful readings of the handkerchief and the play's repressed primal scenes of sexuality, including Snow, "Sexual Anxiety and the Male Order of Things in *Othello*"; Neill, "'Unproper Beds'"; and Little, "'An Essence Unseen.'"

35. See Andrews, "Honest Othello," 279.

36. For a reading of another stage handkerchief as a palimpsest, see Sofer, "Absorbing Interests."

37. On images of blank pages and inscription as the markers of female sexuality, see Gubar, "'The Blank Page' and the Issues of Female Creativity."

38. See Tyson, "Ben Jonson's Black Comedy."

39. Latour, *We Have Never Been Modern*, 78–82.

40. Stallybrass, "Patriarchal Territories."

41. Parker, *Shakespeare from the Margins*, 21–49. For a rhetorical reading of the preposterous erotic energies of both the play and *Othello* criticism, see Altman, "'Preposterous Conclusions.'"

42. Glenn Burger and Steven Kruger similarly argue that the queer is a kind of "logic of the preposterous" that disturbs temporality and "suggests that the stabilization

of a sequential 'pre' and 'post,' cause and effect, might be thought otherwise"; Burger and Kruger, "Introduction," in *Queering the Middle Ages*, xi and xii.

43. Biddick, *The Typological Imaginary.*

44. Snyder, *The Comic Matrix of Shakespeare's Tragedies.*

45. Critics have sidestepped the double-time conundrum by insisting that it would not have been noticeable to an audience in the way it is to readers: see Neill, "Introduction," 34.

46. Lupton, "*Othello* Circumcised," esp. 79.

47. Boehrer, "*Othello*'s Monsters," esp. 131.

48. Fabian, *Time and the Other,* chaps. 1 and 2.

49. See Vitkus, "Turning Turk in *Othello.*"

50. In a now well-known sequence of essays, William Pietz has argued that our modern notions of the fetish derive from the early modern Portuguese *feitisso* or magic; but with the Protestant Reformation and the dramatic reduction in power attributed to objects, the feitisso became twinned with a residual discourse of idolatry, now adapted specifically to demean African talismanic amulets and charms in the new trading contact zones of Guinea and the western coast of Africa. See Pietz, "The Problem of the Fetish, II" and "The Problem of the Fetish, IIIa."

51. Marees, "A Description and Historicall Declaration of the Golden Kingdome of Guinea." Marees's heady brew of magic, African travel narrative, and anti-idolatry is, of course, a persistent feature of *Othello.* Othello powerfully rejects Brabantio's accusation that he used "foul charms" (1.2.73) to win Desdemona; yet once racked with jealousy, he succumbs to magical thought, especially in relation to the handkerchief. "There is magic in the web of it" (3.4.68), he says: the handkerchief has a potentially malign power over those who come into contact with it. He specifically associates this magic with pagan Africa—the spell of an ancient Egyptian charmer and sybil who seem to belong not just to a different place but also to a different, pre-Christian time. And in his imagination, Desdemona comes to resemble Marees's female fetish worshippers: he insists she speaks to the handkerchief, as if it were a subject rather than an object.

52. The link between the "prophetic fury" of Othello's sybil and the "furor profetica" of Ariosto's Cassandra (Ariosto, *Orlando Furioso,* 46.80), has been noted by Prior, "Shakespeare's Debt to Ariosto," and Robinson, *Islam and Early Modern English Literature,* 1–2.

53. Burton, *The Anatomy of Melancholy,* 3.3.2.1.

54. Africanus, *A Geographical Historie of Africa,* 143. Leo Africanus's description of wedding night traditions in Fez is discussed in relation to *Othello*'s handkerchief also by Nelson and Haines, "Othello's Unconsummated Marriage," esp. 8, and Little, "The Primal Scene of Racism in *Othello,*" 312.

55. For an excellent discussion of "trifle" as a term used variously in mercantile, Protestant, and early ethnographic discourse, see Kearney, "The Book and the Fetish."

56. Calvin, *A Very Profitable Treatise,* sig. B2v. See also sigs. A2, A2v, A8, B1v, etc.

57. Appadurai (ed.), *The Social Life of Things*; see especially Igor Kopytoff's contribution to the volume, "The Cultural Biography of Things."

58. Chakrabarty, *Provincializing Europe*, 8.
59. Chakrabarty, *Provincializing Europe*, 108–9.
60. Chakrabarty, *Provincializing Europe*, 250.
61. Nietzsche, *Untimely Meditations*, 60.

CODA. DIS-ORIENTATIONS

1. Ghosh, *In an Antique Land.* I have written elsewhere about Ghosh's ethnography and its potential uses for early modern scholarship; see Harris, "Afterword."
2. Ghosh, *In an Antique Land*, 339.
3. Ghosh, *In an Antique Land*, 95.
4. Ghosh, *In an Antique Land*, 201.
5. Ghosh, *In an Antique Land*, 72–73. Ghosh is asked by the villagers of Lataifa to inspect the pump—which, though its workings are mysterious to him, he affirms in a quasi-religious rite of "silent communion." Conflating modernity and superstition, Ghosh's relation to the water pump provides a nice counterpart to Bruno Latour's account of Robert Boyle's temporally hybrid air pump in *We Have Never Been Modern*, 15–32.
6. Ghosh, *In an Antique Land*, 39.
7. Biddick, *The Typological Imaginary*, 98.
8. Ghosh, *In an Antique Land*, 95.
9. Chakrabarty, *Provincializing Europe*, 243. Chakrabarty and Ghosh have themselves noted the affinities—and tensions—between their conceptions of subaltern history; see Ghosh and Chakrabarty, "A Correspondence on *Provincializing Europe*."

WORKS CITED

Abiteboul, Maurice. "La temporalité dans *Macbeth*." In Nadia J. Rigaud, ed., *Aspects du théâtre anglais*. Aix-en-Provence: Université de Provence, 1987. 11–22.

Adams, Joseph Quincy Adams, ed. *Chief Pre-Shakespearean Dramas*. Boston: Houghton Mifflin, 1924.

Adrian, John M. "Itineraries, Perambulations, and Surveys: The Intersections of Chorography and Cartography in the Sixteenth Century." In Yvonne Bruce, ed., *Images of Matter: Essays on British Literature of the Middle Ages and Renaissance*. Newark: University of Delaware Press, 2005. 29–47.

Africanus, Leo. *A Geographical Historie of Africa, written in Arabicke and Italian by Iohn Leo a More, borne in Granada, and brought vp in Barbarie. . . . Translated and collected by Iohn Pory, lately of Goneuill and Caius College in Cambridge*. London, 1600.

Agamben, Giorgio. *The Man Without Content*. Trans. Georgia Albert. Stanford, Calif.: Stanford University Press, 1999.

———. *The Time That Remains: A Commentary on the Letter to the Romans*. Trans. Patricia Dailey. Stanford, Calif.: Stanford University Press, 2005.

Ahmed, Sara. *Queer Phenomenology: Orientations, Objects, Others*. Durham, N.C.: Duke University Press, 2006.

Alexander, Nigel. "Thomas Rymer and *Othello*." *Shakespeare Survey* 21 (1968): 67–77.

Altman, Joel B. "'Preposterous Conclusions': Eros, *Enargeia*, and the Composition of *Othello*." *Representations* 18 (1987): 129–57.

Andrewes, Lancelot. *Ninety-Six Sermons by the Right Honourable and Reverend Father in God, Lancelot Andrewes*. 5 vols. Oxford: John Henry Parker, 1865.

Andrews, Michael C. "Honest Othello: The Handkerchief Once More." *Studies in English Literature* 13 (1973): 273–84.

Appadurai, Arjun. "Introduction: Commodities and the Politics of Value." In Arjun Appadurai, ed., *The Social Life of Things: Commodities in Cultural Perspective*. Cambridge: Cambridge University Press, 1986. 3–63.

Archer, Ian W. "The Nostalgia of John Stow." In David L. Smith, Richard Strier, and David Bevington, eds., *The Theatrical City: Culture, Theatre and Politics in London, 1576–1649*. Cambridge: Cambridge University Press, 1995. 17–34.

Ariosto, Ludovico. *Orlando Furioso*. Ed. Landfranco Caretti. Milan: Ricciardi, 1963.

Aristotle. *The Basic Works of Aristotle.* Trans. Richard McKeon. 2 vols. New York: Random House, 1941.

———. *De anima.* In *The Basic Works of Aristotle.* Trans. Richard McKeon. 2 vols. New York: Random House, 1941. II. 535–606.

Armstrong, W. A. "Shakespeare and the Acting of Edward Alleyn." *Shakespeare Survey* 7 (1954): 82–89.

Atchley, E. G. Cuthbert F. *A History of the Use of Incense in Divine Worship.* London: Longmans, Green, 1909.

Auerbach, Erich. "Figura." In *Scenes from the Drama of European Literature.* Trans. Ralph Manheim. New York: Meridian, 1959. 11–76.

Augustine. *On Christian Doctrine.* Trans. D. W. Robertson, Jr. Indianapolis: Prentice Hall, 1958.

Badiou, Alain. *Saint Paul: The Foundation of Universalism.* Trans. Ray Brassier. Stanford, Calif.: Stanford University Press, 2003.

Bakhtin, Mikhail. *The Dialogic Imagination: Four Essays.* Trans. Caryl Emerson and Michael Holquist. Austin: University of Texas Press, 1981.

———. *Rabelais and His World.* Trans. Hélène Iswolsky. Cambridge, Mass.: MIT Press, 1968.

Baldensperger, Fernand. "Was Othello an Ethiopian?" *Harvard Studies and Notes in Philology and Literature* 20 (1938): 3–14.

Bale, Antony. "Stow's Medievalism and Antique Judaism in Early Modern London." In Ian Gadd and Alexandra Gillespie, eds., *John Stow (1525–1605) and the Making of the English Past.* London: British Library, 2004. 69–80.

Barkan, Leonard. *Nature's Work of Art: The Human Body as Image of the World.* New Haven: Yale University Press, 1975.

Barnes, Barnabe. *The Devil's Charter: A Critical Edition.* Ed. Jim C. Pogue. New York: Garland, 1980.

Barril, Joan, and Pere Vivas. *Barcelona: The Palimpsest of Barcelona.* Barcelona: Triangle Postals, 2001.

Barthes, Roland. *S/Z.* London: Jonathan Cape, 1974.

Baudelaire, Charles. *Artificial Paradises.* Trans. Stacy Diamond. New York: Citadel Press, 1996.

Baudrillard, Jean. *For a Critique of the Political Economy of the Sign.* Trans. Charles Levin. New York: Telos Press, 1981. 88–101.

Bauer, Dale M., and S. Jaret McKinstry, eds. *Feminism, Bakhtin, and the Dialogic.* Albany: State University of New York Press, 1991.

Beer, Barrett L. "John Stow and the English Reformation, 1547–1559." *Sixteenth-Century Journal* 16 (1985): 257–71.

Benjamin, Walter. *The Arcades Project.* Trans. Howard Eiland and Kevin McLaughlin. Cambridge, Mass.: Harvard University Press, 1999.

———. *Berlin Childhood Around 1900.* Trans. Howard Eiland. Cambridge, Mass.: Harvard University Press, 2006.

———. *Illuminations.* Trans. Harry Zohn. Ed. Hannah Arendt. New York: Schocken, 1969.

———. *Moscow Diary.* Trans. Richard Sieburth. Ed. Gary Smith. Cambridge, Mass.: Harvard University Press, 1986.

———. *The Origins of German Tragic Drama.* Trans. John Osborne. London: Verso, 1977.

———. *Reflections: Essays, Aphorisms, Autobiographical Writing.* Trans. Edmund Jephcott. Ed. Peter Demetz. New York: Schocken, 1986.

Berger, Harry, Jr. *Imaginary Audition: Shakespeare on Stage and Page.* Berkeley: University of California Press, 1989.

———. "Impertinent Trifling: Desdemona's Handkerchief." *Shakespeare Quarterly* 47 (1996): 235–50.

Berry, Herbert. *The Boar's Head Playhouse.* Washington, D.C.: Folger Books, 1986.

Berry, Philippa. "Reversing History: Time, Fortune, and the Doubling of Sovereignty in *Macbeth.*" *European Journal of English Studies* 1 (1997): 367–87.

Biddick, Kathleen. "Coming out of Exile: Dante on the Orient(alism) Express." *American Historical Review* 105 (2000): 1234–49.

———. *The Typological Imaginary: History, Technology, Circumcision.* Philadelphia: University of Pennsylvania Press, 2003.

Bloch, Chana. *Spelling the Word: George Herbert and the Bible.* Berkeley: University of California Press, 1985.

Bloom, Harold. *The Anxiety of Influence: A Theory of Poetry.* New York: Oxford University Press, 1973.

Boehrer, Bruce. "*Othello*'s Monsters: Kenneth Burke, Deleuze and Guattari, and the Impulse to Narrative in Shakespeare." *Journal X* 3:2 (1999): 119–38.

Boose, Lynda E. "Othello's Handkerchief: 'The Recognizance and Pledge of Love.'" *English Literary Renaissance* 5 (1975): 360–74.

Bornstein, George, and Ralph G. Williams, eds. *Palimpsest: Editorial Theory in the Humanities.* Ann Arbor: University of Michigan Press, 1993.

Boyle, Deborah. "Margaret Cavendish's Nonfeminist Natural Philosophy." *Configurations* 12 (2004): 195–227.

Bradley, A. C. *Shakespearean Tragedy: Lectures on* Hamlet, Othello, King Lear, Macbeth. London: Macmillan, 1905.

Bradshaw, Graham. *Misrepresentations: Shakespeare and the Materialists.* Ithaca, N.Y.: Cornell University Press, 1993.

Brathwait, Richard. *Essayes upon the Five Senses.* London, 1635.

Braudel, Fernand. "History and the Social Sciences: The *Longue Durée.*" In Jacques Revel and Lynn Hunt, eds. *Histories: French Constructions of the Past.* Trans. Arthur Goldhammer et al. New York: New Press, 1995. 115–46.

Brown, Bill. "The Dark Wood of Postmodernity: Space, Faith, Allegory." *PMLA* 120 (2005): 734–50.

———. "How to Do Things with Things (A Toy Story)." *Critical Inquiry* 24 (1998): 935–64.

———. *A Sense of Things: The Object Matter of American Literature.* Chicago: Chicago University Press, 2003.

———. "The Tyranny of Things (Trivia in Karl Marx and Mark Twain)." *Critical Inquiry* 28 (2002): 442–69.

Brown, Bill, ed. *Things.* Chicago: University of Chicago Press, 2004.

Bruster, Douglas. "Deep Focus." In *Shakespeare and the Question of Culture: Early Modern Literature and the Cultural Turn.* New York: Palgrave Macmillan, 2003. 29–62.

———. "The Dramatic Life of Objects in the Early Modern Theatre." In Jonathan Gil Harris and Natasha Korda, eds., *Staged Properties in Early Modern English Drama.* Cambridge: Cambridge University Press, 2002. 67–96.

———. "Shakespeare and the End of History." In Hugh Grady and Terence Hawkes, eds., *Shakespeare and Presentism.* London: Routledge, 2007. 168–99.

———. *Shakespeare and the Question of Culture: Early Modern Literature and the Cultural Turn.* New York: Palgrave Macmillan, 2003.

Buchanan, Tony W., Daniel Tranel, and Ralph Adolphs. "A Specific Role for the Human Amygdala in Olfactory Memory." *Learning and Memory* 10 (2003): 319–25.

Burger, Glenn, and Steven F. Kruger, eds. *Queering the Middle Ages.* Minneapolis: University of Minnesota Press, 2001.

Burton, Robert. *The Anatomy of Melancholy.* London, 1632.

Bushnell, Rebecca W. *Tragedies of Tyrants: Political Thought and Theater in the English Renaissance.* Ithaca, N.Y.: Cornell University Press, 1990.

Butler, Judith. *Bodies That Matter: On the Discursive Limits of Sex.* New York: Routledge, 1993.

Butterworth, Philip. *Theatre of Fire: Special Effects in Early English and Scottish Theatre.* London: Society for Theatre Research, 1998.

Calderwood, James L. *Shakespearean Metadrama.* Minneapolis: University of Minnesota Press, 1971.

Calendar of Letter-Books Preserved among the Archives of the Corporation of the City of London at the Guildhall. Letter-Book A. Circa A. D. 1275–1298. Ed. Reginald R. Sharpe. London: John Edward Francis, 1894.

Calendar of State Papers, Domestic Series, November 1667 to September 1668. Ed. Mary Anne Everett Green. London: Printed for Her Majesty's Stationery Office, by Eyre and Spottiswoode, 1893.

Callaghan, Dympna. "Looking Well to Linens: Women and Cultural Production in *Othello.*" In Jean E. Howard and Scott Cutler Shershow, eds. *Marxist Shakespeares.* New York: Routledge, 2001. 53–81.

Calvin, John. *A Very Profitable Treatise, Made by M. Ihon Calvin, declarynge what great profit might come to al christen dome, yf there were a regester made of all Sainctes bodies and other reliques, which are as well in Italy, as in Fraunce, Dutchland, Spaine, and other kingdomes and countreys.* Trans. Steven Withers. London, 1561.

Camden, William. *Britain, Or a Chorographicall Description of the Most Flourishing Kingdomes, England, Scotland, and Ireland.* London, 1607.

———. *Britannia.* London, 1586.

Camões, Luís Vaz de. *The Lusíads.* Trans. Landeg White. Oxford: Oxford University Press, 2002.

Campana. Joseph. "The Bloody Babe and the Crowned Child: Killing Time in *Macbeth.*" Unpublished essay presented at the 2007 Shakespeare Association of America seminar "Shakespeare and the Question of Time."

Campos, Edmund Valentine. "Jews, Spaniards, and Portingales: Ambiguous Identities of Portuguese Marranos in Elizabethan England." *English Literary History* 69 (2002): 599–616.

Carpenter, Nathanael. *Geographie Delineated Forth in Two Bookes, Containing the Sphericall and Topicall Parts Thereof.* Oxford, 1635.

Caruth, Cathy. *Unclaimed Experience: Trauma, Narrative, and History.* Baltimore: Johns Hopkins University Press, 1996.

The Castle of Perseverance. In Mark Eccles, ed., *The Macro Plays.* London: Oxford University Press, 1969.

Cavendish, Margaret. The Blazing World *and Other Writings.* Ed. Kate Lilley. Harmondsworth: Penguin, 1992.

———. *CCXI Sociable Letters.* London, 1664.

———. *Natures Pictures Drawn by Fancies Pencil to the Life.* London, 1656.

———. *Observations upon Experimental Philosophy. To which is added, The Description of a New Blazing World.* London, 1666.

———. *Philosophical Letters: Or, Modest Reflections Upon Some Opinions in Natural Philosophy, Maintained by several Famous and Learned Authors of the Age, Expressed by Way of Letters.* London, 1664.

———. *Poems, and Phancies, Written by the Thrice Noble, Illustrious, and Excellent Princess the Lady Marchioness of Newcastle: The Second Impression, Much Altered and Corrected.* London, 1664.

———. *The World's Olio.* London: 1655.

Celsus, A. Cornelius. *De medicina.* Trans. W. G. Spencer. 2 vols. Cambridge, MA: Harvard University Press, 1935.

Certaine Sermons or Homilies, Appointed to be Read in Churches in the Time of Queen Elizabeth I (1547–1571). Ed. Mary Ellen Rickey and Thomas B. Stroup. Gainesville, Fla.: Scholars' Facsimiles and Reprints, 1968.

Certeau, Michel de. *The Practice of Everyday Life.* Trans. Steven Randall. Berkeley: University of California Press, 1984.

———. *The Writing of History.* Trans. Tom Conley. New York: Columbia University Press, 1988.

Chakrabarty, Dipesh. *Provincializing Europe: Postcolonial Thought and Historical Difference.* Princeton: Princeton University Press, 2000.

Charles, Amy L. *A Life of George Herbert.* Ithaca, N.Y.: Cornell University Press, 1977.

Charleton, Walter. *Physiologia Epicuro-Gassendo-Charletoniana; or, A Fabrick of Natural Science upon the Hypothesis of Atoms.* London, 1654.

Charnes, Linda. *Hamlet's Heirs: Shakespeare and the Politics of a New Millennium.* New York: Routledge, 2006.

———. "Reading for the Wormholes: Micro-periods from the Future." *Early Modern Culture* 6 (2007): http://emc.eserver.org/1-6/charnes.html.

———. "We Were Never Early Modern." In John J. Joughin, ed., *Philosophical Shakespeares.* New York: Routledge, 2000. 51–67.

Cixous, Hélène. "The Laugh of the Medusa." In Robyn R. Warhol and Diane Price Herndl, eds., *Feminisms: An Anthology of Literary Theory and Criticism.* New Brunswick, N.J.: Rutgers University Press, 1991. 334–49.

———. "Sorties: Ways Out/Attacks/ Forays." In Hélène Cixous and Catherine Clément, *The Newly Born Woman.* Trans. Betsy Wing. Minneapolis: University of Minnesota Press, 1986. 63–132.

———. *Vivre l'orange.* Paris: Des Femmes, 1979.

Classen, Constance, David Howes, and Anthony Synnott. *Aroma: The Cultural History of Smell.* London: Routledge, 1994.

Coddon, Karin S. "'Unreal Mockery': Unreason and the Problem of Spectacle in *Macbeth.*" *English Literary History* 56 (1989): 485–501.

Coghill, Nevill. "*Macbeth* at the Globe, 1606–16 (?): Three Questions." In Joseph G. Price, ed., *The Triple Bond: Plays, Mainly Shakespearean, in Performance.* University Park: Pennsylvania State University Press, 1975. 223–39.

Cohen, Jeffrey J. *Medieval Identity Machines.* Minneapolis: University of Minnesota Press, 2002.

Cohen, Robert. *More Power to You.* New York: Applause Theatre and Cinema Books, 2002.

Coletti, Theresa. "Re-reading the Story of Herod in the Middle English Innocents Plays." In Thomas Hahn and Alan Lupack, eds., *Retelling Tales: Essays in Honor of Russell Peck.* Cambridge: D. S. Brewer, 1997. 35–60.

Collinson, Patrick. "John Stow and Nostalgic Antiquarianism." In J. F. Merritt, ed., *Imagining Early Modern London: Perceptions and Portrayals of the City from Stow to Strype, 1598–1720.* New York: Cambridge University Press, 2001. 27–52.

Coote, Lesley. "Merlin, Erceldoune, Nixon: A Tradition of Popular Political Prophecy." *New Medieval Literatures* 4 (2001): 117–37.

Corbin, Alain. *The Foul and the Fragrant: Odor and the French Social Imagination.* Cambridge, Mass.: Harvard University Press, 1986.

Cox, John D. *The Devil and the Sacred in English Drama, 1350–1642.* Cambridge: Cambridge University Press, 2000.

Craig, Hardin, ed. *Two Coventry Corpus Christi Plays.* London: Oxford University Press, 1957.

Crawford, Julie. "'Pleaders, Atturneys, Petitioners and the like': Margaret Cavendish and the Dramatic Petition." In Pamela Allen Brown and Peter Parolin, eds., *Women Players in England, 1500–1650: Beyond the All-Male Stage.* Burlington, Vt.: Ashgate, 2005. 241–60.

Crosse, Henry. *Virtue's Commonwealth.* London, 1603.
Culler, Jonathan. *The Pursuit of Signs: Semiotics, Literature, Deconstruction.* Ithaca, N.Y.: Cornell University Press, 1981.
Dalrymple, William. *City of Djinns: A Year in Delhi.* London: HarperCollins, 1994.
Dant, Tim. *Material Culture in the Social World: Values, Activities, Lifestyles.* Buckingham: Open University Press, 1999.
Daston, Lorraine, ed. *Things That Talk: Object Lessons from Art and Science.* New York: Zone Books, 2004.
Davidson, Clifford, and Thomas H. Seiler, eds. *The Iconography of Hell.* Early Drama, Art, and Music Monograph Series 17. Kalamazoo: Medieval Institute Publications, 1992.
Davilla, Roxanna. "Mexico City as Urban Palimpsest in Salvador Novo's *Nueva Grandeza Mexicana.*" *Studies in the Literary Imagination* (2000) 33: 107–23.
Davis, Kathleen. "Time Behind the Veil: The Media, the Middle Ages, and Orientalism Now." In Jeffrey Jerome Cohen, ed., *The Postcolonial Middle Ages.* New York: Palgrave Macmillan, 2000. 105–22.
de Grazia, Margreta. "The Modern Divide: From Either Side." *Journal of Medieval and Early Modern Studies* 37 (2007): 453–67.
———. "Teleology, Delay, and the *Old Mole.*" *Shakespeare Quarterly* 50 (1999): 251–67.
de Grazia, Margreta, Maureen Quilligan, and Peter Stallybrass, eds. *Subject and Object in Renaissance Culture.* Cambridge: Cambridge University Press, 1996.
Dekker, Thomas. *The Artillery Garden.* London, 1615.
———. *The Dramatic Works of Thomas Dekker.* Ed. Fredson Bowers. 4 vols. London: Cambridge University Press, 1964.
———. *The Shoemaker's Holiday.* Ed. R. L. Smallwood and Stanley Wells. Manchester: Manchester University Press, 1979.
Deleuze, Gilles. *The Fold: Leibniz and the Baroque.* Trans. Tom Conley. Minneapolis: University of Minnesota Press, 1993.
Deleuze, Gilles, and Félix Guattari. *A Thousand Plateaus: Capitalism and Schizophrenia.* Trans. Brian Massumi. Minneapolis: University of Minnesota Press, 1987.
———. *What Is Philosophy?* New York: Columbia University Press, 1996.
Denis, Adrian L. "Treasure City: Havana." *Common-Place* 3 (2004): http://www.common-place.org/vol-03/no-04/havana/.
Derrida, Jacques. "Freud and the Scene of Writing." In *Writing and Difference.* Trans. Alan Bass. Chicago: University of Chicago Press, 1978. 196–231.
———. *Of Grammatology.* Trans. Gayatri Chakravorty Spivak. Baltimore: Johns Hopkins University Press, 1976.
———. *Specters of Marx: The State of the Debt, the Work of Mourning, and the New International.* Trans. Peggy Kamuf. New York: Routledge, 1994.
———. *Writing and Difference.* Trans. Alan Bass. Chicago: University of Chicago Press, 1978.
Dessen, Alan C., and Leslie Thomson. *A Dictionary of Stage Directions in English Drama 1580–1642.* Cambridge: Cambridge University Press, 1999.

Dinshaw, Carolyn. *Getting Medieval: Sexualities and Communities, Pre- and Postmodern.* Durham, N.C.: Duke University Press, 1999.

Dolan, France E. *Whores of Babylon: Catholicism, Gender, and Seventeenth-Century Print Culture.* Ithaca, N.Y.: Cornell University Press, 1999.

Drakakis, John. "Discourse and Authority: The Renaissance of Robert Weimann." *Shakespeare Studies* 26 (1998): 83–104.

Drayton, Michael. *Poly-Olbion, A chorographicall description of tracts, rivers, mountains, forests, and other parts of this renowned isle of Great Britain: with intermixture of the most remarkeable stories, antiquities, wonders, rarities, pleasures, and commodities of the same; divided into two bookes.* London, 1622.

Driver, Tom F. "The Uses of Time." In *The Sense of History in Greek and Shakespearean Drama.* New York: Columbia University Press, 1960. 143–67.

Drummond, William. *The Poetical Works of William Drummond of Hawthornden.* 2 vols. Manchester: Manchester University Press, 1913.

———. *Quinque Sensus.* In Folger MS ADD 1246.24. Catalogued as *Stuart Papers: A Volume of Prints and Manuscripts Relating to the Stuart Reign in England.* Ca. 1619–1685.

Dryden, John. *MacFlecknoe.* London, 1692.

Duby, Georges, and Phillipe Braunstein. "Toward Intimacy: The Fourteenth and Fifteenth Centuries." In Georges Duby, ed., *A History of Private Life II: Revelations of the Medieval World.* Trans. Arthur Goldhammer. Cambridge, Mass.: Belknap Press, 1988. 535–62.

du Cange, Charles. *Glossarium Mediae et Infimae Latinitatis.* Graz: Akademische Druck - u. Verlagsanstalt, 1954.

Duffy, Eamon. *Marking the Hours: English People and Their Prayers, 1240–1570.* New Haven: Yale University Press, 2006.

Dugan, Holly. "The Ephemeral History of Perfume: Scent and Sense in Early Modern England." Unpublished Ph.D. dissertation. University of Michigan, 2005.

Eakins, Emily. "Screwdriver Scholars and Pencil Punditry." *New York Times.* 24 February 2001. B7, B9.

Eastwood, B. S. "Galen on the Elements of Olfactory Sensation." *Rheinisches Museum für Philologie* 124 (1981): 268–90.

Edelman, Lee. *No Future: Queer Theory and the Death Drive.* Durham, N.C.: Duke University Press, 2005.

Egan, Gabriel. Review of Jean E. Howard and Scott Cutler Shershow, eds., *Marxist Shakespeares. Early Modern Literary Studies* 7:2 (2001): 15.1–19, 6. http://purl.oclc.org/emls/07–2/eganrev.htm.

El Gundi, Fadwa. *Veil: Privacy, Modesty, and Resistance.* New York: Berg, 1999.

Endicott [Patterson], Annabel M. "The Structure of George Herbert's *Temple*: A Reconsideration." *University of Toronto Quarterly* 34 (1965): 226–37.

E. S. *The Discovery of the Knights of the Post.* London, 1597.

Evans, Joan. *A History of the Society of Antiquaries.* London: Oxford University Press, 1956.

Faber, M. D., ed. *The Design Within: Psychoanalytic Approaches to Shakespeare*. New York: Science House, 1970.

Fabian, Johannes. *Time and the Other: How Anthropology Makes Its Object*. New York: Columbia University Press, 1983.

Feldman, Abraham B. "Othello's Obsessions." *American Imago* 9 (1952): 159–62.

Ferguson, Margaret W. "Feathers and Flies: Aphra Behn and the Seventeenth-Century Trade in Exotica." In Margreta De Grazia, Maureen Quilligan, and Peter Stallybrass, eds., *Subject and Object in Renaissance Culture*. Cambridge: Cambridge University Press, 1996. 235–59.

Fiedler, Leslie. *The Stranger in Shakespeare*. New York, 1972.

Fish, Stanley. *Self-Consuming Artifacts*. Berkeley: University of California Press, 1972.

———. *The Living Temple: George Herbert and Catechizing*. Berkeley: University of California Press, 1978.

Fitch, Ralph. "The Voyage of Mr Ralph Fitch Merchant of London." In Richard Hakluyt, *Voyages and Discoveries: The Principal Navigations, Voyages, Traffiques and Discoveries of the English Nation*. Ed. Jack Beeching. Harmondsworth: Penguin, 2006. 252–69.

Fletcher, Angus. *Time, Space and Motion in the Age of Shakespeare*. Cambridge, Mass.: Harvard University Press, 2007.

Floyd-Wilson, Mary. "English Epicures and Scottish Witches." *Shakespeare Quarterly* 57 (2006): 131–61.

Foakes, R. A., and R. T. Rickert, eds. *Henslowe's Diary*. Cambridge: Cambridge University Press, 1961.

Folkerth, Wes. *The Sound of Shakespeare*. New York: Routledge, 2002.

Foucault, Michel. *The Order of Things: An Archaeology of the Human Sciences*. New York: Tavistock, 1970.

Foxe, John. *Actes and Monuments of These Latter and Perilous Dayes, Touching Matters of the Church, Wherein are Comprehended and Described the Great Persecution and Horrible Troubles that Have Been Wrought and Practised by the Romishe Prelates, Especiallye in This Realme of England and Scotland*. London, 1563.

Freccero, Carla. *Queer/Early/Modern*. Durham, N.C.: Duke University Press, 2005.

Freeman, Elizabeth. "Queer Temporalities: Introduction." *GLQ: A Journal of Lesbian and Gay Studies* 13 (2007): 159–76.

Freinkel, Lisa. *Reading Shakespeare's Will: The Theology of Figure from Augustine to the Sonnets*. New York: Columbia University Press, 2002.

———. "The Shakespearean Fetish." In Ewan Fernie, ed., *Spiritual Shakespeares*. London: Routledge, 2005. 109–29.

Freud, Sigmund. *Civilization and Its Discontents*. In *The Standard Edition of the Complete Psychological Works of Sigmund Freud, Volume XXI*. Trans. James Strachey. London: Vintage Hogarth Press, 2001. 59–145.

———. "Fetishism." In *On Sexuality*. Pelican Freud Library. Vol. 7. Ed. Angela Richards. Harmondsworth: Penguin, 1977. 351–57.

———. "From the History of an Infantile Neurosis." In *The Standard Edition of the Complete Psychological Works of Sigmund Freud, Volume XVII.* Trans. James Strachey. London: Vintage Hogarth Press, 2001. 1–122.

———. "A Note Upon the 'Mystic Writing-Pad.'" In *The Standard Edition of the Complete Psychological Works of Sigmund Freud, Volume XIX.* Trans. James Strachey. London: Vintage Hogarth Press, 2001. 225–32.

Froehlich, Karlfried. "The State of Biblical Hermeneutics at the Beginning of the Fifteenth Century." In Earl Miner, ed., *Literary Uses of Typology from the Middle Ages to the Present.* Princeton: Princeton University Press. 20–48.

Fukuyama, Francis. *The End of History and the Last Man.* New York: Free Press, 1992.

Fuller, Mary C. "Ralegh's Fugitive Gold: Reference and Deferral in *The Discoverie of Guiana.*" In Stephen Greenblatt, ed., *New World Encounters.* Berkeley: University of California Press, 1993. 218–40.

Fumerton, Patricia, and Simon Hunt, eds. *Renaissance Culture and the Everyday.* Philadelphia: University of Pennsylvania Press, 1999.

Fuss, Diana. *The Sense of an Interior: Four Writers and the Rooms That Shaped Them.* New York: Routledge, 2004.

Galen. *On Anatomical Procedures: The Later Books.* Trans. W. L. H. Duckworth. Ed. M. C. Lyons and B. Towers. Cambridge: Cambridge University Press, 1962.

Gallagher, Catherine. "Embracing the Absolute: The Politics of the Female Subject in Seventeenth-Century England." *Genders* 1 (1988): 24–39.

Gallagher, Catherine, and Stephen Greenblatt. *Practicing the New Historicism.* Chicago: University of Chicago Press, 2000.

Gallagher, Michael P. "Rhetoric, Style, and George Herbert." *English Literary History* 37 (1970): 495–516.

Geertz, Clifford. *The Interpretation of Cultures.* New York: Basic Books, 1973.

Genette, Gérard. *Palimpsests: Literature in the Second Degree.* Trans. Channa Newman and Claude Doubinsky. Lincoln, Neb.: University of Nebraska Press, 1997.

Ghosh, Amitav. *In an Antique Land: History in the Guise of a Traveler's Tale.* New York: Vintage, 1992.

Ghosh, Amitav, and Dipesh Chakrabarty. "A Correspondence on *Provincializing Europe.*" *Radical History Review* 83 (2002): 146–72.

Gilloch, Graeme. *Myth and Metropolis: Walter Benjamin and the City.* Cambridge: Polity, 1996.

Goldberg, Jonathan. "The Commodity of Names: 'Falstaff' and 'Oldcastle' in *1 Henry IV.*" In Jonathan Crewe, ed., *Reconfiguring the Renaissance: Essays in Critical Materialism.* London: Associated University Press, 1992. 76–88

———. "Herbert's 'Decay' and the Articulation of History." *Southern Review* 18 (1985): 3–21.

———. "Lucy Hutchinson Writing Matter." *English Literary History* 73 (2006): 275–301.

———. "Margaret Cavendish, Scribe." *GLQ: A Journal of Lesbian and Gay Studies* 10 (2004): 433–52.

———. "Speculations: *Macbeth* and Source." In Jean E. Howard and Marion F. O'Connor, eds., *Shakespeare Reproduced: The Text in History and Ideology*. London: Methuen, 1987. 242–64.

———. *Voice Terminal Echo: Postmodernism and English Renaissance Texts.* New York: Methuen, 1986. 101–23.

———. *Writing Matter: From the Hands of the English Renaissance.* Stanford, Calif.: Stanford University Press, 1990.

———. "Writing Shakespearean Matter Again: Objects and Their Detachments." *Shakespeare Studies* 28 (2000): 48–51.

Goldberg, Jonathan, and Madhavi Menon. "Queering History." *PMLA* 120 (2005): 1608–17.

Grady, Hugh. *Shakespeare's Universal Wolf: Studies in Early Modern Reification.* Oxford: Clarendon Press, 1996.

Grady, Hugh, and Terence Hawkes, eds. *Presentist Shakespeares.* London: Routledge, 2007.

Graham, Shane. "Memory, Memorialization and the Transformation of Johannesburg: Ivan Vladislavic's *The Restless Supermarket* and *Propaganda by Monuments.*" *Modern Fiction Studies* 53 (2007): 70–99.

Graves, R. B. *Lighting the Shakespearean Stage 1567–1642.* Carbondale, Ill.: Southern Illinois University Press, 1999.

Greenblatt, Stephen. "The Mousetrap." *Shakespeare Studies* 35 (1997): 1–32.

———. *Renaissance Self-Fashioning: From More to Shakespeare.* Chicago: University of Chicago Press, 1980.

———. *Shakespearean Negotiations: The Circulation of Social Energy in Renaissance England.* Berkeley: University of California Press, 1988.

Greene, Robert. *The Comicall Historie of Alphonsus, King of Aragon.* London, 1599.

Griffin, Andrew. "Preserving and Reserving the Past in Stow's *Survey of London.*" In Joan Fitpatrick, ed. *The Idea of the City.* London: Cambridge Scholars Press, forthcoming 2008.

Griffiths, Huw. "The Sonnet in Ruins: Time and the Nation in 1599." *Early Modern Culture* 6 (2007): http://emc.eserver.org/1–6/griffiths.html.

Grosz, Elizabeth. *The Nick of Time: Politics, Evolution, and the Untimely.* Durham, N.C.: Duke University Press, 2004.

Gubar, Susan. "'The Blank Page' and the Issues of Female Creativity." *Critical Inquiry* 8 (1981): 243–63.

Gür, Berin F. "Spatialisation of Power/Knowledge/Discourse." *Space and Culture* 5 (2002): 237–52.

Gurr, Andrew. *The Shakespearean Stage: 1574–1642.* Cambridge: Cambridge University Press, 1992.

———. "*The Tempest*'s Tempest at Blackfriars." *Shakespeare Survey* 41 (1989): 91–102.

———. "Who Strutted and Bellowed?" *Shakespeare Survey* 16 (1963): 95–102.

Hale, J. G. *Renaissance War Studies.* London: Hambledon Press, 1983.

Hall, Joseph. *The Collected Poems of Joseph Hall, Bishop of Exeter and Norwich.* Ed. Arnold Davenport. Liverpool: Liverpool University Press, 1947.

Haller, William. *The Rise of Puritanism, or the Way to the New Jerusalem as Set Forth in Pulpit and Press from Thomas Cartwright to John Lilburne and John Milton, 1570–1643.* New York: Columbia University Press, 1938.

Halpern, Richard. "An Impure History of Ghosts: Derrida, Marx, Shakespeare." In Jean E. Howard and Scott Cutler Shershow, eds., *Marxist Shakespeares.* London: Routledge, 2001. 31–52.

Hankey, Julia. *Shakespeare in Production: Othello.* 2nd ed. Cambridge: Cambridge University Press, 2005.

Harris, Jonathan Gil. "Afterword: Walk Like an Egyptian." In Bryan Reynolds, *Performing Transversally: Reimagining Shakespeare and the Critical Future.* New York: Palgrave, 2003. 271–86.

———. "Atomic Shakespeare." *Shakespeare Studies* 30 (2002): 41–45.

———. *Foreign Bodies and the Body Politic: Discourses of Social Pathology in Early Modern England.* Cambridge: Cambridge University Press, 1998.

———. "'Look not Big, nor Stamp, nor Stare': Acting Up in *The Taming of the Shrew* and the Coventry Herod Plays." *Comparative Drama* 34 (2000–2001): 365–98.

———. "Ludgate Time: Simon Eyre's Oath and the Temporal Economies of *The Shoemaker's Holiday.*" *Huntington Library Quarterly.* Forthcoming 2008.

———. "The New New Historicism's *Wunderkammer* of Objects." *European Journal of English Studies* 4 (2000): 111–23.

———. "(Po)X Marks the Spot: How to 'Read' 'Early Modern' 'Syphilis' in *The Three Ladies of London.*" In Kevin Siena, ed., *Sins of the Flesh: Responses to Sexually Transmitted Disease in Renaissance Europe.* Toronto: Center for Renaissance and Reformation Studies, 2005. 111–34.

———. "Shakespeare's Hair: Staging the Object of Material Culture." *Shakespeare Quarterly* 52 (2001): 479–91.

———. *Sick Economies: Drama, Mercantilism, and Disease in Shakespeare's England.* Philadelphia: University of Pennsylvania Press, 2004.

———. "Untimely Mediations." *Early Modern Culture* 6 (2007): http://emc.eserver.org/1-6/harris.html.

Harris, Jonathan Gil, and Natasha Korda, eds. *Staged Properties in Early Modern English Drama.* Cambridge: Cambridge University Press, 2002.

Harvey, Gabriel. *Pierce's Supererogation or A New Praise of the Old Ass.* London, 1593.

Hattaway, Michael, ed. *The Cambridge Companion to Shakespeare's History Plays.* Cambridge: Cambridge University Press, 2002.

Hawkes, David. "Exchange Value and Empiricism in the Poetry of George Herbert." In Linda Woodbridge, ed., *Money and the Age of Shakespeare: Essays in New Economic Criticism.* New York: Palgrave Macmillan, 2003. 79–96.

———. *Idols of the Marketplace: Idolatry and Commodity Fetishism in English Literature, 1580–1680.* Palgrave Macmillan: New York, 2001.

———. "Materialism and Reification in Renaissance Studies." *Journal of Early Modern Culture* 4 (2004): 114–29.

Hedrick, Donald, and Bryan Reynolds. "'A little touch of Harry in the night': Translucency and Projective Transversality in the Sexual and National Politics of *Henry V.*" In Bryan Reynolds, ed., *Performing Transversally: Reimagining Shakespeare and the Critical Future*. New York: Palgrave Macmillan, 2003. 171–88.

Hegel, G. W. F. *Phenomenology of Spirit*. Ed. J. N. Findlay. Trans. A. V. Miller. New York: Oxford University Press, 1977.

———. *The Philosophy of History*. Trans. J. Sibree. Amherst, N.Y.: Prometheus Books, 1991.

Heilman, Robert. *Magic in the Web: Action and Language in "Othello."* Lexington, Ky.: University of Kentucky Press: 1956.

Helgerson, Richard. "The Buck Basket, the Witch and the Queen of Fairies: The Women's World of Shakespeare's Windsor." In Patricia Fumerton and Simon Hunt, eds., *Renaissance Culture and the Everyday*. Philadelphia: University of Pennsylvania Press, 1999. 162–82.

———. "The Land Speaks: Cartography, Chorography and Subversion in Renaissance England," *Representations* 16 (1986): 50–85.

Herbert, George. *The Country Parson, The Temple*. Ed. John N. Wall Jr. New York: Paulist Press, 1981.

———. *The English Poems of George Herbert*. Ed. C. A. Patrides. London: J. M. Dent and Sons, 1974.

———. *The Latin Poetry of George Herbert*. Trans. Mark McCloskey and Paul R. Murphy. Athens: Ohio University Press, 1965.

———. *Remains*. London, 1652.

———. *The Works of George Herbert*. Ed. F. E. Hutchinson. Oxford: Clarendon Press, 1945.

Herz, R. S., and T. Engen, "Odor Memory: Review and Analysis." *Psychonomic Bulletin and Review* 3 (1996): 300–13.

Heschel, Susannah. "From Jesus to Shylock: Christian Supersessionism in *The Merchant of Venice.*" *Harvard Theological Review* 99 (2006): 407–31.

Heywood, Thomas. *Heywood's Dramatic Works*. 6 vols. London: John Pearson, 1874.

Hidenobu, Jinnai. *Tokyo: A Spatial Anthropology*. Berkeley: University of California Press, 1995.

Hillaby, Joe. "The London Jewry: William I to John." *Jewish Historical Studies: Transactions of the Jewish Historical Society of England* 33 (1992–24): 1–44.

———. "London: The 13th-Century Jewry Revisited." *Jewish Historical Studies: Transactions of the Jewish Historical Society of England* 32 (1990–92): 89–158.

Hillman, Richard. *Intertextuality and Romance in Renaissance Drama: The Staging of Nostalgia*. New York: St. Martin's Press, 1992.

Hodgkins, Christopher. *Authority, Church, and Society in George Herbert: Return to the Middle Way*. Columbia: University of Missouri Press, 1993.

Holsinger, Bruce. *Neomedievalism, Neoconservatism, and the War on Terror*. Chicago: University of Chicago Press, 2007.

Honigmann, E. A. J. "Introduction." In William Shakespeare, *Othello*, ed. E. A. J. Honigmann. London: Routledge, 1997. 1–111.

Hopkin, D. J., Catherine Ingman, and Bryan Reynolds. "Nudge, Nudge, Wink, Wink, Know What I Mean, Know What I Mean? A Theoretical Approach to Performance for Post-Cinema Shakespeare." In Bryan Reynolds, ed., *Performing Transversally: Reimagining Shakespeare and the Critical Future*. New York: Palgrave Macmillan, 2003. 137–70.

Hopkins, Lisa. *Shakespeare on the Edge: Border Crossings in the Tragedies and the Henriad*. Burlington, Vt.: Ashgate, 2005.

Hosking, G. L. *The Life and Times of Edward Alleyn*. London: Jonathan Cape, 1957.

Howard, Jean E. "Competing Ideologies of Commerce in Thomas Heywood's *If You Know Not Me You Know Nobody, Part II*." In Henry S. Turner, ed., *The Culture of Capital: Property, Cities, and Knowledge in Early Modern England*. New York: Routledge, 2002. 163–82.

Hussey, S. S. "How Many Herods in the Middle English Drama?" *Neophilogus* 48 (1963): 252–59.

Hutchinson, Lucy (trans.). *Lucretius: De rerum natura*. Ed. Hugh de Quehen. Ann Arbor: University of Michigan Press, 1996.

Hutton, Sarah. "In Dialogue with Thomas Hobbes: Margaret Cavendish's Natural Philosophy." *Women's Writing* 4 (1997): 421–32.

Huyssen, Andreas. "Modernist Miniatures: Literary Snapshots of Urban Spaces," *PMLA* 122 (2007): 27–42.

———. *Present Pasts: Urban Palimpsests and the Politics of Memory*. Stanford, Calif.: Stanford University Press, 2003.

Impey, Oliver, and Arthur Macgregor. *The Origins of Museums: The Cabinet of Curiosities in Sixteenth- and Seventeenth-Century Europe*. Oxford: Oxford University Press, 1985.

Ingram R. W., ed. *Records of Early English Drama: Coventry*. Toronto: University of Toronto Press, 1981.

Irigaray, Luce. "The Sex That Is Not One." In Robyn R. Warhol and Diane Price Herndl, eds., *Feminisms: An Anthology of Literary Theory and Criticism*. New Brunswick, N.J.: Rutgers University Press, 1991. 351–59.

———. *Speculum of the Other Woman*. Trans. Gillian C. Gill. Ithaca, N.Y.: Cornell University Press, 1985.

Iwasaki, Soji. "*Veritas Filia Temporis* and Shakespeare." *English Literary Renaissance* 3 (1973): 249–63.

Jacobs, Joseph. "The London Jewry, 1290." In *Papers Read at the Anglo-Jewish Historical Exhibition, Royal Albert Hall, London, 1887*. London: Office of the Jewish Chronicle, 1888. 20–52.

Jagose, Anna-Marie. *Inconsequence: Lesbian Representation and the Logic of Sequence*. Ithaca, N.Y.: Cornell University Press, 2002.

James I. *A Counter-blaste to Tobacco*. London, 1604.

———. *His Maiesties Speech in this Last Session of Parliament, as neere his very words as could be gathered at the instant. Together with a Discourse of the Maner of the Discouery of this late intended Treason. . . .* London, 1605.

Jameson, Anna. *Shakespeare's Heroines: With Twenty-Six Portraits of Famous Players.* London: George Bell and Sons, 1897.

Jameson, Fredric. *The Political Unconscious: Narrative as Socially Symbolic Act.* New York: Methuen, 1981.

Jenner, Mark S. R. "Civilization and Deodorization? Smell in Early Modern English Culture." In Peter Burke, Brian Harrison, and Paul Slack, eds., *Civil Histories: Essays Presented to Sir Keith Thomas.* Oxford: Oxford University Press, 2000. 127–44.

Jofen, Jean. "The Case of the Strawberry Handkerchief." *Shakespeare Newsletter* 21 (1971): 14.

Johnson, Lee Ann. "The Relationship of 'The Church Militant' to *The Temple.*" *Studies in Philology* 68 (1971): 200–206.

Jones, Ann Rosalind. "Writing the Body: Toward an Understanding of *l'écriture féminine.*" In Robyn R. Warhol and Diane Price Herndl, eds., *Feminisms: An Anthology of Literary Theory and Criticism.* New Brunswick, N.J.: Rutgers University Press, 1991. 357–70.

Jones, Ann Rosalind, and Peter Stallybrass. "'Rugges of London and the Diuell's Band': Irish Mantles and Yellow Starch as Hybrid London Fashion." In Lena Cowen Orlin, ed., *Material London, ca. 1600.* Philadelphia: University of Pennsylvania Press, 2000. 128–49.

———. *Renaissance Clothing and the Materials of Memory.* Cambridge: Cambridge University Press, 2000.

Jonson, Ben. *Bartholmew Fair,* ed. G. R. Hibbard. London: Ernst Benn Limited, 1977.

———. *Ben Jonson: Selected Masques.* Ed. Stephen Orgel. New Haven: Yale University Press, 1970.

———. *The Complete Plays of Ben Jonson.* Ed. G. A. Wilkes. 4 vols. Oxford: Clarendon Press, 1981.

———. *The Complete Works of Ben Jonson.* Ed . C. H. Herford, Percy Simpson, and Evelyn Simpson. 11 vols. Oxford: Clarendon Press, 1947.

———. *Every Man in His Humor.* Ed. Robert N. Watson. New York: Norton, 1999.

———. *Volpone, or the Fox.* Ed. Philip Brockbank. London: A and C Black, 1991.

Kargon, Robert Hugh. *Atomism in England from Hariot to Newton.* New York: Oxford University Press, 1966.

Kastan, David Scott. "Opening Gates and Stopping Hedges: Grafton, Stow, and the Politics of Elizabethan History Writing." In Elizabeth Fowler and Roland Greene, eds., *The Project of Prose in Early Modern Europe and the New World.* New York: Cambridge University Press, 1997. 66–79.

Kearney, James. "The Book and the Fetish: The Materiality of Prospero's Text." *Journal of Medieval and Early Modern Studies* 32 (2002): 433–68.

Keller, Eve. "Producing Petty Gods: Margaret Cavendish's Critique of Experimental Science." *English Literary History* 64 (1997): 447–71.

Klein, Bernhard. *Maps and the Writing of Space in Early Modern England and Ireland.* Basingstoke: Palgrave Macmillan, 2001.

Kneidel, Gregory. "Herbert and Exactness." *English Literary Renaissance* 36 (2006): 278–303.

Kopytoff, Igor. "The Cultural Biography of Things: Commoditization as Process." In Arjun Appadurai, ed., *The Social Life of Things: Commodities in Cultural Perspective.* Cambridge: Cambridge University Press, 1986. 64–91

Korda, Natasha. *Shakespeare's Domestic Economies: Gender and Property in Early Modern England.* Philadelphia: University of Pennsylvania Press, 2002.

Kristeva, Julia. *Semeiotikè: Recherches pour une sémanalyse, tel quel.* Ed. Phillipe Sollers. Paris: Seuil, 1969.

Kruger, Steven F. *The Spectral Jew: Conversion and Embodiment in Medieval Europe.* Minneapolis: University of Minnesota Press, 2006.

Kuberski, Philip. *The Persistence of Memory: Organism, Myth, Text.* Berkeley: University of California Press, 1992.

Lacan, Jacques. "The Agency of the Letter in the Unconscious." In *Écrits: A Selection.* Trans. Alan Sheridan. New York: Routledge, 1997. 146–78.

———. *Le Séminaire VII: L'éthique de la psychoanalyse.* Paris: Seuil, 1986.

LaCapra, Dominick. *Writing History, Writing Trauma.* Baltimore: Johns Hopkins University Press, 2001.

Lampe, G. W. H., and K. J. Woollcombe, *Essays on Typology.* Naperville: Alec R. Allenson, 1957.

Landa, Manuel de. *A Thousand Years of Nonlinear History.* New York: Swerve, 1997.

Laporte, Dominique. *History of Shit.* Trans. Nadia Benabid and Rodolphe El-Khoury. Cambridge, Mass.: MIT Press, 2000.

Latour, Bruno. *Reassembling the Social: An Introduction to Actor-Network-Theory.* Oxford: Oxford University Press, 2005.

———. *We Have Never Been Modern.* Trans. Catherine Porter. Cambridge, Mass.: Harvard University Press, 1991.

Law, John, and John Hassard, eds. *Actor Network Theory and After.* Oxford: Blackwell, 1999.

Lecercle, Ann. "Hamlet's Play Within the Play as Palimpsest." In François Laroque, ed., *The Show Within: Dramatic and Other Insets: English Renaissance Drama (1550–1642).* Montpellier: Paul-Valéry University Press, 1990. 207–15.

Lemon, Rebecca. "Scaffolds of Treason in *Macbeth.*" *Theatre Journal* 54 (2002): 25–43.

Léry, Jean de. *History of a Voyage to Brazil.* Trans. Janet Whately. Berkeley: University of California Press, 1993.

Levang, Dwight. "George Herbert's 'The Church Militant' and the Chances of History." *Philological Quarterly* 36 (1957): 265–68.

Levin, Richard. "Contemporary Perception of Marlowe's *Tamburlaine.*" *Medieval and Renaissance Drama in England* 1 (1984): 51–70.

Lewalski, Barbara Kiefer. *Protestant Poetics and the Seventeenth-Century Religious Lyric.* Princeton: Princeton University Press, 1979.

Lezra, Jacques. *Unspeakable Subjects: The Genealogy of the Event in Early Modern Europe.* Stanford, Calif.: Stanford University Press, 1997.

Little, Arthur L., Jr. "'An essence unseen': The Primal Scene of Racism in *Othello.*" *Shakespeare Quarterly* 44 (1993): 304–24.

Lupton, Julia Reinhard. *Afterlives of the Saints: Hagiography, Typology, and Renaissance Literature.* Stanford, Calif.: Stanford University Press, 1996.

———. *Citizen-Saints: Shakespeare and Political Theory.* Chicago: University of Chicago Press, 2005.

———. "*Othello* Circumcised: Shakespeare and the Pauline Discourse of Nations," *Representations* 57 (1997): 73–89.

Lynch, Kathleen. "*The Temple*: 'Three Parts Vied and Multiplied.'" *Studies in English Literature* 29 (1989) 139–55.

Lyotard, Jean-François. *The Inhuman: Reflections on Time.* Trans. Geoffrey Bennington and Rachel Bowlby. Stanford, Calif.: Stanford University Press, 1991.

Malcolmson, Cristina. *George Herbert: A Literary Life.* New York: Palgrave Macmillan, 2002.

———. *Heart-Work: George Herbert and the Protestant Ethic.* Stanford, Calif.: Stanford University Press, 1999.

Manley, Lawrence. *Literature and Culture in Early Modern London.* Cambridge: Cambridge University Press, 1997.

———. "Of Sites and Rites." In David L. Smith, Richard Strier, and David Bevington, eds., *The Theatrical City: Culture, Theatre and Politics in London, 1576–1649.* Cambridge: Cambridge University Press, 1995. 35–54.

Manningham, John. *Diary of John Manningham, of the Middle Temple . . . 1602–3.* Ed. John Bruce. London: Camden Society, 1868.

Marchitello, Howard. *Narrative and Meaning in Early Modern Europe: Browne's Skull and Other Histories.* Cambridge: Cambridge University Press, 1997.

———. "Political Maps: The Production of Cartography and Chorography in Early Modern England." In Margaret J. M. Ezell and Katherine O'Brien O'Keeffee, eds., *Cultural Artifacts and the Production of Meaning: The Page, the Image, and the Body.* Ann Arbor: University of Michigan, 1994. 13–40

Marees, Peter. "A Description and Historicall Declaration of the Golden Kingdome of Guinea." In Samuel Purchas, *Hakluytus Posthumus or Purchas His Pilgrimes: Contayning a History of the World in Sea Voyages and Laden Travells by Englishman and Others.* 20 vols. Glasgow: James MacLehose and Sons, 1890–1906. 6:247–97.

Marlowe, Christopher. *Doctor Faustus: A- and B-Texts (1604, 1616).* Ed. David Bevington and Eric Rasmussen. Manchester: Manchester University Press, 1993.

———. *Tamburlaine Parts One and Two.* Ed. Anthony B. Dawson. London: A and C Black, 1997.

Martz, Louis. *The Poetry of Meditation.* New Haven: Yale University Press, 1954.

Marx, Karl. "The Fetishism of Commodities and the Secret Thereof." In *Capital, Volume One*, in Robert C. Tucker, ed., *The Marx-Engels Reader.* 2nd ed. New York: Norton, 1975. 319–29.

———. "Theses on Feuerbach." In *Writings of the Young Karl Marx on Philosophy and Society.* Trans. Loyd D. Easton and Kurt H. Guddat. New York: Doubleday, 1967. 400–402.

Marx, Karl, and Friedrich Engels. "The Communist Manifesto." In Robert C. Tucker, ed., *The Marx-Engels Reader.* 2nd ed. New York: Norton, 1975. 469–500.

Marzynski, Marian, dir. *Shtetl.* Frontline, 1996.

Masuzawa, Tomoko."Troubles with Materiality: The Ghost of Fetishism in the Nineteenth Century." *Comparative Studies in Society and History* 42 (2002): 242–67.

Mendyk, Stan. "Early British Chorography." *Sixteenth-Century Journal* 17 (1986): 459–81.

Menon, Madhavi. *Wanton Words: Rhetoric and Sexuality in English Renaissance Drama.* Toronto: University of Toronto Press, 2004.

Middleton, Thomas. *Women Beware Women.* Ed. Charles Barber. Berkeley: University of California Press, 1969.

Miller, Mary K. "Reading Between the Lines." *Smithsonian* (March 2007): 58–64.

Mills, David, ed. *The Chester Mystery Cycle: A New Edition with Modernised Spelling.* East Lansing, Mich.: Colleagues Press, 1992.

Mintz, Samuel I. "The Duchess of Newcastle's Visit to the Royal Society." *Journal of English and Germanic Philology* 51 (1952): 168–76.

Moi, Toril. *Textual/Sexual Politics* (New York and London: Methuen, 1985).

Montaigne, Michel de. *The Complete Essays.* Ed. M. A. Screech. Harmondsworth: Penguin, 1993.

Mudford, Peter G. "*Othello* and the 'Tragedy of Situation.'" *English* 20 (1971): 1–5.

Mullaney, Steven. "Strange Things, Gross Terms, Curious Customs: The Rehearsal of Cultures in the Late Renaissance." *Representations* 3 (1983): 40–67.

Mundill, R. R. "Anglo-Jewry Under Edward I: Credit Agents and Their Clients." *Jewish Historical Studies: Transactions of the Jewish Historical Society of England* 31 (1988–90): 1–21.

Nagler, Danielle. "Towards the Smell of Mortality: Shakespeare and Ideas of Smell, 1588–1625." *Cambridge Quarterly* (1997): 42–58.

Nakatani, Kiichiroh. "Expressions of Time in *Macbeth.*" *Hiroshima Studies in English Language and Literature* 19:2 (1973): 45–63.

Nashe, Thomas. *The Complete Works of Thomas Nashe.* 5 vols. Ed. Ronald B. McKerrow. London: Bullen, 1904–10.

Nassau, Robert Hamill. "The Philosophy of Fetishism." *Journal of the Royal African Society* 3 (1904): 257–70.

Neill, Michael. "Introduction." In William Shakespeare, *Othello,* ed. Michael Neill. Oxford: Oxford University Press, 2006. 1–190.

———. "'Unproper Beds': Race, Adultery and the Hideous in *Othello.*" *Shakespeare Quarterly* 40 (1989): 383–412.

Nelson, T. G. A. "Death, Dung, the Devil, and Worldly Delights: A Metaphysical Conceit in Harington, Donne, and Herbert." *Studies in Philology* 76 (1979): 272–87.

Nelson, T. G. A., and Charles Haines. "Othello's Unconsummated Marriage." *Essays in Criticism* 33 (1983): 1–18.

Newman, Karen. "'And wash the Ethiop white': Femininity and the Monstrous in *Othello*." In Jean E. Howard and Marion F. O'Connor, eds., *Shakespeare Reproduced: The Text in History and Ideology*. New York: Methuen, 1987. 143–62.

Nietzsche, Friedrich. "On the Uses and Disadvantages of History for Life." In *Untimely Meditations*. Ed. Daniel Breazale. Trans. R. J. Hollingdale. Cambridge: Cambridge University Press, 1997. 57–124.

———. *Untimely Meditations*. Ed. Daniel Breazale. Trans. R. J. Hollingdale. Cambridge: Cambridge University Press, 1997.

"Of Catesby Faux and Garnet." London, British Library. Additional MS 18220 BLa20*161.

Olson, Roberta J. M., Patricia L. Reilly, and Rupert Shepherd, eds. *The Biography of the Object in Late Medieval and Renaissance Italy*. Oxford: Blackwell, 2006.

Orlin, Lena Cowen, ed. *Material London, ca. 1600*. Philadelphia: University of Pennsylvania Press, 2000.

Outlandish Proverbs, Selected. London, 1640.

Pagel, Walter. *William Harvey's Biological Ideas: Selected Aspects and Historical Background*. New York: Hafner, 1967.

Palmer, Barbara D. "The Inhabitants of Hell: Devils." In Clifford Davidson and Thomas H. Seiler, eds., *The Iconography of Hell*. Early Drama, Art, and Music Monograph Series 17. Kalamazoo: Medieval Institute Publications, 1992. 20–40.

Palmer, George Herbert. *The English Works of George Herbert*. Boston: Houghton Mifflin, 1905.

———. *Formative Types in English Poetry*. Boston: Houghton Mifflin, 1918.

Palmer, Richard. "In Bad Odour: Smell and Its Significance in Medicine from Antiquity to the Seventeenth Century." In William F. Bynum and Roy Porter, eds., *Medicine and the Five Senses*. Cambridge: Cambridge University Press, 1993. 61–68.

Papias, Lombardus. *Grammaticus clarus an. 1053*. In du Cange, Charles. *Glossarium Mediae et Infimae Latinitatis*. Graz: Akademische Druck-u. Verlagsanstalt, 1954, VIII. 425.

Parker, Patricia. *Shakespeare from the Margins: Language, Culture, Context*. Chicago: University of Chicago Press, 1996.

Parker, Roscoe E. "The Reputation of Herod in Early English Literature." *Speculum* 8 (1933): 59–67.

Paster, Gail Kern. *The Body Embarrassed: Drama and the Disciplines of Shame in Early Modern England*. Ithaca, N.Y.: Cornell University Press, 1993.

———. *Humoring the Body: Emotions and the Shakespearean Stage*. Chicago: University of Chicago Press, 2004.

Patrides, C. A., ed. *George Herbert: The Critical Heritage*. London: Routledge and Kegan Paul, 1983.

Patrides, C. A., and Joseph Wittreich, eds. *The Apocalypse in English Renaissance Thought and Literature: Patterns, Antecedents and Repercussions*. Manchester: Manchester University Press, 1984.

Paxson, James J. "Theorizing the Mysteries' End in England, the Artificial Demonic, and the Sixteenth-Century Witch-Craze." *Criticism* 39 (1998): 481–502.

Peele, George. *The Battell of Alcazar, Fought in Barbarie, Betweene Sebastian King of Portugall, and Abdelmec King of Marocco.* London, 1594.

Perry, Curtis, ed. *Material Culture and Cultural Materialisms in the Middle Ages and the Renaissance.* Turnhout, Belgium: Brepols, 2000.

Peterson, Douglas L. *Time, Tide, and Tempest.* San Marino, Calif.: Huntington Library, 1973.

Pietz, William. "The Problem of the Fetish, I." *Res* 9 (1985): 5–17.

———. "The Problem of the Fetish, II: The Origin of the Fetish." *Res* 13 (1987): 23–46.

———. "The Problem of the Fetish, IIIa: Bosman's Guinea and the Enlightenment Theory of Fetishism." *Res* 16 (1988): 105–24.

Pollard, Tanya, ed. *Shakespeare's Theater: A Sourcebook.* London: Blackwell, 2003.

Poole, Kristen. "The Devil's in the Archive: *Doctor Faustus* and Ovidian Physics." *Renaissance Drama* n.s. 35 (2006): 191–219.

Powers-Beck, Jeffrey P. *Writing the Flesh: The Herbert Family Dialogue.* Pittsburgh: Duquesne University Press, 1998.

Preston, Thomas. *A Critical Edition of Thomas Preston's* Cambises. Ed. Robert Carl Johnson. Salzburg: Institut für Englische Sprache und Literatur, 1975.

Preus, James Samuel. *From Shadow to Promise: Old Testament Interpretation from Augustine to the Young Luther.* Cambridge, Mass.: Belknap Press, 1969.

Prior, Roger. "A Second Jewish Community in Tudor London." *Jewish Historical Studies: Transactions of the Jewish Historical Society of England* 31 (1988–90): 137–52

———. "Shakespeare's Debt to Ariosto." *Notes and Queries* 246 (2001): 289–92.

Pye, Christopher. "The Sovereign, the Theater, and the Kingdome of Darknesse: Hobbes and the Spectacle of Power." In Stephen Greenblatt, ed., *Representing the English Renaissance.* Berkeley: University of California Press, 1988. 279–301.

Quinones, Ricardo J. *The Renaissance Discovery of Time.* Cambridge, Mass.: Harvard University Press, 1972.

Reynolds, Bryan. *Performing Transversally: Reimagining Shakespeare and the Critical Future.* New York: Palgrave Macmillan, 2003.

Reynolds, Bryan, and William N. West, eds. *Rematerializing Shakespeare: Authority and Representation on the Early Modern English Stage.* New York: Palgrave Macmillan, 2005.

Rindisbacher, Hans J. *The Smell of Books: A Cultural-Historical Study of Olfactory Perception in Literature.* Ann Arbor: University of Michigan Press, 1992.

Rivkin, Julie, and Michael Ryan, eds. *Literary Theory: An Anthology.* 2nd ed. Malden, Mass.: Blackwell, 2004.

Robinson, Benedict S. *Islam and Early Modern English Literature: The Politics of Romance from Spenser to Milton.* New York: Palgrave Macmillan, 2007.

Rogers, John. *The Matter of Revolution: Science, Poetry, and Politics in the Age of Milton.* Ithaca, N.Y.: Cornell University Press, 1996.

Ross, Lawrence. "The Meaning of Strawberries in Shakespeare." *Studies in the Renaissance* 7 (1960): 225–40.

Roth, Cecil. "The Middle Period of Anglo-Jewish History (1290–1655) Reconsidered." *The Jewish Historical Society of England: Transactions* 19 (1960): 1–12.

Rushdie, Salman, *Midnight's Children*. New York: Alfred Knopf, 1980.

Ryle, Gilbert. *Collected Papers*. 2 vols. London: Hutchinson, 1971.

Rymer, Thomas. *A Short View of Tragedy*. London, 1693.

Said, Edward W. *Orientalism*. New York: Vintage, 1979.

Sandler, Florence. "'Solomon Vbique Regnet': Herbert's Use of the Images of the New Covenant." In John R. Roberts, ed., *Essential Articles for the Study of George Herbert's Poetry*. Hamden, Conn.: Archon Books, 1979. 258–67.

Sarasohn, Lisa T. "A Science Turned Upside Down: Feminism and the Natural Philosophy of Margaret Cavendish." *Huntington Library Quarterly* 4 (1994): 289–307.

Schaeffer, William. "Shadow Photographs, Ruins and Shanghai's Projected Past." *PMLA* 122 (2007): 124–34.

Schoenfeldt, Michael C. *Early Modern Bodies and Selves: Physiology and Inwardness in Spenser, Shakespeare, Herbert, and Milton*. Cambridge: Cambridge University Press, 1999.

———. *Prayer and Power: George Herbert and Renaissance Courtship*. Chicago: University of Chicago Press, 1991.

Schwab, Gail M., "Irigarayan Dialogism: Play and Powerplay." In Dale M. Bauer and S. Jaret McKinstry, eds., *Feminism, Bakhtin, and the Dialogic*. Albany, NY: State University of New York Press, 1991. 57–72.

Scoufos, Alice-Lyle. *Shakespeare's Typological Satire: A Study of the Falstaff-Oldcastle Problem*. Athens: Ohio University Press, 1979.

Sedgwick, Eve Kosofsky. *Touching Feeling: Affect, Pedagogy, Performativity*. Durham, N.C.: Duke University Press, 2003.

Serres, Michel. *Angels, A Modern Myth*. Trans. Francis Cowper. Ed. Philippa Hurd. New York: Flammarion, 1995.

———. *The Birth of Physics*. Trans. Jack Hawkes. Manchester: Clinamen, 2000.

———. *Hermes: Literature, Science, Philosophy*. Ed. Josué V. Harari and David F. Bell. Baltimore: Johns Hopkins University Press, 1982.

———. "Le messager," *Bulletin de la Société Francaise de la Philosophie* 62 (1968): 33–71

Serres, Michel, with Bruno Latour. *Conversations on Science, Culture, and Time*. Trans. Roxanne Lapidus. Ann Arbor: University of Michigan Press, 1995.

Shakespeare, William. *The Norton Shakespeare*. Ed. Stephen Greenblatt, Walter Cohen, Jean E. Howard, and Katherine Eisaman Maus. New York: Norton, 1997.

———. *Othello*. Ed. E. A. J. Honigmann. London: Routledge, 1997.

———. *Othello*. Ed. Michael Neill. Oxford: Oxford University Press, 2006.

———. *Titus Andronicus*. Ed. Jonathan Bate. London: Routledge, 1999.

Shapin, Steven. "What Else Is New?" *New Yorker* (May 14, 2007): 144–48.

Shapin, Steven, and Simon Schaffer. *Leviathan and the Air-Pump: Hobbes, Boyle, and the Experimental Life*. Princeton: Princeton University Press, 1985.

Shapiro, James. *Shakespeare and the Jews*. New York: Columbia University Press, 1996.

———. *1599: A Year in the Life of William Shakespeare*. London: Faber and Faber, 2005.

Shaw, John. "'What Is the Matter?' in *Othello*." *Shakespeare Quarterly* 17 (1966): 157–61.

Sherman, Sandra. "Trembling Texts: Margaret Cavendish and the Dialectic of Authorship." *English Literary Renaissance* 7 (1994): 184–210.

Shirley, James. *The Doubtful Heir*. London, 1652.

Shuger, Debra Keller. *Habits of Thought in the English Renaissance: Religion, Politics, and the Dominant Culture*. Berkeley: University of California Press, 1990.

Sidney, Philip. *The Countess of Pembroke's Arcadia*. Ed. Maurice Evans. Harmondsworth: Penguin, 1977.

Sinfield, Alan. *Faultlines: Cultural Materialism and the Politics of Dissident Reading*. Berkeley: University of California Press, 1992.

———. "*Poetaster*, the Author, and the Perils of Cultural Production." In Lena Orlin, ed., *Material London, ca. 1600*. Philadelphia: University of Pennsylvania Press, 2000, 75–90.

Singleton, Marion White. *God's Courtier: Configuring a Different Grace in George Herbert's "The Temple."* Cambridge: Cambridge University Press, 1987.

Sisson, C. J. *The Boar's Head Theatre*. London: Routledge and Kegan Paul, 1972.

———. "A Colony of Jews in Shakespeare's London." *Essays and Studies* 23 (1938): 38–51.

Skey, Miriam. "Herod the Great in Medieval European Drama." *Comparative Drama* 13 (1979): 330–64.

Smith, Bruce R. *The Acoustic World of Early Modern England: Attending to the O-Factor*. Chicago: University of Chicago Press, 1999.

———. "Introduction" to *Forum: Body Work. Shakespeare Studies* 29 (2001): 19–26.

Snow, Edward A. "Sexual Violence and the Male Order of Things in *Othello*." *English Literary Renaissance* 10 (1980): 384–412.

Snyder, Susan. *The Comic Matrix of Shakespeare's Tragedies:* Romeo and Juliet, Hamlet, Othello *and* King Lear. Princeton: Princeton University Press, 1979.

Sofer, Andrew. "Absorbing Interests: Kyd's Bloody Handkerchief as Palimpsest." *Comparative Drama* 34 (2000): 127–53.

Sohmer, Steve. "The 'Double Time' Crux in Othello Solved." *English Literary Renaissance* 32 (2002): 214–38.

Soliman and Perseda. London, 1599.

Spivak, Gayatri Chakravorty. *In Other Worlds: Essays in Cultural Politics*. New York: Routledge, 1986.

Stacy, Robert. "The Conversion of Jews to Christianity in Thirteenth-Century England." *Speculum* 67 (1992): 263–83.

Staines, David. "To Out-Herod Herod: The Development of a Dramatic Character." In Clifford Davidson, C. J. Giankaris, and John H. Stroupe, eds., *The Drama of the Middle Ages: Comparative and Critical Essays*. New York: AMS Press, 1982. 207–31.

Stallybrass, Peter. "*Macbeth* and Witchcraft." In John Russell Brown, ed., *Focus on* Macbeth. London: Routledge and Kegan Paul, 1982. 189–209.

———. "Marx's Coat." In Patricia Spyer, ed., *Border Fetishisms: Material Objects in Unstable Spaces*. New York: Routledge, 1998. 183–207.

———. "Patriarchal Territories: The Body Enclosed." In Margaret W. Ferguson, Maureen Quilligan, and Nancy Vickers, eds., *Rewriting the Renaissance: The Discourses of Sexual Difference in Early Modern Europe.* Chicago: University of Chicago Press, 1986. 123–42.

———. "Publication Circuit in Early Modern Europe." Unpublished manuscript.

———. "The Value of Culture and the Disavowal of Things." In Henry S. Turner, ed., *The Culture of Capital: Property, Cities, and Knowledge in Early Modern England.* New York: Routledge, 2002. 275–92.

———. "'Well Grubbed, Old Mole': Marx, *Hamlet*, and the (Un)Fixing of Representation." *Cultural Studies* 12 (1998): 3–14.

———. "Worn Worlds: Clothes and Identity on the Renaissance Stage." In Margreta de Grazia, Maureen Quilligan, and Peter Stallybrass, eds., *Subject and Object in Renaissance Culture.* Cambridge: Cambridge University Press, 1996. 289–320.

Stallybrass, Peter, and Ann Rosalind Jones. "Fetishizing the Glove in Renaissance Europe." *Critical Inquiry* 28 (2001): 114–32.

Starn, Randolph. "The Early Modern Muddle." *Journal of Early Modern History* 6 (2002): 296–307.

Stein, Arnold. *George Herbert's Lyrics.* Baltimore: Johns Hopkins University Press, 1968.

Stevens, Martin. "Herod as Carnival King in the Medieval Biblical Drama." *Mediaevelia* 18 (1995, for 1992): 43–66.

Stevenson, Jay. "The Mechanist-Vitalist Soul of Margaret Cavendish." *Studies in English Literature* 36 (1996): 527–43.

Stewart, Stanley. "Time and *The Temple.*" *Studies in English Language* 96 (1968): 97–110.

Stockholder, Katherine S. "Egregiously an Ass: Chance and Accident in *Othello.*" *Studies in English Language* 13 (1973): 256–72.

Stones, G. B. "The Atomic View of Matter in the XVth, XVIth, and XVIIth Centuries." *Isis* 10 (1928): 445–65.

Stow, John. *The Suruey of London, containing the originall, antiquitie, encrease, moderne estate, and description of that Citie.* London, 1598.

———. *Survey of London. . . . Begunne first by the paines and industry of Iohn Stovv, in the yeere 1598. Afterwards inlarged by the care and diligence of A.M. in the yeere 1618. And now completely finished by the study and labour of A.M. H.D. and others, this present yeere 1633.* London, 1633.

———. *A Survey of London, by John Stow: Reprinted from the Text of 1603.* Ed. Charles Lethbridge Kingsford. 2 vols. Oxford: Clarendon Press, 1908.

Strier, Richard. *Love Known: Theology and Experience in George Herbert's Poetry.* Chicago: University of Chicago Press, 1983.

Summers, Joseph H. *George Herbert: His Religion and Art.* London: Chatto and Windus, 1954.

Sutton, John. "Porous Memory and the Cognitive Life of Things." In Darren Tofts, Annemarie Jonson, and Alessio Cavallaro, eds., *Prefiguring Cyberculture: An Intellectual History.* Cambridge, Mass.: MIT Press: 2002. 130–41.

Swann, Marjorie. *Curiosities and Texts: The Culture of Collecting in Early Modern England.* Philadelphia: University of Pennsylvania Press, 2001. 22–54.

Sypher, Wylie. *The Ethic of Time: Structures of Experience in Shakespeare.* New York: Seabury Press, 1976.

Tailor, Robert. *The Hog Hath Lost His Pearl.* In Lloyd Edward Kermode, ed. *Three Renaissance Usury Plays.* Manchester: Manchester University Press, 2008.

Targoff, Ramie. *Common Prayer: The Language of Public Devotion in Early Modern England.* Chicago: University of Chicago Press, 2001.

Taylor, Gary. "Divine [ ]sences." *Shakespeare Survey 54: Shakespeare and Religion.* Ed. Peter Holland. Cambridge: Cambridge University Press, 2001. 13–30.

Todd, Richard. *The Opacity of Signs: Acts of Interpretation in George Herbert's* The Temple. Columbia: University of Missouri Press, 1986.

Tomkis, Thomas. *Lingua: Or the Combat of the Tongue, and the five Senses for Superiority.* London, 1607.

Trubowitz, Rachel. "The Reenchantment of Utopia and the Female Monarchical Self: Margaret Cavendish's *Blazing World.*" *Tulsa Studies in Women's Literature* 11 (1992): 229–46.

Turner, Henry S. *The Renaissance Stage: Geometry, Poetics and the Practical Spatial Arts.* Oxford: Oxford University Press, 2006.

———. *Shakespeare's Double Helix.* London: Continuum, 2008.

Tuve, Rosemond. *A Reading of George Herbert.* Chicago: Chicago University Press, 1952.

Tyson, Brian F. "Ben Jonson's Black Comedy: A Connection Between *Othello* and *Volpone.*" *Shakespeare Quarterly* 29 (1978): 60–66.

Vitkus, Daniel J. "Turning Turk in *Othello*: The Conversion and Damnation of the Moor." *Shakespeare Quarterly* 48 (1997): 147–76.

Volosinov, Valentin. *Marxism and the Philosophy of Language.* Trans. Ladislav Atejka and I. R. Titunik. New York: Seminar Press, 1973.

Wagner, Geraldine. "Romancing Multiplicity: Female Subjectivity and the Body Divisible in Margaret Cavendish's *Blazing World.*" *Early Modern Literary Studies* 9:1 (May 2003): 1.1–59. http://purl.oclc.org/emls/09–1/wagnblaz.htm.

Walker, Elsie. "'Now is a time to storm': Julie Taymor's *Titus* (2000)." *Literature/Film Quarterly* (2002): 194–207.

Walker, John David. "The Architechtonics of George Herbert's *The Temple.*" *ELH* 29 (1962): 289–305.

Wall, Wendy. *Staging Domesticity: Household Work and English Identity in Early Modern Drama.* Cambridge: Cambridge University Press, 2004.

Waller, Gary F. *The Strong Necessity of Time: The Philosophy of Time in Shakespeare and Elizabethan Literature.* The Hague: Mouton, 1976.

Walton, Izaak. *The Life of Mr. George Herbert: To which are added some Letters Written by Mr. George Herbert, at his being in Cambridge.* London, 1670.

Warton, Thomas. *History of English Poetry from the Twelfth to the Close of the Sixteenth Century.* London, 1774–81.

Weimann, Robert. *Author's Pen and Actor's Voice: Playing and Writing in Shakespeare's Theatre.* Cambridge: Cambridge University Press, 2000.

———. "Bifold Authority in Shakespeare's Theatre." *Shakespeare Quarterly* 39 (1988): 401–17.

———. *Shakespeare and the Popular Tradition: Studies in the Social Dimension of Dramatic Form and Function.* Ed. Robert Schwartz. Baltimore: Johns Hopkins University Press, 1978.

Westerweel, Bart. *Patterns and Patterning: A Study of Four Poems by George Herbert.* Amsterdam: Rodopi, 1984.

Wheeler, L. Richmond. *Vitalism: Its History and Validity.* London: Witherby, 1939.

White, Hayden. *Metahistory: The Historical Imagination in Nineteenth-Century Europe.* Baltimore: Johns Hopkins University Press, 1973.

Whithorne, Peter. *Certaine Waies for the Ordering of Souldiours in Battelray, and Setting of Battailes, after Diuers Fashions with their Manner of Marching.* London, 1588.

Wickham, Glynne. "Hell-Castle and Its Door-Keeper." *Shakespeare Survey* 19 (1966): 68–74.

Wills, Garry. *Witches and Jesuits: Shakespeare's* Macbeth. New York: Oxford University Press, 1995.

Wilson, Luke. *Theaters of Intention: Drama and the Law in Early Modern England.* Stanford, Calif.: Stanford University Press, 2000.

Withington, Robert. *English Pageantry: An Historical Outline.* 2 vols. Cambridge, Mass.: Harvard University Press, 1920.

Woolf, Virginia. *The Common Reader.* New York: Harcourt and Brace, 1946.

Yachnin, Paul. "Wonder-effects: Othello's Handkerchief." In Jonathan Gil Harris and Natasha Korda, eds., *Staged Properties in Early Modern English Drama.* Cambridge: Cambridge University Press, 2002. 316–34.

Yates, Frances A. *Giordano Bruno and the Hermetic Tradition.* Chicago: University of Chicago Press, 1964.

Yates, Julian. "Accidental Shakespeare." *Shakespeare Studies* 34 (2006): 90–122.

———. *Error, Misuse, Failure: Object Lessons from the English Renaissance.* Minneapolis: University of Minnesota Press, 2002.

Yegenoglu, Meyda. *Colonial Fantasies: Towards a Feminist Reading of Orientalism.* Cambridge: Cambridge University Press, 1988.

Yolton, John. *Thinking Matter: Materialism in Eighteenth-Century Britain.* Oxford: Oxford University Press, 1984.

Zabus, Chantal. *The African Palimpsest: Indigenization of Language in the West African Europhone Novel.* Amsterdam: Rodopi, 2007.

Žižek, Slavoj. *The Sublime Object of Ideology.* London: Verso, 1989.

Žižek, Slavoj, Eric L. Santner, and Kenneth Reinhard. *The Neighbor: Three Inquiries in Political Theology.* Chicago: Chicago University Press, 2005.

Zumthor, Paul. "Le Carrefour des rhétoriqueurs: Intertextualité et rhétorique." *Poétique* 27 (1976): 317–37.

INDEX

ACKNOWLEDGMENTS

This book started, many years ago, as an article about Shakespeare's hair. That article has since been substantially worked and reworked, primped and puffed, teased and trimmed. Traces of it remain faintly discernible in the palimpsest that is *Untimely Matter in the Time of Shakespeare*—even though, as perhaps only befits the time it has taken to complete it, the original hair has long since fallen out.

If this book is a palimpsest, though, its inscriptions are not just my own. My argument has been tested on, and improved in dialogue with, audiences at American University, the Folger Shakespeare Library, the Huntington Library, Johns Hopkins University, Michigan State University, Pennsylvania State University, the University of California at Irvine, the University of London (King's College and Royal Holloway), the University of Maryland, the University of New South Wales, the University of Southern California, and Vanderbilt University. Anonymous question askers at those venues will find some of their queries addressed, and their suggestions taken up, in these pages. Other audience members and event organizers for whose comments and advice I am immensely grateful include Amanda Berry, Bill Brown, Kent Cartwright, Patrick Cheney, Bill Cohen, Theresa Coletti, Frances Dolan, Simon During, Lynn Enterline, Frances Ferguson, Ewan Fernie, Colette Gordon, Laura Gowing, Hugh Grady, Richard Halpern, Elizabeth Hanson, Deborah Harkness, David Hershinow, Heather James, Ahuvia Kahane, Philippa Kelly, Chris Kyle, Ted Leinwand, Arthur Little, Jr., Jonathan Loesberg, Julia Lupton, Gordon McMullan, Michael Neill, Louise Noble, Marianne Noble, John O'Brien, Ellen Pollak, Miri Rubin, Liam Semler, Anita Sherman, Alan Sinfield, Jyotsna Singh, Adam Sutcliffe, and Garrett Sullivan, Jr.

Many friends, colleagues, and students have read and offered invaluable feedback on one or more draft versions of my chapters, amongst them Sadia Abbas, Crystal Bartolovich, Liza Blake, Dympna Callaghan, Joseph Campana, Linda Charnes, Jeffrey Cohen, Holly Dugan, Lee Edelman, Lowell Gallagher, Mimi Godfrey, Andrew Griffin, Huw Griffiths, Deborah Harkness, Jean Howard, Jonathan Hsy, Lindsay Kaplan, Cristina Malcolmson, Nick Moschovakis, Barbara Mowat, Gail Paster, Liz Pohland, Shankar Raman, Bryan Reynolds, Kurt Schreyer, Bruce Smith, Melissa Smith, Peter Stallybrass, Henry Turner, Will West, Julian Yates, and Mimi Yiu. They will all find their fingerprints here, as will members of the seminar entitled "Shakespearean Materialisms" that I codirected with Jacques Lezra at the 2004 Shakespeare Association of America seminar in New Orleans.

This book also bears the distinctive traces of the intellectual communities within which I work. I have been extraordinarily lucky with my colleagues in the Department of English at George Washington University, who have modeled for me intellectual rigor and friendship in equal measure: here I wish to thank in particular Marshall Alcorn, Kavita Daiya, Holly Dugan, Robert McRuer, Faye Moskowitz, Lee Salamon, and Tara Wallace. My chair and good friend Jeffrey Cohen is responsible for so much of my thinking in this book; indeed, I cannot imagine having written it without his many helpful suggestions. My students, graduate and undergraduate, have given me countless opportunities to rethink my ideas about the untimely. Particular thanks go to Taylor Asen, Liza Blake, Ashley Denham Busse, Jennifer Cho, Barkuzar al-Dubbati, Lowell Duckert, Laura Ewald, John Figura, Mo Kentoff, Nedda Mehdizadeh, Nirmala Menon, Duc Nguyen, Almila Ozdek, Aaron Potenza, Vijay Simhan, Mike Smith, Niles Tomlinson, Aliya Weise, and Gabriella Wyatt. I owe a large debt also to my colleagues at the Folger Shakespeare Library, especially the editorial team at *Shakespeare Quarterly*—Gail Kern Paster, Barbara Mowat, Bill Sherman, Mimi Godfrey, and Liz Pohland—and the library staff, including the indomitable Georgianna Ziegler, who has no peer in her ability to track down elusive texts and illustrations.

The University of Pennsylvania Press has once again given me and my work a dream home. I am indebted to the two anonymous readers for the press, whose thoughtful suggestions made my argument much, much stronger than it would otherwise have been. The resourceful Mariana Martinez helped guide the project from manuscript to book form, as did my project editor Noreen O'Connor-Abel and my copyeditor Otto Bohlmann. William Boehm and the other members of the press's graphic design team gave the book its distinctive look. Above all, I thank Jerry Singerman. With his keen eye, fine wit, and punctual (*zeitgemässe*?) responses to even my most simpleminded queries, Jerry is the best editor a writer could hope for.

I also owe deep thanks to a group of friends who have sustained me emotionally, intellectually, and materially throughout the writing of this book. I am glad to list their names here: Shekhar Aiyar, Sunny Balijapalli, Asma Barlas, Carrie Bramen, Amanda Claybaugh, Kavita Daiya, Lee Edelman, Jonathan Goldberg, Stephen Guy-Bray, Natasha Korda, Joe Litvak, Ulises Mejias, Michael Moon, Martin Murray, Anna Neill, Franziska Ohnsorge, Natsu Onoda, Margaret Aziza Pappano, Martin Puchner, Rashmi Ripley-Nair, Bob Ripley, Priyanka Ripley, Sameera Ripley, David Schmid, Ashley Shelden, Ayanna Thompson, Gordon Turnbull, Henry Turner, Rebecca Walkowitz, and Tara Wallace. I thank Tom Kemple, who suggested the title *Untimely Matter* during a conversation late one night in Bermuda. And I am immensely grateful to Peter Stallybrass, who kindly allowed me to use the picture he took of the magnificent breviary housed in Smith College's Rare Books collection.

I am immensely grateful to my families, antipodean and Indian, who have done so much to make this book conceptually possible. My father, Norman Harris, helped nurture my love for Shakespeare many decades ago; my mother, Stella Shulamit Harris, remains my primary expert on all matters Hebrew; and my sister, Miriam Harris, has helped me better understand the possibilities of polychronicity, thanks to her love of the brilliant Canadian multimedia artist and time traveler, Janet Cardiff. My little sister, Naomi Harris, has lent an extra, painful dimension to my experience of the untimely; that she is no longer here to read this has not stopped me from regarding her as one of my ideal interlocutors. Finally, my extended *desi* out-law family—T. M. C. Menon, Indira Menon, Kalyani Menon, Nandini Gopinadh, Rajeev Gopinadh, Maya Gopinadh, Kutten Gopinadh, Gita Muralidharan, Arvind Menon, Nalini Menon, and Jai Menon—have provided me not only with roofs under which much of this book has been written, but also with many sublime menus and with much love.

My biggest debt of all is to Madhavi Menon. This book may be about the untimely, but it would not be what it is without Madhavi's timely interventions. She has read and reread every page of my manuscript, offering robust criticism and rousing consolation, and always at the right time. Every page of this book is the product of my ongoing dialogue with her. Not only have her ruminations on the unhistorical provided the indispensable foil to my own on the untimely; her love, liveliness, and laughter have also been my life raft through many turbulent waters. Madhavi has had to put up for several years with my time-consuming obsession with time. Now that that obsession has (one hopes) run its course, I look forward to our spending much more time together. I dedicate this book to her.

Some chapters in this book have already appeared in print, albeit in very different redactions. An earlier version of Chapter 2, entitled "Rematerializing Shakespeare's Intertheatricality: The Occidental/Oriental Halimpsest," was published in Bryan Reynolds and William N. West (eds.), *Rematerializing Shakespeare: Authority and Representation in Early Modern England* (New York: Palgrave Macmillan, 2005), 75–94; a shorter version of Chapter 4, entitled "The Smell of *Macbeth*," appeared in *Shakespeare Quarterly* 58, no. 4 (2007): 465–86; and a somewhat different version of Chapter 5, entitled "Cleopatran Affinities: Hélène Cixous, Margaret Cavendish, and the Writing of Dialogic Matter," was published in Dympna Callaghan (ed.), *The Impact of Feminism in English Renaissance Studies* (New York: Palgrave Macmillan, 2006), 33–52. I thank Palgrave Macmillan and Johns Hopkins University Press for permission to rework those publications here.

www.ingramcontent.com/pod-product-compliance
Ingram Content Group UK Ltd.
Pitfield, Milton Keynes, MK11 3LW, UK
UKHW032028240225
455518UK00001B/104

9 780812 221466